Jürgen Franke · Wolfgang Härdle ·
Christian Hafner

Statistics
of Financial
Markets

An Introduction

Springer

Professor Dr. Jürgen Franke
University of Kaiserslautern
P.O. Box 3049
67653 Kaiserslautern
Germany
e-mail: franke@mathematik.uni-kl.de

Professor Dr. Wolfgang Härdle
Humboldt-Universität zu Berlin
CASE-Center for Applied Statistics and Economics
Spandauer Str. 1
10178 Berlin
Germany
e-mail: haerdle@wiwi.hu-berlin.de

Professor Dr. Christian M. Hafner
Erasmus University Rotterdam
Econometric Institute, Faculty of Economics
P.O. Box 1738
3000 DR Rotterdam
The Netherlands
e-mail: chafner@few.eur.nl

Library of Congress Control Number: 2004105112

The photo on the cover of the bull and bear in front of the Frankfurt Stock Exchange was taken by Professor Wolfgang Härdle.

ISBN 3-540-21675-8 Springer-Verlag Berlin Heidelberg New York

Mathematics Subject Classification (2000): 62M10, 62P05, 91B28, 91B84

Springer-Verlag
is a part of Springer Science+Business Media

springeronline.com

© Springer-Verlag Berlin Heidelberg 2004
Printed in Germany

Cover design: Erich Kirchner, Heidelberg
Typeset by the authors using a LaTeX macro package

Printed on acid-free paper   40/3142at - 5 4 3 2 1 0

Universitext

Uni

Subje

ht

Springer
Berlin
Heidelberg
New York
Hong Kong
London
Milan
Paris
Tokyo

Figure 0.1: Notes of a student for the exam of a course based on this book.

Figure 0.2: Notes of a student for the exam of a course based on this book.

Figure 0.3: Notes of a student for the exam of a course based on this book.

Figure 0.4: Notes of a student for the exam of a course based on this book.

Figure 0.5: Notes of a student for the exam of a course based on this book.

Preface

Until about the 1970s, financial mathematics has been rather modest compared with other mathematical disciplines. This changed rapidly after the path-breaking works of F. Black, M. Scholes, and R. Merton on derivative pricing, for which they received the Nobel prize of economics in 1997. Since 1973, the publication year of the famous Black and Scholes article, the importance of derivative instruments in financial markets has not ceased to grow. Higher risks associated with, for example, flexible instead of fixed exchange rates after the fall of the Bretton Woods system required a risk management and the use of hedging instruments for internationally active companies. More recently, globalization and the increasingly complex dependence of financial markets are reasons for using sophisticated mathematical and statistical methods and models to evaluate risks.

The necessity to improve and develop the mathematical foundation of existing risk management was emphasized in the turbulent 1990s with, for example, the Asian crisis, the hedging disasters of Metallgesellschaft and Orange County, and the fall of the Long-Term Capital Management hedge fund (controlled by Merton and Scholes!). This saw the legislator obliged to take action. In continental Europe, this development is mainly influenced by the Basel Committee on Banking Supervision, whose recommendations form the basis in the European Union for legislation, with which financial institutions are obliged to do a global, thorough risk management. As a result, there is an increasing demand for experts in financial engineering, who control risks internally, search for profitable investment opportunities and guarantee the obligations of legislation. In the future, such risk management is likely to become obligatory for other, deregulated markets such as telecommunication and energy markets. Being aware of the increasing price, volume, and credit risks in these markets, large companies usually have already created new departments dealing with asset and liability management as well as risk management.

The present text is supposed to deliver the necessary mathematical and statistical basis for a position in financial engineering. Our goal is to give a comprehensive introduction into important ideas of financial mathematics and statistics. We do not aim at covering all practically relevant details, and we also do not discuss the technical subtleties of stochastic analysis. For both purposes there is already a vast variety of textbooks. Instead, we want to give students of mathematics, statistics, and economics a primer for the modelling and statistical analysis of financial data. Also, the book is meant for practitioners, who want to deepen their acquired practical knowledge. Apart from an introduction to the theory of pricing derivatives, we emphasize the statistical aspects of mathematical methods, i.e., the selection of appropriate models as well as fitting and validation using data.

The present book consists of three parts. The first two are organized such that they can be read independently. Each one can be used for a course of roughly 30 hours. We deliberately accept an occasional redundancy if a topic is covered in both parts but from a different perspective. The third part presents selected applications to current practical problems. Both _option pricing_ as _statistical modelling of financial time series_ have often been topic of seminars and lectures in the international study program _financial mathematics_ of Universität Kaiserslautern (www.mathematik.uni-kl.de) as well as in the economics and statistics program of Humboldt-Universität zu Berlin (ise.wiwi.hu-berlin.de). Moreover, they formed the basis of lectures for banking practitioners which were given by the authors in various European countries.

The first part covers the classical theory of pricing derivatives. Next to the Black and Scholes option pricing formula for conventional European and American options and their numerical solution via the approximation using binomial processes, we also discuss the evaluation of some exotic options. Stochastic models for interest rates and the pricing of interest rate derivatives conclude the first part. The necessary tools of stochastic analysis, in particular the Wiener process, stochastic differential equations and Itô's Lemma will be motivated heuristically and not derived in a rigorous way. In order to render the text accessible to non-mathematicians, we do not explicitly cover advanced methods of financial mathematics such as martingale theory and the resulting elegant characterization of absence of arbitrage in complete markets.

The second part presents the already classical analysis of financial time series, which originated in the work of T. Bollerslev, R. Engle, and C. Granger. Starting with conventional linear processes, we motivate why financial time series rarely can be described using such linear models. Alternatively, we discuss the related model class of stochastic volatility models. Apart from standard ARCH and GARCH models, we discuss extensions that allow for an asymmetric impact of lagged returns on volatility. We also review multivariate GARCH models that can be applied, for example, to estimate and test the capital asset pricing model (CAPM) or to portfolio selection problems. As a support for explorative data analysis and the search and validation of parsimonious parametric models, we emphasize the use of nonparametric models for financial time series and their fit to data using kernel estimators or other smoothing methods.

In the third part of the book, we discuss applications and practical issues such as option pricing, risk management, and credit scoring. We apply flexible GARCH type models to evaluate options and to overcome the Black and Scholes restriction of constant volatility. We give an overview of Value at Risk (VaR) and backtesting, and show that copulas can improve the estimation of VaR. A correct understanding of the statistical behavior of extremes such as September 11, 2001, is essential for risk management, and we give an overview of extreme value theory with financial applications. As a particularly popular nonparametric modelling tool in financial institutions, we discuss neural networks from a statistical viewpoint with applications to the prediction of financial time series. Next, we show how a principal components analysis can be used to explain the dynamics of implied volatilities. Finally, we present nonparametric extensions of conventional discrete choice models and apply them to the credit scoring problem.

We decided to collect some technical results concerning stochastic integration in the appendix. Here we also present Girsanov's theorem and the martingale representation theorem, with which dynamic portfolio strategies as well as an alternative proof of the Black and Scholes formula are developed. This appendix is based on work by Klaus Schindler, Saarbrücken.

In designing the book as e-book, we are going new ways of scientific publishing together with Springer Verlag and MD*Tech. The book is provided with an individual license key, which enables the reader to download the html and pdf versions of the text as well as all slides for a 60 to 90 hours lecture from the e-book server at www.quantlet.com. All examples, tables and graphs can be reproduced and changed interactively using the XploRe quantlet technology.

The present book would not exist without the cooperating contributions of P. Čížek, M. Fengler, Z. Hlávka, E. Kreutzberger, S. Klinke, D. Mercurio and D. Peithmann. The first part of the book arose from an extended vocational training which was developed together with G. Maercker, K. Schindler and N. Siedow. In particular, we want to thank Torsten Kleinow, who accompanied the writing of the text in all phases, developed the e-book platform and improved the presentation by various valuable contributions. Important impulses for an improved presentation were given by Klaus Schindler of the

University of Saarbrücken, which we gratefully acknowledge. The chapter
on copulas is based on a contribution by Jörn Rank, Andersen Consulting,
and Thomas Siegl, BHF Bank, which we adopted with their kind approval.
The quantlets for multivariate GARCH models were contributed by Matthias
Fengler and Helmut Herwartz. All graphs were created by Ying Chen, who
also led the text management. We would like to express our thanks to these
colleagues. We also benefitted from many constructive comments by our students of the universities in Kaiserslautern, Berlin, and Rotterdam. As an
example of their enthusiasm we depict the preparation sheet of a student for
the exam at the front pages of the book. Graphs and formulae are combined
to create a spirit of the "art of quantitative finance".

Finally, for the technical realization of the text we want to thank Beate Siegler
and Anja Ossetrova.

Kaiserslautern, Berlin and Rotterdam, April 2004

Frequently Used Notation

$x \stackrel{\text{def}}{=} \ldots$ x is defined as ...

$\mathbb{R}$ real numbers

$\overline{\mathbb{R}} \stackrel{\text{def}}{=} \mathbb{R} \cup \{\infty, \infty\}$

$A^\top$ transpose of matrix A

$X \sim D$ the random variable X has distribution D

$\mathsf{E}[X]$ expected value of random variable X

$Var(X)$ variance of random variable X

$\mathrm{Cov}(X, Y)$ covariance of two random variables X and Y

$\mathrm{N}(\mu, \Sigma)$ normal distribution with expectation μ and covariance matrix Σ, a similar notation is used if Σ is the correlation matrix

$\mathsf{P}[A]$ or $\mathsf{P}(A)$ probability of a set A

$\mathbf{1}$ indicator function

$(F \circ G)(x) \stackrel{\text{def}}{=} F\{G(x)\}$ for functions F and G

$x \approx y$ x is approximately equal to y

$\alpha_n = \mathcal{O}(\beta_n)$ iff $\frac{\alpha_n}{\beta_n} \longrightarrow$ constant, as $n \longrightarrow \infty$

$\alpha_n = o(\beta_n)$ iff $\frac{\alpha_n}{\beta_n} \longrightarrow 0$, as $n \longrightarrow \infty$

$\mathcal{F}_t$ is the information set generated by all information available at time t

Let A_n and B_n be sequences of random variables.

$A_n = \mathcal{O}_p(B_n)$ iff $\forall \varepsilon > 0 \; \exists M, \; \exists N$ such that $\mathsf{P}[|A_n/B_n| > M] < \varepsilon, \; \forall n > N$.

$A_n = o_p(B_n)$ iff $\forall \varepsilon > 0 \; : \; \lim_{n \to \infty} \mathsf{P}[|A_n/B_n| > \varepsilon] = 0$.

Contents

Part I

Option Pricing

1 Derivatives

Classical financial mathematics deals first of all with basic financial instruments like stocks, foreign currencies and bonds. A *derivative* (*derivative security* or *contingent claim*) is a financial instrument whose value depends on the value of others, more basic *underlying* variables. In this chapter we consider forward contracts, futures contracts and options as well as some combinations.

Simple derivatives have been known on European stock exchanges since the turn of the 19th century. While they lost popularity between World War I and II, they revived in the seventies accompanied by the work of Black, Scholes and Merton, who developed a theoretical foundation to price such instruments. Their entrepreneurial approach, which is not only applied to price derivatives but everywhere in finance where the risk of complex financial instruments is measured and controlled, was awarded the Nobel price in economics in 1997. At the same time, it triggered the development of modern financial mathematics whose basics we describe in the first part of this book. Since we concentrate only on the mathematical modelling ideas, we introduce the required financial terminology as we pass by. We leave out numerous details which are of practical importance but which are of no interest for the mathematical modelling, and refer to, for example, Hull (2000), Welcker, Kloy and Schindler (1992).

Particularly simple derivative securities are *forward* and *future contracts*. Both contracts are agreements involving two parties and calling for future delivery of an asset at an agreed–upon price. Stocks, currencies and bonds, as well as agricultural products (grain, meat) and raw materials (oil, copper, electric energy) are underlying in the contract.

Definition 1.1 (Forward contract)
A forward contract *is an agreement between two parties in which one of the parties assumes a long position (the other party assumes a short position) and obliges to purchase (sell) the underlying asset at a specified future date $T > t$, (expiration date or maturity) for a specified price K (delivery price).*

At time t, the value $V_{K,T}(S_t, \tau)$ of such a contract depends on the current value of the underlying S_t, the time to maturity $\tau = T - t$ and of the parameters K, T specified in the contract.

Futures contracts closely resemble forward contracts. While the latter do not entail any more payments until maturity once the agreement is signed, futures contracts are traded on an exchange and mark to the market on a daily basis. Under certain assumptions forward and futures prices are identical.

Example 1.1
An investor enter into a long forward contract on September 1, 2003, which obliges him to buy 1 000 000 EUR at a specified exchange rate of 1.2 USD/EUR in 90 days. The investor gains if the exchange rate is up to 1.3 USD/EUR on November 30, 2003. Since he can sell the 1 000 000 EUR for USD 1 300 000. In this case $t = $ September 1, 2003 $\tau = $ 90 days, $T = $ November 30, and $K = $ USD 1 200 000.

Definition 1.2 (Spot Price, Forward Price, Future Price)
The current price of the underlying (stock, currency, raw material) S_t is often referred to as the spot price. *The delivery price giving a forward contract a value of zero is called* forward price *and denoted F_t. That is, F_t solves $V_{F_t,T}(S_t, \tau) = 0$. The* future price *is defined accordingly.*

Later we will compute the value of a forward contract, which determines the forward price. Since under certain assumptions forward and future contracts have the same value, their prices are equal. When such a contract is initiated in time $t = 0$, often the delivery price is set to $K = F_0$. The contract has a value of zero for both the seller and the buyer, i.e. no payments occur. In the course of time, as additional transactions take place on the exchange, the delivery price K and the forward price F_t can be different.

Contrary to forward and futures contracts where both parties are obligated to carry out the transaction, an option gives one party the right to buy or sell the security. Obviously, it's important to distinguish whether the buyer or seller of the option has the right to exercise. There are two types of options: call and put options. Furthermore, European options are delimited from American options. While European options are like forward contracts, American options can be exercised at any date before maturity. These terms are derived from historical, not geographical roots.

Definition 1.3 (Call Option, Put Option)
A European call option is an agreement which gives the holder the right to buy

*the underlying asset at a specified date $T > t$, (expiration date or maturity),
for a specified price K, (strike price or exercise price). If the holder does not
exercise, the option expires worthless.*

European put option *is an agreement which gives the holder the right to sell
the underlying asset at a specified date T for a specified price K.*

The holder of an American call *or* put option *has the right to exercise the
option at any time between t and T.*

The option types defined above are also called *plain vanilla options*. In
practice, many more complex derivatives exist and numerous new financial
instruments are still emerging. *Over-the-counter (OTC) derivatives* are tai-
lor made instruments designed by banking institutions to satisfy a particular
consumer need. A compound option, for example, is such an OTC–derivative.
It gives the holder the right to buy or sell at time T an underlying option
which matures in $T' > T$. The mathematical treatment of these *exotic options* is particularly difficult, since the current value of this instrument does
not only depend on the value of the underlying S_t but also on the entire path
of the underlying, $S_{t'}, 0 \leq t' \leq t$.

Asian, lookback and knock–out options are path-dependent derivatives. While
the delivery price K of an asian option depends on the average value of the
security of a certain period of time, it depends in the case of a lookback option on the minimum or maximum value of the security for a certain period
of time. Knock–out options expire worthless if the price level ever hits a
specified level.

To get used to forward and futures contracts, plain vanilla options and simple
combinations of them, it is convenient to have a look at the *payoff* of an
instrument, i.e. the value of the derivative at maturity T. The payoff of a
long position in a forward contract is just $S_T - K$, with S_T the security's
spot price at expiration date T. The holder of the contract pays K for the
security and can sell it for S_T. Thus, he makes a profit if the value of the
security S_T at expiration is greater than the delivery price K. Being short
in a forward contract implies a payoff $K - S_T$. Both payoff functions are
depicted in Figure 1.1.

The call option payoff function is denoted:

$$\max\{S_T - K, 0\} = (S_T - K)^+.$$

Thus, the option holder only exercises if the delivery price K is less than the
value of the security S_T at expiration date T. In this case, he receives the
same cash amount as in the case of a forward or future contract. If $K < S_T$,

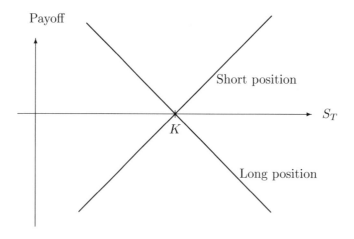

Figure 1.1: Value of forward contract at maturity

he will clearly choose not to exercise and the option expires worthless. The
put option payoff function is:

$$\max\{K - S_T, 0\} = (K - S_T)^+.$$

In contrast to forward and future contracts, options have to be bought for
a positive amount $C(S_0, T)$, called the *option price* or *option prime*. Often,
the options profit function is defined as $(S_T - K)^+ - C(S_0, T)$. However,
this definition adds cash flows of different points in time. The correct profit
is obtained by compounding the cash outflow in time $t = 0$ up to time
$t = T$, since the investor could have invested the option option at the risk–
free interest rate r. Assuming continuous compounding at a constant interest
rate r, the profit function of a call option is denoted: $(S_T - K)^+ - C(S_0, T)e^{rT}$.

Example 1.2
*Consider a long call option with delivery price K and option price C_0 in
time $t = 0$. The payoff and profit function are given in Figure 1.2 and 1.3,
respectively.*

Example 1.3
Combining a long call and a long put with the same delivery price K is called

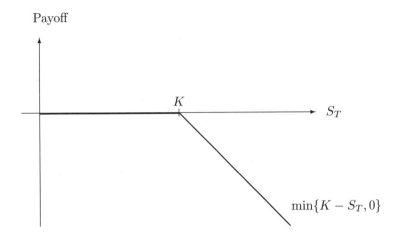

Figure 1.2: Payoff of a short position in a call option

a straddle. Figure 1.4 shows the straddle profit function. C_0 and P_0 denote the call and put option option respectively.

Another fundamental financial instrument which is used in option pricing is a *bond*. Apart from interest yields, the bond holder possibly receives coupon payments at fixed points in time. In particular, we will consider zero–coupon bonds, i.e. bonds which promise a single payment at a fixed future date.

Definition 1.4 (Zero coupon Bond, Discount Bond)
A zero coupon bond *or* discount bond *is a bond without coupon payments which pays an interest r. The investor pays in time 0 an amount B_0 and receives at maturity T the amount B_T which is the sum of B_0 and the interest earned on B_0. The bonds' value at maturity is termed* face value.

Buying a zero–coupon bond corresponds to lending money at a fixed interest rate for a fixed period of time. Conversely, selling a zero-coupon bond is equivalent to borrowing money at rate r. Since bonds are traded on an exchange, they can be sold prior to maturity at price B_t, i.e. B_0 plus accrued interest up to time t.

In practice, interest rates are compounded at discrete points in time, for

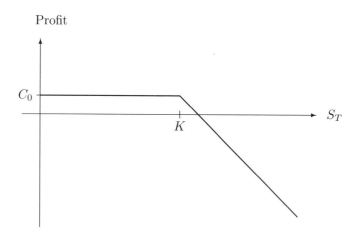

Profit

C_0

K

S_T

Figure 1.3: Profit of a short position in a call option

example annually, semiannually or monthly. If the interest rate r is compounded annually, the initial investment B_0 has n years later a value of $B_n^{(1)} = B_0(1 + r)^n$. If it is compounded k times per annum (p.a.), the investment pays an interest rate of $\frac{r}{k}$ each $\frac{1}{k}$ years, and has a terminal value of $B_n^{(k)} = B_0(1 + \frac{r}{k})^{nk}$ after n years. However, when options and other complex derivatives are priced, continuous compounding is used, which denoted for $k \to \infty$. In this case, the initial investment B_0 grows in n years to $B_n = B_0 \cdot e^{nr}$, and r is called *short rate*. The difference between discrete and continuous compounding is small when k is large. While an investment of $B_0 = 1000$ EUR at a yearly rate $r = 10\%$ grows to 1100 EUR within a year when annually compounded, it grows to 1105.17 EUR when continuously compounded.

In light of this, the continuous compounded rate r can be modified to account for these deviations. Assuming annual compounding at rate r_1, for both continuous and annual compounding, a continuous compounded rate $r = \log(1 + r_1)$ has to be applied, in order to obtain the same terminal value $B_n = B_n^{(1)}$.

If not stated otherwise, continuous compounding will be assumed from here on. For comparing cash flows occurring at different points in time, they

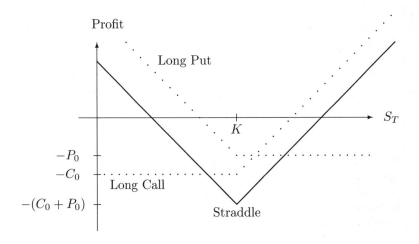

Figure 1.4: Profit of a straddle

have to be compounded or discounted to the same point in time. That is, interest payments are added or subtracted. With continuous compounding, an investment of B in time t in $\Delta t > 0$ is

compounded   to time $t + \Delta t$: $B\,e^{r\Delta t}$

discounted   to time $t - \Delta t$: $B\,e^{-r\Delta t}$.

Before finishing the chapter, some more financial terms will be introduced. A *portfolio* is a combination of one or more financial instruments - its value is considered as an individual financial instrument. One element of a portfolio is also called a *position*. An investor assumes a *long position* when he buys an instrument, and a *short position* when he sells it. A *long call* results from buying a call option, a *long put* from buying a put option, and *a short forward* from selling a forward contract.

An investor closes out a position of his portfolio by making the future portfolio performance independent of the instrument. If the latter is traded on an exchange, he can sell (e.g. a stock or a bond) or buy (e.g. borrowed money) it. Should the instrument not be traded, however, the investor can close out the position by adding to the portfolio the inverse instrument. Thus, both sum up to zero, and do not influence the portfolio performance any more.

Example 1.4
Consider an investor who bought on February 1 a 1 000 000 USD forward contract with a delivery price of 1 200 000 EUR and which matures in one year. On June 1, he wishes to close out the position. He can sell *another forward contract of the same size with the same delivery price and the maturity date, namely January 31. The long and the short positions sum up to zero at any time.*

Short selling is a trading strategy that involves selling financial instruments, for example stocks, which he does not own. At a later point in time, he buys back these objects. In practice, this requires the intervention of a broker who mediates another client owing the objects and willing to lend them to the investor. The short selling investor commits to pay to the client any foregone income, as dividends for example, that would be received in the meantime.

Example 1.5
An investor selling short 1000 stocks, lends them from the owner and sells them immediately for 1000 S_0 in the market (S_t denotes the stock price at time t). Later, at time $t > 0$, he closes out the position, by buying back the stocks for 1000 S_t and returning them to the owner. The strategy is profitable if S_t is clearly below S_0. If in time t_0, $0 < t_0 < t$, a dividend D per share is paid, the investor pays 1000 D to the owner. Short selling is in practice subject to numerous restrictions. In the following, it is only the possibility of short selling that will be of interest.

1.1   Recommended Literature

Basic textbooks on derivatives are, among others, Hull (2000), Jarrow (1992) and Cox and Rubinstein (1985). Neftci (1996) and Duffie (1996) are more advanced regarding the mathematical level. A rather practical but still theoretically well–founded introduction is given by Briys, Bellalah, Mai and de Varenne (1998).

2 Introduction to Option Management

2.1 Arbitrage Relations

In this section we consider the fundamental notion of no–arbitrage. An *arbitrage opportunity* arises if it is possible to make a riskless profit. In an ideal financial market, in which all investors dispose of the same pieces of information and in which all investors can react instantaneously, there should not be any arbitrage opportunity. Since otherwise each investor would try to realize the riskless profit instantaneously. The resulting transactions would change the prices of the involved financial instruments such that the arbitrage opportunity disappears.

Additionally to no–arbitrage we presume in the remaining chapter that the financial market fulfills further simplifying assumptions which are in this context of minor importance and solely serve to ease the argumentation. If these assumptions hold we speak of a perfect financial market.

ASSUMPTION (*perfect financial market*)
There are no arbitrage opportunities, no transaction costs, no taxes, and no restrictions on short selling. Lending rates equal borrowing rates and all securities are perfectly divisible.

The assumption of a perfect financial market is sufficient to determine the value of future and forward contracts as well as some important relations between the prices of some types of options. Above all no mathematical model for the price of the financial instrument is needed. However, in order to determine the value of options more than only economic assumptions are necessary. A detailed mathematical modelling becomes inevitable. Each mathematical approach though has to be in line with certain fundamental arbitrage relations being developed in this chapter. If the model implies values of future and forward contracts or option prices which do not fulfill these relations the model's assumptions must be wrong.

An important conclusion drawn from the assumption of a perfect financial market and thus from no–arbitrage will be used frequently in the proofs to come. It is the fact that two portfolios which have at a certain time T the same value must have the same value at a prior time $t < T$ as well. Due to its importance we will further illustrate this reasoning. We proceed from two portfolios A and B consisting of arbitrary financial instruments. Their value in time t will be denoted by $W_A(t)$ and $W_B(t)$ respectively. For any fixed point of time T, we assume that $W_A(T) = W_B(T)$ independently of the prior time T values of each financial instrument contained in A and B. For any prior point of time $t < T$ we assume without loss of generality that $W_A(t) \leq W_B(t)$. In time t an investor can construct without own financial resources a portfolio which is a combination of A and B by buying one unit of every instrument of A, selling one unit of every instrument of B (short selling) and by investing the difference $\Delta(t) = W_B(t) - W_A(t) \geq 0$ at a fixed rate r. The combined portfolio has at time t a value of

$$W_A(t) - W_B(t) + \Delta(t) = 0,$$

i.e. the investor has no initial costs. At time T the part of the combined portfolio which is invested at rate r has the compounded value $\Delta(T) = \Delta(t)e^{r(T-t)}$, and hence the combined portfolio has a value of

$$W_A(T) - W_B(T) + \Delta(T) = \Delta(t)e^{r(T-t)} > 0,$$

if $\Delta(t) > 0$. The investor made a riskless gain by investing in the combined portfolio which contradicts the no–arbitrage assumption. Therefore, it must hold $\Delta(t) = 0$, i.e. $W_A(t) = W_B(t)$.

The previous reasoning can be used to determine the unknown value of a financial derivative. For this, a portfolio A is constructed which contains instruments with known price along with one unit of the derivative under investigation. Portfolio A will be compared to another portfolio B, called the *duplicating portfolio*, which contains exclusively instruments with known prices. Since the duplicating portfolio B is constructed such that for certain it has the same value at a fixed point of time T as portfolio A the no–arbitrage assumption implies that both portfolios must have the same value at any prior point of time. The value of the financial derivative can thus be computed at any time $t \leq T$. We illustrate this procedure in the following example of a forward contract.

Theorem 2.1
We consider a long forward contract to buy an object which has a price of S_t at time t. Let K be the delivery price, and let T be the maturity date. $V(s, \tau)$

denotes the value of the long forward contract at time t as a function of the current price $S_t = s$ and the time to maturity $\tau = T - t$. We assume constant interest rates r during the time to maturity.

1. *If the underlying object does not pay any dividends and does not involve any costs during the time to maturity τ, then it holds*

$$V(S_t, \tau) = V_{K,T}(S_t, \tau) = S_t - Ke^{-r\tau} \tag{2.1}$$

The forward price is equal to $F_t = S_t e^{r\tau}$.

2. *If during the time to maturity the underlying pays at discrete time points dividends or involves any costs whose current time t discounted total value is equal to D_t, then it holds*

$$V(S_t, \tau) = V_{K,T}(S_t, \tau) = S_t - D_t - Ke^{-r\tau} \tag{2.2}$$

The forward price is equal to $F_t = (S_t - D_t)e^{r\tau}$.

3. *If the underlying involves continuous costs at rate b, then it holds*

$$V(S_t, \tau) = V_{K,T}(S_t, \tau) = S_t e^{(b-r)\tau} - Ke^{-r\tau} \tag{2.3}$$

The forward price is equal to $F_t = S_t e^{b\tau}$.

Proof:
For simplicity we assume the underlying object to be a stock paying either discrete dividend yields whose value discounted to time t is D_t or paying a continuous dividend yield at rate b. In the latter case the stock involves continuous costs equal to $b = r - d$. The investor having a long position in the stock gains dividends (as negative costs) at rate d but simultaneously loses interests at rate r since he invested his capital in the stock instead of in a bond with a fixed interest rate. In place of stocks, bonds, currencies or other simple instruments can be considered as well.

1. We consider at time t the following two portfolios A and B:

Portfolio A: One long forward contract on a stock with delivery price K, maturing in time T.
One long zero bond with face value K, maturing in time T.

Portfolio B: A long position in one unit of the stock.

At maturity T portfolio A contains a zero bond of value K. Selling this zero bond for K the obligation to buy the stock for K can be fulfilled. Following these transactions portfolio A consists as well as portfolio B of one unit of the stock. Thus both portfolios have at time T the same value and must therefore, due to the no–arbitrage assumption, have the same value at any time t prior to T :

$$V(S_t, \tau) + Ke^{-r\tau} = S_t \,, \qquad (2.4)$$

since the value of the zero bond at time t is given by discounting K at rate r, $Ke^{-r\tau}$. The forward price is by definition the solution of

$$0 = V_{F_t, T}(S_t, \tau) = S_t - F_t e^{-r\tau}.$$

2. We consider at time t the two portfolios A and B as given above and add one position to portfolio B :

Portfolio B: A long position in one unit of the stock and one short position of size D_t in a zero bond with interest rate r (lending an amount of money of D_t).

At maturity T the dividend yields of the stock in portfolio B, which compounded to time T amount to $D_t e^{r\tau}$, are used to pay back the bond. Thus, both portfolios A and B consist again of one unit of the stock, and therefore they must have the same value at any time $t < T$:

$$V(S_t, \tau) + Ke^{-r\tau} = S_t - D_t \,. \qquad (2.5)$$

The forward price results as in part 1 from the definition.

3. If the stock pays dividends continuously at a rate d, then the reasoning is similar as in part 2. Once again, we consider at time t two portfolios A and B. And again, A is left unchanged, B is now composed of the following position:

Portfolio B: A long position in $e^{-d\tau}$ stocks.

Reinvesting the dividends yields continuously in the stock portfolio B consists again of exactly one stock at time T. Heuristically, this can be illustrated as follows: In the time interval $[t, t + \delta]$ the stock pays approximately, for a small δ, a dividend of $d \cdot \delta \cdot S_t$. Thus, the current total amount of stocks in the portfolio, $e^{-d\tau} = e^{-d(T-t)}$, pays a total dividend yield of $d \cdot \delta \cdot S_t \cdot e^{-d(T-t)}$, which is reinvested in the stock. Assuming that the stock price does not change significantly in the interval $[t, t+\delta]$, i.e. $S_{t+\delta} \approx S_t$, portfolio B contains in time $t + \delta$

$$(1 + d \cdot \delta) \cdot e^{-d(T-t)} \approx e^{d\delta} \cdot e^{-d(T-t)} = e^{-d(T-t-\delta)}$$

stocks. The above reasoning can be done exactly by taking the limit $\delta \to 0$, and it can be shown that portfolio B contains at any time s between t and T exactly $e^{-d(T-s)}$ stocks. That is, for $s = T$ portfolio B is composed of exactly one stock. The same reasoning as in part 1 leads to the conclusion that portfolio A and B must have the same value at any time t. Thus, we have

$$V(S_t, \tau) + Ke^{-r\tau} = e^{-d\tau}S_t . \tag{2.6}$$

where we have to set $b = r - d$. The forward price results as in part 1 from the definition. □

Example 2.1 *We consider a long forward contract on a 5 year bond which is currently traded at a price of 900 EUR. The delivery price is 910 EUR, the time to maturity of the forward contract is one year. The coupon payments of the bond of 60 EUR occur after 6 and 12 months (the latter shortly before maturity of the forward contract). The continuously compounded annual interest rates for 6 and 12 months are 9% and 10% respectively. In this example we have*

$$S_t = 900 , \ K = 910 , \ r = 0.10 , \ \tau = 1 , \ D_t = 60e^{-0.09 \cdot \frac{1}{2}} + 60e^{-0.10} = 111.65 \tag{2.7}$$

Thus, the value of the forward contract is given by

$$V(S_t, \tau) = 900 - 111.65 - 910e^{-0.10} = -35.05. \tag{2.8}$$

The value of the respective short position in the forward contract is +35.05. The price F_t of the forward contract is equal to $F_t = (S_t - D_t)e^{r\tau} = 871.26$.

Example 2.2 *Consider a long forward contract to buy 1000 Dollar. If the investor buys the 1000 Dollar and invests this amount in a American bond, the American interest rate can be interpreted as a dividend yield d which is continuously paid. Let r be the home interest rate. The investment involves costs $b = r - d$, which are the difference between the American and the home interest rate. Denoting the dollar exchange rate by S_t the price of the forward contract is then given by*

$$F_t = S_t e^{b\tau} = S_t e^{(r-d)\tau}. \tag{2.9}$$

While for $r > d$ a report $S_t < F_t$ results, for $r < d$ a backwardation $S_t > F_t$ results. If $r > d$ and the delivery price is chosen to equal the current exchange rate, i.e. $K = S_t$, then the value of the forward contract is

$$V_{S_t, T}(S_t, \tau) = S_t(e^{-d\tau} - e^{-r\tau}) > 0.$$

Buying the forward contract at a price of S_t is thus more expensive than buying the dollars immediately for the same price since in the former case the investor can invest the money up to time T in a domestic bond paying an interest rate which is higher than the American interest rate.

The following result states that forward and future contracts with the same delivery price and the same time to maturity are equal, if interest rates are constant during the contract period. We will use the fact that by definition forward and future contracts do not cost anything if the delivery price is chosen to be equal to the current price of the forward contract respectively the price of the future contract.

Theorem 2.2
If interest rates are constant during contract period, then forward and future prices are equal.

Proof:
We proceed from the assumption that the future contract is agreed on at time 0, and that is has a time to maturity of N days. We assume that profits and losses are settled (marked to market) on a daily basis at a daily interest rate of ρ. While the forward price at the end of day 0 is denoted by F, the future price at the end of day t, $t = 0, 1, \cdots, N$ is denoted by F_t. The goal is to show that $F = F_0$. For that we construct two portfolios again:

Portfolio A: A long position in $e^{N\rho}$ forward contracts with delivery price F and maturity date N.
A long position in a zero bond with face value $Fe^{N\rho}$ maturing in N days.

Portfolio B: A long position in futures contracts with delivery price F_t and maturity date N. The contracts are bought daily such that the portfolio contains at the end of the t–th day exactly $e^{(t+1)\rho}$ future contracts $(t = 0, 1, \cdots, N)$.
A long position in a zero bond with face value $F_0 e^{N\rho}$ maturing in N days.

Purchasing a forward or a future contract does not cost anything since their delivery prices are set to equal the current forward or future price. Due to the marking to market procedure the holder of portfolio B receives from day $t - 1$ to day t for each future contract an amount of $F_t - F_{t-1}$ which can possibly be negative (i.e. he has to pay).

At maturity, i.e. at the end of day N, the zero bond of portfolio A is sold at the face value $Fe^{N\rho}$ to fulfill the terms of the forward contract and to buy $e^{N\rho}$ stocks at a the delivery price F. Then A contains exclusively these stocks and has a value of $S_N e^{N\rho}$. Following, we show that portfolio B has the same value.

At the beginning of day t portfolio B contains $e^{t\rho}$ future contracts, and the holder receives due to the marking to market procedure the amount $(F_t - F_{t-1})e^{t\rho}$ which can possibly be negative. During the day he increases his long position in the future contracts at zero costs such that the portfolio contains $e^{(t+1)\rho}$ future contracts at the end of the day. The earnings at day t compounded to the maturity date have a value of:

$$(F_t - F_{t-1})e^{t\rho} \cdot e^{(N-t)\rho} = (F_t - F_{t-1})e^{N\rho}. \qquad (2.10)$$

At maturity the terms of the future contracts are fulfilled due to the marking to market procedure. All profits and losses compounded to day N have a value of:

$$\sum_{t=1}^{N}(F_t - F_{t-1})e^{N\rho} = (F_N - F_0)e^{N\rho}. \qquad (2.11)$$

Together with the zero bond portfolio B has at day N a value of

$$(F_N - F_0)e^{N\rho} + F_0 e^{N\rho} = F_N e^{N\rho} = S_N e^{N\rho},$$

since at maturity the future price F_N and the price S_N of the underlying are obviously equal.

Hence, both portfolios have at day N the same value and thus due to the no–arbitrage assumption their day 0 values must be equal as well. Since the forward contract with delivery price F has a value of 0 at day 0 due to the definition of the forward price, the value of portfolio A is equal to the value of the zero bond, i.e. F (face value $Fe^{N\rho}$ discounted to day 0). Correspondingly, the e^{ρ} futures contained in portfolio B have at the end of day 0 a value of 0 due to the definition of the future price. Again, the value of portfolio B reduces to the value of the zero bond. The latter has a value of F_0 (face value $F_0 e^{N\rho}$ discounted to day 0). Putting things together, we conclude that $F = F_0$. □

Now, we want to proof some relationship between option prices using similar methods. The most elementary properties are summarized in the following remark without a proof. For that, we need the notion of the *intrinsic value* of an option.

Definition 2.1 (Intrinsic Value)
The intrinsic value *of a call option at time t is given by* $\max(S_t - K, 0)$, *the intrinsic value of a put option is given by* $\max(K - S_t, 0)$. *If the intrinsic value of an option is positive we say that the option is* in the money. *If* $S_t = K$, *then the option is* at the money. *If the intrinsic value is negative, then the option is said to be* out of the money.

Remark 2.1
Options satisfy the following elementary relations. $C(s, \tau) = C_{K,T}(s, \tau)$ *and* $P(s, \tau) = P_{K,T}(s, \tau)$ *denote the time t value of a call and a put with delivery price K and maturity date T, if* $\tau = T - t$ *is the time to maturity and the price of the underlying is s, i.e.* $S_t = s$.

1. *Option prices are non negative since an exercise only takes place if it is in the interest of the holder. An option gives the right to exercise. The holder is not obligated to do so.*

2. *American and European options have the same value at maturity T since in T they give the same rights to the holder. At maturity T the value of the option is equal to the intrinsic value:*

$$C_{K,T}(S_T, 0) = \max(S_T - K, 0), \quad P_{K,T}(S_T, 0) = \max(K - S_T, 0).$$

3. *An American option must be traded at least at its intrinsic value since otherwise a riskless profit can be realized by buying and immediately exercising the option. This relation does not hold in general for European options. The reason is that a European option can be exercised only indirectly by means of a future contract. The thereby involved discounting rate can possibly lead to the option being worth less than its intrinsic value.*

4. *The value of two American options which have different time to maturities, $T_1 \leq T_2$, is monotonous in time to maturity:*

$$C_{K,T_1}(s, T_1 - t) \leq C_{K,T_2}(s, T_2 - t), \quad P_{K,T_1}(s, T_1 - t) \leq P_{K,T_2}(s, T_2 - t).$$

This follows, for calls, say, using 2., 3. from the inequality which holds at time $t = T_1$ with $s = S_{T_1}$

$$C_{K,T_2}(s, T_2 - T_1) \geq \text{ intrinsic value } = \max(s - K, 0) = C_{K,T_1}(s, 0) \tag{2.12}$$

Due to the no–arbitrage assumption the inequality must hold for any point in time $t \leq T_1$. For European options this result does not hold in general.

5. *An American option is at least as valuable as the identically specified European option since the American option gives more rights to the holder.*

6. *The value of a call is a monotonously decreasing function of the delivery price since the right to buy is the more valuable the lower the agreed upon delivery price. Accordingly, the value of a put is a monotonously increasing function of the delivery price.*

$$C_{K_1,T}(s,\tau) \geq C_{K_2,T}(s,\tau) \,, \quad P_{K_1,T}(s,\tau) \leq P_{K_2,T}(s,\tau)$$

for $K_1 \leq K_2$. This holds for American as well as for European options.

The value of European call and put options on the same underlying with the same time to maturity and delivery price are closely linked to each other without using a complicated mathematical model.

Theorem 2.3 (Put–Call Parity for European Options)
For the value of a European call and put option which have the same maturity date T, the same delivery price K, the same underlying the following holds (where r denotes the continuous interest rate):

1. *If the underlying pays a dividend yield with a time t discounted total value of D_t during the time to maturity $\tau = T - t$ then it holds*

$$C(S_t,\tau) = P(S_t,\tau) + S_t - D_t - Ke^{-r\tau} \qquad (2.13)$$

Q SFEPutCall.xpl

2. *If the underlying involves continuous costs of carry at rate b during the time to maturity $\tau = T - t$ then it holds*

$$C(S_t,\tau) = P(S_t,\tau) + S_t e^{(b-r)\tau} - Ke^{-r\tau} \qquad (2.14)$$

Proof:
For simplicity, we again assume the underlying to be a stock. We consider a portfolio A consisting of one call which will be duplicated by a suitable portfolio B containing a put among others.

1. In the case of discrete dividend yields we consider at time t the following portfolio B :

1. Buy the put.

	Value at time t T	
Position	$K < S_T$	$K \geq S_T$
a)	0	$K - S_T$
b)	$-K$	$-K$
c)	S_T	S_T
d)	0	0
Sum	$S_T - K$	0

Table 2.1: Value of portfolio B at time T (Theorem 2.3).

2. Sell a zero bond with face value K maturing T.

3. Buy one stock.

4. Sell a zero bond at the current price D_t.

The stock in portfolio B pays dividends whose value discounted to time t is D_t. At time T these dividend yields are used to pay back the zero bond of position d). Hence this position has a value of zero at time T. Table 2.1 shows the value of portfolio B at time T where we distinguished the situations where the put is exercised ($K \geq S_T$) and where it is not exercised. At time T portfolio B has thus the same value $\max(S_T - K, 0)$ as the call. To avoid arbitrage opportunities both portfolios A and B must have the same value at any time t prior T, that is it holds

$$C(S_t, \tau) = P(S_t, \tau) - Ke^{-r\tau} + S_t - D_t \qquad (2.15)$$

2. In the case of continuous dividends at rate d and corresponding costs of carry $b = r - d$ we consider the same portfolio B as in part 1. but this time without position d). Instead we buy $e^{-d\tau}$ stocks in position c) whose dividends are immediately reinvested in the same stock. If d is negative, then the costs are financed by selling stocks. Thus, portfolio B contains exactly one stock at time T, and we conclude as in part 1. that the value of portfolio B is at time t equal to the value of the call. $\square$

The proof of the put–call parity holds only for European options. For American options it may happen that the put or call are exercised prior maturity and that both portfolios are not hold until maturity.

The following result makes it possible to check whether prices of options on the same underlying are consistent. If the convexity formulated below is

Position	Value at time t'			
	$S_{t'} \le K_1$	$K_1 < S_{t'} \le K_\lambda$	$K_\lambda < S_{t'} \le K_0$	$K_0 < S_{t'}$
B 1.	0	$\lambda(S_{t'} - K_1)$	$\lambda(S_{t'} - K_1)$	$\lambda(S_{t'} - K_1)$
B 2.	0	0	0	$(1 - \lambda)(S_{t'} - K_0)$
$-A$	0	0	$-(S_{t'} - K_\lambda)$	$-(S_{t'} - K_\lambda)$
Sum	0	$\lambda(S_{t'} - K_1)$	$(1 - \lambda)(K_0 - S_{t'})$	0

Table 2.2: Difference in the values of portfolios B and A at time t' (Theorem 2.4).

violated, then arbitrage opportunities arise as we will show in the example following the proof of the next theorem.

Theorem 2.4
The price of a (American or European) Option is a convex function of the delivery price.

Proof:
It suffices to consider calls since the proof is analogous for puts. The put–call parity for European options is linear in the term which depends explicitly on K. Hence, for European options it follows immediately that puts are convex in K given that calls are convex in K.

For $0 \le \lambda \le 1$ and $K_1 < K_0$ we define $K_\lambda \stackrel{\text{def}}{=} \lambda K_1 + (1 - \lambda)K_0$. We consider a portfolio A which at time $t < T$ consists of one call with delivery price K_λ and maturity date T. At time t we duplicate this portfolio by the following portfolio B :

1. A long position in λ calls with delivery price K_1 maturing in T.

2. A long position in $(1 - \lambda)$ calls delivery price K_0 maturing in T.

By liquidating both portfolios at an arbitrary point of time $t', t \le t' \le T$ we can compute the difference in the values of portfolio A and B which is given in Table 2.2

Since $\lambda(S_{t'} - K_1) \ge 0$ und $(1 - \lambda)(K_0 - S_{t'})) \ge 0$ in the last row of Table 2.2 the difference in the values of portfolio A and B at time t' and thus for any point of time $t < t'$ is greater than or equal to zero. Hence, denoting $\tau = T - t$ it holds

$$\lambda C_{K_1, T}(S_t, \tau) + (1 - \lambda)C_{K_0, T}(S_t, \tau) - C_{K_\lambda, T}(S_t, \tau) \ge 0 \qquad (2.16)$$

Delivery price	Option price
$K_1 = 190$	30.6 EUR
$K_\lambda = 200$	26.0 EUR
$K_0 = 220$	14.4 EUR

Table 2.3: Data of Example 2.3.

$\square$

Example 2.3

We consider three European call options on the MD*TECH A.G. having all the same time to maturity and delivery prices $K_1 = 190$, $K_\lambda = 200$, $K_0 = 220$, i.e. $\lambda = \frac{2}{3}$. Table 2.3 shows the data of this example. Due to the last theorem it must hold:

$$\tfrac{2}{3}C_{K_1,T}(S_t, \tau) + \tfrac{1}{3}C_{K_0,T}(S_t, \tau) \geq C_{K_\lambda,T}(S_t, \tau) \qquad (2.17)$$

Since this condition is obviously violated an arbitrage opportunity exists, and with the following portfolio a riskless gain can be realized:

1. *A long position in $\lambda = \frac{2}{3}$ calls with delivery price K_1.*

2. *A long position in $1 - \lambda = \frac{1}{3}$ calls with delivery price K_0.*

3. *A short position in 1 call with delivery price $K_\lambda \stackrel{\text{def}}{=} \frac{2}{3}K_1 + \frac{1}{3}K_0$.*

By setting up this portfolio at the current time t we realize an immediate profit of +0.80 EUR. The portfolio value at options' maturity T is given by Table 2.4 from which we can extract that we realize further profits for stock prices S_T between 190 and 220 of at most $\dfrac{20}{3}$ EUR.

We already said that option prices are monotonous functions of the delivery price. The following theorem for European options is more precise on this subject.

Theorem 2.5

For two European calls (puts) with the same maturity date T and delivery prices $K_1 \leq K_2$ it holds at time $t \leq T$:

$$0 \leq C_{K_1,T}(S_t, \tau) - C_{K_2,T}(S_t, \tau) \leq (K_2 - K_1)e^{-r\tau} \qquad (2.18)$$

Position	Value at time T			
	$S_T \leq 190$	$190 < S_T \leq 200$	$200 < S_T \leq 220$	$220 < S_T$
1.	0	$\frac{2}{3}(S_T - 190)$	$\frac{2}{3}(S_T - 190)$	$\frac{2}{3}(S_T - 190)$
2.	0	0	0	$\frac{1}{3}(S_T - 220)$
3.	0	0	$-(S_T - 200)$	$-(S_T - 200)$
Sum	0	$\frac{2}{3}(S_T - 190)$	$\frac{1}{3}(220 - S_T)$	0

Table 2.4: Portfolio value at time T of Example 2.3.

or

$$0 \leq P_{K_2,T}(S_t, \tau) - P_{K_1,T}(S_t, \tau) \leq (K_2 - K_1)e^{-r\tau} \qquad (2.19)$$

with $\tau = T - t$ and r denoting the time to maturity and the interest rate respectively. If call (put) option prices are differentiable as a function of the delivery price, then by taking the limit $K_2 - K_1 \to 0$ it follows

$$1 \leq -e^{-r\tau} \leq \frac{\partial C}{\partial K} \leq 0 \quad bzw. \quad 0 \leq \frac{\partial P}{\partial K} \leq e^{-r\tau} \leq 1 \qquad (2.20)$$

Proof:
We proof the theorem for calls since for puts the reasoning is analogous. For this we consider a portfolio A containing one call with delivery price K_1 which we compare to a duplicating portfolio B. At time t the latter portfolio consists of the following two positions:

1. A long position in one call with delivery price K_2.

2. A long position in one zero bond with face value $(K_2 - K_1)$ maturing in T.

The difference of the value of portfolios B and A at time T is shown in Table 2.5. At time T portfolio B is clearly as valuable as portfolio A which given the no–arbitrage assumption must hold at time t as well. We conclude:

$$C_{K_2,T}(S_t, \tau) + (K_2 - K_1)e^{-r\tau} \geq C_{K_1,T}(S_t, \tau).$$

$\square$

2.2   Portfolio Insurance

A major purpose of options is hedging, i.e. the protection of investments against market risk caused by random price movements. An example for

Position	Value at time T		
	$S_T \leq K_1$	$K < S_T < K_2$	$K_2 \leq S_T$
B 1.	0	0	$S_T - K_2$
B 2.	$K_2 - K_1$	$K_2 - K_1$	$K_2 - K_1$
$-A$	0	$-(S_T - K_1)$	$-(S_T - K_1)$
Sum	$K_2 - K_1$	$K_2 - S_T$	0

Table 2.5: Difference in the values of portfolios B and A at time T (Theorem 2.5).

active hedging with options is the portfolio insurance. That is to strike deals in order to change at a certain point of time the risk structure of a portfolio such that at a future point of time

- the positive profits are reduced by a small amount (which can be interpreted as an insurance premium) and in that way

- the portfolio value does not drop below a certain *floor*.

The portfolio insurance creates a risk structure of the portfolio which prevents extreme losses. For illustration purposes we consider at first a simple example.

Example 2.4
An investor has a capital of 10 500 EUR at his disposal to buy stocks whose current price is 100 EUR. Furthermore, put options on the same stock with a delivery price of $K = 100$ and a time to maturity of one year are quoted at a market price of 5 EUR per contract. We consider two investment alternatives.

Portfolio A: *Buying 105 stocks.*

Portfolio B: *Buying 100 stocks for 10 000 EUR and buying 100 put options for 500 EUR.*

The price of the put options can be interpreted as the premium to insure the stocks against falling below a level of 10 000 EUR. Denoting the stock price in one year by S_T the value of the non–insured portfolio is $105 \cdot S_T$. This portfolio bears the full market risk that the stock price drops significantly below 100 EUR. The insured portfolio, however, is at least as worth as 10 000 EUR

Stock price S_T [EUR]	Non–insured portfolio		Insured portfolio		Insured portfolio in % of the non–insured portfolio
	Value [EUR]	Return % p.a.	Value [EUR]	Return % p.a.	
50	5250	−50	10000	−4.8	190
60	6300	−40	10000	−4.8	159
70	7350	−30	10000	−4.8	136
80	8400	−20	10000	−4.8	119
90	9450	−10	10000	−4.8	106
100	10500	0	10000	-4.8	95
110	11550	+10	11000	+4.8	95
120	12600	+20	12000	+14.3	95
130	13650	+30	13000	+23.8	95
140	14700	+40	14000	+33.3	95

Table 2.6: The effect of a portfolio insurance on portfolio value and return.

since if $S_T < 100$ the holder exercises the put options and sells the 100 stocks for 100 EUR each.

Should the stock price increase above 100 EUR the investor does not exercise the put which thus expires worthless. By buying the put some of the capital of portfolio B is sacrificed to insure against high losses. But, while the probabilities of high profits slightly decrease, the probabilities of high losses decrease to zero. Investing in portfolio B the investor looses at most 500 EUR which he paid for the put. Table 2.6 shows the impact of the stock price S_T in one year on both the insured and the non–insured portfolio values and returns.

The numerous conceivable strategies to insure portfolios can be classified by the frequency with which the positions in the portfolio have to rebalanced. Two approaches can be distinguished:

- Static strategies rebalance the portfolio positions at most once before expiration of the investment horizon.

- Dynamic strategies rebalance the portfolio positions very frequently, ideally continuously, according to certain rules.

The static strategy sketched in the previous example can be modified. Instead of hedging by means of put options the investor can chose between the following two strategies:

Strategy 1: The investor buys an equal number of *stocks and puts.*

Strategy 2: The investor buys *bonds* with a face value equal to the floor he
is aiming at and for the remaining money he buys calls on the stock.

All strategies commonly practiced rely on modifications of the above basic
strategies. While following the first strategy it is the put which guarantees
that the invested capital does not drop below the floor, applying the second strategy it is the bond which insures the investor against falling prices.
The stocks respectively the calls make up for the profits in case of rising
prices. The equivalence of both strategies follows from the put–call parity,
see Theorem 2.3.

Before deciding about what kind of portfolio insurance will be used some
points have to be clarified:

1. Which financial instruments are provided by the market, and what are
   their characteristics (coupons, volatilities, correlation with the market
   etc.)?

2. Which ideas does the investor have about

   - the composition of the portfolio (which financial instruments),
   - the amount of capital to invest,
   - the investment horizon,
   - the floor (lower bound of the portfolio value) or rather the mini-
     mum return he is aiming at the end of the investment. Given the
     floor F and the capital invested V the possibly negative minimum
     return of a one year investment is given by $\rho = \frac{F-V}{V}$.

The strategies 1 and 2 described above we illustrate in another example.

Example 2.5
*We proceed from the assumption that the investor has decided to invest in
stock. Depending on the type of return of the object we distinguish two cases
(for negative returns, as storage costs of real values for example, the approach
can be applied analogously):*

i) *continuous dividend yield d*

ii) *ex ante known discrete yields with a time 0 discounted total value of D_0.*

Data of Example 2.5:	
Current point of time t	0
Available capital V	100 000 EUR
Target floor F	95 000 EUR
Investment horizon T	2 years
Current stock price S_0	100 EUR
Continuously compounded annual interest rate r	0.10
Annual stock volatility σ	0.30
Dividends during time to maturity	
Case i): continuous dividends d	0.02
Fall ii): dividends with present value D_0	5 EUR

Table 2.7: Data of Example 2.5

The data of the example is shown in Table 2.7. The volatility can be inter-preted as a measure of variability of the stock price. The notion of volatility is an essential part of option pricing and will be treated extensively later. Placing our considerations at the beginning $t = 0$ of the investment the time to maturity is $\tau = T - t = T$. For both strategies the goal is to determine the number n of stocks and/or (European) options and their delivery price K.

Case i)
The stock pays a continuous dividend at rate $d = 2\%$ p.a. which he reinvests immediately. At maturity T the position in the stock grew from n stocks to $ne^{d\tau}$ with $\tau = T - 0 = T$. Thus, for strategy 1 he has to buy in $t = 0$ the same number of put options. Since the amount he wants to invest in $t = 0$ is V it must hold

$$n \cdot S_0 + ne^{d\tau} \cdot P_{K,T}(S_0, \tau) = V. \qquad (2.21)$$

The investor chooses the put options delivery price K such that his capital after two years does not drop below the floor F he is aiming at. That is, exercising the puts in time T (if $S_T \leq K$) must give the floor F which gives the second condition

$$ne^{d\tau} \cdot K = F \iff n = \frac{F}{K}e^{-d\tau}. \qquad (2.22)$$

Substituting equation (2.22) into equation (2.21) gives

$$e^{-d\tau}S_0 + P_{K,T}(S_0, \tau) - \frac{V}{F} \cdot K = 0. \qquad (2.23)$$

Thanks to the Black–Scholes pricing formula for European options that will be derived later in Section 6.2 the put price is expressed as a function of

Stock price S_T [EUR]	Non–insured portfolio		Insured portfolio		Insured portfolio in % of the non– insured portfolio
	Value [EUR]	Return % p.a.	Value [EUR]	Return % p.a.	
70	72857	−27	95000	−5	130
80	83265	−17	95000	−5	114
90	93673	−6	95000	−5	101
100	104081	+4	95400	−5	92
110	114489	+15	104940	+5	92
120	124897	+25	114480	+14	92
130	135305	+35	124020	+24	92
140	145714	+46	133560	+34	92

Table 2.8: The effect of a portfolio insurance in case i) on portfolio value and return.   Q SFEoptman.xpl

the parameter K. The delivery price which he is looking for can be computed by solving equation (2.23) numerically, for example by means of the Newton–Raphson method. In this case, K is equal to 99.56. To be sure that the capital value does not drop below the floor $F = 95\,000$ EUR he buys $n = \frac{F}{K}e^{-d\tau} = 916.6$ stocks and $n \cdot e^{d\tau} = 954$ puts with delivery price $K = 99.56$. The price of the put option given by the Black–Scholes formula is 8.72 EUR/put.   Q SFEexerput.xpl

Following the corresponding strategy 2 he invests $Fe^{-r\tau} = 77\,779.42$ EUR in bonds at time 0 which gives compounded to time T exactly the floor $F = 95\,000$ EUR. For the remaining capital of $V - Fe^{-r\tau} = 22\,220.58$ EUR he buys 954 calls with delivery price $K = 99.56$ which have a price of 23.29 EUR/call according to the Black–Scholes formula. From the put–call parity follows the equivalence of both strategies, i.e. both portfolios consisting of stocks and puts respectively zero bonds and calls have at each time t the same value:

$$n \cdot S_t + ne^{d\tau}P_{K,T}(S_t, \tau) = nKe^{-b\tau} + ne^{d\tau}C_{K,T}(S_0, \tau) \qquad (2.24)$$

where $\tau = T - t, b = r - d$ and $nKe^{-b\tau} = Fe^{-r\tau}$ due to equation (2.22). Table 2.8 shows the risk decreasing effect of the insurance.

Case ii)

Until maturity the stock pays dividends with a time 0 discounted total value $D_0 = 5$ EUR which are after distribution immediately invested in bonds. At time T the dividend yield has a compounded value of $D_T = D_0e^{r\tau} = 6.107$

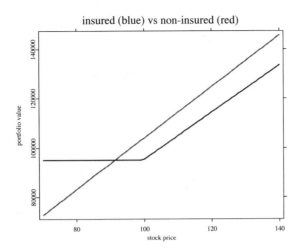

Figure 2.1: The effect of a portfolio insurance: While the straight line represents the value of the insured portfolio as a function of the stock price, the dotted line represents the value of the non–insured portfolio as a function of the stock price.   **Q** SFEoptman.xpl

EUR *where* $\tau = T$ *denotes the time to maturity. Reasoning as in case i) and taking the dividend* D_T *into account he buys n stocks respectively n puts, and obtains the following equations*

$$n \cdot S_0 + nP_{K,T}(S_0 - D_0, \tau) = V \qquad (2.25)$$

and

$$nK + nD_T = F. \qquad (2.26)$$

The substraction of the cash dividend D_0 *from the stock price* S_0 *in the option price formula cannot be justified until we introduced the binomial model in Chapter 7. Briefly, in a perfect market the stock price decreases instantaneously by the amount of the distributed dividend. Otherwise, an arbitrage opportunity arises. Substituting equation (2.26) into equation (2.25) gives:*

$$S_0 + P_{K,T}(S_0 - D_0, \tau) - \frac{V}{F} \cdot (K + D_T) = 0 \qquad (2.27)$$

Solving the equations analogously as in case i) the number n of stocks and puts and the delivery price K for strategy 1 are obtained:

$$K = 96.42 \quad und \quad n = \frac{F}{K + D_T} = 926.55$$

Stock price S_T [EUR]	Non–insured portfolio		Insured portfolio		Insured portfolio in % of the non– insured portfolio
	Value [EUR]	Return % p.a.	Value [EUR]	Return % p.a.	
70	76107	−24	94996	−5	125
80	86107	−14	94996	−5	110
90	96107	−4	94996	−5	99
96.42	102527	+3	94996	−5	93
100	106107	+6	98313	−2	93
110	116107	+16	107579	+8	93
120	126107	+26	116844	+17	93
130	136107	+36	126110	+26	93
140	146107	+46	135375	+35	93

Table 2.9: The effect of a portfolio insurance in case ii) on portfolio value and
return.

For strategy 2 he buys 926.55 *calls at a price of* 23.99 EUR/*call with a delivery
price* $K = 96.42$. *He invests* 95 000$e^{-r\tau} = 77\,779.42$ *in bonds. For case ii)
the effect of the portfolio insurance for both strategies is shown in Table 2.9
taking into account the time* T *compounded total dividend.*

The example shows how a portfolio insurance can be carried out by means
of options in principle. In practice, the following problems frequently occur:

- The number n of stocks and options is not an integer. In a perfect
  financial market financial instruments are perfectly divisible, in reality,
  however, this is not the case. The error resulting from rounding up or
  down to closest integer can be neglected only in large portfolios.

- Puts and calls traded on the market do not cover the whole range of
  delivery prices. Thus, options with the computed delivery price are
  possibly not available. Furthermore, options typically expire in less
  than one year which makes static strategies only limited applicable
  when long–term investments are involved.

- Finally, the market provides first of all American options which are
  more expensive than European options which are sufficient to insure the
  portfolio. The additional exercise opportunities offered by American
  options, are only of interest if the investor possibly has to close the
  portfolio early.

The fact that options are not traded at all delivery prices suggests to produce them by the delta hedge process described in Chapter 6. But since a dynamic strategy is involved transaction costs have to be taken into account and give rise to other problems. Finally, we point out that when insuring large portfolios it is convenient to hedge by means of index options, i.e. puts and calls on the DAX for example, not only from a cost saving point of view but also those options replace options on a single underlying which are not traded on the market. To compute the exact effect of an index option hedge the correlation of the portfolio with the index is needed. The latter correlation is obtained from the correlations of each individual stock contained in the portfolio with the index. Besides detailed model assumptions as the Capital Asset Pricing Model (CAPM see Section 10.4.1) which among others concern the stock returns are required.

2.3   Recommended Literature

The fundamental arbitrage relations of financial derivatives can be found in every modern finance textbook, as for example Hull (2000). In principle each option pricing theory is based on theses relations, as it is the case for the model of Black and Scholes (1973) for example, see also the fundamental article of Merton (1973). The idea of portfolio assurance was introduced by Leland (1980). It is nowadays covered above all by practical risk management textbooks as Das (1997).

3 Basic Concepts of Probability Theory

3.1   Real Valued Random Variables

Thanks to Newton's laws, dropping a stone from a latitude of 10 m, the point of time of its impact on the ground is known before executing the experiment. Quantities in complex systems (such as stock prices at a certain date, daily maximum temperature at a certain place) are however not deterministically predictable, although it is known which values are more likely to occur than others. Contrary to the falling stone, data which cannot be described successfully by deterministic mechanism, can be modelled by random variables.

Let X be such a random variable which, (as a model for stock prices), takes values on the real time. The appraisal of which values of X are more and which are less likely, is expressed by the *probability* of events as $\{a < X < b\}$ or $\{X \leq b\}$. The set of all probabilities

$$\mathrm{P}(a \leq X \leq b) \,, \quad -\infty < a \leq b < \infty \,,$$

determines the *distribution* of X. In other words, the distribution is defined by the probabilities of all events which depend on X. In the following, we denote the probability distribution of X by $\mathcal{L}(X)$.

The probability distribution is uniquely defined by the *cumulative probability distribution*

$$F(x) = \mathrm{P}(X \leq x) \,, \quad -\infty < x < \infty \,.$$

$F(x)$ is monotonously increasing and converges for $x \to -\infty$ to 0, and for $x \to \infty$ to 1. If there is a function p, such that the probabilities can be computed by means of an integral

$$\mathrm{P}(a < X < b) = \int_a^b p(x)dx \,,$$

p is called a *probability density*, or briefly density of X. Then the cumulative distribution function is a primitive of p:

$$F(x) = \int_{-\infty}^{x} p(y)dy.$$

For small h it holds:

$$P(x - h < X < x + h) \approx 2h \cdot p(x).$$

Thus $p(x)$ is a measure of the likelihood that X takes values close to x.

The most important family of distributions with densities, is the *normal distribution* family. It is characterized by two parameters μ, σ^2. The densities are given by

$$\varphi_{\mu,\sigma^2}(x) = \frac{1}{\sqrt{2\pi\sigma^2}} e^{-\frac{(x-\mu)^2}{2\sigma^2}} = \frac{1}{\sigma} \varphi\left(\frac{x-\mu}{\sigma}\right),$$

$$\varphi(x) = \varphi_{0,1}(x) = \frac{1}{\sqrt{2\pi}} e^{-\frac{x^2}{2}}.$$

The distribution with density $\varphi(x)$ is called *standard normal distribution*. "X is a normal random variable with parameters μ, σ^2" is commonly abbreviated by "X is $N(\mu, \sigma^2)$ distributed". The cumulative distribution function of a standard normal distribution is denoted by Φ and it holds:

$$\Phi(x) = \int_{-\infty}^{x} \varphi(y)dy.$$

If X is $N(\mu, \sigma^2)$ distributed, then the centered and scaled random variable $(X - \mu)/\sigma$ is standard normal distributed. Therefore, its cumulative distribution function is given by:

$$F(x) = P(X \leq x) = P\left(\frac{X - \mu}{\sigma} \leq \frac{x - \mu}{\sigma}\right) = \Phi\left(\frac{x - \mu}{\sigma}\right).$$

A distribution which is of importance in modelling stock prices is the *lognormal distribution*. Let X be a positive random variable whose natural logarithm $\ln(X)$ is normally distributed with parameters μ, σ^2. We say that X is lognormally distributed with parameters μ, σ^2. Its cumulative distribution function follows directly from the above definition:

$$F(x) = P(X \leq x) = P(\ln X \leq \ln x) = \Phi\left(\frac{\ln x - \mu}{\sigma}\right), \quad x > 0.$$

Deriving $F(x)$ once, we obtain its density function with parameters μ, σ^2:

$$p(x) = \frac{1}{\sqrt{2\pi\sigma^2}} \frac{1}{x} e^{-\frac{(\ln x - \mu)^2}{2\sigma^2}} = \frac{1}{\sigma x} \varphi\left(\frac{\ln x - \mu}{\sigma}\right), \quad x > 0.$$

If X is a random variable that takes only finitely or countably infinite values $x_1, \ldots, x_n$, X is said to be a discrete random variable and its distribution is fully determined by the probabilities:

$$P(X = x_k), \quad k = 1, \ldots, n.$$

The simplest discrete random variables take only 2 or 3 values, for example ± 1 or $-1, 0, +1$. They constitute the basis of binomial or trinomial trees which can be used to construct discrete random processes in computers. Such tree methods are reasonable approximations to continuous processes which are used to model stock prices.

In this context, *binomially distributed* random variables appear. Let $Y_1, \ldots, Y_n$ be independent random variables taking two values, 0 or 1, with probabilities

$$p = P(Y_k = 1), \ 1 - p = P(Y_k = 0), \quad k = 1, \ldots, n.$$

We call such random variables *Bernoulli distributed* with parameter p. The number of ones appearing in the sample $Y_1, \ldots, Y_n$, equals the sum $X = \sum_{k=1}^{n} Y_k$ which is binomial distributed with parameters n, p:

$$X = \sum_{k=1}^{n} Y_k, \ P(X = m) = \binom{n}{m} p^m (1 - p)^{n-m}, \quad m = 0, \ldots, n.$$

Q SFEBinomial.xpl

Instead of saying X is binomial distributed with parameters n, p, we use the notation "X is $B(n, p)$ distributed". Hence, a Bernoulli distributed random variable is $B(1, p)$ distributed.

If n is large enough, a $B(n, p)$ distributed random variable can be approximated by a $N(np, np(1 - p))$ distributed random variable Z, in the sense that

$$P(a < X < b) \approx P(a < Z < b). \tag{3.1}$$

The central limit theorem is more precise on that matter. In classical statistics it is used to avoid, for large n, the tedious calculation of binomial probabilities. Conversely, it is possible to approximate the normal distribution by an easy simulated binomial tree.   **Q** SFEclt.xpl

3.2 Expectation and Variance

The mathematical *expectation* or the *mean* $\mathsf{E}[X]$ of a real random variable X is a measure for the location of the distribution of X. Adding to X a real constant c, it holds for the expectation: $\mathsf{E}[X+c] = \mathsf{E}[X]+c$, i.e. the location of the distribution is translated. If X has a density $p(x)$, its expectation is defined as:

$$\mathsf{E}(X) = \int_{-\infty}^{\infty} x p(x) dx.$$

If the integral does not exist, neither does the expectation. In practice, this is rather rarely the case.

Let $X_1, \ldots, X_n$ be a sample of identically independently distributed (i.i.d.) random variables (see Section 3.4) having the same distribution as X, then $\mathsf{E}[X]$ can be estimated by means of the sample mean:

$$\hat{\mu} = \frac{1}{n} \sum_{t=1}^{n} X_t.$$

A measure for the dispersion of a random variable X around its mean is given by the *variance* $\mathrm{Var}(X)$:

$$
\begin{aligned}
\mathrm{Var}(X) &= \mathsf{E}[(X - \mathsf{E}\,X)^2] \\
\text{Variance} &= \text{mean squarred deviation of a random variable} \\
&\quad \text{around its expectation.}
\end{aligned}
$$

If X has a density $p(x)$, its variance can be computed as follows:

$$\mathrm{Var}(X) = \int_{-\infty}^{\infty} (x - \mathsf{E}\,X)^2 p(x) dx.$$

The integral can be infinite. There are empirical studies giving rise to doubt that some random variables appearing in financial and actuarial mathematics and which model losses in highly risky businesses dispose of a finite variance.

As a quadratic quantity the variance's unity is different from that of X itself. It is better to use the standard deviation of X which is measured in the same unity as X:

$$\sigma(X) = \sqrt{\mathrm{Var}(X)}.$$

Given a sample of i.i.d. variables $X_1, \ldots, X_n$ which have the same distribution as X, the sample variance can be estimated by:

$$\hat{\sigma}^2 = \frac{1}{n} \sum_{t=1}^{n} (X_t - \hat{\mu})^2.$$

A $N(\mu, \sigma^2)$ distributed random variable X has mean μ and variance σ^2. The 2σ area around μ contains with probability of a little more than 95% observations of X:

$$\mathsf{P}(\mu - 2\sigma < X < \mu + 2\sigma) \approx 0.95 \,.$$

A lognormally distributed random variable X with parameters μ and σ^2 has mean and variance

$$\mathsf{E}(X) = e^{\mu + \frac{1}{2}\sigma^2}, \quad \mathrm{Var}(X) = e^{2\mu + \sigma^2}(e^{\sigma^2} - 1).$$

A $B(n, p)$ distributed variable X has mean np and variance $np(1 - p)$. The approximation (3.1) is chosen such that the binomial and normal distribution have identical mean and variance.

3.3   Skewness and Kurtosis

Definition 3.1 (Skewness)
The skewness of a random variable X with mean μ and variance σ^2 is defined as

$$S(X) = \frac{\mathsf{E}[(X - \mu)^3]}{\sigma^3}.$$

If the skewness is negative (positive) the distribution is skewed to the left (right). Normally distributed random variables have a skewness of zero since the distribution is symmetrical around the mean. Given a sample of i.i.d. variables $X_1, \ldots, X_n$, Skewness can be estimated by (see Section 3.4)

$$\hat{S}(X) = \frac{\frac{1}{n} \sum_{t=1}^{n} (X_t - \hat{\mu})^3}{\hat{\sigma}^3}, \tag{3.2}$$

with $\hat{\mu}, \hat{\sigma}^2$ as defined in the previous section.

Definition 3.2 (Kurtosis)
The kurtosis of a random variable X with mean μ and variance σ^2 is defined as

$$\mathrm{Kurt}(X) = \frac{\mathsf{E}[(X - \mu)^4]}{\sigma^4}.$$

Normally distributed random variables have a kurtosis of 3. Financial data often exhibits higher kurtosis values, indicating that values close to the mean and extreme positive and negative outliers appear more frequently than for normally distributed random variables. Kurtosis can be estimated by

$$\widehat{\mathrm{Kurt}}(X) = \frac{\frac{1}{n}\sum_{t=1}^{n}(X_t - \hat{\mu})^4}{\hat{\sigma}^4}. \tag{3.3}$$

Example 3.1 *The empirical standard deviation of monthly DAX data from 1979:1 to 2000:10 is $\hat{\sigma} = 0.056$, which corresponds to a yearly volatility of $\hat{\sigma} \cdot \sqrt{12} = 0.195$. Later in Section(6.3.4), we will explain the factor $\sqrt{12}$ in detail. The kurtosis of the data is much greater than 3 which suggests a non-normality of the DAX returns.*

Q SFEsumm.xpl

3.4 Random Vectors, Dependence, Correlation

A *random vector* $(X_1, \ldots, X_n)$ from $\mathbb{R}^n$ can be useful in describing the mutual dependencies of several random variables $X_1, \ldots, X_n$, for example several underlying stocks. The joint distribution of the random variables $X_1, \ldots, X_n$ is as in the univariate case, uniquely determined by the probabilities

$$\mathrm{P}(a_1 \le X_1 \le b_1, \ldots, a_n \le X_n \le b_n), \quad -\infty < a_i \le b_i < \infty, \, i = 1, ..., n.$$

If the random vector $(X_1, \ldots, X_n)$ has a density $p(x_1, \ldots, x_n)$, the probabilities can be computed by means of the following integrals:

$$\mathrm{P}(a_1 \le X_1 \le b_1, \ldots, a_n \le X_n \le b_n) = \int_{a_n}^{b_n} \ldots \int_{a_1}^{b_1} p(x_1, \ldots, x_n) dx_1 \ldots dx_n.$$

The univariate or marginal distribution of X_j can be computed from the joint density by integrating out the variable not of interest.

$$\mathrm{P}(a_j \le X_j \le b_j) = \int_{-\infty}^{\infty} \ldots \int_{a_j}^{b_j} \ldots \int_{-\infty}^{\infty} p(x_1, \ldots, x_n) dx_1 \ldots dx_n.$$

The intuitive notion of *independence* of two random variables X_1, X_2 is formalized by requiring:

$$\mathrm{P}(a_1 \le X_1 \le b_1, a_2 \le X_2 \le b_2) = \mathrm{P}(a_1 \le X_1 \le b_1) \cdot \mathrm{P}(a_2 \le X_2 \le b_2),$$

i.e. the joint probability of two events depending on the random vector (X_1, X_2) can be factorized. It is sufficient to consider the univariate distributions of X_1 and X_2 exclusively. If the random vector (X_1, X_2) has a density $p(x_1, x_2)$, then X_1 and X_2 have densities $p_1(x)$ and $p_2(x)$ as well. In this case, independence of both random variables is equivalent to a joint density which can be factorized:

$$p(x_1, x_2) = p_1(x_1) p_2(x_2).$$

Dependence of two random variables X_1, X_2 can be very complicated. If X_1, X_2 are jointly normally distributed, their dependency structure can be rather easily quantified by their covariance:

$$\mathrm{Cov}(X_1, X_2) = \mathsf{E}[(X_1 - \mathsf{E}[X_1])(X_2 - \mathsf{E}[X_2])],$$

as well as by their correlation:

$$\mathrm{Corr}(X_1, X_2) = \frac{\mathrm{Cov}(X_1, X_2)}{\sigma(X_1) \cdot \sigma(X_2)}.$$

The correlation has the advantage of taking values between -1 and +1, which is scale invariant. For jointly normally distributed random variables, independence is equivalent to zero correlation, while complete dependence is equivalent to either a correlation of +1 (X_1 is large when X_2 is large) or a correlation of -1 (X_1 is large when X_2 is small).

In general, it holds for *independent* random variables $X_1, \ldots, X_n$

$$\mathrm{Cov}(X_i, X_j) = 0 \qquad \text{for } i \neq j.$$

This implies a useful computation rule:

$$\mathrm{Var}\left(\sum_{j=1}^{n} X_j\right) = \sum_{j=1}^{n} \mathrm{Var}(X_j).$$

If $X_1, \ldots, X_n$ are independent and have all the same distribution:

$$\mathrm{P}(a \leq X_i \leq b) = \mathrm{P}(a \leq X_j \leq b) \qquad \text{for all } i, j,$$

we call them *independently and identically distributed (i.i.d.)*.

3.5   Conditional Probabilities and Expectations

The *conditional probability* that a random variable Y takes values between a and b conditioned on the event that a random variable X takes values between x and $x + \Delta_x$, is defined as

$$P(a \le Y \le b | x \le X \le x + \Delta_x) = \frac{P(a \le Y \le b,\, x \le X \le x + \Delta_x)}{P(x \le X \le x + \Delta_x)}, \quad (3.4)$$

provided the denominator is different from zero. The conditional probability of events of the kind $a \le Y \le b$ reflects our opinion of which values are more plausible than others, given that another random variable X has taken a certain value. If Y is independent of X, the probabilities of Y are not influenced by a priori knowledge about X. It holds:

$$P(a \le Y \le b | x \le X \le x + \Delta x) = P(a \le Y \le b).$$

As Δx goes to 0 in equation (3.4), the left side of equation (3.4) converges heuristically to $P(a \le Y \le b | X = x)$. In the case of a continuous random variable X having a density p_X, the left side of equation (3.4) is not defined since $P(X = x) = 0$ for all x. But, it is possible to give a sound mathematical definition of the conditional distribution of Y given $X = x$. If the random variables Y and X have a joint distribution $p(x, y)$, then the conditional distribution has the density

$$p_{Y|X}(y|x) = \frac{p(x, y)}{p_X(x)} \quad \text{for} \quad p_X(x) \ne 0$$

and $p_{Y|X}(y|x) = 0$ otherwise. Consequently, it holds

$$P(a \le Y \le b | X = x) = \int_a^b p_{Y|X}(y|x)dy.$$

The expectation with respect to the conditional distribution can be computed by

$$E(Y|X = x) = \int_{-\infty}^{\infty} y\, p_{Y|X}(y|x)dy \stackrel{\text{def}}{=} \eta(x).$$

The function $\eta(x) = E(Y|X = x)$ is called the *conditional expectation of Y given X − x*. Intuitively, it is the expectation of the random variable Y knowing that X has taken the value x.

Considering $\eta(x)$ as a function of the random variable X the conditional expectation of Y given X is obtained:

$$E(Y|X) = \eta(X).$$

$E(Y|X)$ is a random variable, which can be regarded as a function having the same expectation as Y. The conditional expectation has some useful properties, which we summarize in the following theorem.

Theorem 3.1 *Let X, Y, Z be real valued continuous random variables having a joint density.*

a) *If X, Y are independent, then $\mathsf{E}(Y|X = x) = \mathsf{E}(Y)$*

b) *If $Y = g(X)$ is a function of X, then*

$$\mathsf{E}[Y|X = x] = \mathsf{E}[g(X)|X = x] = g(x).$$

In general, it holds for random variables of the kind $Y = Zg(X)$:

$$\mathsf{E}[Y|X = x] = \mathsf{E}[Zg(X)|X = x] = g(x)\,\mathsf{E}[Z|X = x].$$

c) *The conditional expectation is linear, i.e. for any real numbers a, b it holds:*

$$\mathsf{E}(aY + bZ|X = x) = a\,\mathsf{E}(Y|X = x) + b\,\mathsf{E}(Z|X = x).$$

d) *The law of iterated expectations: $\mathsf{E}[\mathsf{E}(Y|X)] = \mathsf{E}(Y)$.*

The concept of the conditional expectation can be generalized analogously for multivariate random vectors Y and X. Let $S_t, t = 0, 1, 2, ...$ be a sequence of chronologically ordered random variables, for instance as a model of daily stock prices, let $Y = S_{t+1}$ and $X = (S_t, ..., S_{t-p+1})^\top$, then the conditional expectation

$$\mathsf{E}(Y|X = x) = \mathsf{E}(S_{t+1}|S_t = x_1, ..., S_{t-p+1} = x_p)$$

represents the expected stock price of the following day $t + 1$ given the stock prices $x = (x_1, ..., x_p)^\top$ of the previous p days. Since the information available at time t (relevant for the future evolution of the stock price) can consist of more than only a few past stock prices, we make frequent use of the notation $\mathsf{E}(Y|\mathcal{F}_t)$ for the expectation of Y given the information available up to time t. For all t, $\mathcal{F}_t$ denotes a family of events (having the structure of a $\sigma-$ algebra, i.e. certain combinations of events of $\mathcal{F}_t$ are again elements of $\mathcal{F}_t$) representing the information available up to time t. $\mathcal{F}_t$ consists of events of which it is known whether they occur up to time t or not. Since more information unveils as time evolves, we must have $\mathcal{F}_s \subset \mathcal{F}_t$ for $s < t$, see Definition 5.1. Leaving out the exact definition of $\mathsf{E}(Y|\mathcal{F}_t)$ we confine to emphasize that the computation rules given in Theorem 3.1, appropriately reformulated, can be applied to the general conditional expectation.

3.6   Recommended Literature

Ross (1994), Pitman (1997), Krengel (2000) and Krengel (1995), among others, give an introduction to probability theory. An introduction to martingale theory which is imperative for the understanding of advanced mathematical finance is given by Williams (1991).

4 Stochastic Processes in Discrete Time

A *stochastic process* or random process consists of chronologically ordered random variables $\{X_t; \ t \geq 0\}$. For simplicity we assume that the process starts at time $t = 0$ in $X_0 = 0$. In this chapter, we consider exclusively processes in *discrete time*, i.e. processes which are observed at equally spaced points of time $t = 0, 1, 2, \dots$. Typical examples are daily, monthly or yearly observed economic data as stock prices, rates of unemployment or sales amount.

4.1 Binomial Processes

One of the simplest stochastic processes is an *ordinary random walk*, a process whose increments $Z_t = X_t - X_{t-1}$ from time $t - 1$ to time t take exclusively the values $+1$ or -1. Additionally, we assume the increments to be i.i.d. and independent of the starting value X_0. Hence, the ordinary random walk can be written as:

$$X_t = X_0 + \sum_{k=1}^{t} Z_k \qquad , \ t = 1, 2, \dots \qquad (4.1)$$

$X_0, Z_1, Z_2, \dots$ independent and

$$\mathrm{P}(Z_k = 1) = p \quad , \quad \mathrm{P}(Z_k = -1) = 1 - p \qquad \text{for all } k \,.$$

Letting the process go up by u and go down by d, instead, we obtain a more general class of *binomial processes*:

$$\mathrm{P}(Z_k = u) = p, \quad \mathrm{P}(Z_k = -d) = 1 - p \quad \text{für alle } k \,,$$

where u and d are constant (u=up, d=down).

Linear interpolation of the points (t, X_t) reflects the time evolution of the process and is called a *path* of an ordinary random walk. Starting in $X_0 = a$, the process moves on the grid of points (t, b_t), $t = 0, 1, 2, \ldots$, $b_t = a - t$, $a - t + 1, \ldots, a + t$. Up to time t, X_t can grow at most up to $a + t$ (if $Z_1 = \ldots = Z_t = 1$) or can fall at least to $a - t$ (if $Z_1 = \ldots = Z_t = -1$). Three paths of an ordinary random walk are shown in Figure 4.1 ($p = 0.5$), 4.2 ($p = 0.4$) and Figure 4.3 ($p = 0.6$).

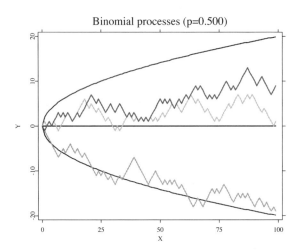

Figure 4.1:   Three paths of a symmetric ordinary random walk. (2σ)–
            intervals around the drift (which is zero) are given as well.
                                                    Q SFEBinomp.xpl

For generalized binomial processes the grid of possible paths is more complicated. The values which the process X_t starting in a can possibly take up to
time t are given by

$$b_t = a + n \cdot u - m \cdot d, \text{ where } n, m \geq 0, \quad n + m = t.$$

If, from time 0 to time t, the process goes up n times and goes down m times
then $X_t = a + n \cdot u - m \cdot d$. That is, n of t increments $Z_1, \ldots, Z_t$ take the
value u, and m increments take the value $-d$. The grid of possible paths is
also called a binomial tree.

The mean of the *symmetric ordinary random walk* ($p = \frac{1}{2}$) starting in 0
($X_0 = 0$) is for all times t equal to 0 :

$$\mathsf{E}[X_t] = 0 \qquad \text{for all } t.$$

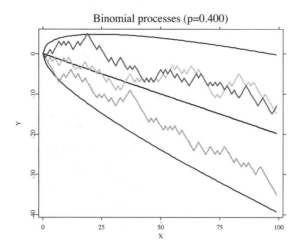

Figure 4.2:   Three paths of an ordinary random walk with $p = 0.4$. (2σ)–
intervals around the drift (which is the line with negative slope)
are given as well.   **Q** SFEBinomp.xpl

Otherwise, the *random walk* has a *trend* or *drift*, for $(p > \frac{1}{2})$ it has a positive
drift and for $(p < \frac{1}{2})$ it has a negative drift. The process grows or falls in
average:
$$\mathsf{E}[X_t] = t \cdot (2p - 1) \,,$$
since it holds for all increments $\mathsf{E}[Z_k] = 2p - 1$. Hence, the trend is linear in
time. It is the upward sloping line in Figure 4.3 $(p = 0.6)$ and the downward
sloping line in Figure 4.2 $(p = 0.6)$.

For the generalized *binomial process* with general starting value X_0 it holds
analogously $\mathsf{E}[Z_k] = (u + d)p - d$ and thus:
$$\mathsf{E}[X_t] = \mathsf{E}[X_0] + t \cdot \{(u + d)p - d\} \,.$$

As time evolves the set of values X_t grows, and its variability increases. Since
the summands in (4.1) are independent and $\text{Var}(Z_k) = \text{Var}(Z_1)$ for all k, the
variance of X_t is given by (refer to Section 3.4):
$$\text{Var}(X_t) = \text{Var}(X_0) + t \cdot \text{Var}(Z_1) \,.$$

Hence, the variance of X_t grows linearly with time. So does the standard
deviation. For the random walks depicted in Figure 4.1 $(p = 0.5)$, Figure

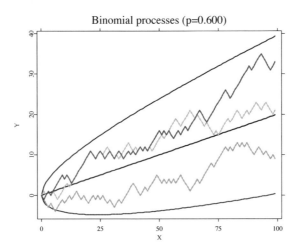

Figure 4.3: Three paths of an ordinary random walk with $p = 0.6$. (2σ)–
            intervals around the drift (which is the line with positive slope)
            are given as well.   **Q** SFEBinomp.xpl

4.2 ($p = 0.4$) and Figure 4.3 ($p = 0.6$) the intervals $[\mathsf{E}[X_t] - 2\sigma(X_t); \mathsf{E}[X_t] + 2\sigma(X_t)]$ are shown as well. For large t , these intervals should contain 95% of the realizations of processes.

The variance of the increments can be easily computed. We use the following result which holds for the binomial distribution. Define

$$Y_k = \frac{Z_k + d}{u + d} = \begin{cases} 1 & \text{if } Z_k = u \\ 0 & \text{if } Z_k = -d \end{cases}$$

or

$$Z_k = (u + d)\,Y_k - d \tag{4.2}$$

we obtain the following representation of the binomial process

$$X_t = X_0 + (u + d)\,B_t - td \tag{4.3}$$

where

$$B_t = \sum_{k=1}^{t} Y_k \tag{4.4}$$

is a $B(t, p)$ distributed random variable.

Given the distribution of X_0, the distribution of X_t is specified for all t. It can be derived by means of a simple transformation of the binomial distribution $B(t, p)$. From equations (4.2) to (4.4) we obtain for $X_0 = 0$:

$$\mathrm{Var}(X_t) = t(u + d)^2\, p(1 - p)$$

and for large t the distribution of X_t can be approximated by:

$$\mathcal{L}(X_t) \approx N(t\{(u + d)p - d\},\, t(u + d)^2\, p(1 - p)).$$

For $p = \frac{1}{2}, u = d = \Delta x$, the following approximation holds for $\mathcal{L}(X_t)$:

$$N(0, t \cdot (\Delta x)^2).$$

Figure 4.4 shows the fit for $t = 100$.

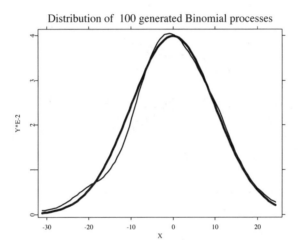

Figure 4.4: The distribution of 100 paths of an ordinary symmetric random walk of length 100 and a kernel density estimation of 100 normally distributed random variables.   **Q** SFEbinomv.xpl

4.2 Trinomial Processes

In contrast to binomial processes, a *trinomial process* allows a quantity to stay constant within a given period of time. In the latter case, the increments are described by:

$$P(Z_k = u) = p \,, \, P(Z_k = -d) = q \,, \, P(Z_k = 0) = r = 1 - p - q \,,$$

and the process X_t is again given by:

$$X_t = X_0 + \sum_{k=1}^{t} Z_k$$

where $X_0, Z_1, Z_2, \ldots$ are mutually independent. To solve the Black–Scholes equation, some algorithms use trinomial schemes with time and state dependent probabilities p, q and r. Figure 4.5 shows five simulated paths of a trinomial process with $u = d = 1$ and $p = q = 0.25$.

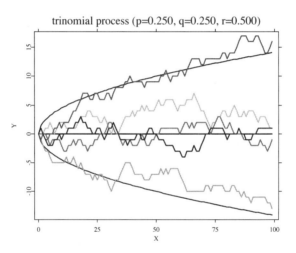

Figure 4.5:   Five paths of a trinomial process with $p = q = 0.25$. (2σ)–intervals around the trend (which is zero) are given as well.

⧉ SFETrinomp.xpl

The exact distribution of X_t cannot be derived from the binomial distribution but for the trinomial process a similar relations hold:

$$
\begin{aligned}
\mathsf{E}[X_t] &= \mathsf{E}[X_0] + t \cdot \mathsf{E}[Z_1] = \mathsf{E}[X_0] + t \cdot (pu - qd) \\
\mathrm{Var}(X_t) &= \mathrm{Var}(X_0) + t \cdot \mathrm{Var}(Z_1), \text{ where} \\
\mathrm{Var}(Z_1) &= p(1 - p)u^2 + q(1 - q)d^2 + 2pq \, ud \,.
\end{aligned}
$$

For large t, X_t is approximately $\mathrm{N}(\mathsf{E}[X_t], \mathrm{Var}(X_t))$–distributed.

4.3   General Random Walks

Binomial and trinomial processes are simple examples for *general random walks*, i.e. stochastic processes $\{X_t; \, t \geq 0\}$ satisfying:

$$X_t = X_0 + \sum_{k=1}^{t} Z_k \,, \qquad t = 1, 2, \ldots$$

where X_0 is independent of $Z_1, Z_2, \ldots$ which are i.i.d. The increments have a distribution of a real valued random variable. Z_k can take a finite or countably infinite number of values; but it is also possible for Z_k to take values out of a continuous set.

As an example, consider a *Gaussian random walk* with $X_0 = 0$, where the finitely many $X_1, \ldots, X_t$ are jointly normally distributed. Such a random walk can be constructed by assuming identically, independently and normally distributed increments. By the properties of the normal distribution, it follows that X_t is $N(\mu t, \, \sigma^2 t)$–distributed for each t. If $X_0 = 0$ and $\mathrm{Var}(Z_1)$ is finite, it holds approximately for all random walks for t large enough:

$$\mathcal{L}(X_t) \approx N(t \cdot \mathsf{E}[Z_1], \, t \cdot \mathrm{Var}(Z_1)).$$

This result follows directly from the central limit theorem for i.i.d. random variables.

Random walks are processes with *independent increments*. That means, the increment Z_{t+1} of the process from time t to time $t+1$ is independent of the past values $X_0, \ldots, X_t$ up to time t. In general, it holds for any $s > 0$ that the increment of the process from time t to time $t + s$

$$X_{t+s} - X_t = Z_{t+1} + \ldots + Z_{t+s}$$

is independent of $X_0, \ldots, X_t$. It follows that the best prediction, in terms of mean squared error, for X_{t+1} given $X_0, \ldots, X_t$ is just $X_t + \mathsf{E}[Z_{t+1}]$. As long as the price of only one stock is considered, this prediction rule works quite well. Already hundred years ago, Bachelier postulated (assuming $\mathsf{E}[Z_k] = 0$ for all k):"The best prediction for the stock price of tomorrow is the price of today."

Processes with independent increments are also *Markov–processes*. In other words, the future evolution of the process in time t depends exclusively on X_t, and the value of X_t is independent of the past values $X_0, \ldots, X_{t-1}$. If the increments Z_k and the starting value X_0, and hence all X_t, can take a finite or countably infinite number of values, then the *Markov–property* is formally expressed by:

$$P(a_{t+1} < X_{t+1} < b_{t+1} | X_t = c, a_{t-1} < X_{t-1} < b_{t-1}, \ldots, a_0 < X_0 < b_0)$$

$$= P(a_{t+1} < X_{t+1} < b_{t+1} | X_t = c).$$

If $X_t = c$ is known, additional information about $X_0, \ldots, X_{t-1}$ does not influence the opinion about the range in which X_t will probably fall.

4.4   Geometric Random Walks

The essential idea underlying the random walk for real processes is the assumption of mutually independent increments of the order of magnitude for each point of time. However, economic time series in particular do not satisfy the latter assumption. Seasonal fluctuations of monthly sales figures for example are in *absolute terms* significantly greater if the yearly average sales figure is high. By contrast, the relative or percentage changes are stable over time and do not depend on the current level of X_t. Analogously to the random walk with i.i.d. absolute increments $Z_t = X_t - X_{t-1}$, a *geometric random walk* $\{X_t; t \geq 0\}$ is assumed to have i.i.d. relative increments

$$R_t = \frac{X_t}{X_{t-1}}, \quad t = 1, 2, \ldots.$$

For example, a geometric *binomial random walk* is given by

$$X_t = R_t \cdot X_{t-1} = X_0 \cdot \Pi_{k=1}^t R_k \tag{4.5}$$

where $X_0, R_1, R_2, \ldots$ are mutually independent and for $u > 1, d < 1$:

$$P(R_k = u) = p \,, \ P(R_k = d) = 1 - p \,.$$

Given the independence assumption and $\mathsf{E}[R_k] = (u - d)p + d$ it follows from equation (4.5) that $\mathsf{E}[X_t]$ increases or decreases exponentially as the case may be $\mathsf{E}[R_k] > 1$ or $\mathsf{E}[R_k] < 1$:

$$\mathsf{E}[X_t] = \mathsf{E}[X_0] \cdot (\mathsf{E}[R_1])^t = \mathsf{E}[X_0] \cdot \{(u - d)p + d\}^t.$$

If $\mathsf{E}[R_k] = 1$ the process is on average stable, which is the case for

$$p = \frac{1 - d}{u - d}.$$

For a recombining process, i.e. $d = \frac{1}{u}$, this relationship simplifies to

$$p = \frac{1}{u + 1}.$$

Taking logarithms in equation (4.5) yields:

$$\ln X_t = \ln X_0 + \sum_{k=1}^{t} \ln R_k \ .$$

The process $\tilde{X}_t = \ln X_t$ is itself an ordinary binomial process with starting value $\ln X_0$ and increments $Z_k = \ln R_k$ for which hold:

$$P(Z_k = \ln u) = p, \quad P(Z_k = \ln d) = 1 - p \ .$$

For t large, $\tilde{X}_t$ is approximately normally distributed, i.e. $X_t = \exp(\tilde{X}_t)$ is approximately lognormally distributed.

4.5   Binomial Models with State Dependent Increments

Binomial processes and more general random walks model the stock price at best locally. They proceed from the assumption that the distribution of the increments $Z_t = X_t - X_{t-1}$ are the same for each value X_t, regardless of whether the stock price is substantially greater or smaller than X_0. Absolute increments $X_t - X_{t-1} = (R_t - 1) X_{t-1}$ of a geometric random walk depend on the level of X_{t-1}. Thus, geometric random walks are processes which do not have independent absolute increments. Unfortunately, modelling the stock price dynamics globally the latter processes are too simple to explain the impact of the current price level on the future stock price evolution. A class of processes which take this effect into account are binomial processes with state dependent (and possibly time dependent) increments:

$$X_t = X_{t-1} + Z_t \ , \quad t = 1, 2, \ldots \tag{4.6}$$

$$P(Z_t = u) = p(X_{t-1}, t), \ \ P(Z_t = -d) = 1 - p(X_{t-1}, t) \ .$$

Since the distribution of Z_t depends on the state X_{t-1} and possibly on time t, increments are neither independent nor identically distributed. The deterministic functions $p(x, t)$ associate a probability to each possible value of the process at time t and to each t. Stochastic processes $\{X_t; \ t \geq 0\}$ which are constructed as in (4.6) are still *markovian* but without having independent increments.

Accordingly, geometric binomial processes with state dependent relative increments can be defined (for $u > 1$, $d < 1$):

$$X_t = R_t \cdot X_{t-1} \tag{4.7}$$

$$P(R_t = u) = p(X_{t-1}, t), \;\; P(R_t = d) = 1 - p(X_{t-1}, t).$$

Processes as defined in (4.6) and (4.7) are mainly of theoretic interest, since without further assumptions it is rather difficult to estimate the probabilities $p(x, t)$ from observed stock prices. But generalized binomial models (as well as the trinomial models) can be used to solve differential equations numerically, as the Black–Scholes equation for American options for example.

5 Stochastic Integrals and Differential Equations

This chapter provides the tools which are used in option pricing. The field of stochastic processes in continuous time which are defined as solutions of stochastic differential equations plays an important role. To illustrate these notions we use repeatedly approximations by stochastic processes in discrete time and refer to the results from Chapter 4.

A stochastic process in continuous time $\{X_t; \ t \geq 0\}$ consists of chronologically ordered random variables, but here the variable t is continuous, i.e. t is a positive real number.

Stock prices are actually processes in discrete time. But to derive the Black-Scholes equation they are approximated by continuous time processes which are easier to handle analytically. However the simulation on a computer of such processes or the numerical computation of say American options, is carried out by means of discrete time approximations. We therefore switch the time scale between discrete and continuous depending on what is more convenient for the actual computation.

5.1 Wiener Process

We begin with a simple symmetric random walk $\{X_n; \ n \geq 0\}$ starting in 0 $(X_0 = 0)$. The increments $Z_n = X_n - X_{n-1}$ are i.i.d. with :

$$P(Z_n = 1) = P(Z_n = -1) = \frac{1}{2} .$$

By shortening the period of time of two successive observations we accelerate the process. Simultaneously, the increments of the process become smaller during the shorter period of time. More precisely, we consider a stochastic process $\{X_t^{\Delta}; \ t \geq 0\}$ in continuous time which increases or decreases in a time step Δt with probability $\frac{1}{2}$ by Δx. Between these jumps the process is constant (alternatively we could interpolate linearly). At time $t = n \cdot \Delta t$ the process is:

$$X_t^\Delta = \sum_{k=1}^n Z_k \cdot \Delta x = X_n \cdot \Delta x$$

where the increments $Z_1 \Delta x, Z_2 \Delta x, \ldots$ are mutually independent and take the values Δx or $-\Delta x$ with probability $\frac{1}{2}$ respectively. From Section 4.1 we know:

$$\mathsf{E}[X_t^\Delta] = 0 , \qquad \mathrm{Var}(X_t^\Delta) = (\Delta x)^2 \cdot \mathrm{Var}(X_n) = (\Delta x)^2 \cdot n = t \cdot \frac{(\Delta x)^2}{\Delta t} .$$

Now, we let Δt and Δx become smaller. For the process in the limit to exist in a reasonable sense, $\mathrm{Var}(X_t^\Delta)$ must be finite. On the other hand, $\mathrm{Var}(X_t^\Delta)$ should not converge to 0, since the process would then not be random any more. Hence, we must choose:

$$\Delta t \to 0, \ \Delta x = c \cdot \sqrt{\Delta t}, \ \text{such that} \ \mathrm{Var}(X_t^\Delta) \to c^2 t .$$

If Δt is small, then $n = t/\Delta t$ is large. Thus, the random variable X_n of the ordinary symmetric random walk is approximately $\mathrm{N}(0, n)$ distributed, and therefore for all t (not only for t such that $t = n \, \Delta t$):

$$\mathcal{L}(X_t^\Delta) \approx \mathrm{N}(0, \ n(\Delta x)^2) \approx \mathrm{N}(0, \ c^2 t) .$$

Thus the limiting process $\{X_t; \ t \geq 0\}$ which we obtain from $\{X_t^\Delta; \ t \geq 0\}$ for $\Delta t \to 0, \ \Delta x = c \sqrt{\Delta t}$ has the following properties:

(i) X_t is $\mathrm{N}(0, c^2 t)$ distributed for all $t \geq 0$.

(ii) $\{X_t; \ t \geq 0\}$ has *independent increments*, i.e. for $0 \leq s < t$, $X_t - X_s$ is independent of X_s (since the random walk $\{X_n; \ n \geq 0\}$ defining $\{X_t^\Delta; \ t \geq 0\}$ has independent increments).

(iii) For $0 \leq s < t$ the increment $(X_t - X_s)$ is $\mathrm{N}(0, \ c^2 \cdot (t - s))$ distributed, i.e. its distribution depends exclusively on the length $t - s$ of the time interval in which the increment is observed (this follows from (i) and (ii) and the properties of the normal distribution).

A stochastic process $\{X_t; \ t \geq 0\}$ in continuous time satisfying (i)–(iii) is called *Wiener process* or *Brownian motion* starting in 0 ($X_0 = 0$). The standard Wiener process resulting from $c = 1$ will be denoted by $\{W_t; \ t \geq 0\}$. For this process it holds for all $0 \leq s < t$

$$\mathsf{E}[W_t] = 0, \ \mathrm{Var}(W_t) = t$$

$$\begin{aligned}
\mathrm{Cov}(W_t, W_s) &= \mathrm{Cov}(W_t - W_s + W_s, W_s) \\
&= \mathrm{Cov}(W_t - W_s, W_s) + \mathrm{Cov}(W_s, W_s) \\
&= 0 + \mathrm{Var}(W_s) = s
\end{aligned}$$

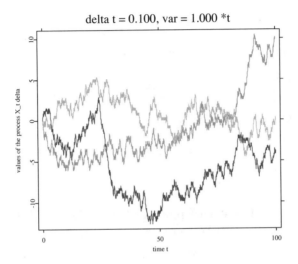

Figure 5.1: Typical paths of a Wiener process. Q SFEWienerProcess.xpl

As for every stochastic process in continuous time, we can consider a path or realization of the Wiener process as a *randomly chosen function* of time. With some major mathematical instruments it is possible to show that the paths of a Wiener process are continuous with probability 1:

$$P(W_t \text{ is continuous as a function of } t) = 1.$$

That is to say, the Wiener process has no jumps. But W_t fluctuates heavily: the paths are continuous but highly erratic. In fact, it is possible to show that the paths are not differentiable with probability 1.

Being a process with independent increments the Wiener process is *markovian*. For $0 \le s < t$ it holds $W_t = W_s + (W_t - W_s)$, i.e. W_t depends only on W_s and on the increment from time s to time t:

$$\begin{aligned}
&P(a < W_t < b \,|\, W_s = x \,, \text{ information about } W_{t'},\ 0 \le t' < s) \\
&= P(a < W_t < b \,|\, W_s = x\,)
\end{aligned}$$

Using properties (i)–(iii), the distribution of W_t given the outcome $W_s = x$ can be formulated explicitly. Since the increment $(W_t - W_s)$ is $\mathrm{N}(0, t - s)$ distributed, W_t is $\mathrm{N}(x, t - s)$ distributed given $W_s = x$:

$$P(a < W_t < b \,|W_s = x) = \int_a^b \frac{1}{\sqrt{t-s}} \varphi\Big(\frac{y-x}{\sqrt{t-s}}\Big) dy.$$

Proceeding from the assumption of a random walk $\{X_n; \, n \geq 0\}$ with drift $\mathsf{E}[X_n] = n(2p - 1)$ instead of a symmetric random walk results in a process X_t^Δ which is no more zero on average, but

$$\mathsf{E}[X_t^\Delta] \;=\; n \cdot (2p - 1) \cdot \Delta x = (2p - 1) \cdot t \, \frac{\Delta x}{\Delta t}$$

$$\mathrm{Var}(X_t^\Delta) \;=\; n \, 4p(1 - p) \cdot (\Delta x)^2 = 4p(1 - p) \cdot t \cdot \frac{(\Delta x)^2}{\Delta t}.$$

For $\Delta t \to 0$, $\Delta x = \sqrt{\Delta t}$, $p = \frac{1}{2}(1 + \mu\sqrt{\Delta t})$ we obtain for all t:

$$\mathsf{E}[X_t^\Delta] \to \mu t \,, \;\; \mathrm{Var}(X_t^\Delta) \to t.$$

The limiting process is a Wiener process $\{X_t; \, t \geq 0\}$ with *drift* or *trend* μt. It results from the standard Wiener process:

$$X_t = \mu t + W_t.$$

Hence, it behaves in the same way as the standard Wiener process but it fluctuates on average around μ instead of 0. If $(\mu > 0)$ the process is increasing linearly on average, and if $(\mu < 0)$ it is decreasing linearly on average.

5.2 Stochastic Integration

In order to introduce a stochastic process as a solution of a stochastic differential equation as we introduce the concept of the Itô–integral: a stochastic integral with respect to a Wiener process. Formally the construction of the Itô–integral is similar to the one of the Stieltjes–integral. But instead of integrating with respect to a deterministic function (Stieltjes–integral), the Itô–integral integrates with respect to a random function, more precisely, the path of a Wiener process. Since the integrant itself can be random, i.e. it can be a path of a stochastic process, one has to analyze the mutual dependencies of the integrant and the Wiener process.

Let $\{Y_t; \, t \geq 0\}$ be the process to integrate and let $\{W_t; \, t \geq 0\}$ be a standard Wiener process. The definition of a stochastic integral assumes that

$\{Y_t;\ t \geq 0\}$ is not anticipating. Intuitively, it means that the process up to time s does not contain any information about future increments $W_t - W_s$, $t > s$, of the Wiener process. In particular, Y_s is independent of $W_t - W_s$.

An integral of a function is usually defined as the limit of the sum of the suitably weighted function. Similarly, the *Itô integral* with respect to a Wiener process is defined as the limit of the sum of the (randomly) weighted (random) function $\{Y_t;\ t \geq 0\}$:

$$I_n = \sum_{k=1}^{n} Y_{(k-1)\Delta t} \cdot (W_{k\Delta t} - W_{(k-1)\Delta t}) \ , \quad \Delta t = \frac{t}{n} \qquad (5.1)$$

$$\int_0^t Y_s \ dW_s = \lim_{n \to \infty} I_n \ ,$$

where the limit is to be understood as the limit of a random variable in terms of mean squared error, i.e. it holds

$$\mathsf{E}\{ \big[\int_0^t Y_s \ dW_s - I_n \big]^2 \} \to 0, \quad n \to \infty.$$

It is important to note, that each summand of I_n is a product of two independent random variables. More precisely, $Y_{(k-1)\Delta t}$, the process to integrate at the left border of the small interval $[(k-1)\Delta t,\ k\Delta t]$ is independent of the increment $W_{k\Delta t} - W_{(k-1)\Delta t}$ of the Wiener process in this interval.

It is not hard to be more precise on the non anticipating property of $\{Y_t;\ t \geq 0\}$.

Definition 5.1 (Information structure, non–anticipating)
For each $t \geq 0$, $\mathcal{F}_t$ denotes a family of events (having the structure of a σ–algebra, i.e. certain combinations of events contained in $\mathcal{F}_t$ are again in $\mathcal{F}_t$) which contain the available information up to time t. $\mathcal{F}_t$ consists of events from which is known up to time t whether they occurred or not. We assume:

$\mathcal{F}_s \subset \mathcal{F}_t$ *for $s < t$*   *(information grows as time evolves)*

$\{a < Y_t < b\} \in \mathcal{F}_t$ *(Y_t contains no information about events occurring after time t)*

$\{a < W_t < b\} \in \mathcal{F}_t$
$W_t - W_s$ *independent of $\mathcal{F}_s$*   *for $s < t$*   *(the Wiener process is adapted to evolution of information)*

Then, we call $\mathcal{F}_t$ the information structure at time t and the process $\{Y_t;\ t \geq 0\}$ non–anticipating with respect to the information structure $\mathcal{F}_t;\ t \geq 0$.

The process $\{Y_t\}$ is called non–anticipating since due to the second assumption it does not anticipate any future information. The evolving information structure $\mathcal{F}_t$ and the random variables Y_t, W_t are adapted to each other.

The integral depends crucially on the point of the interval $[(k-1)\Delta t, \; k\Delta t]$ at which the random variable Y_s is evaluated in (5.1). Consider the example $Y_t = W_t, \; t \geq 0$, i.e. we integrate the Wiener process with respect to itself. As a gedankenexperiment we replace in (5.1) $(k-1)\Delta t$ by an arbitrary point $t(n,k)$ of the interval $[(k-1)\Delta t, \; k\Delta t]$. If we defined:

$$\int_0^t W_s \, dW_s = \lim_{n \to \infty} \sum_{k=1}^n W_{t(n,k)} \left(W_{k\Delta t} - W_{(k-1)\Delta t} \right)$$

the expected values would converge as well. Hence by interchanging the sum with the covariance operator we get:

$$\mathsf{E}\left[\sum_{k=1}^n W_{t(n,k)} \left(W_{k\Delta t} - W_{(k-1)\Delta t} \right) \right] = \sum_{k=1}^n \mathrm{Cov}(W_{t(n,k)}, W_{k\Delta t} - W_{(k-1)\Delta t})$$

$$= \sum_{k=1}^n \{ t(n,k) - (k-1)\Delta t \} \to \mathsf{E}\left[\int_0^t W_s \, dW_s \right].$$

For $t(n,k) = (k-1)\Delta t$ – which is the case for the Itô–integral – we obtain 0, for $t(n,k) = k\Delta t$ we obtain $n \cdot \Delta t = t$, and for suitably chosen sequences $t(n,k)$ we could obtain for the expectation of the stochastic integral any value between 0 and t. In order to assign to $\int_0^t W_s \, dW_s$ a unique value, we have to agree on a certain sequence $t(n,k)$.

To illustrate how Itô–integrals are computed, and that other than the usual computation rules have to be applied, we show that:

$$\int_0^t W_s \, dW_s = \frac{1}{2}(W_t^2 - W_0^2) \; - \; \frac{t}{2} = \frac{1}{2}(W_t^2 - t) \tag{5.2}$$

Summing the differences $W_{k\Delta t}^2 - W_{(k-1)\Delta t}^2$, all terms but the first and the last cancel out and remembering that $n\Delta t = t$ we get

$$
\begin{aligned}
\frac{1}{2}(W_t^2 - W_0^2) &= \frac{1}{2}\sum_{k=1}^{n}(W_{k\Delta t}^2 - W_{(k-1)\Delta t}^2) \\
&= \frac{1}{2}\sum_{k=1}^{n}(W_{k\Delta t} - W_{(k-1)\Delta t})(W_{k\Delta t} + W_{(k-1)\Delta t}) \\
&= \frac{1}{2}\sum_{k=1}^{n}(W_{k\Delta t} - W_{(k-1)\Delta t})^2 \\
&\quad + \sum_{k=1}^{n}(W_{k\Delta t} - W_{(k-1)\Delta t})\, W_{(k-1)\Delta t}\,.
\end{aligned}
$$

While the second term converges to $\int_0^t W_s\, dW_s$, the first term is a sum of n independent identically distributed random variables and which is thus approximated due to the law of large numbers by its expected value

$$
\frac{n}{2}\, \mathsf{E}[(W_{k\Delta t} - W_{(k-1)\Delta t})^2] = \frac{n}{2}\Delta t = \frac{t}{2}\,.
$$

For smooth functions f_s, for example continuously differentiable functions, it holds $\int_0^t f_s\, df_s = \frac{1}{2}(f_t^2 - f_0^2)$. However, the stochastic integral (5.2) contains the additional term $-\frac{t}{2}$ since the local increment of the Wiener process over an interval of length Δt is of the size of its standard deviation – that is $\sqrt{\Delta t}$. The increment of a smooth function f_s is proportional to Δt, and therefore considerably smaller than the increment of the Wiener process for $\Delta t \to 0$.

5.3   Stochastic Differential Equations

Since the Wiener process fluctuates around its expectation 0 it can be approximated by means of symmetric random walks. As for random walks we are interested in stochastic processes in continuous time which are growing on average, i.e. which have a *trend* or *drift*. Proceeding from a Wiener process with arbitrary σ (see Section 5.1) we obtain the generalized Wiener process $\{X_t;\ t \geq 0\}$ with *drift rate* μ and variance σ^2 :

$$
X_t = \mu \cdot t + \sigma \cdot W_t \quad,\quad t \geq 0. \tag{5.3}
$$

The general Wiener process X_t is at time t, $N(\mu t,\ \sigma^2 t)$–distributed. For its increment in a small time interval Δt we obtain

$$
X_{t+\Delta t} - X_t = \mu \cdot \Delta t + \sigma(W_{t+\Delta t} - W_t)\,.
$$

For $\Delta t \rightarrow 0$ use the differential notation:

$$dX_t = \mu \cdot dt + \sigma \cdot dW_t \tag{5.4}$$

This is only a different expression for the relationship (5.3) which we can also write in integral form:

$$X_t = \int_0^t \mu \, ds + \int_0^t \sigma dW_s \tag{5.5}$$

Note, that from the definition of the stochastic integral it follows directly that $\int_0^t d \, W_s = W_t - W_0 = W_t$.

The differential notation (5.4) proceeds from the assumption that both the local drift rate given by μ and the local variance given by σ^2 are constant. A considerably larger class of stochastic processes which is more suited to model numerous economic and natural processes is obtained if μ and σ^2 in (5.4) are allowed to be time and state dependent. Such processes $\{X_t; \ t \geq 0\}$, which we call Itô–processes, are defined as solutions of *stochastic differential equations*:

$$dX_t = \mu(X_t, t)dt + \sigma(X_t, t)dW_t \tag{5.6}$$

Intuitively, this means:

$$X_{t+\Delta t} - X_t = \mu(X_t, t)\Delta t + \sigma(X_t, t)(W_{t+\Delta t} - W_t),$$

i.e. the process' increment in a small interval of length Δt after time t is $\mu(X_t, t) \cdot \Delta t$ plus a random fluctuation which is N(0, $\sigma^2(X_t, t) \cdot \Delta t$) distributed. A precise definition of a solution of (5.6) is a stochastic process fulfilling the integral equation

$$X_t - X_0 = \int_0^t \mu(X_s, s)ds + \int_0^t \sigma(X_s, s)dW_s \tag{5.7}$$

In this sense (5.6) is only an abbreviation of (5.7). For $0 \leq t' < t$, it follows immediately:

$$X_t = X_{t'} + \int_{t'}^t \mu(X_s, s)ds + \int_{t'}^t \sigma(X_s, s)dW_s \, .$$

Since the increment of the Wiener process between t' and t does not dependent on the events which occurred up to time t', it follows that an Itô–process is *Markovian*.

Discrete approximations of (5.6) and (5.7) which can be used to simulate Itô–processes are obtained by observing the process between 0 and t only at evenly spaced points in time $k\Delta t$, $k = 0, \ldots, n$, $n\Delta t = t$.

With $X_k = X_{k\Delta t}$ and $Z_k = (W_{k\Delta t} - W_{(k-1)\Delta t})/\sqrt{\Delta t}$ we get

$$X_{k+1} - X_k = \mu(X_k, k) \cdot \Delta t + \sigma(X_k, k) \cdot Z_{k+1} \cdot \sqrt{\Delta t}$$

or rather with the abbreviations $\mu_k(X) = \mu(X, k)\Delta t$, $\sigma_k(X) = \sigma(X, k)\sqrt{\Delta t}$:

$$X_n - X_0 = \sum_{k=1}^{n} \mu_{k-1}(X_{k-1}) + \sum_{k=1}^{n} \sigma_{k-1}(X_{k-1}) \cdot Z_k$$

with identical independently distributed $N(0, 1)$–random variables $Z_1, Z_2, \dots$.
Q SFESimCIR.xpl, **Q** SFMSimOU.xpl

5.4   The Stock Price as a Stochastic Process

Stock prices are stochastic processes in *discrete time* which take only *discrete values* due to the limited measurement scale. Nevertheless, stochastic processes in *continuous time* are used as models since they are analytically easier to handle than discrete models, e.g. the binomial or trinomial process. However, the latter are more intuitive and prove to be very useful in simulations.

Two features of the general Wiener process $dX_t = \mu dt + \sigma \, dW_t$ make it an unsuitable model for stock prices. First, it allows for negative stock prices, and second the local variability is higher for high stock prices. Hence, stock prices S_t are modeled by means of the more general Itô–process:

$$dS_t = \mu(S_t, t)dt + \sigma(S_t, t)dW_t .$$

This model does depend on the unknown functions $\mu(X, t)$ and $\sigma(X, t)$. A useful and simpler variant utilizing only two unknown real model parameters μ and σ can be justified by the following reflection: The percentage return on the invested capital should on average not depend on the stock price at which the investment is done, and of course, should not depend on the *currency unit* (EUR, USD, ...) in which the stock price is quoted. Furthermore, the average return should be proportional to the investment horizon, as it is the case for other investment instruments. Putting things together, we request:

$$\frac{\mathsf{E}[dS_t]}{S_t} = \frac{\mathsf{E}[S_{t+dt} - S_t]}{S_t} = \mu \cdot dt .$$

Since $\mathsf{E}[dW_t] = 0$ this condition is satisfied if

$$\mu(S_t, t) = \mu \cdot S_t ,$$

for given S_t. Additionally,

$$\sigma(S_t, t) = \sigma \cdot S_t$$

takes into consideration that the absolute size of the stock price fluctuation is proportional to the currency unit in which the stock price is quoted. In summary, we model the stock price S_t as a solution of the stochastic differential equation

$$dS_t = \mu \cdot S_t \, dt + \sigma \cdot S_t \cdot dW_t \,,$$

where μ is the *expected return* on the stock, and σ the *volatility*. Such a process is called *geometric Brownian motion* because

$$\frac{dS_t}{S_t} = \mu \, dt + \sigma \, dW_t \,.$$

By applying Itôs lemma, which we introduce in Section 5.5, it can be shown that for a suitable Wiener process $\{Y_t; \ t \geq 0\}$ it holds

$$S_t = e^{Y_t} \quad \text{bzw.} \quad Y_t = \ln S_t \,.$$

Since Y_t is normally distributed, S_t is lognormally distributed. As random walks can be used to approximate the general Wiener process, geometric random walks can be used to approximate geometric Brownian motion and thus this simple model for the stock price.

5.5   Itôs Lemma

A crucial tool in dealing with stochastic differential equations is Itôs lemma. If $\{X_t, \ t \geq 0\}$ is an Itô–process:

$$dX_t = \mu(X_t, t)dt + \sigma(X_t, t) \, dW_t \,, \tag{5.8}$$

one is often interested in the dynamics of stochastic processes which are functions of X_t: $Y_t = g(X_t)$. Then $\{Y_t; \ t \geq 0\}$ can also be described by a solution of a stochastic differential equation from which interesting properties of Y_t can be derived as for example the average growth in time t.

For a heuristic derivation of the equation for $\{Y_t; \ t \geq 0\}$ we assume that g is differentiable as many times as necessary. From a Taylor expansion it follows:

$$\begin{aligned}
Y_{t+dt} - Y_t &= g(X_{t+dt}) - g(X_t) \\
&= g(X_t + dX_t) - g(X_t) \\
&= \frac{dg}{dX}(X_t) \cdot dX_t + \frac{1}{2}\frac{d^2g}{dX^2}(X_t) \cdot (dX_t)^2 + \dots
\end{aligned} \tag{5.9}$$

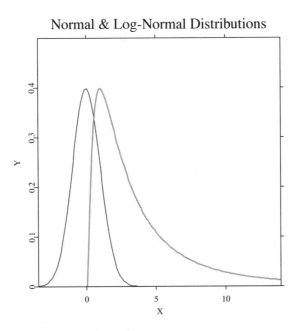

Figure 5.2: Density comparison of lognormally and normally distributed random variables.   **Q** SFELogNormal.xpl

where the dots indicate the terms which can be neglected (for $dt \to 0$). Due to equation (5.8) the drift term $\mu(X_t, t)dt$ and the volatility term $\sigma(X_t, t)dW_t$ are the dominant terms since for $dt \to 0$ they are of size dt and $\sqrt{dt}$ respectively.

In doing this, we use the fact that $\mathsf{E}[(dW_t)^2] = dt$ and $dW_t = W_{t+dt} - W_t$ is of the size of its standard deviation, $\sqrt{dt}$. We neglect terms which are of smaller size than dt. Thus, we can express $(dX_t)^2$ by a simpler term:

$$
\begin{aligned}
(dX_t)^2 &= (\mu(X_t, t)dt + \sigma(X_t, t)\,dW_t)^2 \\
&= \mu^2(X_t, t)(dt)^2 + 2\mu(X_t, t)\,\sigma(X_t, t)\,dt\,dW_t + \sigma^2(X_t, t)(dW_t)^2.
\end{aligned}
$$

We see that the first and the second term are of size $(dt)^2$ and $dt \cdot \sqrt{dt}$ respectively. Therefore, both can be neglected. However, the third term is of size dt. More precisely, it can be shown that $dt \to 0$:

$$
(dW_t)^2 = dt.
$$

Thanks to this identity, calculus rules for stochastic integrals can be derived from the rules for deterministic functions (as Taylor expansions for example). Neglecting terms which are of smaller size than dt we obtain from (5.9) the following version of *Itôs lemma*:

Lemma 5.1 (Itôs Lemma)

$$
\begin{aligned}
dY_t &= dg(X_t) \\
&= \left(\frac{dg}{dX}(X_t) \cdot \mu(X_t, t) + \frac{1}{2} \frac{d^2 g}{dX^2}(X_t) \cdot \sigma^2(X_t, t) \right) dt \\
&\quad + \frac{dg}{dX}(X_t) \cdot \sigma(X_t, t) \, dW_t
\end{aligned}
$$

or - dropping the time index t and the argument X_t of the function g and its derivatives:

$$
dg = \left(\frac{dg}{dX} \mu(X, t) + \frac{1}{2} \frac{d^2 g}{dX^2} \sigma^2(X, t) \right) dt + \frac{dg}{dX} \sigma(X, t) dW .
$$

Example 5.1

Consider $Y_t = \ln S_t$ the logarithm of the geometric Brownian motion. For $g(X) = \ln X$ we obtain $\frac{dg}{dX} = \frac{1}{X}$, $\frac{d^2 g}{dX^2} = -\frac{1}{X^2}$. Applying Itôs lemma for the geometric Brownian motion with $\mu(X, t) = \mu X$, $\sigma(X, t) = \sigma X$ we get:

$$
\begin{aligned}
dY_t &= \left(\frac{1}{S_t} \mu S_t - \frac{1}{2} \frac{1}{S_t^2} \sigma^2 S_t^2 \right) dt + \frac{1}{S_t} \cdot \sigma S_t \, dW_t \\
&= \left(\mu - \frac{1}{2} \sigma^2 \right) dt + \sigma \, dW_t
\end{aligned}
$$

The logarithm of the stock price *is a generalized Wiener process with drift rate $\mu^* = \mu - \frac{1}{2} \sigma^2$ and variance rate σ^2. Since Y_t is $N(\mu^* t, \sigma^2 t)$–distributed S_t is itself* lognormally distributed *with parameters $\mu^* t$ and $\sigma^2 t$.*

A generalized version of Itôs lemma for functions $g(X, t)$ which are allowed to depend on time t is:

Lemma 5.2 (Itôs lemma for functions depending explicitly on time)

$$
dg = \left(\frac{\partial g}{\partial X} \cdot \mu(X, t) + \frac{1}{2} \frac{\partial^2 g}{\partial X^2} \sigma^2(X, t) + \frac{\partial g}{\partial t} \right) dt + \frac{\partial g}{\partial X} \sigma(X, t) dW \quad (5.10)
$$

$Y_t = g(X_t, t)$ is again an Itô process, but this time the drift rate is augmented by an additional term $\frac{\partial g}{\partial t}(X_t, t)$.

5.6   Recommended Literature

This chapter briefly summarized results which belong to the main topics of stochastic analysis. Numerous textbooks of different levels introduce to the calculus of stochastic integrals and stochastic differential equations, see for example von Weizsäcker and Winkler (1990), Mikosch (1998) or Karatzas and Shreve (1999).

6 Black–Scholes Option Pricing Model

6.1 Black–Scholes Differential Equation

Simple generally accepted economic assumptions are insufficient to develop a rational option pricing theory. Assuming a perfect financial market in Section 2.1 lead to elementary arbitrage relations which options have to fulfill. While these relations can be used as a verification tool for sophisticated mathematical models, they do not provide an explicit option pricing function depending on parameters such as time and the stock price as well as the options underlying parameters K, T. To obtain such a pricing function the value of the underlying financial instrument (stock, currency, ...) has to be modelled. In general, the underlying instrument is assumed to follow a stochastic process either in discrete or in continuous time. While the latter are analytically easier to handle, the former, which we will consider as approximations of continuous time processes for the time being, are particularly useful for numerical computations. In the second part of this text, the discrete time version will be discussed as financial time series models.

A model for stock prices which is frequently used and is also the basis of the classical Black–Scholes approach, is the so–called geometric Brownian motion. In this model the stock price S_t is a solution of the stochastic differential equation

$$dS_t = \mu S_t dt + \sigma S_t dW_t. \tag{6.1}$$

Equivalently, the process of stock price returns can be assumed to follow a standard Brownian motion, i.e.

$$\frac{dS_t}{S_t} = \mu dt + \sigma dW_t. \tag{6.2}$$

The drift μ is the expected return on the stock in the time interval dt. The volatility σ is a measure of the return variability around its expectation μ.

Both parameters μ and σ are dependent on each other and are important factors of the investors' risk preferences involved in the investment decision: The higher the expected return μ, the higher, in general, the risk quantified by σ.

Modelling the underlying as geometric Brownian motion provides a useful approximation to stock prices accepted by practitioners for short and medium maturity. In real practice, numerous model departures are known: in some situations the volatility function $\sigma(x,t)$ of the general model (5.8) is different from the linear specification $\sigma \cdot x$ of geometric Brownian motion. The Black–Scholes' approach is still used to approximate option prices. The basic idea to derive option prices can be applied to more general stock price models.

Black–Scholes' approach relies on the idea introduced in Chapter 2, i.e. duplicating the portfolio consisting of the option by means of a second portfolio consisting exclusively of financial instruments whose values are known. The duplicating portfolio is chosen such that both portfolios have equal values at options maturity T. Then, it follows from the assumption of a perfect financial market, and in particular of no–arbitrage opportunities, that both portfolios must have equal values at any time prior to time T. The duplicating portfolio can be created in two equivalent ways which we illustrate in an example of a call option on a stock with price S_t:

1. Consider a portfolio consisting of one call of which the price is to be computed. The duplicating portfolio is composed of stocks and risk–less zero bonds of which the quantity adapts continuously to changes in the stock price. Without loss of generality, the zero bond's face value can be set equal to one since the number of zero bond's in the duplicating portfolio is free parameter. At time t the two portfolios consist of:

Portfolio A: One call option (long position) with delivery price K and maturity date T.

Portfolio B: $n_t = n(S_t, t)$ stocks and $m_t = m(S_t, t)$ zero bonds with face value $B_T = 1$ and maturity date T.

2. Consider a perfect hedge–portfolio, which consists of stocks and written calls (by means of short selling). Due to a dynamic hedge–strategy the portfolio bears no risk at any time, i.e. profits due to the calls are neutralized by losses due to the stocks. Correspondingly, the duplicating portfolio is also risk–less and consists exclusively of zero bonds. Again, the positions are adjusted continuously to changes in the stock price. At time t the two portfolios

are composed of:

Portfolio A: One stock and $n_t = n(S_t, t)$ (by means of short selling) written call options on the stock with delivery price K and maturity date T.

Portfolio B: $m_t = m(S_t, t)$ zero bonds with face value $B_T = 1$ and maturity dates T.

Let $T^* = T$ be the time when the call option expires worthless, and otherwise let T^* be the time at which the option is exercised. While for a European call option it holds $T^* = T$ at any time, an American option can be exercised prior to maturity. We will see that both in 1. the call value is equal to the value of the duplicating portfolio, and in 2. the hedge–portfolio's value equals the value of the risk–less zero bond portfolio at any time $t \le T^*$, and thus the same partial differential equation for the call value results, which is called *Black–Scholes equation*.

The Black–Scholes approach can be applied to any financial instrument $\mathcal{U}$ contingent on an underlying with price S_t if the latter price follows a geometric Brownian motion, and if the derivatives price F_t is a function only of the price S_t and time: $F_t = F(S_t, t)$. Then, according to the theorem below, a portfolio duplicating the financial instrument exists, and the approach illustrated in 1. can be applied to price the instrument. Pricing an arbitrary derivative the duplicating portfolio must have not only the same value as the derivative at exercising time T^*, but also the same cash flow pattern, i.e. the duplicating portfolio has to generate equal amounts of withdrawal profits or contributing costs as the derivative. The existence of a perfect hedge–portfolio of approach 2. can be shown analogously.

Theorem 6.1
Let the value S_t of an object be a geometric Brownian motion (6.1). Let $\mathcal{U}$ be a derivative contingent on the object and maturing in T. Let $T^* \le T$ be the time at which the derivative is exercised, or rather $T^* = T$ if it is not. Let the derivative's value at any time $t \le T^*$ be given by a function $F(S_t, t)$ of the object's price and time.

   a) It exists a portfolio consisting of the underlying object and risk–less bonds which duplicates the derivative in the sense that it generates up to time T^* the same cash flow pattern as $\mathcal{U}$, and that it has the same time T^* value as $\mathcal{U}$.

b) *The derivatives value function $F(S,t)$ satisfies Black–Scholes partial differential equation*

$$\frac{\partial F(S,t)}{\partial t} - rF(S,t) + bS\frac{\partial F(S,t)}{\partial S} + \frac{1}{2}\sigma^2 S^2 \frac{\partial^2 F(S,t)}{\partial S^2} = 0, \quad t \leq T^*.$$
(6.3)

Proof:

To simplify we proceed from the assumption that the object is a stock paying a continuous dividend yield d, and thus involving costs of carry $b = r - d$ with r the continuous compounded risk–free interest rate. Furthermore, we consider only the case where $\mathcal{U}$ is a derivative on the stock, and that $\mathcal{U}$ does not generate any payoff before time T^*.

We construct a portfolio consisting of $n_t = n(S_t, t)$ shares of the stock and $m_t = m(S_t, t)$ zero bonds with maturity date T and a face value of $B_T = 1$. Let

$$B_t = B_T e^{-r(T-t)} = e^{-r(t-T)}$$

be the zero bond's value discounted to time t. We denote the time t portfolio value by

$$V_t \overset{\text{def}}{=} V(S_t, t) = n(S_t, t) \cdot S_t + m(S_t, t) \cdot B_t.$$

It is to show that n_t and m_t can be chosen such that at exercise time respectively at maturity of $\mathcal{U}$ the portfolio value is equal to the derivative's value, i.e. $V(S_{T^*}, T^*) = F(S_{T^*}, T^*)$. Furthermore, it is shown that the portfolio does not generate any cash flow prior to T^*, i.e. it is neither allowed to withdraw nor to add any money before time T^*. All changes in the positions must be realized by buying or selling stocks or bonds, or by means of dividend yields.

First of all, we investigate how the portfolio value V_t changes in a small period of time dt. By doing this, we use the notation $dV_t = V_{t+dt} - V_t$, $dn_t = n_{t+dt} - n_t$ etc.

$$\begin{aligned}
dV_t &= n_{t+dt}S_{t+dt} + m_{t+dt}B_{t+dt} - n_t S_t - m_t B_t \\
&= dn_t S_{t+dt} + n_t dS_t + dm_t B_{t+dt} + m_t dB_t,
\end{aligned}$$

and thus

$$dV_t = dn_t(S_t + dS_t) + n_t dS_t + dm_t(B_t + dB_t) + m_t dB_t. \quad (6.4)$$

Since the stochastic process S_t is a geometric Brownian motion and therefore an Itô–process (5.8) with $\mu(x,t) = \mu x$ and $\sigma(x,t) = \sigma x$, it follows from the generalized Itô lemma (5.10) and equation (6.1)

$$dn_t = \frac{\partial n_t}{\partial t}dt + \frac{\partial n_t}{\partial S}dS_t + \frac{1}{2}\frac{\partial^2 n_t}{\partial S^2}\sigma^2 S_t^2 dt, \quad (6.5)$$

and an analogous relation for m_t. Using

$$(dS_t)^2 = (\mu S_t dt + \sigma S_t dW_t)^2 = \sigma^2 S_t^2 (dW_t)^2 + o(dt) = \sigma^2 S_t^2 dt + o(dt),$$

$$dB_t = rB_t dt, \; dS_t \cdot dt = o(dt) \text{ and } dt^2 = o(dt)$$

and neglecting terms of size smaller than dt it follows:

$$dn_t(S_t + dS_t) = \left(\frac{\partial n_t}{\partial t} dt + \frac{\partial n_t}{\partial S} dS_t + \frac{1}{2} \frac{\partial^2 n_t}{\partial S^2} \sigma^2 S_t^2 dt \right) S_t + \frac{\partial n_t}{\partial S} \sigma^2 S_t^2 dt, \quad (6.6)$$

$$dm_t(B_t + dB_t) = \left(\frac{\partial m_t}{\partial t} dt + \frac{\partial m_t}{\partial S} dS_t + \frac{1}{2} \frac{\partial^2 m_t}{\partial S^2} \sigma^2 S_t^2 dt \right) B_t. \quad (6.7)$$

The fact that neither the derivative nor the duplicating portfolio generates any cash flow before time T^* means that the terms $dn_t(S_t + dS_t)$ and $dm_t(B_t + dB_t)$ of dV_t in equation (6.4) which correspond to purchases and sales of stocks and bonds have to be financed by the dividend yields. Since one share of the stock pays in a small time interval dt a dividend amount of $d \cdot S_t \cdot dt$, we have

$$d \cdot n_t S_t \cdot dt = (r - b) \cdot n_t S_t \cdot dt = dn_t(S_t + dS_t) + dm_t(B_t + dB_t).$$

Substituting equations (6.6) and (6.7) in the latter equation, it holds:

$$0 = (b - r)n_t S_t dt + \left(\frac{\partial m_t}{\partial t} dt + \frac{\partial m_t}{\partial S} dS_t + \frac{1}{2} \frac{\partial^2 m_t}{\partial S^2} \sigma^2 S_t^2 dt \right) B_t$$

$$+ \left(\frac{\partial n_t}{\partial t} dt + \frac{\partial n_t}{\partial S} dS_t + \frac{1}{2} \frac{\partial^2 n_t}{\partial S^2} \sigma^2 S_t^2 dt \right) S_t + \frac{\partial n_t}{\partial S} \sigma^2 S_t^2 dt.$$

Using equation (6.1) and summarizing the stochastic terms with differential dW_t as well as the deterministic terms with differential dt containing the drift parameter μ, and all other deterministic terms gives:

$$0 = \left(\frac{\partial n_t}{\partial S} S_t + \frac{\partial m_t}{\partial S} B_t \right) \mu S_t dt$$

$$+ \left\{ \left(\frac{\partial n_t}{\partial t} + \frac{1}{2} \frac{\partial^2 n_t}{\partial S^2} \sigma^2 S_t^2 \right) S_t + \frac{\partial n_t}{\partial S} \sigma^2 S_t^2 \right.$$

$$+ \left(\frac{\partial m_t}{\partial t} + \frac{1}{2} \frac{\partial^2 m_t}{\partial S^2} \sigma^2 S_t^2 \right) B_t + (b - r)n_t S_t \left. \right\} dt$$

$$+ \left(\frac{\partial n_t}{\partial S} S_t + \frac{\partial m_t}{\partial S} B_t \right) \sigma S_t dW_t. \quad (6.8)$$

This is only possible if the stochastic terms disappear, i.e.

$$\frac{\partial n_t}{\partial S} S_t + \frac{\partial m_t}{\partial S} B_t = 0. \tag{6.9}$$

Thus the first term in (6.8) is neutralized as well. Hence the middle term must also be zero:

$$\left(\frac{\partial n_t}{\partial t} + \frac{1}{2}\frac{\partial^2 n_t}{\partial S^2}\sigma^2 S_t^2\right) S_t + \frac{\partial n_t}{\partial S}\sigma^2 S_t^2$$
$$+\left(\frac{\partial m_t}{\partial t} + \frac{1}{2}\frac{\partial^2 m_t}{\partial S^2}\sigma^2 S_t^2\right) B_t + (b - r)n_t S_t = 0. \tag{6.10}$$

To further simplify we compute the partial derivative of equation (6.9) with respect to S :

$$\frac{\partial^2 n_t}{\partial S^2} S_t + \frac{\partial n_t}{\partial S} + \frac{\partial^2 m_t}{\partial S^2} B_t = 0 \tag{6.11}$$

and substitute this in equation (6.10). We then obtain

$$\frac{\partial n_t}{\partial t} S_t + \frac{\partial m_t}{\partial t} B_t + \frac{1}{2}\frac{\partial n_t}{\partial S}\sigma^2 S_t^2 + (b - r)n_t S_t = 0. \tag{6.12}$$

Since the stock price S_t does not depend explicitly on time, i.e. $\partial S_t/\partial t = 0$, the derivative of the portfolio value $V_t = n_t S_t + m_t B_t$ with respect to time gives:

$$\frac{\partial V_t}{\partial t} = \frac{\partial n_t}{\partial t} S_t + \frac{\partial m_t}{\partial t} B_t + m_t \frac{\partial B_t}{\partial t} = \frac{\partial n_t}{\partial t} S_t + \frac{\partial m_t}{\partial t} B_t + m_t r B_t.$$

This implies

$$\frac{\partial n_t}{\partial t} S_t + \frac{\partial m_t}{\partial t} B_t = \frac{\partial V_t}{\partial t} - r m_t B_t = \frac{\partial V_t}{\partial t} - r(V_t - n_t S_t).$$

Substituting this equation in equation (6.12) we eliminate m_t and obtain

$$\frac{1}{2}\sigma^2 S_t^2 \frac{\partial n}{\partial S} + \frac{\partial V_t}{\partial t} + bn_t S_t - rV_t = 0. \tag{6.13}$$

Since the zero bond value B_t is independent of the stock price S_t, i.e. $\partial B_t/\partial S = 0$, the derivative of the portfolio value $V_t = n_t S_t + m_t B_t$ with respect to the stock price gives (using equation (6.9))

$$\frac{\partial V_t}{\partial S} = \frac{\partial n_t}{\partial S} S_t + n_t + \frac{\partial m_t}{\partial S} B_t = n_t,$$

and thus

$$n_t = \frac{\partial V_t}{\partial S}. \tag{6.14}$$

That is, n_t is equal to the so–called *delta* or hedge–ratio of the portfolio (see Section 6.3.1). Since

$$m_t = \frac{V_t - n_t S_t}{B_t}$$

we can construct a duplicating portfolio if we know $V_t = V(S_t, t)$. We can obtain this function of stock price and time as a solution of the Black–Scholes differential equation

$$\frac{\partial V(S, t)}{\partial t} - rV(S, t) + bS \frac{\partial V(S, t)}{\partial S} + \frac{1}{2}\sigma^2 S^2 \frac{\partial^2 V(S, t)}{\partial S^2} = 0 \qquad (6.15)$$

which results from substituting equation (6.14) in equation (6.13). To determine V we have to take into account a boundary condition which is obtained from the fact that the cash flows at exercising time respectively maturity, i.e. at time T^*, of the duplicating portfolio and the derivative are equal:

$$V(S_{T^*}, T^*) = F(S_{T^*}, T^*). \qquad (6.16)$$

Since the derivative has at any time the same cash flow as the duplicating portfolio, $F(S, t)$ also satisfies the Black–Scholes differential equation, and at any time $t \leq T^*$ it holds $F_t = F(S_t, t) = V(S_t, t) = V_t$. $\qquad \square$

Black–Scholes' differential equation fundamentally relies on the assumption that the stock price can be modelled by a geometric Brownian motion. This assumption is justified, however, if the theory building on it reproduces the arbitrage relations derived in Chapter 2. Considering an example we verify this feature. Let $V(S_t, t)$ be the value of a future contract with delivery price K and maturity date T. The underlying object involves costs of carry at a continuous rate b. Since $V(S_t, t)$ depends only on the price of the underlying and time it satisfies the conditions of Theorem 6.1. From Theorem 2.1 and substituting $\tau = T - t$ for the time to maturity it follows

$$V(S, t) = Se^{(r-b)(t-T)} - Ke^{r(t-T)}.$$

Substituting the above equation into equation (6.3) it can be easily seen that it is the unique solution of Black–Scholes' differential equation with boundary condition $V(S, T) = S - K$. Hence, Black–Scholes' approach gives the same price for the future contract as the model free no–arbitrage approach.

Finally, we point out that modelling stock prices by geometric Brownian motion gives reasonable solutions for short and medium terms. Applying the model to other underlyings such as currencies or bonds is more difficult. Bond options typically have significant longer time to maturity than stock options. Their value does not only depend on the bond price but also on interest rates which have to be considered stochastic. Modelling interest rates reasonably involves other stochastic process, which we will discuss in later chapters.

Generally exchange rates cannot be modelled by geometric Brownian motion. Empirical studies show that the performance of this model depends on the currency and on the time to maturity. Hence, applying Black–Scholes' approach to currency options has to be verified in each case. If the model is used, the foreign currency has to be understood as the option underlying with a continuous foreign interest rate d corresponding to the continuous dividend yield of a stock. Thus, continuous costs of carry with rate $b = r - d$ equal the interest rate differential between the domestic and the foreign market. If the investor buys the foreign currency early, then he cannot invest his capital at home any more, and thus he looses the domestic interest rate r. However, he can invest his capital abroad and gain the foreign interest rate d. The value of the currency option results from solving Black–Scholes' differential equation (6.3) respecting the boundary condition implied by the option type.

6.2 Black–Scholes Formulae for European Options

In this section we are going to use Black–Scholes' equation to compute the price of European options. We keep the notation introduced in the previous chapter. That is, we denote

$$C(S,t) = C_{K,T}(S,t), \qquad\qquad P(S,t) = P_{K,T}(S,t)$$

the value of a European call respectively put option with exercise price K and maturity date T at time $t \leq T$, where the underlying, for example a stock, at time t has a value of $S_t = S$. The value of a call option thus satisfies for all prices S with $0 < S < \infty$ the differential equation

$$rC(S,t) - bS\frac{\partial C(S,t)}{\partial S} - \frac{1}{2}\sigma^2 S^2 \frac{\partial^2 C(S,t)}{\partial S^2} = \frac{\partial C(S,t)}{\partial t}, \ 0 \leq t \leq T, \quad (6.17)$$

$$C(S,T) = \max\{0, S - K\}, \ 0 < S < \infty, \quad (6.18)$$

$$C(0,t) = 0, \quad \lim_{S\to\infty} C(S,t) - S = 0, \ 0 \leq t \leq T. \quad (6.19)$$

The first boundary condition (6.18) follows directly from the definition of a call option, which will only be exercised if $S_T > K$ thereby procuring the gain $S_T - K$. The definition of Brownian motion implies that the process is absorbed by zero. In other words, if $S_t = 0$ for one $t < T$ it follows $S_T = 0$. That is the call will not be exercised, which is formulated in the first part of condition (6.19). Whereas the second part of (6.19) results from the reflection that the probability that the Brownian motion falls below K is fairly small if it attained a level significantly above the exercise price. If $S_t \gg K$ for a $t < T$ then it holds with a high probability that $S_T \gg K$. The call will be, thus, exercised and procures the cash flow $S_T - K \approx S_T$.

The differential equation (6.17) subject to boundary conditions (6.18). (6.19) can be solved analytically. To achieve this, we transform it into a differential equation known from the literature. First of all, we substitute the time variable t for the time to maturity $\tau = T - t$. By doing this, the problem with final condition (6.18) in $t = T$ changes to a problem subject to an initial condition in $\tau = 0$. Following, we multiply (6.17) by $2/\sigma^2$ and substitute the parameters r, b for

$$\alpha = \frac{2r}{\sigma^2}, \ \beta = \frac{2b}{\sigma^2},$$

as well as the variables τ, S for

$$v = \sigma^2(\beta - 1)^2\frac{\tau}{2}, \qquad\qquad u = (\beta - 1)\ln\frac{S}{K} + v.$$

While for the original parameters hold $0 \le S < \infty, 0 \le t \le T$, for now the new parameters it holds

$$-\infty < u < \infty, \qquad\qquad 0 \le v \le \frac{1}{2}\sigma^2(\beta - 1)^2 T \stackrel{\text{def}}{=} v_T.$$

Finally, we set

$$g(u, v) = e^{r\tau}C(S, T - \tau)$$

and obtain the new differential equation

$$\frac{\partial^2 g(u, v)}{\partial u^2} = \frac{\partial g(u, v)}{\partial v}. \tag{6.20}$$

with the initial condition

$$g(u, 0) = K\max\{0, e^{\frac{u}{\beta - 1}} - 1\} \stackrel{\text{def}}{=} g_0(u), \quad -\infty < u < \infty. \tag{6.21}$$

Problems with initial conditions of this kind are well known from the literature on partial differential equations. They appear, for example, in modelling heat conduction and diffusion processes. The solution is given by

$$g(u, v) = \int_{-\infty}^{\infty} \frac{1}{2\sqrt{\pi v}} g_0(\xi)e^{-\frac{(\xi - u)^2}{4v}} d\xi.$$

The option price can be obtained by undoing the above variables and parameter substitutions. In the following we denote, as in Chapter 2, by $C(S, \tau)$ the call option price being a function of the time to maturity $\tau = T - t$ instead of time t. Then it holds

$$C(S, \tau) = e^{-r\tau} g(u, v) = e^{-r\tau} \int_{-\infty}^{\infty} \frac{1}{2\sqrt{\pi v}} g_0(\xi) e^{-\frac{(\xi - u)^2}{4v}} d\xi.$$

Substituting $\xi = (\beta - 1) \ln(x/K)$ we obtain the original terminal condition $\max\{0, x - K\}$. Furthermore, replacing u and v by the variables S and τ we obtain

$$
\begin{aligned}
C(S, \tau) \;=\; & e^{-r\tau} \int_{0}^{\infty} \max(0, x - K) \frac{1}{\sqrt{2\pi}\sigma\sqrt{\tau}x} \\
& \exp\left\{ -\frac{[\ln x - \{\ln S + (b - \frac{1}{2}\sigma^2)\tau\}]^2}{2\sigma^2\tau} \right\} dx.
\end{aligned}
\tag{6.22}
$$

In the case of Brownian motion $S_T - S_t$ is lognormally distributed, i.e. $\ln(S_T - S_t)$ is normally distributed with parameters $(b - \frac{1}{2}\sigma^2)\tau$ and $\sigma^2\tau$. The conditional distribution of S_T given $S_t = S$ is therefore lognormal as well but with parameters $\ln S + (b - \frac{1}{2}\sigma^2)\tau$ and $\sigma^2\tau$. However, the integrant in equation (6.22) is except for the term $\max(0, x - K)$ the density of the latter distribution. Thus, we can interpret the price of a call as the discounted expected option payoff $\max(0, S_T - K)$, which is the terminal condition, given the current stock price S :

$$C(S, \tau) = e^{-r\tau} \, \mathsf{E}[\max(0, S_T - K) \,|\, S_t = S]. \tag{6.23}$$

This property is useful when deriving numerical methods to compute option prices. But before doing that, we exploit the fact that equation (6.22) contains an integral with respect to the density of the lognormal distribution to further simplify the equation. By means of a suitable substitution we transform the term in an integral with respect to the density of the normal distribution and we obtain

$$C(S, \tau) = e^{(b-r)\tau} S \Phi(y + \sigma\sqrt{\tau}) - e^{-r\tau} K \Phi(y), \tag{6.24}$$

where we use y as a shortcut for

$$y = \frac{\ln \frac{S}{K} + (b - \frac{1}{2}\sigma^2)\tau}{\sigma\sqrt{\tau}}. \tag{6.25}$$

Φ denotes the standard normal distribution

$$\Phi(y) = \frac{1}{\sqrt{2\pi}} \int_{-\infty}^{y} e^{-\frac{z^2}{2}} \, dz.$$

Equations (6.24) and (6.25) are called the *Black–Scholes Formulae*. For the limit cases $S \gg K$ and $S = 0$ it holds:

- If $S \gg K$ then $y \gg 0$ and thus $\Phi(y + \sigma\sqrt{\tau}) \approx \Phi(y) \approx 1$. It follows that the value of a call option on a non dividend paying stock, $b = r$, approaches $S - e^{-r\tau}K$. That is, it can be approximated by the current stock price minus the discounted exercise price.

- If $S = 0$ then $y = -\infty$ and therefore $\Phi(y) = 0$. Thus the option is worthless: $C(0, \tau) = 0$.

The corresponding Black–Scholes Formula for the price $P(S, \tau)$ of a European put option can be derived by solving Black–Scholes differential equation subject to suitable boundary conditions. However, using the put–call parity (Theorem 2.3) is more convenient:

$$P(S, \tau) = C(S, \tau) - Se^{(b-r)\tau} + Ke^{-r\tau}.$$

From this and equation (6.24) we obtain

$$P(S, \tau) = e^{-r\tau} K\Phi(-y) - e^{(b-r)\tau} S\Phi(-y - \sigma\sqrt{\tau}). \qquad (6.26)$$

As we see the value of European put and call options can be computed by explicit formulae. The terms in equation (6.24) for, say the value of a call option, can be interpreted in the following way. Restricting to the case of a non dividend paying stock, $b = r$, the first term, $S\Phi(y + \sigma\sqrt{\tau})$, represents the value of the stock which the option holder obtains when he decides to exercise the option. The other term, $e^{-r\tau}K\Phi(y)$, represents the value of the exercise price. The quotient S/K influences both terms via the variable y.

Deriving Black–Scholes' differential equation we saw in particular that the value of a call option had been duplicated by means of bonds and stocks. The amount of money invested in stocks was $\frac{\partial C}{\partial S}S$ with $\frac{\partial C}{\partial S}$ being the hedge ratio. This ratio, also called delta, determines the relation of bonds and stocks necessary to hedge the option position. Computing the first derivative of Black–Scholes' formula in equation (6.24) with respect to S we obtain

$$\frac{\partial C(S, t)}{\partial S} = \Phi(y + \sigma\sqrt{\tau}).$$

Thus the first term in equation (6.24) reflects the amount of money of the duplicating portfolio invested in stocks, the second term the amount invested in bonds.

Since the standard normal distribution can be evaluated only numerically, the implementation of Black–Scholes' formula depending on the standard normal distribution requires an approximation of the latter. This approximation can have an impact on the computed option value. To illustrate we consider several approximation formulae (see for example Hastings (1955))

a.) The normal distribution can be approximated in the following way:

$$\Phi(y) \approx 1 - (a_1 t + a_2 t^2 + a_3 t^3)e^{-\frac{y^2}{2}}, \quad \text{where}$$

$$t = (1 + by)^{-1}, \qquad b = 0.332672527,$$
$$a_1 = 0.17401209, \qquad a_2 = -0.04793922,$$
$$a_3 = 0.373927817.$$

The approximating error is independently of y of size $\mathcal{O}(10^{-5})$.

🔍 SFENormalApprox1.xpl

b.)

$$\Phi(y) \approx 1 - (a_1 t + a_2 t^2 + a_3 t^3 + a_4 t^4 + a_5 t^5)e^{-\frac{y^2}{2}}, \quad \text{where}$$

$$t = (1 + by)^{-1}, \qquad b = 0.231641888,$$
$$a_1 = 0.127414796, \qquad a_2 = -0.142248368, \qquad a_3 = 0.71070687,$$
$$a_4 = -0.726576013, \qquad a_5 = 0.530702714.$$

The error of this approximation is of size $\mathcal{O}(10^{-7})$. 🔍 SFENormalApprox2.xpl

c.) An approximation of the normal distribution, with error size $\mathcal{O}(10^{-5})$ is given by:

$$\Phi(y) \approx 1 - \frac{1}{2(a_1 t + a_2 t^2 + a_3 t^3 + a_4 t^4 + a_5 t^5)^8}, \quad \text{where}$$

$$a_1 = 0.099792714, \qquad a_2 = 0.044320135, \qquad a_3 = 0.009699203,$$
$$a_4 = -0.000098615, \qquad a_5 = 0.00581551.$$

🔍 SFENormalApprox3.xpl

d.) Finally we present the Taylor expansion:

$$\begin{aligned}
\Phi(y) &\approx \frac{1}{2} + \frac{1}{\sqrt{2\pi}}\left(y - \frac{y^3}{1!2^1 3} + \frac{y^5}{2!2^2 5} - \frac{y^7}{3!2^3 7} + \cdots\right) \\
&= \frac{1}{2} + \frac{1}{\sqrt{2\pi}}\sum_{n=0}^{\infty}(-1)^n \frac{y^{2n+1}}{n!2^n(2n+1)}.
\end{aligned}$$

x	norm-a	norm-b	norm-c	norm-d	iter
1.0000	0.8413517179	0.8413447362	0.8413516627	0.8413441191	6
1.1000	0.8643435425	0.8643338948	0.8643375717	0.8643341004	7
1.2000	0.8849409364	0.8849302650	0.8849298369	0.8849309179	7
1.3000	0.9032095757	0.9031994476	0.9031951398	0.9031993341	8
1.4000	0.9192515822	0.9192432862	0.9192361959	0.9192427095	8
1.5000	0.9331983332	0.9331927690	0.9331845052	0.9331930259	9
1.6000	0.9452030611	0.9452007087	0.9451929907	0.9452014728	9
1.7000	0.9554336171	0.9554345667	0.9554288709	0.9554342221	10
1.8000	0.9640657107	0.9640697332	0.9640670474	0.9640686479	10
1.9000	0.9712768696	0.9712835061	0.9712842148	0.9712839202	11
2.0000	0.9772412821	0.9772499371	0.9772538334	0.9772496294	12

Table 6.1: Several approximations to the normal distribution

Stock price S_t		230.00	EUR	
Exercise price K		210.00	EUR	
Time to maturity $\tau = T - t$		0.50000		
Continuous interest rate r		0.04545		
Volatility σ		0.25000		
No dividends				
	norm-a	norm-b	norm-c	norm-d
Option prices	30.74262	30.74158	30.74352	30.74157

Table 6.2: Prices of a European call option for different approximations of the normal distribution   **Q** SFEBSCopt1.xpl

By means of this series the normal distribution can be approximated arbitrarily close depending on the number of terms used in the summation. Increasing the number of terms increases as well the number of arithmetic operations.

Q SFENormalApprox4.xpl

Table 6.1 compares all four approximation formulae. The Taylor series was truncated after the first term whose absolute value is smaller than 10^{-5}. The last column shows the number of terms used.

Table 6.2 shows the price of a particular European call option computed by means of the four approximations presented above.

Current time t	6 weeks
Maturity T	26 weeks
Time to maturity $\tau = T - t$	20 weeks = 0.3846
Continuous annual interest rate r	0.05
Annualized stock volatility σ	0.20
Current stock price S_t	98 EUR
Exercise price K	100 EUR

Table 6.3: Data of the example

6.3 Risk Management and Hedging

Trading options is particularly risky due to the possibly high random component. Advanced strategies to reduce and manage this risk can be derived from Black–Scholes formula (6.24). To illustrate this issue we consider an example and some traditional strategies.

Example 6.1
A bank sells a European call option to buy 100 000 shares of a non dividend paying stock for 600 000 EUR. The details of this option are given in Table 6.3.

Applying Black–Scholes' formula (6.24) for a non dividend paying stock, $b = r$, gives a theoretical value of 480 119 EUR, approximately 480 000 EUR, of the above option. That is, the bank sold the option about 120 000 EUR above its theoretical value. But it takes the risk to incur substantial losses.

A strategy to manage the risk due to the option would be to do nothing, i.e. to take a naked *position. Should the option be exercised at maturity the bank has to buy the shares for the stock price prevailing at maturity. Assume the stock trades at $S_T = 120$ EUR. Then an options' exercise costs the bank $100\,000 \cdot (S_T - K) = 2\,000\,000$ EUR, which is a multiple of what the bank received for selling the derivative. However, if the stock trades below $K = 100$ EUR the option will not be exercised and the bank books a net gain of 600 000 EUR.*   **Q** SFEBSCopt2.xpl

In contrast to the naked position it is possible to set up a covered *position by buying 100 000 shares at $100\,000 \cdot S_t = 9\,800\,000$ EUR at the same time the option is sold. In case $S_T > K$ the option will be exercised and the stocks will be delivered at a price of $100\,000 \cdot K = 10\,000\,000$ EUR, which discounted to time t is about 9 800 000 EUR. Thus the bank's net gain is equal to 600 000 EUR, the price at which the option is sold. If the stock price* *decreases to $S_T = 80$ EUR then the option will not be exercised. However, the bank incurs a loss of 2 000 000 EUR due to the lower stock price, which is as above a multiple of the option price. Note that from put–call parity for European options (Theorem 2.3) it follows that the risk due to a covered short call option position is identical to the risk due to naked long put option position.*

Both risk management strategies are unsatisfying because the cost varies significantly between 0 and large values. According to Black–Scholes the option costs on average around 480 000 EUR, and a perfect hedge eliminates the impact of random events such that the option costs exactly this amount.

An expensive hedging strategy, i.e. a strategy to decrease the risk associated with the sale of a call, is the so–called *stop–loss strategy.* The bank selling the option takes an uncovered position as long as the stock price is below the exercise price, $S_t < K$, and sets up a covered position as soon as the call is in–the–money, $S_t > K$.

The shares to be delivered in case of options exercise are bought as soon as the stock S_t trades above the exercise price K, and are sold as soon as S_t falls below the exercise price K.

Since all stocks are sold and bought at K after time 0 and at maturity T either the stock position is zero, $(S_t < K)$, or the stocks are sold at K to the option holder, $(S_t > K)$, this strategy bears no costs.

Note that playing a stop–loss strategy bears a cost if $S_0 > K$, i.e. stocks are bought at S_0 and sold at K :

$$\text{costs of a stop–loss hedging strategy:} \ \ \max(S_0 - K, \ 0).$$

Because these costs are smaller than the Black–Scholes price $C(S_0, T)$ arbitrage would be possible by running a stop–loss strategy. However, this reasoning ignores some aspects:

- Buying and selling stocks bear transaction costs,

- Buying stocks before time T involves binding capital leading to renounce of interest rate revenue,

- practically it is not possible to buy or sell stocks exactly at K rather stocks are bought at $K + \delta$ if stocks are increasing and stocks are sold at $K - \delta$ if stocks are decreasing, for a $\delta > 0$.

In practice, purchases and sales take place only after Δt time units. The larger Δt, the greater δ in general, and the less transaction costs have to

Δt (weeks)	5	4	2	1	$\frac{1}{2}$	$\frac{1}{4}$
L		1.02	0.93	0.82	0.77	0.76	0.76

Table 6.4: Performance of the stop–loss strategy

be paid. Hull (2000) investigated in a Monte Carlo study with $M = 1000$ simulated stock price paths the stop–loss strategy's ability to reduce the risk associated with the sale of a call option. For each simulated path the costs $\Lambda_m, m = 1, ..., M$, caused by applying the stop–loss strategy are registered and their sample variance

$$\hat{v}_\Lambda^2 = \frac{1}{M} \sum_{m=1}^{M} (\Lambda_m - \frac{1}{M} \sum_{j=1}^{M} \Lambda_j)^2$$

is computed. Dividing the sample standard deviation by the call price measures the remaining risk of the stop–loss hedged short call position

$$L = \frac{\sqrt{\hat{v}_\Lambda^2}}{C(S_0, T)}.$$

Table 6.4 shows the results. A perfect hedge would reduce the risk to zero, i.e. $L = 0$.

6.3.1　Delta Hedging

In order to reduce the risk associated with option trading more complex hedging strategies than those considered so far are applied. Let us have a look at the following example. Sell a call option on a stock, and try to make the value of this portfolio for small time intervals as insensitive as possible to small changes in the price of the underlying stock. This is what is called delta hedging. Later on, we consider further *Greeks* (gamma, theta, vega, rho) to fine tune the hedged portfolio.

By the *delta* or the *hedge ratio* we understand the derivative of the option price with respect to the stock price. In a discrete time model we use the differential quotient of the change in the option price ΔC with respect to a change in the stock price ΔS:

$$\Delta = \frac{\partial C}{\partial S} \quad \text{oder} \quad \Delta = \frac{\Delta C}{\Delta S}.$$

The delta of other financial instruments is defined accordingly. The stock itself has the value S. Consequently it holds $\Delta = \partial S/\partial S = 1$. A futures contract on a non dividend paying stock has a value of $V = S - K \cdot e^{-r\tau}$ (see Theorem 2.1) and thus its delta is $\Delta = \partial V/\partial S = 1$ as well. Stocks and future contracts can therefore be used equivalently in delta hedging strategies. If the latter are available they are preferable due to lower transaction costs.

Example 6.2
A bank sells calls on 2000 shares of a stock for a price of $C = 10$ EUR/share at a stock price of $S_0 = 100$ EUR/share. Let the call's delta be $\Delta = 0.4$. To hedge the sold call options $\Delta \cdot 2000 = 800$ shares of the stock are added to the portfolio. Small changes in the option value will be offset by corresponding changes in the value of the portfolio's stock shares. Should the stock price increase by 1 EUR, i.e. the value of the stock position in the portfolio increases by 800 EUR, the value of one call on 1 share increases by $\Delta C = \Delta \cdot \Delta S = 0.4$ EUR and following the value of the portfolio's short call position decreases by 800 EUR. That is, gains and losses offset because the delta of the option position is neutralized by the delta of the stock position. The portfolio has a $\Delta = 0$, and the bank takes a delta neutral position.

Since the delta of an option depends on the stock price and time, among others, the position is only for a short period of time delta neutral. In practice, the portfolio has to be *re-balanced* frequently in order to adapt to the changing environment. Strategies to manage portfolio risk which involve frequent re-balancing are known as *dynamic hedging*. We point out that the Black–Scholes differential equation (6.3) can be derived by means of a dynamic hedge portfolio whose position is kept continuously delta neutral. This approach is analogous to reproducing the option by a duplicating portfolio.

Example 6.3
The price of the underlying stock rises within a week to 110 EUR. Due to the time decay and the increased stock price the option delta increased to $\Delta = 0.5$. In order to reobtain a delta neutral position $(0.5 - 0.4) \cdot 2000 = 200$ shares of the stock have to be bought.

From the Black–Scholes formulae for the value of European call and put options on non dividend paying stocks it follows for the delta:

$$\Delta = \frac{\partial C}{\partial S} \;=\; \Phi(y + \sigma\sqrt{\tau}) \qquad\qquad (6.27)$$

$$\text{bzw. } \Delta = \frac{\partial P}{\partial S} \;=\; \Phi(y + \sigma\sqrt{\tau}) - 1,$$

with y being defined in equation (6.25).

Figure 6.1 displays the delta (6.27) as a function of time and stock price. For an increasing stock price delta converges to 1, for decreasing stock prices it converges to 0. Put differently, if the option is deep in–the–money (ITM) it will be exercised at maturity with a high probability. That is the reason why the seller of such an option should be long in the underlying to cover the exercise risk. On the other hand, if the option is far out–of–the–money it will probably not be exercised, and the seller can restrict himself to holding a smaller part of the underlying.

Delta

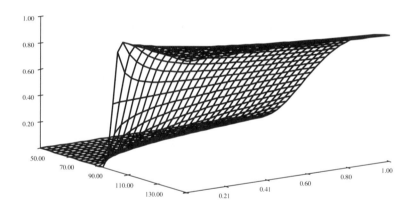

Figure 6.1:   Delta as a function of the stock price (right axis) and time to maturity (left axis).   **Q** SFEdelta.xpl

Furthermore, the probability p that an out–of–the–money (OTM) option will be exercised and an ITM option will not be exercised at maturity is higher the longer the time to maturity. This explains why the delta for longer times to maturity becomes more flat (linear).

Table 6.5 according to Hull (2000) shows (in the same spirit as Table 6.4) the performance of the delta hedging strategy contingent on the time increments Δt between re–balancing trades. If Δt is small enough the risk associated with a sold call option can be managed quite well. In the limit $\Delta t \to 0$ continuous re–balancing underlying the derivation of the Black–Scholes formula follows, and the risk is perfectly eliminated $(L = 0)$. The linearity of

Δt (weeks)	5	4	2	1	$\frac{1}{2}$	$\frac{1}{4}$
L		0.43	0.39	0.26	0.19	0.14	0.09

Table 6.5: Performance of the delta–hedging strategy

the mathematical derivative implies for the delta Δ_p of a portfolio consisting of $w_1, \ldots, w_m$ contracts of m financial derivatives $1, \ldots, m$ with deltas $\Delta_1, \ldots, \Delta_m$:

$$\Delta_p = \sum_{j=1}^{m} w_j \Delta_j.$$

Example 6.4
Consider a portfolio consisting of the following USD *options*

1. *200 000 bought calls (long position) with exercise price 1.70* EUR *maturing in 4 months. The delta of an option on 1 Doller is $\Delta_1 = 0.54$.*

2. *100 000 written calls (short position) with exercise price 1.75* EUR *maturing in 6 months and a delta of $\Delta_2 = 0.48$.*

3. *100 000 written puts (short position) with exercise price 1.75* EUR *maturing in 3 months with $\Delta_3 = -0.51$.*

The portfolio's delta is (increases in values of written options have a negative impact on the portfolio value):

$$\begin{aligned}\Delta_p &= 200\,000 \cdot \Delta_1 - 100\,000 \cdot \Delta_2 - 100\,000 \cdot \Delta_3 \\ &= 111\,000\end{aligned}$$

The portfolio can be made delta neutral by selling 111 000 USD *or by selling a corresponding future contract on* USD *(both have a delta of $\Delta = 1$).*

6.3.2 Gamma and Theta

Using the delta to hedge an option position the option price is locally approximated by a function which is linear in the stock price S. Should the time Δt passing by until the next portfolio re–balancing be not very short this approximation is no longer adequate (see Table 6.5). That is why a more accurate approximation, the Taylor expansion of C as a function of S and t, is considered:

$$\Delta C = C(S+\Delta S,\ t+\Delta t)-C(S,t) = \frac{\partial C}{\partial S}\cdot\Delta S+\frac{\partial C}{\partial t}\cdot\Delta t+\frac{1}{2}\frac{\partial^2 C}{\partial S^2}(\Delta S)^2+\mathcal{O}(\Delta t),$$

where (as we already saw in the demonstration of Theorem 6.1) ΔS is of size $\sqrt{\Delta t}$ and the terms summarized in $\mathcal{O}(\Delta t)$ are of size smaller than Δt. Neglecting all terms but the first, which is of size $\sqrt{\Delta t}$, the approximation used in delta hedging is obtained:

$$\Delta C \approx \Delta \cdot \Delta S.$$

Taking also the terms of size Δt into account it follows

$$\Delta C \approx \Delta \cdot \Delta S + \Theta \cdot \Delta t + \frac{1}{2}\Gamma(\Delta S)2,$$

where $\Theta = \partial C/\partial t$ is the options *theta* and $\Gamma = \partial^2 C/\partial S^2$ is the options *gamma*. Θ is also called the options *time decay*. For a call option on a non dividend paying stock it follows from the Black–Scholes formula (6.24):

$$\Theta = -\frac{\sigma S}{2\sqrt{\tau}}\,\varphi(y + \sigma\sqrt{\tau}) - rKe^{-r\tau}\Phi(y)$$

and

$$\Gamma = \frac{1}{\sigma S\sqrt{\tau}}\,\varphi(y + \sigma\sqrt{\tau}), \qquad\qquad (6.28)$$

where y is defined in equation (6.25).

Figure 6.2 displays the gamma given by equation (6.28) as a function of stock price and time to maturity. Most sensitive to movements in stock prices are at–the–money options with a short time to maturity. Consequently, to hedge such options the portfolio has to be rebalanced frequently.

Assuming a delta neutral portfolio *gamma hedging* consists of buying or selling further derivatives to achieve a gamma neutral portfolio, i.e. $\Gamma = 0$, and thereby making the portfolio value even more insensitive to changes in the stock price. Note that on the one hand neither stocks nor future contracts can be used for gamma hedging strategies since both have a constant Δ and thus a zero gamma $\Gamma = 0$. On the other hand, however, those instruments can be used to make a gamma neutral portfolio delta neutral without affecting the portfolio's gamma neutrality. Consider an option position with a gamma of Γ. Using w contracts of an option traded on a stock exchange with a gamma of Γ_B, the portfolio's gamma is $\Gamma + w\Gamma_B$. By setting $w = -\Gamma/\Gamma_B$ the resulting gamma for the portfolio is 0.

Gamma

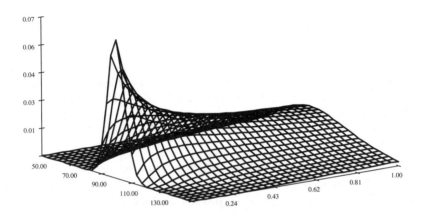

Figure 6.2:   Gamma as a function of stock price (right axis) and time to maturity (left axis).   **Q** SFEgamma.xpl

Example 6.5
Let a portfolio of USD options and US–Dollars be delta neutral with a gamma of $\Gamma = -150\,000$. On the exchange trades a USD–call with $\Delta_B = 0.52$ and $\Gamma_B = 1.20$. By adding $-\Gamma/\Gamma_B = 125\,000$ contracts of this option the portfolio becomes gamma neutral. Unfortunately, its delta will be $125\,000 \cdot \Delta_B = 65\,000$. The delta neutrality can be achieved by selling 65 000 USD without changing the gamma.

Contrary to the evolution of the stock price the expiry of time is deterministic, and time does not involve any risk increasing randomness. If both Δ and Γ are 0 then the option value changes (approximately risk free) at a rate $\Theta = \Delta C/\Delta t$. The parameter Θ is for most options negative, i.e. the option value decreases as the maturity date approaches.

From Black–Scholes's formula (6.24) it follows for a delta neutral portfolio consisting of stock options

$$rV = \Theta + \frac{1}{2}\sigma^2 S^2 \Gamma,$$

with V denoting the portfolio value. Δ and Γ depend on each other in a straightforward way. Consequently, Δ can be used instead of Γ to gamma hedge a delta neutral portfolio.

6.3.3   Rho and Vega

Black–Scholes' approach proceeds from the assumption of a constant volatility σ. The appearance of smiles indicates that this assumption does not hold in practice. Therefore, it can be useful to make the portfolio value insensitive to changes in volatility. By doing this, the *vega* of a portfolio (in literature sometimes also called lambda or kappa) is used, which is for a call option defined by $\mathcal{V} = \frac{\partial C}{\partial \sigma}$.

For stocks and future contracts it holds $\mathcal{V} = 0$. Thus, in order to set up a vega hedge one has to make use of traded options. Since a vega neutral portfolio is not necessarily delta neutral two distinct options have to be involved to achieve simultaneously $\mathcal{V} = 0$ and $\Gamma = 0$.

From Black–Scholes' formula (6.24) and the variable y defined in equation (6.25) it follows that the vega of a call option on a non dividend paying stock is given by:

$$\mathcal{V} = S\sqrt{\tau}\varphi(y + \sigma\sqrt{\tau}). \tag{6.29}$$

Since the Black–Scholes formula was derived under the assumption of a constant volatility it is actually not justified to compute the derivative of (6.24) with respect to σ. However, the above formula for $\mathcal{V}$ is quite similar to an equation for $\mathcal{V}$ following from a more general stochastic volatility model. For that reason, equation (6.29) can be used as an approximation to the real vega.

Figure 6.3 displays the vega given by equation (6.29) as a function of stock price and time to maturity. At–the–money options with a long time to maturity are most sensitive to changes in volatility.

Finally, the call option's risk associated with movements in interest rates can be reduced by using *rho* to hedge the position:

$$\rho = \frac{\partial C}{\partial r}.$$

For a call on a non dividend paying stock it follows from equation (6.24)

$$\rho = K\,\tau\,e^{-r\tau}\Phi(y).$$

Vega

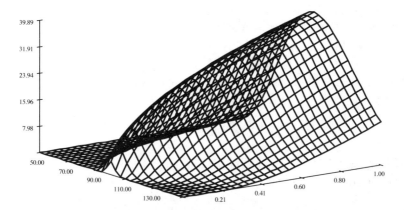

Figure 6.3: Vega as a function of stock price (right axis) and time to maturity
(left axis).   **Q** SFEvega.xpl

When hedging currency options domestic as well as foreign interest rates
have to be taken into account. Consequently, rho hedging strategies need to
consider two distinct values ρ_1 and ρ_2.

6.3.4   Historical and Implied Volatility

A property of the Black–Scholes formulae (6.22), (6.24) is that all option
parameters are known except the volatility parameter σ. In practical applications σ is estimated from available stock price observations or from prices
of similar products traded on an exchange.

Historical volatility is an estimator for σ based on the variability of the
underlying stock in the past. Let $S_0, \ldots, S_n$ be the stock prices at times
$0, \Delta t, 2\Delta t, \ldots, n\Delta t$. If the stock price S_t is modelled as Brownian motion,

the logarithmic relative increments

$$R_t = \ln \frac{S_t}{S_{t-1}}, \quad t = 1, \ldots, n$$

are independent and identical normally distributed random variables. R_t is the increment $Y_t - Y_{t-1}$ of the logarithmic stock price $Y_t = \ln S_t$ which as we saw in Section 5.4 is in a small time interval of length Δt a Wiener process with variance σ^2. Consequently the variance of R_t is given by

$$v = \text{Var}(R_t) = \sigma^2 \cdot \Delta t.$$

A good estimator for $\text{Var}(R_t)$ is the sample variance

$$\hat{v} = \frac{1}{n-1} \sum_{t=1}^{n} (R_t - \bar{R}_n)^2$$

with $\bar{R}_n = \frac{1}{n} \sum_{t=1}^{n} R_t$ being the sample average. $\hat{v}$ is unbiased, i.e. $\text{E}[\hat{v}] = v$, and the random variable

$$(n-1) \frac{\hat{v}}{v}$$

is χ^2_{n-1} distributed (chi-square distribution with $n - 1$ degrees of freedom). In particular this implies that the mean squared relative estimation error of $\hat{v}$ is given by

$$\text{E}\left(\frac{\hat{v} - v}{v}\right)^2 = \frac{1}{(n-1)^2} \text{Var}\left((n-1)\frac{\hat{v}}{v}\right) = \frac{2}{n-1}.$$

Since it holds $v = \sigma^2 \Delta t$ an estimator for the volatility σ based on historical stock prices is

$$\hat{\sigma} = \sqrt{\hat{v}/\Delta t}.$$

By means of a Taylor expansion of the square root function and by means of the known quantities $\text{E}[\hat{v}]$ and $\text{Var}(\hat{v}/v)$ it follows that $\hat{\sigma}$ is unbiased neglecting terms of size n^{-1} :

$$\text{E}\hat{\sigma} = \sigma + \mathcal{O}\left(\frac{1}{n}\right),$$

and that the mean squared relative estimation error of $\hat{\sigma}$ is given by

$$\text{E}\left(\frac{\hat{\sigma} - \sigma}{\sigma}\right)^2 = \frac{1}{2(n-1)} + \mathcal{O}\left(\frac{1}{n}\right),$$

again neglecting terms of size smaller than n^{-1}. Thanks to this relationship the reliability of the estimator $\hat{\sigma}$ can be evaluated.

Sample parameter selection:

a) As data daily settlement prices $S_0, \ldots, S_n$ are often used. Since σ is in general expressed as an annualized volatility Δt corresponds to one day on a yearly basis. Working with calender day count convention $\Delta t = \frac{1}{365}$. Unfortunately, for weekends and holidays no data is available. The following empirical argument favors to ignore weekends and holidays: If the stock dynamics behaved on Saturdays and Sundays as it does on trading days even if the dynamics were not observed then standard deviation of the change in the stock price from Friday to Monday would three times as large as the standard deviation between two trading days, say Monday to Tuesday. This follows from the fact that for the Wiener process $Y_t = \ln S_t$ the standard deviation of the increment $Y_{t+\delta} - Y_t$ is $\sigma \cdot \delta$. Empirical studies of stock markets show, however, that both standard deviations are proportional with a constant of around 1 but in any case significantly smaller than 3. Put in other words, the volatility decreases on weekend days. A conclusion is that trading increases volatility, and that the stock variability is not solely driven by external economic influences. Estimating volatility should therefore be done by considering exclusively trading days. Usually a year is supposed to have 252 trading days, i.e. $\Delta t = \frac{1}{252}$.

Concerning monthly data, $\Delta t = \frac{1}{12}$ is applied. In Section 3.3 we have calculated an annual volatility of 19% based on the monthly DAX data.

Q SFEsumm.xpl

b) Theoretically, the larger n the more reliable $\hat{\sigma}$. However, empirically the volatility is not constant over longer time periods. That is to say that stock prices from the recent past contain more information about the current σ as do stock prices from long ago. As a compromise closing prices of the last 90 days respectively 180 days are used. Some authors advise to use historical data of a period which has the same length as the period in the future in which the estimated volatility will be applied. In other words, if you want to compute the value of a call expiring in 9 months you should use closing prices of the past 9 months.

The *implied volatility* of an option is computed from its market price observed on an exchange and not from the prices of the underlying as it is case for the historical volatility. Consider a European call on a non dividend paying stock ($d = 0$, $b = r$), which has a quoted market price of C_B, then its implied volatility σ_I is given by solving

$$S \ \Phi(y + \sigma_I\sqrt{\tau}) - e^{-r\tau} K \ \Phi(y) = C_B$$

$$\text{with} \qquad y = \frac{1}{\sigma_I\sqrt{\tau}} \{\ln \frac{S}{K} + (r - \frac{1}{2}\sigma_I^2)\tau\}.$$

σ_I is the value of the volatility which if substituted into the Black-Scholes formula (6.24) would give a price equal to the observed market price C_B. σ_I is implicitly defined as a solution of the above equation, and has to be computed numerically due to the fact that the Black–Scholes formula cannot be inverted.

The implied volatility can be used to get an idea of the market view of the stock volatility. It is possible to construct an estimator using implied volatilities of options on the same stock but which are different in time to maturity τ and exercise price K. A weighting scheme takes the option price dependence on the volatility into account.

Q SFEVolSurfPlot.xpl

Example 6.6
Consider two traded options on the same underlying. One is at–the–money (ATM) and the other is deep ITM with volatilities of $\sigma_{I1} = 0.25$ respectively $\sigma_{I2} = 0.21$. At–the–money the dependence of option price and volatility is particular strong. That is, the price of the first option contains more information about the stock volatility and σ_{I1} can be considered a more reliable volatility estimate. Thus the estimator combining both implied volatilities should attribute a higher weight to σ_{I1}, as for example

$$\tilde{\sigma} = 0.8 \cdot \sigma_{I1} + 0.2 \cdot \sigma_{I2}.$$

Some authors suggest to set $\tilde{\sigma} = \sigma_{Im}$ with σ_{Im} being the volatility of the option which is most sensitive to changes in σ, i.e. the option with the highest vega $\partial C/\partial \sigma$ in absolute terms.

In order to apply the concept of risk neutrality (see Cox and Ross (1976)) the probability measure has to be transformed such that the price process under this new measure is a martingale. By doing this the absence of arbitrage opportunities is guaranteed. In incomplete markets, however, a multitude of such transformations exist (see Harrison and Kreps (1979)). In contrast to complete markets the trader cannot build up a self–financing portfolio reproducing the options payoff at maturity when the market is incomplete. Therefore hedging is no more riskless, and option prices depend on risk preferences. In this context we want to point out that the lack of a perfect hedge is of great importance in practice.

6.4 Recommended Literature

The classical papers of Black and Scholes (1973) and Merton (1973) which established modern derivatives pricing theory are worth reading. As does this book, Wilmott, Howison and Dewynne (1995) present an extensive introduction to mathematics of financial derivatives without martingale theory. Two influential works contributing to modern financial mathematics but which apply more advanced results of the theory of stochastic processes are Harrison and Pliska (1981) and Delbaen and Schachermayer (1994). A discussion of the mathematical foundations of absence of arbitrage is given by Jensen and Nielsen (1996). Korn and Korn (1999) and Korn and Korn (2001) provide a compact introduction to modern financial mathematics. For the advanced mathematician Duffie (1996) and Baxter and Rennie (1996) represent good starts into derivative pricing using martingale theory. Korn (1999) puts the focus on problems arising in hedging and portfolio optimization.

7 Binomial Model for European Options

There exists a big zoo of options of which the boundary conditions of the Black-Scholes differential equation are too complex to solve analytically. An example is the American option. For this reason one has to rely on numerical price computation. The best known methods approximate the stock price process by a discrete time stochastic process, or, as in the approach followed by Cox, Ross, Rubinstein, model the stock price process as a discrete time process from the start. By doing this, the options time to maturity T is decomposed into n equidistant time steps of length

$$\Delta t = \frac{T}{n}.$$

We consider therefore the discrete time points

$$t_j = j\Delta t, \; j = 0, ..., n.$$

By S_j we denote the stock price at time t_j. At the same time, we discretize the set of values the stock price can take such that it takes on the finitely many values $S_j^k, k = 1, ..., m_j$, with j denoting the point of time and k representing the value. If the stock price is in time t_j equal to S_j^k, then it can jump in the next time step to one of m_{j+1} new states S_{j+1}^l, $l = 1, ..., m_{j+1}$. The probabilities associated to these movements are denoted by p_{kl}^j:

$$p_{kl}^j = \mathrm{P}(S_{j+1} = S_{j+1}^l | S_j = S_j^k),$$

with

$$\sum_{l=1}^{m_{j+1}} p_{kl}^j = 1, \quad 0 \le p_{kl}^j \le 1.$$

If we know the stock price at the current time, we can build up a tree of possible stock prices up to a certain point of time, for example the maturity date $T = t_n$. Such a tree is also called *stock price tree*. Should the option price

be known at the final point of time t_n of the stock price tree, for example
by means of the options intrinsic value, the option value at time t_{n-1} can
be computed (according to (6.24)) as the discounted conditional expectation
of the corresponding option prices at time t_n given the stock price at time
t_{n-1}:

$$
\begin{aligned}
V(S^k_{n-1}, t_{n-1}) &= e^{-r\Delta t}\mathsf{E}\{V(S_n, t_n) \,|\, S_{n-1} = S^k_{n-1}\} \\
&= e^{-r\Delta t}\sum_{l=1}^{m_n} p^{n-1}_{kl} V(S^l_n, t_n).
\end{aligned}
\tag{7.1}
$$

$V(S,t)$ again denotes the option value at time t if the underlying has a price
of S. Repeating this step for the remaining time steps t_j, $j = n-2, n-3, ..., 0$,
the option prices up to time $t = 0$ can be approximated.

7.1   Cox–Ross–Rubinstein Approach to Option Pricing

As the simplest example to price an option we consider the approach of Cox,
Ross and Rubinstein (CRR) which is based on the assumption of a *binomial
model*, and which can be interpreted as a numerical method to solve the
Black–Scholes equation. We treat exclusively European options and assume
for the time being that the underlying pays no dividends within the time
to maturity. Again, we discretize time and consider solely the points in
time $t_0 = 0, t_1 = \Delta t, t_2 = 2\Delta t, ..., t_n = n\Delta t = T$ with $\Delta t = \frac{T}{n}$. The binomial
model proceeds from the assumption that the discrete time stock price process
S_j follows a geometric random walk (see Chapter 4), which is the discrete
analogue of the geometric Brownian motion. The binomial model has the
feature that at any point of time the stock price has only two possibilities to
move:

- either the price moves at rate u and with probability p in one direction
  (for example it moves *up*)

- or the price moves at rate d and with probability $1 - p$ in another
  direction (for example it moves *down*).

Using the notation introduced above, if the stock price in time t_j is equal to S^k_j
then in time t_{j+1} it can take only the values $u \cdot S^k_j$ and $d \cdot S^k_j$. The probabilities
p and q are independent of j. All other probabilities p^j_{kl} associated to $S^l_{j+1} \neq$
$u \cdot S^k_j$ and $\neq d \cdot S^k_j$ are 0.

In order to approximate the Black–Scholes differential equation by means of the Cox–Ross–Rubinstein approach, the probabilities p, q as well as the rates u, d have to be chosen such that in the limit $\Delta t \to 0$ the binomial model converges to a geometric Brownian motion. That is, arguing as in (6.23) the conditional distribution of $\ln S_{j+1}$ given S_j must be asympotically a normal distribution with expectation parameter $\ln S_j + (b - \frac{1}{2}\sigma^2)\Delta t$ and variance parameter $\sigma^2 \Delta t$. However, the conditional distribution of $\ln S_{j+1}$ given S_j implied by the binomial model is determined by $\ln(u \cdot S_j), \ln(d \cdot S_j)$ and their associated probabilities p and q. We set the parameters of the geometric random walk such that the conditional expectations and variances implied by the binomial model are equal to their asymptotic values for $\Delta t \to 0$. Taking into account that $p + q = 1$ we obtain three equations for the four unknown variables p, q, u and d :

$$p + q = 1,$$

$$E \overset{\text{def}}{=} p \ln(u \cdot S_j) + q \ln(d \cdot S_j) = \ln(S_j) + (b - \frac{1}{2}\sigma^2)\Delta t,$$

$$p\{\ln(u \cdot S_j) - E\}^2 + q\{\ln(d \cdot S_j) - E\}^2 = \sigma^2 \Delta t.$$

Due to the first equation, the current stock price S_j disappears from the remaining equations. By substituting $q = 1 - p$ into the latter two equations, we obtain, after some rearrangements, two equations and three unknown variables:

$$p \ln(\frac{u}{d}) + \ln d = (b - \frac{1}{2}\sigma^2)\Delta t,$$

$$(1 - p)p\{\ln\left(\frac{u}{d}\right)\}^2 = \sigma^2 \Delta t.$$

To solve this nonlinear system of equations we introduce a further condition

$$u \cdot d = 1,$$

i.e. if the stock price moves up and subsequently down, or down and subsequently up, then it takes its initial value two steps later. This recombining feature is more than only intuitively appealing. It simplifies the price tree significantly. At time t_j there are only $m_j = j + 1$ possible values the stock price S_j can take. More precisely, given the starting value S_0 at time t_0 the set of possible prices at time t_j is

$$S_j^k = S_0 u^k d^{j-k}, \ k = 0, ..., j,$$

because it holds $S_{j+1}^{k+1} = u \cdot S_j^k$ and $S_{j+1}^k = S_j^k / u$. In the general case there would be $m_j = 2j$ possible states since the not only the number of up and

down movements would determine the final state but also the order of up
and down movements.

Solving the system of three equations for p, u, d and neglecting terms being
small compared to Δt it holds approximatively:

$$p = \frac{1}{2} + \frac{1}{2}(b - \frac{1}{2}\sigma^2)\frac{\sqrt{\Delta t}}{\sigma}, \quad u = e^{\sigma\sqrt{\Delta t}}, \quad d = \frac{1}{u}. \qquad (7.2)$$

For the option price at time t_j and a stock price $S_j = S_j^k$ we use the shortcut
$V_j^k = V(S_j^k, t_j)$. As in equation (7.1) we obtain the option price at time t_j
by discounting the conditional expectation of the option price at time t_{j+1} :

$$V_j^k = e^{-r\Delta t}\{pV_{j+1}^{k+1} + (1 - p)V_{j+1}^k\}. \qquad (7.3)$$

At maturity $T = t_n$ the option price is known. In case of a European option
we have

$$V_n^k = \max\{0, S_n^k - K\}, \ k = 0, ..., n. \qquad (7.4)$$

Beginning with equation (7.1) and applying equation (7.3) recursively all
option values V_j^k, $k = 0, ..., j$, $j = n - 1, n - 2, ..., 0$ can be determined.

Example 7.1
*An example of a call option is given in Table 7.1. First the tree of stock
prices is computed. Since $\Delta t = \tau/n = 0.1$ it follows from equation (7.2)
that $u = 1.0823$. Given the current stock price $S_0 = 230$ the stock can either
increase to $S_1^1 = uS_0 = 248.92$ or decrease to $S_1^0 = S_0/u = 212.52$ after the
first time step. After the second time step, proceeding from state $S_1 = S_1^1$
the stock price can take the values $S_2^2 = uS_1 = 269.40$ or $S_2^1 = S_1/u = 230$,
proceeding from $S_1 = S_1^0$ it can move to $S_2^1 = 230$ or $S_2^0 = 196.36$ and so
on. At maturity, after 5 time steps, the stock price S_5 can take the following
six values $S_5^5 = u^5 S_0 = 341.51, S_5^4 = u^3 S_0 = 291.56, ..., S_5^0 = S_0/u^5 = 154.90$.*

*Following, given the tree of stock prices, we compute the option price at matu-
rity applying equation (7.4), for example $V_5^4 = V(S_5^4, t_5) = S_5^4 - K = 81.561$
or $V_5^1 = 0$, since $S_5^1 = 181.44 < K$. Equation (7.2) implies $p = 0.50898$,
since the cost of carry b are equal to the risk free interest rate r when no
dividends are paid. Proceeding from the options' intrinsic values at maturity we compute recursively the option values at preceding points of time by
means of equation (7.3). With $V_5^4 = 81.561, V_5^3 = 38.921$ we obtain the
option value $V_4^3 = 60.349$ at time $t_4 = 0.4$ corresponding to a stock price
$S_4 = S_4^3 = 269.40$ by substituting the known values of $p, r, \Delta t$. Analogously
we obtain the option value $V_0^0 = 30.378$ at time $t_0 = 0$ and current stock
price $S_0 = 230$ by means of equation (7.3) and the time $t_1 = 0.1$ option
values $V_1^1 = 44.328, V_1^0 = 16.200$.*

*Using only 5 time steps 30.378 is just a rough approximation to the theoretical
call value. However, comparing prices implied by the Black–Scholes formula
(6.24) to prices implied by the Cox–Ross–Rubinstein approach for different
time steps n the convergence of the numerical binomial model solution to the
Black–Scholes solution for increasing n is evident (see Table 7.2).*

Current stock price S_t	230.00
Exercise price K	210.00
Time to maturity τ	0.50
Volatility σ	0.25
Risk free rate r	0.04545
Dividend	none
Time steps	5
Option type	European call

Stock prices	Option prices					
341.50558						131.506
315.54682					106.497	
291.56126				83.457		81.561
269.39890			62.237		60.349	
248.92117		44.328		40.818		38.921
230.00000	30.378		26.175		20.951	
212.51708		16.200		11.238		2.517
196.36309			6.010		1.275	
181.43700				0.646		0.000
167.64549					0.000	
154.90230						0.000
Time	0.00	0.10	0.20	0.30	0.40	0.50

Table 7.1: Evolution of option prices (no dividend paying underlying)

Q SFEBiTree.xpl

The numerical procedure to price an option described above does not change
if the underlying pays a continuous dividend at rate d. It is sufficient to set
$b = r - d$ instead of $b = r$ for the cost of carry. Dividends paid at discrete
points of time, however, require substantial modifications in the recursive
option price computation, which we going to discuss in the following section.

Example 7.2
*We consider a call on US–Dollar with a time to maturity of 4 months, i.e. $\tau =
1/3$ years, a current exchange rate of $S = 1.50$ EUR/USD and an exercise*

Time steps	5	10	20	50	100	150	Black-Scholes
Option value	30.378	30.817	30.724	30.751	30.769	30.740	30.741

Table 7.2: Convergence of the price implied by the binomial model to the price implied by the Black–Scholes formula

price $K = 1.50$ EUR/USD. *The continuous dividend yield, which corresponds to the US interest rate, is assumed to be 1%, and the domestic interest rate is 9%. It follows that the cost of carry being the difference between the domestic and the foreign interest rate is equal to $b = r - d = 8\%$. Table 7.3 gives as in the previous example the option prices implied by the binomial model.*

Current EUR/USD–price S_t	1.50
Exercise price K	1.50
Time to maturity τ	0.33
Volatility σ	0.20
Risk free interest rate r	0.09
Continuous dividend d	0.01
Time steps	6
Option type	European call

Price	Option prices						
1.99034							0.490
1.89869						0.405	
1.81127					0.324		0.311
1.72786				0.247		0.234	
1.64830			0.180		0.161		0.148
1.57240		0.127		0.105		0.079	
1.50000	0.087		0.067		0.042		0.000
1.43093		0.041		0.022		0.000	
1.36504			0.012		0.000		0.000
1.30219				0.000		0.000	
1.24223					0.000		0.000
1.18503						0.000	
1.13046							0.000
Time	0.00	0.06	0.11	0.17	0.22	0.28	0.33

Table 7.3: Evolution of option prices (with continuous dividends)

Q SFEBiTree.xpl

7.2   Discrete Dividends

In case of dividend payments at discrete points of time the tree of stock prices changes. By changing the price tree we have to distinguish two different cases. In the first case, dividends are paid as a percentage of the stock price. In the second case, dividends are paid as a fixed amount of money. We confine ourselves to the case that dividends are paid only once during the time to maturity, say, at time $t^*, 0 < t^* \leq T$. Dividends paid at several points of time can be dealt with analogously. We assume that the underlying is a stock.

Using arbitrage arguments it can be shown that the stock price jumps down by the amount of the dividend at the time the dividend is paid. Let's consider the following argument to visualize this. At time $t^* - dt$, which is immediately before the dividend is paid, we buy the stock, cash in the dividend, and sell the stock at time $t^* + dt$. By doing this, we make a gain of $D + S_{t^*+dt} - S_{t^*-dt}$, which has to be zero if arbitrage is excluded. Therefore, for $dt \to 0$ it is sufficient if S_t jumps down by D at time t^*.

7.2.1   Dividends as a Percentage of the Stock Price

Suppose that t^* is contained, say, in the ith time interval, i.e. $t_{i-1} < t^* \leq t_i$. Let the dividend paid at time t_i be a percentage δ of the stock price, that is the dividend amount that is paid is equal to δS_i. It follows that the stock price at time t_i is smaller by the dividend amount than the stock price without the dividend payment. Accordingly, all stock prices in the tree after time t_i change in the same way: all prices S_j^k, $j \geq i$, are multiplied by the factor $(1 - \delta)$. Following this correction the option values can be determined recursively as in the no dividend case.

Example 7.3
We consider a call option on a stock paying a dividend of $\delta = 1\%$ of the stock price at time 0.15. All other parameters of this example are those already given in Table 7.1. The results are shown in Table 7.4. First we ignore the dividend and compute the stock price tree as shown in Table 7.1. Following, all stock prices from the dividend date on, i.e. from time $t_2 = 0.2$ on (note that we divided the time period into 5 time steps $0 \leq t \leq 0.5$), are multiplied by the factor $(1 - \delta)$. In Table 7.4 the values in parentheses correspond to the stock prices that are decreased by the dividend amount, i.e. S_j^k, $j < i = 2$ respectively $0.99 \cdot S_j^k$, $j \geq i = 2$. Thus, the option prices at maturity change due to equation (7.4), for example $V_5^4 = V(0.99 \cdot S_5^4, t_5) = 0.99 \cdot 291.56 - K = 78.646$. Having determined the option values at maturity the

preceding option values are again computed by recursively applying equation (7.2). Note, V_j^k corresponds to the stock price $0.99 \cdot S_j^k$ rather than to S_j^k, for $j \geq 2$, i.e. $t_j \geq t^*$. However, the current time $t_0 = 0 < t^* = 0.15$ is not concerned, i.e. $V_0^0 = 28.384$ is still the option price corresponding to the current stock price $S_0 = 230$.

Current stock price S_t	230.00
Exercise price K	210.00
Time to maturity τ	0.50
Volatility σ	0.25
Risk free interest rate r	0.04545
Discrete dividend δ	0.01
Dividend date t^*	0.15
Time steps	5
Option type	European call

Stock prices	Option prices					
341.50558						128.091
315.54682					103.341	(338.09)
291.56126				80.542	(312.39)	78.646
269.39890			59.543	(288.65)	57.655	(288.65)
248.92117		41.942	(266.70)	38.329	(266.70)	36.432
230.00000	28.384	(248.92)	24.087	(246.43)	18.651	(246.43)
212.51708	(230.00)	14.592	(227.70)	9.547	(227.70)	0.392
196.36309		(212.52)	4.886	(210.39)	0.199	(210.39)
181.43700			(194.40)	0.101	(194.40)	0.000
167.64549				(179.62)	0.000	(179.62)
154.90230					(165.97)	0.000
						(153.35)
Time	0.00	0.10	0.20	0.30	0.40	0.50
Dividend	1.00	1.00	0.99	0.99	0.99	0.99

Table 7.4: Evolution of option prices (dividends as a percentage of the stock price)

Q SFEBiTree.xpl

7.2.2   Dividends as a Fixed Money Amount

We assume now that at an ex ante fixed point in time t^* a fixed amount of money (for example 5.00 EUR) is paid. Now, the stock price jumps down by an amount which is independent of the stock price. It follows that the tree is not totally recombining anymore. The stock price tree splits up which can be visualized in a simple example. Suppose at time t^*, $t_1 < t^* \leq t_2 < T$, a fixed dividend of D is paid. Figure 7.1 shows the stock price tree for this example. Before the dividend payment at time t_1 the nodes correspond to stock prices of the kind uS_0 and S_0/u. After the dividend payment, however, stock prices at time t_2 are given by $u^2 S_0 - D, S_0 - D$ and $S_0/u^2 - D$. Proceeding from these 3 prices the tree consists of 6 possible prices in time t_3, at time t_4 it consists of 9 and so on. The stock price tree gets very vast the more time steps are considered, and is less useful for practical computations. To overcome this problem, we use the fact that the dividend is independent of the stock price and therefore not random anymore. We decompose the stock price S_j in a random and a deterministic component:

$$S_j = \tilde{S}_j + D_j,$$

with D_j being the current present value of the dividend payment, i.e. before dividend payment, it is the time $t_j \leq t^*$ discounted value of D, afterwards it is 0:

$$D_j = \begin{cases} De^{-r(t^* - t_j)} & \text{, for } t_j \leq t^*, \\ 0 & \text{, for } t^* < t_j. \end{cases} \qquad (7.5)$$

In particular, at maturity it holds $D_n = 0$ and $S_n = \tilde{S}_n$. In order to compute

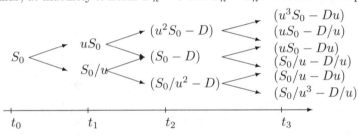

Figure 7.1: Evolution of the stock price tree (dividends as a fixed amount of money

the option price we first construct a stock price tree of the random stock price component $\tilde{S}_n$ beginning in $\tilde{S}_0 = S_0 - D_0$. Starting at maturity $T = t_n$ we obtain:

$$\tilde{V}_{n-1} = e^{-r\Delta t} \mathsf{E}[\max(0, \tilde{S}_n - K) | \tilde{S}_{n-1}]$$

The other option prices are given as in the no dividend case by:

$$\tilde{V}_{j-1} = e^{-r\Delta t} \mathsf{E}[\tilde{V}_j | \tilde{S}_{j-1}].$$

The original option prices then correspond to $\tilde{V}_j^k$ given above. However, they do not correspond to the stock price $\tilde{S}_j^k$, rather than to the actual stock price

$$S_j^k = \tilde{S}_j^k + D_j.$$

Example 7.4

In this example, there are two dividend payments at time $t_1^* = 0.25$ and $t_2^* = 0.75$. Both dividends are $D^{(1)} = D^{(2)} = 1.00$ EUR. The parameters and results are given in Table 7.5. First, we compute the time t_j present value of all dividends with equation (7.5): $D_j = D^{(1)}e^{-r(t_1^*-t_j)} + D^{(2)}e^{-r(t_2^*-t_j)}$ for $t_j \leq t_1^*$, $D_j = D^{(2)}e^{-r(t_2^*-t_j)}$ for $t_1^* < t_j \leq t_2^*$ and $D_j = 0$ for $t_2^* < t_j$. In

Current stock price S_t	100.00
Exercise price K	100.00
Time to maturity τ	1.00
Volatility σ	0.30
Risk free interest rate r	0.10
Discrete dividend $D^{(1)}$	1.00
Payment date t_1^*	0.25
Discrete dividend $D^{(2)}$	1.00
payment date t_2^*	0.75
Time steps	6
Option type	European Put

Prices	Option prices					
204.55						0.000
180.97					0.000	(204.55)
160.12				0.000	(180.97)	0.000
141.65			0.179	(161.10)	0.000	(160.11)
125.32		1.373	(142.63)	0.394	(141.65)	0.000
110.88	3.906	(126.28)	2.810	(126.32)	0.866	(125.32)
98.10	7.631	(112.81)	6.990	(111.85)	5.720	(110.88)	1.903
86.79	(100)	12.236	(99.06)	12.100	(99.09)	11.567	(98.10)
76.78		(88.72)	18.775	(87.76)	19.953	(86.79)	23.215
67.93			(77.74)	27.211	(77.78)	30.421	(76.78)
60.10				(68.91)	36.631	(67.93)	39.897
53.17					(61.09)	45.178	(60.10)
47.05						(53.17)	52.955
						(47.05)
Zeit	0.00	0.17	0.33	0.50	0.67	0.83	1.00
Div. D_j	1.903	1.935	0.960	0.975	0.992	0.00	0.00

Table 7.5: Evolution of option prices (discrete dividends as a fixed money amount)

🔍 SFEBiTree4.xpl

particular, it holds $D_j = 0$ for $t_j > t_2^*$. Following, we construct the stock price tree as in Table 7.1, but this time we start in $\tilde{S}_0 = S_0 - D_0 = 98.10$ rather than in $S_0 = 100$. Proceeding from the boundary values $\tilde{V}_6^k = K - \tilde{S}_n^k$, $k = 0, ..., 3$, $\tilde{V}_6^k = 0$, $k = 4, ..., 6$ we compute once again recursively the put prices at earlier points in time by means of equation (7.3). We have to take into account that for example the option price $\tilde{V}_3^2 = 2.810$ belongs to the stock price $S_3^2 = \tilde{S}_3^2 + D_3 = 111.85$ and not to $\tilde{S}_3^2 = 110.88$, which accounts for the *dividend. It follows that the put option price at a current stock price $S_0 = 100$ is equal to $\tilde{V}_0^0 = 7.631$.*

7.3 Recommended Literature

Starting point to price options by means of binomial processes is the classic work of Cox, Ross and Rubinstein (1979) who introduce this approach as an independent method rather than only as a numeric approximation to the Black–Scholes equations. Baxter and Rennie (1996) provide a detailed and modern description of option pricing with binomial trees. The numerical aspects are extensively discussed by Dewynne, Howison and Wilmott (1993).

8 American Options

8.1 Arbitrage Relationship for American Options

It is complex to price American options since they can be exercised at any time point up to expiry date. The time the holder chooses to exercise the options depends on the spot price of the underlying asset S_t. In this sense the exercising time is a random variable itself. It is obvious that the Black-Scholes differential equations still hold as long as the options are not exercised. However the boundary conditions are so complicated that an analytical solution is not possible. In this section we study American options in more detail. The numerical procedures of pricing will also be discussed in the next section.

As shown in Section 2.1, the right to early exercise implies that the value of an American option can never drop below its intrinsic value. For example the value of an American put should not go below $\max(K - S_t, 0)$ with the exercise price K. In contrast this condition does not hold for European options. Thus American puts would be exercised before expiry date if the value of the option would drop below the intrinsic value.

Let's consider an American put on a stock with expiry date T. If the stock price S_{t^*} at time t^* is zero, then $S_t = 0$ holds for $t \geq t^*$ since the price process follows a geometric Brownian motion. It is then not worth waiting for a later exercise any more. If the put holder waits, he will loose the interests on the value K that can be received from a bond investment for example. If $S_{t^*} = 0$, the value of the put at t^* is K which is the same as the intrinsic value. Since the respective European put cannot be exercised early, e.g. at time t^*, we can only get K on the expiry date. If we discount it to time t^* with $\tau^* = T - t^*$, we only get $Ke^{-r\tau^*}$ that is the value of the European put at time t^*. Obviously this value is smaller than the value of an American put and its intrinsic value. Figure 8.1 shows the put value with a continuous cost of carry b.

As we can see an early exercise of the put is maybe necessary even before $S_t = 0$. For a certain critical stock price S^{**}, the lost of interests on the

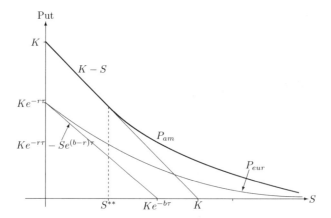

Figure 8.1: European put and early exercise of an American put with costs
of carry b_1 and b_2.

intrinsic value, which the holder can receive by exercising it immediately,
is higher than the possible increase of the option value due to the eventual
underlying fluctuations. That is one of the reasons why the critical underlying
price is dependent on time: $S^{**} = S^{**}(t)$.

From the derivation of the Black-Scholes differential equations it follows that
they are valid as long as the option is not exercised. Given that there are no
transaction costs in perfect markets, a revenue can be realized from an early
exercise, which equals to the intrinsic value of the option. One says in this
case that the option falls back to its intrinsic value by early exercising. Thus
the pricing of American options is an open boundary problem. The Black-
Scholes differential equations are valid where the underlying S is either higher
than the critical put-price $S^{**} = S^{**}(t)$ or lower than the critical call-price
$S^* = S^*(t)$. The boundaries defined through $S^{**}(t)$ and $S^*(t)$ are unknown.

Figure 8.2 shows the regions where the option price $C = C(S, t)$ for an
American call satisfies the Black-Scholes differential equations.

- In the interior $\{(S, t)|0 \leq S < S^*(t), t < T\}$ the Black-Scholes differen-
  tial equations hold.

- At the boundaries $\{(S, t)|S = S^*(t), t < T\}$ and $\{(S, t)|0 \leq S, t = T\}$
  the call falls back to the intrinsic value $\max(S - K, 0)$.

- $C(S,t)$ and $\dfrac{\partial C(S,t)}{\partial S}$ are continuous in the whole region including the boundaries.

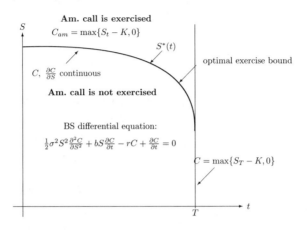

Figure 8.2: The exercise boundary $S^*(t)$ for an American call.

The numerical solution for such boundary problems is described in the next section. Based on the assumptions of perfect markets and arbitrage free argument in Section 2.1 we derive some properties of American options without considering any specific mathematical models for the price process S_t.

Theorem 8.1

1. *An American call on an asset that does not bring any positive incomes is not early exercised and has the same value as an equivalent European call.*

2. *For an American call on an asset that brings positive incomes at discrete time points $t_1, \cdots, t_n$ the optimal exercise time lays just before these points. Consequently in the case of continuous positive payments, any time point can be an optimal exercise time.*

Proof:
Let K denote the exercise price, T the expiry date, $\tau = T - t$ the time to maturity of a call and S_t the price of the underlying asset. $C_{am}(S,\tau)$ and $C_{eur}(S,\tau)$ denote the value of the respective American and European calls

at time t with time to maturity $\tau = T - t$ and the spot price $S_t = S$. Using the put-call parity for European options we find

1. in the case of discrete dividends D with the discounted value $D_t \leq 0$ at time t, i.e. they are costs. Furthermore it holds based on Theorem 2.3:

$$C(S_t, \tau) = P(S_t, \tau) + S_t - D_t - Ke^{-r\tau} \geq S_t - Ke^{-r\tau} > S_t - K \quad (8.1)$$

where $C = C_{eur}$ and P is the respective put price.

In the case of continuous dividends with rate $d \leq 0$, it follows from $b - r = -d \geq 0$ that:

$$\begin{aligned} C(S_t, \tau) &= P(S_t, \tau) + S_t e^{(b-r)\tau} - Ke^{-r\tau} \\ &\geq S_t e^{(b-r)\tau} - Ke^{-r\tau} > S_t - K \end{aligned} \quad (8.2)$$

In both cases we verify that $C(S_t, \tau) > S_t - K$ for European calls. Since $C_{am} \geq C$, we conclude that

$$C_{am}(S_t, \tau) > S_t - K,$$

i.e. the value of an American call is higher than the intrinsic value during the whole maturity. Therefore early exercise is avoided.

2. without any restriction we consider the case where t_1 is the next payment time. $\tilde{t} < t_1$ represents any early time. $\tilde{C}(S_t, \tilde{\tau})$ with $\tilde{\tau} = \tilde{t} - t$ is the value of a European call with the same exercise price K but with a different maturity date at $\tilde{t}$. Since there are no payments before $\tilde{t}$ at all, it follows from part 1 that $\tilde{C}(S_t, \tilde{\tau}) > S_t - K$ for $t < \tilde{t}$. Due to the longer time to maturity and the possibility of early exercise of American calls, it follows

$$C_{am}(S_t, \tau) \geq \tilde{C}(S_t, \tilde{\tau}) > S_t - K \quad (8.3)$$

As in part 1, the value of an American call at any time $t < \tilde{t}$ lays strictly over the intrinsic value, which excludes an early exercise. Since $\tilde{t} < t_1$ can take any value, $C_{am}(S_t, \tau)$ falls to the intrinsic value just at time t_1 (or in a respectively later time point).

□

Figure 8.3 shows a graphical representation of the first part of the theorem.

- If $b \geq r$ which is equivalent to $d \leq 0$, then $C_{am} = C_{eur}$.

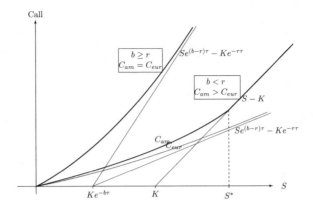

Figure 8.3: A European call and an early exercised American Call.

- If $b < r$ which is equivalent to $d > 0$, then $C_{am} > C_{eur}$.

It is also possible to derive a formula similar to the put call parity for American options. Given that the model is unknown for the critical price $S^*(t)$, $S^{**}(t)$ and consequently the time point for early exercise, the formula is just an inequality.

Theorem 8.2 (Put-Call Parity for American options)
We consider an American call and an American put with the same maturity date T and the same exercise price K on the same underlying asset. Let $C_{am}(S, \tau)$ and $P_{am}(S, \tau)$ denote the option prices at time t when the spot price is $S_t = S$ and the time to maturity is $\tau = T - t$. It holds

1. *if there are incomes or costs during the time to maturity $\tau = T - t$ with the discounted value D_t at time t, then*

$$P_{am}(S_t, \tau) + S_t - Ke^{-r\tau} \geq C_{am}(S_t, \tau) \geq P_{am}(S_t, \tau) + S_t - D_t - K \quad (8.4)$$

2. *if there are continuous costs of carry with rate b on the underlying asset,*

Position	$\tilde{t} = t_1 - \Delta t$ early exercise of the call	t_1	Call is exercised early $S_T \leq K$	$S_T > K$	Call is not exercised early $S_T \leq K$	$S_T > K$
1.	≥ 0	–	$K - S_T$	0	$K - S_T$	0
2.	$S_{\tilde{t}}$	D_1	–	–	S_T	S_T
3.	$-Ke^{-r(T-\tilde{t})}$	–	$-K$	$-K$	$-K$	$-K$
4.	$-(S_{\tilde{t}} - K)$	–	$Ke^{r(T-\tilde{t})}$	$Ke^{r(T-\tilde{t})}$	0	$-(S_T - K)$
Sum	≥ 0	≥ 0	≥ 0	≥ 0	0	0

Table 8.1: Portfolio value at time $\tilde{t}$, t_1 and T.

Q SFEamerican.xpl

then

$$
\begin{aligned}
P_{am}(S_t, \tau) + S_t - Ke^{-r\tau} &\geq C_{am}(S_t, \tau) \\
&\geq P_{am}(S_t, \tau) + S_t e^{(b-r)\tau} - K \\
&\qquad \text{if } b < r \qquad (8.5) \\
P_{am}(S_t, \tau) + S_t e^{(b-r)\tau} - Ke^{-r\tau} &\geq C_{am}(S_t, \tau) \\
&\geq P_{am}(S_t) + S_t - K \ \text{if } b \geq r
\end{aligned}
$$

Proof:

Supposing without any restriction that the underlying asset is a stock paying dividends D_1 at time t_1.

1. We show first the left inequality. We consider a portfolio consisting of the following four positions:

1. buy an American put

2. buy a stock

3. sell bonds (i.e. borrow money) with the nominal value K and the maturity date T

4. sell an American call

In this portfolio, the position 1 is held until time T despite the underoptimal conditions, i.e. the put is not exercised early even when the call holder exercises it early. Note from Theorem 8.1 that an early exercise of the call is only possible at time $\tilde{t} := t_1 - \Delta t$ where $\Delta t \approx 0$, i.e. directly before the

Pos.	$\tilde{t}=t_1-\Delta t$ early exercise of a put	Put is exercised early $S_T \leq K$	$S_T > K$	Put is not exercised early $S_T \leq K$	$S_T > K$
1.	≥ 0	0	$S_T - K$	0	$S_T - K$
2.	$-S_{\tilde{t}} - D_t e^{r(\tilde{t}-t)}$	$-S_T$ $-D_t e^{r\tau}$	$-S_T$ $-D_t e^{r\tau}$	$-S_T$ $-D_t e^{r\tau}$	$-S_T$ $-D_t e^{r\tau}$
3.	$(D_t + K)e^{r(\tilde{t}-t)}$	$(D_t+K)e^{r\tau}$	$(D_t+K)e^{r\tau}$	$(D_t+K)e^{r\tau}$	$(D_t+K)e^{r\tau}$
4.	$-(K-S_{\tilde{t}})$	0	0	$-(K-S_T)$	0
Sum	≥ 0	≥ 0	≥ 0	≥ 0	≥ 0

Table 8.2: Portfolio value at time $\tilde{t}$, t_1 and T.

payment at time t_1. In this case we deliver the stock of the portfolio. The value of the portfolio at time T is given in the Table 8.1.

Therefore it holds for every time t as mentioned:

$$P_{am}(S_t,\tau) + S_t - Ke^{-r\tau} - C_{am}(S_t,\tau) \geq 0 \tag{8.6}$$

The proof of the second inequality is analogous but with opposite positions. Here we consider that the put can be exercised early, see Table 8.2.

1. buy an American call

2. sell a stock

3. buy a bond (i.e. lend money) at present value $K + D_t$ with maturity date T

4. sell an American put

Therefore we have for every time t as mentioned:

$$C_{am}(S_t,\tau) - P_{am}(S_t,\tau) - S_t + K + D_t \geq 0 \tag{8.7}$$

2. For continuous cost of carry we first consider the case where $b \geq r \iff d \leq 0$. We prove the left inequality at first

$$P_{am}(S_t,\tau) + S_t e^{(b-r)\tau} - Ke^{-r\tau} \geq C_{am}(S_t,\tau) \tag{8.8}$$

Consider the following portfolio at time t:

1. buy an American put

2. buy $e^{(b-r)\tau}$ stocks

3. sell bonds at nominal value K with expiring date T

4. sell an American call

As in part 1 it follows that the value of the portfolio at time T is zero if the call is *not* exercised early. The continuous costs of carry ($d \leq 0$) are financed through the sell of the stocks so that only one stock is left in the portfolio at time T.

If, on the other hand, the call is exercised early at time $\tilde{t}$, the whole portfolio is then liquidated and we get:

$$
\begin{aligned}
P_{am}(S_{\tilde{t}}, \tau) - (S_{\tilde{t}} - K) + S_{\tilde{t}} e^{(b-r)(T-\tilde{t})} - K e^{-r(T-\tilde{t})} &= \\
P_{am}(S_{\tilde{t}}, \tau) + K(1 - e^{-r(T-\tilde{t})}) + S_{\tilde{t}}(e^{(b-r)(T-\tilde{t})} - 1) &\geq 0
\end{aligned} \tag{8.9}
$$

The value of the portfolio at time t is:

$$
P_{am}(S_t, \tau) + S_t e^{(b-r)\tau} - K e^{-r\tau} - C_{am}(S_t, \tau) \geq 0 \tag{8.10}
$$

If $b < r \iff d > 0$ the left inequality is similarly proved,

$$
P_{am}(S_t, \tau) + S_t - K e^{r\tau} \geq C_{am}(S_t, \tau) \tag{8.11}
$$

it is enough to hold one stock in the portfolio because of $d > 0$.

We show now the right inequality for the case $b \geq r$

$$
C_{am}(S_t, \tau) \geq P_{am}(S_t, \tau) + S_t - K \tag{8.12}
$$

We consider the following portfolio at time t:

1. buy an American call

2. sell an American put

3. sell a stock (short sales)

4. buy a bond with nominal value $Ke^{r\tau}$ and expiring at time T

If the put is not exercised early, it holds at time T:

$$
\begin{array}{ccccccc}
0 & - & (K - S_T) & -S_T e^{-(b-r)\tau} + K e^{r\tau} & \geq & 0 & \text{if} \quad S_T < K \\
(S_T - K) & + & 0 & -S_T e^{-(b-r)\tau} + K e^{r\tau} & \geq & 0 & \text{if} \quad S_T \geq K
\end{array} \tag{8.13}
$$

If the put is exercised early at time $\tilde{t}$, the whole portfolio is liquidated and we get:

$$C_{am}(S_{\tilde{t}}, \tau) - (K - S_{\tilde{t}}) - S_{\tilde{t}} e^{-(b-r)(\tilde{t}-t)} + K e^{r(\tilde{t}-t)} \geq 0 \qquad (8.14)$$

Thus the value of the portfolio at time t is:

$$C_{am}(S_t, \tau) - P_{am}(S_t, \tau) - S_t + K \geq 0 \qquad (8.15)$$

Analogously one gets for the right inequality when $b < r$

$$C_{am}(S_t, \tau) \geq P_{am}(S_t, \tau) + S_t e^{(b-r)\tau} - K \qquad (8.16)$$

where the position of the stock is reduced to $e^{(b-r)\tau}$.   □

8.2   The Trinomial Model for American Options

The American option price can only be determined numerically. Similar to the European options, the binomial model after Cox-Ross-Rubinstein can be used. In this section we introduce a less complex but numerically efficient approach based on trinomial trees, see Dewynne et al. (1993). It is related to the classical numerical procedures for solving partial differential equations, which are also used to solve the Black-Scholes differential equations.

The trinomial model (see Section 4.2) follows the procedure of the binomial model whereby the price at each time point $t_j = j\Delta t, j = 0, ..., n$ can change to three instead of two directions with $\Delta t = T/n$, see Figure 8.4. The value S_j^k at time t_j can reach to the values $u_1 \cdot S_j^k, u_2 \cdot S_j^k, u_3 \cdot S_j^k$ at t_{j+1}, where $u_i > 0, i = 1, 2, 3$, are the suitable parameters of the model. The probability with which the price moves from S_j^k to $u_i \cdot S_j^k$ is represented as $p_i, i = 1, 2, 3$. The price process $S_j, j = 0, ..., n$ in discrete time is also a trinomial process, i.e. the logarithms of the price $Z_j = \ln S_j, j = 0, ..., n$ is an ordinary trinomial process with possible increments $\ln u_i, i = 1, 2, 3$.

As in the binomial model three conditions must be fulfilled: The sum of the probabilities $p_i, i = 1, 2, 3$, is one, the expectation and variance of the logarithms increments Z_j must be the same as those of the logarithms of the geometric Brownian motion over the time interval Δt. From these conditions we get three equations:

$$p_1 + p_2 + p_3 = 1, \qquad (8.17)$$

$$p_1 \ln u_1 + p_2 \ln u_2 + p_3 \ln u_3 = (b - \frac{1}{2}\sigma^2)\Delta t, \qquad (8.18)$$

$$p_1(\ln u_1)^2 + p_2(\ln u_2)^2 + p_3(\ln u_3)^2 = \sigma^2 \Delta t + (b - \frac{1}{2}\sigma^2)^2 \Delta t^2. \,(8.19)$$

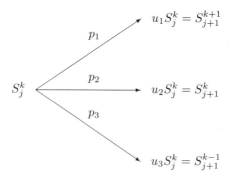

$$u_1 S_j^k = S_{j+1}^{k+1}$$

$$u_2 S_j^k = S_{j+1}^k$$

$$u_3 S_j^k = S_{j+1}^{k-1}$$

Figure 8.4: Possible price movements in the trinomial model.

In the last equation we use $\mathsf{E}(Z_j^2) = var(Z_j) + (\mathsf{E}\, Z_j)^2$. Since there are 6 unknown parameters in the trinomial model, we have the freedom to introduce three extra conditions in order to identify a unique and possibly simple solution of the equation system. To be able to construct a clear price tree, we require the recombination property

$$u_1 u_3 = u_2^2.$$

From this, the number of possible prices at time t_n is reduced from maximal 3^n to $2n+1$ and consequently the memory spaces and computation time are saved. To determine the parameters of the model we still need two more conditions. We discuss two approaches of which one comes from binomial models while the other from the numerical results of partial differential equations.

a.) The first approach requires that a time step of Δt in the trinomial model corresponds to two time steps in the binomial model: u_1 represents two upwards increments, u_3 two downwards increments and u_2 one upward and one downward increment (or reversed). The binomial model fulfills the recombination condition $d = 1/u$. Since now the length of the time step is $\Delta t/2$, it holds following Section 7.1

$$u = e^{\sigma \sqrt{\Delta t/2}}$$

and the probability with which the price moves upwards in the binomial model is:

$$p = \frac{1}{2} + \frac{1}{2}(b - \frac{1}{2}\sigma^2)\frac{\sqrt{\Delta t/2}}{\sigma}.$$

Then we get the conditions for the parameters of the trinomial model

$$
\begin{aligned}
u_1 &= u^2, \, u_2 = 1, \, u_3 = u^{-2}, \\
p_1 &= p^2, \, p_2 = 2p(1 - p), \, p_3 = (1 - p)^2.
\end{aligned}
$$

With these parameters, the trinomial model performs the same as the corresponding binomial model for the European option, requiring however only the half of the time step. It converges therefore more quickly than the binomial model against the Black-Scholes solution.

Example 8.1 *Given the parameters from Table 7.1, the trinomial model delivers a price of 30,769 for a European call option after $n = 50$ steps. This corresponds exactly the value the binomial model reaches after $n = 100$ steps, see Table 7.2.*

American options differ from the European in that the options can be exercised at any time t^*, $0 < t^* \le T$. Consequently the value of a call falls back to the intrinsic value if it is early exercised:

$$
C(S, t^*) = \max\{0, S(t^*) - K\}.
$$

Mathematically we have solved the free boundary problem, which is only numerically possible.

V_j^k denotes the option value at time t_j if the spot price of stock is $S_j = S_j^k$. As in the binomial model on European options we use V_j^k to denote the discounted expectation that is calculated from the prices attainable in the next time step, V_{j+1}^{k+1}, V_{j+1}^k and V_{j+1}^{k-1}. Different from the European options, the expectation of American options may not fall under the intrinsic value. The recursion of American call price is thus:

$$
C_j^k = \max\{S_j^k - K, \, e^{-r\Delta t}[p_1 C_{j+1}^{k+1} + p_2 C_{j+1}^k + p_3 C_{j+1}^{k-1}]\}.
$$

Example 8.2 *Table 8.3 gives the parameters and the value of an American call option determined with steps $n = 50$ in a trinomial model. It coincides with Theorem 8.1 giving the same value 30.769 as a European option because the underlying stock issues no dividend during the running time.*

The American put is on the other hand more valuable than the European. With the parameters from Table 8.3 one gets $P_{eur} = 6.05140$ and $P_{am} = 6.21159$.

spot stock price S_t	230.00
exercise price K	210.00
time to maturity τ	0.50
volatility σ	0.25
interest rate r	0.04545
dividend	no
steps	50
option type	American call
option price	30.769

Table 8.3: The value of an American call option.

b.) In the second approach the trinomial parameters p_i and u_i are certainly decided through additional conditions. Here a certain upwards trend is shown in the whole price tree since we replace the condition $u_2 = 1$ by

$$u_2 = u \stackrel{\text{def}}{=} e^{(b-\frac{1}{2}\sigma^2)\Delta t}.$$

Furthermore we assume $p_1 = p_3$ and receive therefore together with the four above-mentioned conditions:

$$p_1 = p_3 = p, \quad p_2 = 1 - 2p, \quad \text{with} \ \ p = \frac{\Delta t}{Th^2},$$

$$u_1 = u e^{\sigma h \sqrt{T/2}}, \ \ u_2 = u, \ \ u_3 = u e^{-\sigma h \sqrt{T/2}},$$

Where h is another free parameter. The p_i and u_i fulfill the equation system (8.17) - (8.19) exactly so that p_1, p_2, p_3 are not trivial probabilities, i.e they must be between 0 and 1 and $0 < p < 1/2$. That means h must fulfill the following condition:

$$h > \sqrt{\frac{2\Delta t}{T}}. \tag{8.20}$$

We consider now a European option. Here the trinomial model delivers the following recursion for the possible option value dependent on the probabilities p_i and the change rates u_i:

$$V_j^k = e^{-r\Delta t}\left(\frac{\Delta t}{Th^2}V_{j+1}^{k+1} + (1 - 2\frac{\Delta t}{Th^2})V_{j+1}^k + \frac{\Delta t}{Th^2}V_{j+1}^{k-1}\right). \tag{8.21}$$

We consider $\Delta t = -(T - t_{j+1}) + (T - t_j)$ for all $j = 0, ..., n - 1$ and we put $h^* = \Delta t/T$ as well as

$$Z_j^k = V_j^k e^{-r(T-t_j)}, \ \ Z_{j+1}^k = V_{j+1}^k e^{-r(T-t_{j+1})}.$$

The recursion (8.21) for the option value V_j^k becomes then

$$\frac{Z_j^k - Z_{j+1}^k}{h^*} = \frac{Z_{j+1}^{k+1} - 2Z_{j+1}^k + Z_{j+1}^{k-1}}{h^2}. \tag{8.22}$$

This is the explicit difference approximation of the parabolic differential equation (6.15), see Samaskij (1984). The condition (8.20) corresponds to the well-known stability requirement for explicit difference operations. Compared to the previously discussed approach, the probabilities p_i in the variant of the trinomial models and the calculation in (8.21) are not dependent on the volatility. The recursion (8.21) depends only on the starting condition, i.e. $S_n = S_T$ at the exercise moment as an observation depends on σ from the geometric Brownian motion.

8.3   Recommended Literature

American options are classic financial derivative instruments and play a central role in the literatures referenced in Chapter 6. The trinomial model as numerical procedures to approximate the option prices is introduced in detail in Dewynne et al. (1993) and Wilmott et al. (1995).

9 Exotic Options and Interest Rate Derivatives

A whole series of complex options exist, so called exotic options, and are mainly used in OTC-trading (over the counter) to meet the special needs of corporate customers. The most important types are:

- Compound Options

- Chooser Options

- Barrier Options

- Asian Options

- Lookback Options

9.1 Examples of Exotic Options

9.1.1 Compound Options, Option on Option

With a compound option one has the right to acquire an ordinary option at a later date. To illustrate such a compound option consider a *Call-on-a-Call* with the parameters:

$$\text{maturity dates } T_1 < T_2$$
$$\text{strike prices } K_1, K_2.$$

Such a compound option gives the owner the right at time T_1 for the price K_1 to buy a Call that has a maturity date T_2 and a strike price K_2.

The value $V(S,t)$ of this option at time t with an actual price $S_t = S$ can be calculated by applying the Black-Scholes formula twice:

1) Beginning at time $t = T_2$, calculate (explicitly or numerically) the value of the Call, which can be bought at time T_1, at time $t = T_1$. This value is $C(S, T_1)$.

2) The purchasing option of the Call at time T_1 is only exercised when

$$C(S, T_1) > K_1$$

Thus it holds that

$$V(S, T_1) = \max\{C(S, T_1) - K_1, \ 0\}.$$

Calculate $V(S, t)$ for $t < T_1$ using the Black-Scholes equation with these restrictions at $t = T_1$ analog to the normal Call.

Remark 9.1 *Since $V(S, t)$ is only dependent on t and the price S_t at time t, this value function fulfills the Black-Scholes equation so that our approach is justified.*

9.1.2   Chooser Options or "As you wish" Options

A Chooser Option is a form of the compound option, where the buyer can decide at a later date which type of option he would like to have. To illustrate consider a *regular Chooser Option* with the parameters:

$$\begin{aligned} \text{maturity dates } T_1 < T_2 \\ \text{strike prices } K_1, K_2. \end{aligned}$$

This option gives one the right at time T_1 for the price K_1 to buy a Call or a Put (as one likes), which has a maturity T_2 and a strike price K_2: in the language of compound options this is referred to as a *Call-on-a-Call* or *Put*.

The value $V(S, t)$ can be found by applying the Black-Scholes formula three times:

1) Determine the value $C(S, T_1)$ and $P(S, T_1)$ of a Call and a Put with a maturity T_2, and strike price K_2.

2) Solve the Black-Scholes equation for $t < T_1$ with the restriction

$$V(S, T_1) = \max\{C(S, T_1) - K_1, \ P(S, T_1) - K_1, 0\}$$

9.1.3 Barrier Options

A barrier Option changes its value in leaps as soon as the stock price reaches a given barrier, which can also be time dependent. As an example consider a simple European barrier Option which at

maturity T, strike price K and
barrier B

gives the holder the right to buy a stock at time T for the price K provided that

- *down-and-out:* $S_t > B$ for all $0 \leq t \leq T$

- *up-and-out:* $S_t < B$ for all $0 \leq t \leq T$

This type of Knock-out Option is worthless as soon as the price S_t reaches the barrier. A Knock-in-Option is just the opposite. It is worthless up until the barrier is reached.

For example, a European *Knock-in-Call* consists of the right to buy stock provided that

- *down-and-in:* $S_t \leq B$ for some $0 \leq t \leq T$

- *up-and-in:* $S_t \geq B$ for some $0 \leq t \leq T$

The value of a barrier Option is no longer dependent on a stock price at a specific point in time, but on the overall development of the stock price during the option's life span. Thus in principle it does not fulfill the Black-Scholes differential equation. The dependence however, is essentially simple enough to work with the conventional Black-Scholes application. As an example consider a *Down-and-out-Call* with $K > B$. As long as $S_t > B$, $V(S,t)$ fulfills the Black-Scholes equation with the restriction:

$$V(S,T) = \max(S_T - K, \ 0)$$

In the event that the price reaches the barrier B, the option of course becomes worthless:

$$V(B,t) = 0 \ , \qquad 0 \leq t \leq T,$$

is therefore an additional restriction that needs to be taken into consideration when solving the differential equation (6.22). The explicit solution is given as:

$$V(S,t) = C(S,t) - \left(\frac{B}{S}\right)^{\alpha} C\left(\frac{B^2}{S}, t\right)$$

with $\alpha = \dfrac{2r}{\sigma^2} - 1$, where $C(S,t)$ represents the value of a common European Call on the stock in question. The value $\bar{V}(S,t)$ of an European Down-and-in Call can be calculated analogously. If one already knows $V(S,t)$, one can also use the equation

$$\bar{V}(S,t) + V(S,t) = C(S,t).$$

It is fulfilled since a Down-and-in and a Down-and-out Call together have the same effect as a normal Call.

9.1.4   Asian Options

With Asian options the value depends on the average stock price calculated over the entire life span of the option. With an *average strike option* over the time period $0 \leq t \leq T$ the payoff, for example, has at the time to maturity the form

$$\max\left(S_t - \frac{1}{t}\int_0^t S_s\, ds\,,\, 0\right), t = T.$$

With an American Average Strike Option this is also the payoff when the option is exercised ahead of time at some arbitrary time $t \leq T$.

To calculate the value of an Asian Option consider a general class of European Options with a payoff at time T that is dependent on S_T and I_T with

$$I_t = \int_0^t f(S_s, s)ds.$$

Analogous to the Black-Scholes equation we derive an equation for the value at time t of such a *path dependent Option* $V(S, I, t)$. At time t with a stock price S_t this results in

$$I_t + dI_t \stackrel{\text{def}}{=} I_{t+dt} = \int_0^{t+dt} f(S_s, s)ds$$

$$= I_t + \int_t^{t+dt} f(S_s, s)dt$$

$$= I_t + f(S_t, t)dt + \mathcal{O}(dt).$$

Thus the differential of I_t is equal to $dI_t = f(S_t, t)dt$.

Using Itôs Lemma it follows for $V_t = V(S_t, I_t, t)$ that:

$$dV_t = \sigma S_t \frac{\partial V_t}{\partial S} dW_t + f(S_t, t) \frac{\partial V_t}{\partial I} dt$$

$$+ \left(\frac{1}{2} \sigma^2 S^2 \frac{\partial^2 V_t}{\partial S} + \frac{\partial V_t}{\partial t} \right) dt$$

Analogous to the derivation of the Black-Scholes formula continuous Delta hedging produces a risk free portfolio from an option and $\Delta_t = \partial V_t / \partial S$ sold stocks. Together with the restriction of no arbitrage it follows for the case of no dividends ($b = r$) that:

$$\frac{\partial V_t}{\partial t} + f(S_t, t) \frac{\partial V_t}{\partial I} + \frac{1}{2} \sigma^2 S_t^2 \frac{\partial^2 V_t}{\partial S^2} + r S_t \frac{\partial V_t}{\partial S} - r\, V_t = 0$$

This is the Black-Scholes equation with an additional term $f(S_t, t) \frac{\partial V_t}{\partial I}$. The boundaries in this case are

$$V(S, I, T) = g(S, I, T).$$

For an Average Strike Call we have:

$$g(S, I, t) = \max(S - \frac{1}{t} I,\ 0) \quad \text{und} \quad f(S, t) = S.$$

For European options an explicit analytical solution of the differential equation exists in which complicated, specialized functions appear, the so called confluent hypergeometric functions. The numerical solution, however, is easier and faster to obtain.

The integral $\int_0^t S_s ds$ in practice is calculated as the sum over all quoted prices, for example, at 30 second time intervals. Discrete time Asian Options use in place of this a substantially larger time scale. I_t changes only once a day or once a week:

$$I_t = \sum_{j=1}^{n(t)} S_{t_j}\ ,\quad t_{n(t)} \le t < t_{n(t)+1}$$

with $t_{j+1} - t_j = 1$ day or $= 1$ week and closing price S_{t_j}.

Such a discrete time Asian Option is largely consistent with a common option with discrete dividend payments at time periods $t_1, t_2, \ldots$. From the assumption of no arbitrage follows a continuity restriction at t_j:

$$V(S, I, t_j-) = V(S, I + S,\ t_j^+)$$

To determine the value of the option one begins as usual at the time to maturity where the value of the option is known:

1) $T = t_n$

$$V(S, I, T) = \max(S - \frac{1}{T}I_T, \ 0)$$

$$I_T = \sum_{j=1}^{n} S_{t_j}$$

Solve the Black-Scholes equation backwards to time t_{n-1} and obtain

$$V(S, I + S, \ t_{n-1}^{+})$$

2) Calculate using the continuity restriction the new terminal value $V(S, I, t_{n-1}^{-})$. Solve the Black-Scholes equation backwards to time t_{n-2} and obtain

$$V(S, I + S, \ t_{n-2}^{+})$$

etc.

9.1.5   Lookback Options

The value of a lookback Option depends on the maximum or minimum of the stock price over the entire life span of the option, for example, a *lookback put* over the time period $0 \le t \le T$ has at maturity the payoff

$$\max(M_T - S_T, \ 0) \quad \text{with} \quad M_t = \max_{0 \le s \le t} S_s.$$

To calculate the value of such an option first consider a path dependent option with

$$I_t(n) = \int_0^t S_s^n ds, \quad \text{i.e.} \quad f(S, t) = S^n.$$

With $M_t(n) = (I_t(n))^{\frac{1}{n}}$ it holds that:

$$M_t = \lim_{n \to \infty} M_t(n).$$

Form the differential equation for $I_t(n)$ and $n \to \infty$ it follows that the value $V_t = V(S_t, M_t, t)$ of an European lookback put fulfills the following equation:

$$\frac{\partial V_t}{\partial t} + \frac{1}{2}\sigma^2 S_t^2 \frac{\partial^2 V_t}{\partial S^2} + r \ S_t \frac{\partial V_t}{\partial S} - r \ V_t = 0$$

This is the normal Black-Scholes equation. M only appears as an argument of V and in the boundary conditions:

$$V(S, M, T) = \max(M - S,\ 0)$$

The solution is for a remaining time period of $\tau = T - t$, $\alpha = 2r/\sigma^2$:

$$V(S, M, t) = S\left(\Phi(y_1) \cdot (1 + \frac{1}{\alpha}) - 1\right)$$
$$+ M\ e^{-r\tau}\left(\Phi(y_3) - \frac{1}{\alpha}\left(\frac{M}{S}\right)^{\alpha-1}\Phi(y_2)\right)$$

$$\text{with} \quad y_1 = \frac{1}{\sigma\sqrt{\tau}}\{\ln\frac{S}{M} + (r + \frac{1}{2}\sigma^2)\tau\}$$

$$y_2 = \frac{1}{\sigma\sqrt{\tau}}\{\ln\frac{S}{M} - (r + \frac{1}{2}\sigma^2)\tau\}$$

$$y_3 = \frac{1}{\sigma\sqrt{\tau}}\{\ln\frac{M}{S} - (r + \frac{1}{2}\sigma^2)\tau\}$$

9.2 Models for the Interest Rate and Interest Rate Derivatives

As we saw in the previous chapter, important assumptions of the Black and Scholes application are

- constant risk free domestic interest rate r (approximately fulfilled by stock options with life spans of ≤ 9 months)

- independence of the price of the option's underlying from the interest rate r (empirical research shows that for stocks this is approximately fulfilled).

Both assumptions are violated for *bond options* and the longer time periods which are typically found in the analysis of these options.

A *bond* produces at the time of maturity T a fixed amount Z, the nominal value, and if applicable at predetermined dates before T dividend payments (*coupon*). If there are no coupons, the bond is referred to as a zero coupon bond or *zero bond* for short.

When valuing a Bond Option coupons can be treated as discrete dividend payments when valuing stock options.

9.2.1 Bond Value with Known Time Dependent Interest Rate

To begin we calculate the bond value $V(t)$ at time t with a time dependent but known interest rate $r(t)$.

From the assumption of no arbitrage we conclude that a bond's change in value over the time period $[t, t+dt]$ with possible coupon payments $K(t)dt$ coincides with the change in value of a bank account with a value $V(t)$ and with an interest of $r(t)$:

$$V(t+dt) - V(t) = \left(\frac{dV}{dt} + K(t) \right) dt = r(t)V(t)\ dt$$

Together with the boundary restrictions $V(T) = Z$ it follows that:

$$V(t) = e^{I(t)}\{Z + \int_t^T K(s)\, e^{-I(s)} ds\} \tag{9.1}$$

with $I(t) = -\int_t^T r(s)ds$, the antiderivative of $r(t)$.

For a zero bond this simplifies to: $V(t) = Z \cdot e^{I(t)}$

9.2.2 Stochastic Interest Rate Model

Due to the uncertainty associated with the future development of the interest rate, $r(t)$ is modelled as a random variable. In order to have an unambiguous, fixed interest rate, one usually considers the interest rate of an investment over the shortest possible time period:

$r(t) = spot\ rate = $ Interest rate for the shortest possible investment.

$r(t)$ does not follow a geometric Brownian motion so that the Black-Scholes application cannot be used. There are a number of models for $r(t)$, that are special cases of the following general *Ansatz* which models the interest rate as a general Itô Process:

$$dr(t) = \mu(r(t), t)dt + \sigma(r(t), t)dW_t \tag{9.2}$$

$\{W_t\}$ represents as usual a standard Wiener process.

Three of the most used models are simple, special cases and indeed are the coefficient functions of the models from

- *Vasicek*:

$$\mu(r,t) = a(b-r) \ , \ \ \sigma(r,t) = \sigma \tag{9.3}$$
$$a, b, \sigma \ \ \text{constants}$$

- *Cox, Ingersoll, Ross*:

$$\mu(r,t) = a(b-r), \ \ \sigma(r,t) = \sigma\sqrt{r} \tag{9.4}$$
$$a, b, \sigma \ \ \text{constants}$$

- *Hull, White*:

$$\mu(r,t) = \delta(t) - ar, \ \ \sigma(r,t) = \sigma \tag{9.5}$$
$$a, \sigma \ \ \text{constants}, \ \ \delta(t) \ \ \text{from market data}$$
$$\text{deducible known function}$$

In general $\mu(r,t)$ and $\sigma(r,t)$ can be conveniently chosen, in order to replicate in the model empirically observed phenomena. In the following we write $w(r,t)$ for $\sigma(r,t)$, in order to clearly differentiate between the function $w \stackrel{\text{def}}{=} \sigma$ and the constant σ, which appears as a parameter in the three models mentioned above.

9.2.3   The Bond's Value Equation

A stock option can be hedged with stocks, and Black and Scholes use this in deriving the option pricing formula. Since there is no underlying financial instrument associated with a bond, bonds with varying life spans have to be used to mutually hedge each other, in order to derive the equation for valuing bonds.

Consider a portfolio made up of a zero bond with a remaining life time of τ_1 and $-\Delta$ zero bonds (i.e., Δ sold zero bonds) with a remaining life time of τ_2. The value of the portfolio at time t for the current interest rate $r(t) = r$ is:

$$\Pi(r,t) = V_1(r,t) - \Delta \cdot V_2(r,t).$$

where $V_i, i = 1, 2$ stands for the value function of both bonds. We write $\Pi_t = \Pi\{r(t), t\}, V_{it} = V_i\{r(t), t\}, i = 1, 2, \ \mu_t = \mu\{r(t), t\}, \ w_t = w\{r(t), t\}$. Using Itôs Lemma it follows that

$$dll_t = \frac{\partial V_{1t}}{\partial t} dt + \frac{\partial V_{1t}}{\partial r} dr(t) + \frac{1}{2} w_t^2 \cdot \frac{\partial^2 V_{1t}}{\partial r^2} dt$$

$$- \Delta \left(\frac{\partial V_{2t}}{\partial t} dt + \frac{\partial V_{2t}}{\partial r} dr(t) + \frac{1}{2} w_t^2 \frac{\partial^2 V_{2t}}{\partial r^2} dt \right)$$

By hedging the risks the random component disappears. This is achieved by choosing

$$\Delta = \frac{\partial V_{1t}}{\partial r} \Big/ \frac{\partial V_{2t}}{\partial r}.$$

The insertion and comparison of the portfolio with a risk free investment and taking advantage of the no arbitrage assumption, that is the equality of the change in value of the portfolio and investment:

$$d\Pi_t = r(t) \cdot \Pi_t \, dt,$$

produces altogether

$$\left(\frac{\partial V_{1t}}{\partial t} + \frac{1}{2} w_t^2 \frac{\partial^2 V_{1t}}{\partial r^2} - r(t) \, V_{1t} \right) \Big/ \frac{\partial V_{1t}}{\partial r}$$

$$= \left(\frac{\partial V_{2t}}{\partial t} + \frac{1}{2} w_t^2 \frac{\partial^2 V_{2t}}{\partial r^2} - r(t) \, V_{2t} \right) \Big/ \frac{\partial V_{2t}}{\partial r}. \qquad (9.6)$$

This is only correct when both sides are independent of the remaining life times τ_1, τ_2. V_{1t}, V_{2t} therefore satisfy both of the following differential equations

$$\frac{\partial V_t}{\partial t} + \frac{1}{2} w_t^2 \frac{\partial^2 V_t}{\partial r^2} - r(t) \, V_t = -a\{r(t), t\} \cdot \frac{\partial V_t}{\partial r}$$

for the function $a(r, t)$ which is independent of one of the remaining life times. With the economically interpretable value

$$\lambda(r, t) = \frac{\mu(r, t) - a(r, t)}{w(r, t)}$$

this produces with the abbreviation $\lambda_t = \lambda\{r(t), t\}$ the *zero bond's value equation* for $V(r, t)$:

$$\frac{\partial V(r, t)}{\partial t} + \frac{1}{2} w_t^2 \frac{\partial^2 V(r, t)}{\partial r^2} - (\mu_t - \lambda_t w_t) \frac{\partial V(r, t)}{\partial r} - r(t) \, V(r, t) = 0 \qquad (9.7)$$

with the boundary restrictions $V(r, T) = Z$ at the time of maturity and with additional boundary restrictions dependent on μ, w. It should be noted that in the equation μ_t, w_t, λ_t stand for functions of r and t.

The value $\lambda(r, t)$ has the following interpretation. Consider a risky portfolio, that is not hedged, consisting of a bond with the value $V_t = V\{r(t), t\}$. For the change in value within the time period dt we obtain using Itôs Lemma and the zero bond's value equation:

$$dV_t = r(t) \ V_t \ dt + w_t \cdot \frac{\partial V_t}{\partial r}(dW_t + \lambda\{r(t), t\} \, dt)$$

Since $\mathsf{E}[dW_t] = 0$, the mean change in value $\mathsf{E}[dV_t]$ is

$$\left(w_t \frac{\partial V_t}{\partial r}\right) \cdot \lambda\{r(t), t\} \, dt$$

above the increase in value $r(t) \ V_t \ dt$ of a risk free investment. $\lambda(r, t) \, dt$ is therefore the bonus on the increase in value, which one receives at time t with a current interest rate $r(t) = r$ for taking on the associated risks. $\lambda(r, t)$ is thus interpreted as the *market price of risk*.

9.2.4   Solving the Zero Bond's Value Equation

Consider the special case:

$$w(r, t) = \sqrt{\alpha(t)r - \beta(t)}$$

$$\mu(r, t) = -\gamma(t) \cdot r + \eta(t) + \lambda(r, t)w(r, t).$$

Inserting the solution assumption

$$V(r, t) = Z \cdot e^{A(t) - rB(t)}$$

into the zero bond's value equation results in the two equations

$$\frac{\partial A(t)}{\partial t} = \eta(t) \ B(t) + \frac{1}{2} \beta(t) \ B^2(t)$$

$$\frac{\partial B(t)}{\partial t} = \frac{1}{2}\alpha(t) \ B^2(t) + \gamma(t) \ B(t) - 1$$

with boundary restrictions $A(T) = B(T) = 0$ (since $V(r, T) = Z$).

For the time independent $\alpha, \beta, \gamma, \eta$ there is an explicit solution, which with a remaining life time of $\tau = T - t$ has the form

$$B(t) = \frac{2(e^{\psi_1 \tau} - 1)}{(\gamma + \psi_1)(e^{\psi_1 \tau} - 1) + 2\psi_1}, \quad \psi_1 = \sqrt{\gamma^2 + \alpha}$$

$$\frac{2}{\alpha}A(t) = b_2\psi_2 \ln(b_2 - B) + (\psi_2 - \frac{\beta}{2})b_1 \ln(\frac{B}{b_1} + 1)$$

$$+\frac{1}{2}B\,\beta - b_2\psi_2 \ln b_2$$

with

$$b_{1/2} = \frac{\pm\gamma + \sqrt{\gamma^2 + 2\alpha}}{\alpha}, \quad \psi_2 = \frac{\eta + b_2\beta/2}{b_1 + b_2}$$

Choice of parameters:

1) The spot rate volatility is $\sqrt{\alpha r(t) - \beta}$. With this representation α, β can be estimated from historical data, in a fashion similar to the historical volatility of stocks.

2) Taking the *yield curve* (see Section 10.4.3) into consideration, the discussion of which goes beyond the scope of this section, estimators for γ and η can be derived.

9.2.5   Valuing Bond Options

As an example consider a European Call with a strike price K and a maturity T_C on a zero bond with a maturity of $T_B > T_C$,, i.e., the right is given to buy the bond at time T_C at a price K.

$V_B(r, t) =$ Value of the bond at time t with the current interest rate $r(t) = r$

$C_B(r, t) =$ Value of the Call at time t with the current interest rate $r(t) = r$

C_B is only dependent on the random variable $r(t)$ and time t and therefore itself also satisfies the zero bond's value equation, but with the boundary restrictions

$$C_B(r, T_C) = \max(V_B(r, T_C) - K, \ 0).$$

This equation, analogous to the corresponding Black-Scholes equation can be numerically solved.

9.3   Recommended Literature

Exotic options such as bond options are discussed in detail in Hull (2000). The numerical methods necessary for valuing complex path-dependent derivatives are briefly reviewed in Wilmott et al. (1995) and are discussed in more detail in Dewynne et al. (1993). The classical stochastic interest rate models are introduced in Vasicek (1977), Cox, Ingersoll and Ross (1985) and Hull and White (1990). A standard work taking a modern point of view of the interest rate in financial mathematics is Heath and Morton (1992).

Part II

Statistical Model of Financial Time Series

10 Introduction: Definitions and Concepts

Financial markets can be regarded from various points of view. First of all there are economic theories which make assertions about security pricing. Different economic theories exist in different markets (currency, interest rates, stocks, derivatives, etc.). The well known examples include the purchasing power parity for exchange rates, interest rate term structure models, the *capital asset pricing model* (CAPM) and the Black-Scholes option pricing model. Most of these models are based on theoretical concepts which, for example, involve the formation of expectations, utility functions and risk preferences. Normally it is assumed that individuals in the economy act 'rationally', have rational expectations and are risk averse. Under this situation prices and returns can be determined in equilibrium models (as, for example, the CAPM) which clear the markets, i.e., supply equals aggregate demand. A different Ansatz pursues the arbitrage theory (for example, the Black-Scholes model), which assumes that a riskless profit would be noticed immediately by market participants and be eliminated through adjustments in the price. Arbitrage theory and equilibrium theory are closely connected. The arbitrage theory can often get away with fewer assumptions, whereas the equilibrium theories reach more explicitly defined solutions for complex situations.

The classical econometric models are formulated with the economically interpreted parameters. One is interested in the following empirical questions:

1. How well can a specific model describe a given set of data (cross section or time series)?

2. Does the model help the market participants in meeting the relative size of assertions made on future developments?

3. What do the empirical findings imply for the econometric model? Will it eventually have to be modified? Can suggestions actually be made which will influence the functioning and structural organization of the markets?

In order to handle these empirical questions, a statistical inquiry is needed. Since as a rule with financial market data the dynamic characteristics are the most important, we will concentrate mainly on the time series analysis. First of all, we will introduce the concepts of univariate analysis. Then we will move to the multivariate time series. The interdependence of financial items can be modelled explicitly as a system.

Certain terms, which are often used in time series analysis and in the analysis of financial time series, are introduced in a compact form. We will briefly define them in the next section.

10.1   Certain Definitions

First we will need to look closer at stochastic processes, the basic object in time series analysis.

Definition 10.1 (stochastic process)
A stochastic process X_t, $t \in \mathbb{Z}$, is a family of random variables, defined in a probability space $(\Omega, \mathcal{F}, \mathrm{P})$.

At a specific time point t, X_t is a random variable with a specific density function. Given a specific $\omega \in \Omega$, $X(\omega) = \{X_t(\omega), t \in \mathbb{Z}\}$ is a realization or a path of the process.

Definition 10.2 (cdf of a stochastic process)
The joint cumulative distribution function (cdf) of a stochastic process X_t is defined as

$$F_{t_1,\ldots,t_n}(x_1,\ldots,x_n) = \mathrm{P}(X_{t_1} \leq x_1, \ldots, X_{t_n} \leq x_n).$$

The stochastic process X_t is clearly identified, when the system of its density functions is known. If for any $t_1, \ldots, t_n \in \mathbb{Z}$ the joint distribution function $F_{t_1,\ldots,t_n}(x_1,\ldots,x_n)$ is known, the underlying stochastic process is uniquely determined.

Definition 10.3 (conditional cdf)
The conditional cdf of a stochastic process X_t for any $t_1,\ldots,t_n \in \mathbb{Z}$ with $t_1 < t_2 < \ldots < t_n$ is defined as

$$F_{t_n|t_{n-1},\ldots,t_1}(x_n \mid x_{n-1},\ldots,x_1) = \mathrm{P}(X_{t_n} \leq x_n \mid X_{t_{n-1}} = x_{n-1}, \ldots, X_{t_1} = x_1).$$

Next we will define moment functions of real stochastic process. Here we will assume that the moments exist. If this is not the case, then the corresponding function is not defined.

Definition 10.4 (Mean function)
The mean function μ_t of a stochastic process X_t is defined as

$$\mu_t = \mathsf{E}[X_t] = \int_{\mathbb{R}} x dF_t(x). \tag{10.1}$$

In general μ_t depends on time t, as, for example, processes with a seasonal or periodical structure or processes with a deterministic trend.

Definition 10.5 (Autocovariance function)
The autocovariance function of a stochastic process X is defined as

$$
\begin{aligned}
\gamma(t,\tau) &= \mathsf{E}[(X_t - \mu_t)(X_{t-\tau} - \mu_{t-\tau})] \\
&= \int_{\mathbb{R}^2} (x_1 - \mu_t)(x_2 - \mu_{t-\tau}) dF_{t,t-\tau}(x_1, x_2) \tag{10.2}
\end{aligned}
$$

for $\tau \in \mathbb{Z}$.

The autocovariance function is symmetric, i.e., $\gamma(t,\tau) = \gamma(t-\tau, -\tau)$. For the special case $\tau = 0$ the result is the variance function $\gamma(t,0) = \text{Var}(X_t)$. In general $\gamma(t,\tau)$ is dependent on t as well as on τ. In the following we define the important concept of stationarity, which will simplify the moment functions in many cases.

Definition 10.6 (Stationary)
A stochastic process X is covariance stationary if

1. $\mu_t = \mu$, and

2. $\gamma(t,\tau) = \gamma_\tau$.

A stochastic process X_t is strictly stationary if for any $t_1, \ldots, t_n$ and for all $n, s \in \mathbb{Z}$ it holds that

$$F_{t_1,\ldots,t_n}(x_1, \ldots, x_n) = F_{t_1+s,\ldots,t_n+s}(x_1, \ldots, x_n).$$

For covariance stationary the term weakly stationary is often used. One should notice, however, that a stochastic process can be strictly stationary without being covariance stationary, namely then, when the variance (or covariance) does not exist. If the first two moment functions exist, then covariance stationary follows from strictly stationary.

Definition 10.7 (Autocorrelation function (ACF))
The autocorrelation function ρ of a covariance stationary stochastic process is defined as

$$\rho_\tau = \frac{\gamma_\tau}{\gamma_0}.$$

The ACF is normalized on the interval [-1,1] and thus simplifies the interpretation of the autocovariance structure from various stochastic processes. Since the process is required to be covariance stationary, the ACF depends only on one parameter, the lag τ. Often the ACF is plotted as a function of τ, the so called *correlogram*. This is an important graphical instrument to illustrate linear dependency structures of the process.

Next we define two important stochastic processes which build the foundation for further modelling.

Definition 10.8 (White noise (WN))
The stochastic process X_t is white noise if the following holds

1. $\mu_t = 0$, and

2. $\gamma_\tau = \begin{cases} \sigma^2 & \text{when } \tau = 0 \\ 0 & \text{when } \tau \neq 0. \end{cases}$

$\mathbf{Q}$ SFEtimewr.xpl

If X_t is a process from i.i.d. random values with expectation 0 and finite variance, then it is a white noise. This special case is called *independent white noise*. On the contrary the white noise could have dependent third or higher moments, and in this case it would not be independent.

Definition 10.9 (Random Walk)
The stochastic process X_t follows a random walk, *if it can be represented as*

$$X_t = c + X_{t-1} + \varepsilon_t$$

with a constant c and white noise ε_t.

If c is not zero, then the variables $Z_t = X_t - X_{t-1} = c + \varepsilon_t$ have a non-zero mean. We call it a random walk with a drift (see Section 4.1). In contrast to Section 4.3 we do not require here that the variables are independent. The random walk defined here is the boundary case for an AR(1) process introduced in Example 10.1 as $\alpha \to 1$. When we require, as in Section 4.3, that ε_t is independent white noise, then we will call X_t a random walk with independent increments. Historically the random walk plays a special role, since at the beginning of the last century it was the first stochastic model to represent the development of stock prices. Even today the random walk is often assumed as an underlying hypothesis. However the applications are rejected in its strongest form with independent increments.

In order to determine the moment functions of a random walk, we will simply assume that the constant c and the initial value X_0 are set to zero. Then through recursive substitutions we will get the representation

$$X_t = \varepsilon_t + \varepsilon_{t-1} + \ldots + \varepsilon_1.$$

The mean function is simply

$$\mu_t = \mathsf{E}[X_t] = 0, \tag{10.3}$$

and for the variance function, since there is no correlation of ε_t, we obtain

$$\mathrm{Var}(X_t) = \mathrm{Var}(\sum_{i=1}^{t} \varepsilon_i) = \sum_{i=1}^{t} \mathrm{Var}(\varepsilon_i) = t\sigma^2. \tag{10.4}$$

The variance of the random walk increases linearly with time. For the auto-covariance function the following holds for $\tau < t$:

$$
\begin{aligned}
\gamma(t, \tau) &= \mathrm{Cov}(X_t, X_{t-\tau}) \\
&= \mathrm{Cov}(\sum_{i=1}^{t} \varepsilon_i, \sum_{j=1}^{t-\tau} \varepsilon_j) \\
&= \sum_{j=1}^{t-\tau} \sum_{i=1}^{t} \mathrm{Cov}(\varepsilon_i, \varepsilon_j) \\
&= \sum_{j=1}^{t-\tau} \sigma^2 = (t - \tau)\sigma^2.
\end{aligned}
$$

For $\tau < t$ the autocovariance is thus strictly positive. Since the covariance function depends on time t (and not only on the lags τ), the random walk is not covariance stationary. For the autocorrelation function ρ we obtain

$$\rho(t, \tau) = \frac{(t - \tau)\sigma^2}{\sqrt{t\sigma^2 (t - \tau)\sigma^2}} = \frac{(t - \tau)}{\sqrt{t(t - \tau)}} = \sqrt{1 - \frac{\tau}{t}}.$$

Again ρ depends on t as well as on τ, thus the random walk is not covariance stationary.

As further illustration we consider a simple, but important stochastic process.

Example 10.1 (AR(1) Process)
The stochastic process X_t follows an autoregressive process of first order, written AR(1) process, if

$$X_t = c + \alpha X_{t-1} + \varepsilon_t$$

with a constant parameter α, $|\alpha| < 1$. The process X_t can also, through iterative substitutions, be written as

$$
\begin{aligned}
X_t &= c(1 + \alpha + \alpha^2 + \ldots + \alpha^{k-1}) \\
&\quad + \alpha^k X_{t-k} + \varepsilon_t + \alpha \varepsilon_{t-1} + \ldots + \alpha^{k-1} \varepsilon_{t-k+1} \\
&= c\left(\sum_{i=0}^{k-1} \alpha^i\right) + \alpha^k X_{t-k} + \sum_{i=0}^{k-1} \alpha^i \varepsilon_{t-i} \\
&= c\,\frac{1 - \alpha^k}{1 - \alpha} + \alpha^k X_{t-k} + \sum_{i=0}^{k-1} \alpha^i \varepsilon_{t-i}
\end{aligned}
$$

If X_{t-k} is given for a particular k (for example, the initial value of the process), the characteristics of the process are obviously dependent on this value. This influence disappears, however, over time, since we have assumed that $|\alpha| < 1$ and thus $\alpha^k \to 0$ for $k \to \infty$. For $k \to \infty$ there exists a limit in the sense of squared deviation, thus we can write the process X_t as

$$X_t = c\frac{1}{1 - \alpha} + \sum_{i=0}^{\infty} \alpha^i \varepsilon_{t-i}.$$

For the moment functions we then have

$$\mu_t = c\frac{1}{1 - \alpha},$$

and

$$\gamma_\tau = \frac{\sigma^2}{1 - \alpha^2} \alpha^\tau.$$

The ACF is thus simply $\rho_\tau = \alpha^\tau$. For positive α this function is strictly positive, for negative α it alternates around zero. In every case it converges to zero, but with $\alpha = 0.5$, for example, convergence is very fast, and with $\alpha = 0.99$ it is quite slow.   **Q** SFEacfar1.xpl

Definition 10.10 (Markov Process)
A stochastic process has the Markov property if for all $t \in \mathbb{Z}$ and $k \geq 1$

$$F_{t|t-1,\ldots,t-k}(x_t|x_{t-1},\ldots,x_{t-k}) = F_{t|t-1}(x_t|x_{t-1}).$$

In other words, the conditional distribution of a Markov process at a specific point in time is completely determined by the condition of the system at the previous date. One can also define Markov processes of higher order, from which the conditional distribution only depends on the finite number of past levels. Two examples for the Markov process of first order are the above mentioned random walk with independent variables and the AR(1) process with independent white noise.

Definition 10.11 (Martingale)
The stochastic process X_t is a martingale if the following holds

$$\mathsf{E}[X_t|X_{t-1} = x_{t-1},\ldots,X_{t-k} = x_{t-k}] = x_{t-1}$$

for every $k > 0$.

The martingale is also a frequently used instrument in describing prices in financial markets. One should notice, that for a martingale process only one statement about the conditional expectation is made, while for a Markov process statements on the entire conditional distribution are made. An example of a martingale is the random walk without a drift. The AR(1) process with $0 < \alpha < 1$ is not a Martingale, since $\mathsf{E}[X_t|x_{t-1},\ldots,x_{t-k}] = c + \alpha x_{t-1}$.

Definition 10.12 (fair game)
The stochastic process X_t is a fair game if the following holds

$$\mathsf{E}[X_t|X_{t-1} = x_{t-1},\ldots,X_{t-k} = x_{t-k}] = 0$$

for every $k > 0$.

Sometimes a fair game is also called a martingale difference. If X_t is namely a martingale, then $Z_t = X_t - X_{t-1}$ is a fair game.

Definition 10.13 (Lag-Operator)
The operator L moves the process X_t back by one unit of time, i.e., $LX_t = X_{t-1}$ and $L^k X_t = X_{t-k}$. In addition we define the difference operator Δ as $\Delta = 1 - L$, i.e., $\Delta X_t = X_t - X_{t-1}$, and $\Delta^k = (1 - L)^k$.

After these mathematical definitions we arrive at the more econometric definitions, and in particular, at the term return. We start with a time series of prices $P_1, \ldots, P_n$ and are interested in calculating the return between two periods.

Definition 10.14 (simple return)
The simple return R_t is defined as

$$R_t = \frac{P_t - P_{t-1}}{P_{t-1}}.$$

Should the average return $R_t(k)$ need to be calculated over k periods, then the geometric mean is taken from the simple gross return, i.e.,

$$R_t(k) = \left(\prod_{j=0}^{k-1} (1 + R_{t-j}) \right)^{1/k} - 1.$$

In general the geometric mean is not equal to the arithmetic mean $k^{-1} \sum_{j=0}^{k-1} R_{t-j}$.

Definition 10.15 (log return)
The log return r_t is defined as

$$r_t = \ln \frac{P_t}{P_{t-1}} = \ln(1 + R_t).$$

⌕ SFEContDiscRet.xpl

The log return is defined for the case of continuous compounding. For the average return over several periods we have

$$
\begin{aligned}
r_t(k) &= \ln\{1 + R_t(k)\} = \frac{1}{k} \ln \prod_{j=0}^{k-1} (1 + R_{t-j}) \\
&= \frac{1}{k} \sum_{j=0}^{k-1} \ln(1 + R_{t-j}) \\
&= \frac{1}{k} \sum_{j=0}^{k-1} r_{t-j},
\end{aligned}
$$

i.e., for log returns the arithmetic average return is applied.

For small price changes the difference of the simple return and log return is negligible. According to the Taylor approximation it follows that

$$
\begin{aligned}
\ln(1+x) &= \ln(1) + \frac{\partial \ln x}{\partial x}(1)x + \frac{\partial^2 \ln x}{\partial x^2}(1)\frac{x^2}{2!} + \cdots \\
&= x - \frac{x^2}{2!} + \frac{x^3}{3!} + \cdots.
\end{aligned}
$$

For x close to zero a first order approximation is sufficient, i.e., $\ln(1+x) \approx x$. As a general rule one could say, that with returns under 10% it does not really matter whether the simple or the log returns are used. This is above all the case when one is studying financial time series with a high frequency, as, for example, with daily values.

10.2   Statistical Analysis of German Stock Returns

In this section we describe several classical characteristics of financial time series using daily returns of German stocks from 1974 to 1996. We will concentrate, on the one hand, on the linear, chronological (in)dependence of the returns, and on the other hand, on the distribution characteristics. Table 10.1 displays the summarized descriptive statistics. The autocorrelation of first order is for all stock returns close to zero. The largest positive autocorrelation is with PREUSSAG (0.08), the largest negative autocorrelation is with ALLIANZ (-0.06). The majority of autocorrelations are positive (14 as compared to 6 negative). This is an empirical phenomenon which is also documented for the American market.

While the first order autocorrelation of the returns of all stock returns are all close to zero, the autocorrelations of the squared and absolute returns of all stocks are positive and significantly larger than zero. Obviously there is a linear relationship in the absolute values of the chronologically sequential returns. Since the autocorrelation is positive, it can be concluded, that small (positive or negative) returns are followed by small returns and large returns follow large ones again. In other words, there are quiet periods with small prices changes and turbulent periods with large oscillations. Indeed one can further conclude that these periods are of relatively longer duration, i.e., the autocorrelations of squared returns from mainly very large orders are still positive. These effects have already been examined by Mandelbrot and Fama in the sixties. They can be modelled using, among others, the ARCH models studied in Chapter 12. Furthermore we will consider estimates for

	$\rho_1(r_t)$	$\rho_1(r_t^2)$	$\rho_1(|r_t|)$	S	K	BJ
ALLIANZ	-0.0632	0.3699	0.3349	0.0781	32.409	207116.0
BASF	-0.0280	0.2461	0.2284	-0.1727	8.658	7693.5
BAYER	-0.0333	0.3356	0.2487	0.0499	9.604	10447.0
BMW	-0.0134	0.3449	0.2560	-0.0107	17.029	47128.0
COMMERZBANK	0.0483	0.1310	0.2141	-0.2449	10.033	11902.0
DAIMLER	-0.0273	0.4050	0.3195	0.0381	26.673	134201.0
DEUTSCHE BANK	0.0304	0.2881	0.2408	-0.3099	13.773	27881.0
DEGUSSA	0.0250	0.3149	0.2349	-0.3949	19.127	62427.0
DRESDNER	0.0636	0.1846	0.2214	0.1223	8.829	8150.2
HOECHST	0.0118	0.2028	0.1977	-0.1205	9.988	11708.0
KARSTADT	0.0060	0.2963	0.1964	-0.4042	20.436	72958.0
LINDE	-0.0340	0.1907	0.2308	-0.2433	14.565	32086.0
MAN	0.0280	0.2824	0.2507	-0.5911	18.034	54454.0
MANNESMANN	0.0582	0.1737	0.2048	-0.2702	13.692	27442.0
PREUSSAG	0.0827	0.1419	0.1932	0.1386	10.341	12923.0
RWE	0.0408	0.1642	0.2385	-0.1926	16.727	45154.0
SCHERING	0.0696	0.2493	0.2217	-0.0359	9.577	10360.0
SIEMENS	0.0648	0.1575	0.1803	-0.5474	10.306	13070.0
THYSSEN	0.0426	0.1590	0.1553	-0.0501	6.103	2308.0
VOLKSWAGEN	0.0596	0.1890	0.1687	-0.3275	10.235	12637.0

Table 10.1: First order autocorrelation of the returns $\rho_1(r_t)$, the squared returns $\rho_1(r_t^2)$ and the absolute returns $\rho_1(|r_t|)$ as well as skewness (S), kurtosis (K) and the Bera-Jarque test statistic (BJ) for the daily returns of German stocks 1974-1996.

Q SFEReturns.xpl

the skewness and kurtosis. Whereas the skewness in most cases is close to zero and is sometimes positive, sometimes negative, the kurtosis is in every case significantly larger than 3. The smallest estimated kurtosis is by THYSSEN ($\widehat{\mathrm{Kurt}} = 6.1$), the largest by ALLIANZ ($\widehat{\mathrm{Kurt}} = 32.4$). Under the null hypothesis of the normal distribution, the estimates in (3.2) and (3.3) are independent and asymptotically normally distributed with

$$\sqrt{n}\hat{S} \xrightarrow{\mathcal{L}} N(0,6)$$

and

$$\sqrt{n}(\widehat{\mathrm{Kurt}} - 3) \xrightarrow{\mathcal{L}} N(0,24).$$

From this the combined test of the normal distribution from Bera and Jarque (BJ) can be derived:

$$BJ = n\left(\frac{\hat{S}^2}{6} + \frac{(\widehat{\mathrm{Kurt}} - 3)^2}{24}\right).$$

BJ is asymptotically χ^2 distribution with two degrees of freedom. The last column in Table 10.1 shows, that in all cases the normal distribution hypothesis is clearly rejected by a significance level of 1% (critical value 9.21). This is above all caused by the value of the kurtosis. Typically in financial time series, the kurtosis is significantly larger than 3, which is caused by the frequent appearance of outliers. Furthermore, there are more frequent appearances of very small returns than what one would expect under the normal distribution hypothesis. One says that the empirical distribution of the returns is *leptokurtic*, which means that the distribution is more mass around the center and in the tails than the normal distribution. The opposite, a weaker asymmetry or *platykurtic* distribution rarely appears in financial markets.

10.3 Expectations and Efficient Markets

Market efficiency is a very general concept in economic theory. A market is called efficient if at every point in time all relevant information is completely reflected in the price of the traded object. This general definition must be defined more concretely, in order to say what "completely reflected" means. To this end we require the concept of *rational expectations*. In general one speaks of rational expectations when by the forecast of a stochastic process P_t all relative and available information $\mathcal{F}_{t-1}$ (see Definition 5.1) is 'optimally' used. Optimal means that the mean squared error of the forecast is minimized. This is the case when the conditional expectation (see Section 3.5) $E[P_t|\mathcal{F}_{t-1}]$ is used as the forecast.

Theorem 10.1
For every $h > 0$ using the conditional expectation $E[P_{t+h} \mid \mathcal{F}_t]$ as a forecast, $P^*_{t+h|t}$ minimizes the mean squared error $E[(P_{t+h} - P^*_{t+h|t})^2]$ given all relevant information $\mathcal{F}_t$ at time t.

Proof:
Given any forecast $P^*_{t+h|t}$, that can be written as a (in general nonlinear) function of the random variables at time t, which determines the information set $\mathcal{F}_t$, then the mean squared error can be written as

$$
\begin{aligned}
E[(P_{t+h} - P^*_{t+h|t})^2] &= E[(P_{t+h} - E[P_{t+h}|\mathcal{F}_t] + E[P_{t+h}|\mathcal{F}_t] - P^*_{t+h|t})^2] \\
&= E[(P_{t+h} - E[P_{t+h}|\mathcal{F}_t])^2] \\
&\quad + E[(E[P_{t+h}|\mathcal{F}_t] - P^*_{t+h|t})^2],
\end{aligned} \tag{10.5}
$$

since the cross product is equal to zero:

$$
\begin{aligned}
2\mathsf{E}[(P_{t+h} - \mathsf{E}[P_{t+h}|\mathcal{F}_t])\,(\mathsf{E}[P_{t+h}|\mathcal{F}_t] - P^*_{t+h|t})] &= \\
2\mathsf{E}[\mathsf{E}[P_{t+h} - \mathsf{E}[P_{t+h}|\mathcal{F}_t]|\mathcal{F}_t](\mathsf{E}[P_{t+h}|\mathcal{F}_t] - P^*_{t+h|t})] &= \\
2\mathsf{E}[0 \cdot (\mathsf{E}[P_{t+h}|\mathcal{F}_t] - P^*_{t+h|t})] &= 0.
\end{aligned}
$$

The second term on the right hand side of (10.5) is nonnegative and is equal to zero when $\mathsf{E}[P_{t+h}|\mathcal{F}_t] = P^*_{t+h|t}$.

$\square$

Not all economic variables have sufficient information available to estimate $\mathsf{E}[P_t \mid \mathcal{F}_{t-1}]$. This has to do with the type of underlying process that determines P_t and the relative level of the necessary information for the forecast. In order to shed light upon this conceptual problem, hypotheses have been developed in the macro-economic theory, which do not require the use of mathematical expectations $\mathsf{E}[P_t \mid \mathcal{F}_{t-1}]$. The hypothesis on *adaptive expectations* assumes for instance that the forecast at time $t-1$ of P_t, $\mathsf{E}^a_{t-1}[P_t]$, is generated by the following mechanism:

$$
\mathsf{E}^a_{t-1}[P_t] - \mathsf{E}^a_{t-2}[P_{t-1}] = \theta(P_{t-1} - \mathsf{E}^a_{t-2}[P_{t-1}]) \tag{10.6}
$$

with a constant parameter θ, $0 < \theta < 1$. Changes in the forecast result from the last forecast error weighted by θ.

Theorem 10.2
The adaptive expectation in (10.6) is optimal in the sense of the mean squared error exactly when P_t follows the process

$$
P_t = P_{t-1} + \varepsilon_t - (1 - \theta)\varepsilon_{t-1} \tag{10.7}
$$

where ε_t is white noise.

Proof:
With the Lag-Operator L (see Definition 10.13), (10.6) can be represented as

$$
\{1 - (1 - \theta)L\}\,\mathsf{E}^a_{t-1}[P_t] = \theta P_{t-1}.
$$

Since $0 < \theta < 1$ and $\{1 - (1 - \theta)z\}^{-1} = \sum_{i=0}^{\infty}(1 - \theta)^i z^i$ this can be written as

$$
\mathsf{E}^a_{t-1}[P_t] = \theta \sum_{i=0}^{\infty}(1 - \theta)^i P_{t-i-1}.
$$

The process (10.7) can be rewritten as

$$\{1 - (1 - \theta)L\}\,\varepsilon_t = P_t - P_{t-1}$$

and

$$
\begin{aligned}
\varepsilon_t &= \sum_{j=0}^{\infty}(1-\theta)^j(P_{t-j} - P_{t-j-1}) \\
&= P_t - \theta\sum_{j=0}^{\infty}(1-\theta)^j P_{t-j-1},
\end{aligned}
$$

so that $P_t - \mathsf{E}_{t-1}^a[P_t]$ is white noise. Thus $\mathsf{E}_{t-1}^a[P_t]$ is the best forecast for P_t in the sense of the mean squared error.

$\square$

The process (10.7) is also referred to as the integrated autoregressive moving average process (ARIMA) of order (0,1,1). The family of ARIMA models will be discussed in more detail in Chapter 11. In general exogenous factors, for example, supply shocks, could also be involved in determining the equilibrium prices. In this case adaptive expectations would be suboptimal. If X_t is the stochastic exogenous factor and $\mathcal{F}_t$ is a family of results which are determined from the observations $\{p_t, p_{t-1}, \ldots, x_t, x_{t-1}, \ldots\}$ available at time t, then the optimal process $\mathsf{E}[P_t \mid \mathcal{F}_{t-1}]$ is in general a function of $\{p_t, p_{t-1}, \ldots\}$ and of $\{x_t, x_{t-1}, \ldots\}$. Special cases do exist in which adaptive expectations coincide with rational expectations, for example, in a linear supply/demand system with X_t as an exogenous shock that follows a random walk. If X_t is instead an AR(1) process, then forecasts with adaptive expectations have a larger mean squared error than forecasts with rational expectations. If the factor X_t is *common knowledge*, i.e., available to the public, then rational expectations in this example would mean that the price would be optimally forecasted by using this information.

However, when the factor X_t is not observable for everyone, in principle the uninformed agent could *learn* from the prices offered by the informed agent. This means that through observation of prices they could obtain information on the status of ω, above and beyond what is in their private information set F_i. Here it is assumed that the information function of prices is correctly interpreted.

In order to illustrate what role the price plays in forming expectations, imagine purchasing a bottle of wine. In the store there are three bottles to choose with the prices EUR 300, EUR 30 and EUR 3. Since the bottle for EUR

Type	P1	P2
I	300	50
II	50	300
III	150	250

Table 10.2: Payments in periods P1 and P2 according to type of investor

300 exceeds the budget, only two bottles for EUR 3 and EUR 30 are considered. Now assume that someone who is not a wine expert could not evaluate the quality of the wine from instructions written on the label. Since one is pressed by time, collecting information from other people is time consuming. What remains is the information included in the price. Assume further that one has learned through previous shopping experiences that the more expensive wine tends to be better than the cheaper wine. Thus one constructs a function of the price with respect to the quality, i.e., how good the wine is. One would choose the wine for EUR 30 if the better quality and more expensive wine was valued more in the utility function than the price advantage of the cheaper wine. The buyer behaved *rationally*, since he optimized his decision (here maximizing his utility function) with the help of the available information and the price function, assuming that the function was right.

In addition let's take a look at another example of an experimental market which is taken from the literature. We have a security that is traded in two periods P1 and P2 and in each period it pays various dividends according to the type of investor. The trading system is an auction in which at the time of an offer both bid and ask prices are verbally given. There are three types of investors and from each type there are three investors, i.e., a total of nine investors can trade the security, among other instruments. Each investor has an initial capital of 10 000 Franks (1 'Frank' = 0.002 USD) and two securities. The initial capital of 10 000 Franks must be paid back at the end of the second period. Every profit which results from trading the security may be kept. When the investor is in possession of the security at the end of P1 or P2, he will receive the dividend with respect to what type of investor he is. Table 10.2 displays information on the dividend payments.

Every investor knows only his own dividend payment, no one else. The question is, whether and if so how fast the investors 'learn' about the pricing structure, i.e., gain information on the value of the security to the other investors. There are two underlying hypotheses:

1. Investors tell each other through their bids about their individual dividends only in P1 and P2 ('naive behavior').

2. The investors draw conclusions through the observed price on the value of the security for the other investors and use this information in their own bids ('rational behavior').

Since the experiment is over after the period P2, only the individual dividend payments of each investor are of interest, so that in P2 both hypotheses coincide: The equilibrium price is 300 Franks, since type II is just willing to buy at this price and there is competition among the type II investors. At the beginning of P1, before any trading begins, each investor has information only on his own dividends, so that at first one applies naive behavior: type I and type II would offer a maximum of 350, type III would offer a maximum of 400, thus the equilibrium price according to the hypothesis of naive behavior is 400 Franks. This hypothesis performed well in empirical experiments. When the experiment is repeated with the same dividend matrix, the investors can learn through the prices of the previous experiment, which value the security has for the other types of investors in P2. In particular under the hypothesis of rational behavior, type I could learn that the equilibrium price in P2 is higher than what his own dividend would be, thus he could sell the security at a higher price. The equilibrium price in P1 is under the rational hypothesis 600 Franks. Type I buys at the price in P1 and sells in P2 to type II at a price of 300.

In repeated experiments it was discovered that the participants actually tended from naive behavior to rational behavior, although the transition did not occur immediately after the first experiment, it was gradual and took about 8 repetitions. Other experiments were run, including a *forward and futures market* in which in the first period P1 the price of the security in P2 could already be determined. Here it was shown that through the immediate transparency of the security's value in future periods the transition to rational expectations equilibrium was much quicker.

The observed market price is created through the interaction of various supplies and demands an aggregation of the individual heterogenous information sets. Assume that the price at time t is a function of the state of the economy, the *price function* $p_t(\omega)$, $\omega \in \Omega$. We define in the following an equilibrium with rational expectations.

Definition 10.16 (RE-Equilibrium)
An equilibrium at t with rational expectations (RE-equilibrium) is an equilibrium in which every agent i optimizes his objective function given the information set $\mathcal{F}_{i,t}$ and the price function $p_t(\omega)$.

Definition 10.16 assumes in particular that every agent includes the information function of the prices correctly in his objective function.

The concept of *efficient markets* is closely related to the concept of rational expectations. According to the original and general definition, a market is efficient if at every point in time all relevant information is reflected in the price. This means, for example, that new information is immediately incorporated into the price. In the following we define efficient markets with respect to an information set $\mathcal{G}$.

Definition 10.17 (Efficient Markets)
A market is efficient with respect to $\mathcal{G} = (G_t)$, $t \in \mathbb{N}$, $G_t \subset \mathcal{F}_t$, if at every time t the market is in RE-equilibrium with the price function $p_t(\omega)$ and if for every agent i and every time t the following holds

$$G_t \subset \{\mathcal{F}_{i,t} \cup p_t(\omega)\}.$$

Typically three cases are identified as weak, semi-strong and strong efficiency.

1. The market is *weak efficient*, when efficiency refers only to historical prices, i.e., the set $\mathcal{G} = (G_t)$,
   $G_t = \{p_t, p_{t-1}, p_{t-2}, \ldots\}$. This is, for example, achieved when for all i it holds that $\{p_t, p_{t-1}, p_{t-2}, \ldots\} \subset F_{i,t}$, that is when the historical prices are contained in every private information set.

2. The market is *semi-strong efficient*, when efficiency refers to the set $\mathcal{G} = (G_t)$, $(\cap_i F_{i,t}) \subset G_t \subset (\cup_i F_{i,t})$, which includes all publicly available information.

3. The market is *strong efficient*, when efficiency refers to the set $\mathcal{G} = (G_t)$, $G_t = \cup_i F_{i,t}$, i.e., when all information (public and private) is reflected in the price function. In this case one speaks of a *fully revealing* RE-equilibrium.

An equivalent definition says that under efficient markets no abnormal returns can be achieved. In order to test it one must first determine what a 'normal' return is, i.e., one must define an econometric model. Efficient markets can then be tested only with respect to this model. If this combined hypothesis is rejected, it could be that markets are inefficient or that the econometric model is inadequate.

The following is a brief summary of the typical econometric models that have been proposed for financial data. For each of the most interesting financial instruments, stocks, exchange rates, interest rates and options, a corresponding theory will be presented, which are considered to be classic theory in the respective areas. In later chapters we will refer back to these theories when we discuss empirically motivated expansions.

10.4 Econometric Models: A Brief Summary

10.4.1 Stock Prices: the CAPM

The *capital asset pricing model* (CAPM), developed independently by various authors in the sixties, is a classical equilibrium model for the valuation of risky securities (stocks). It is based on the following assumptions:

1. There exists homogenous information among the market participants. This assumption can be weakened by assuming that under homogenous information a rational equilibrium is *fully revealing* (see the strong version of Definition 10.17).

2. The market has no frictions, i.e., there are no transaction costs, no taxes, no restrictions on short selling or on the divisibility of stocks.

3. There is complete competition.

4. There are no arbitrage opportunities.

5. There are a finite number of stocks (K) and a riskless security with return r.

6. Every investor has a strictly concave utility function as a function of the risky future cash flows. This means that every investor is risk averse.

7. Every investor maximizes his expected utility, which is dependent only on the expectation and the variance of the risky future cash flows. This is the crucial assumption of the CAPM. Sufficient conditions for this ($\mu - \sigma$)-criterion are either of the following:

   a) Every investor has a quadratic utility function.

   b) The stock returns are normally distributed.

In the following $X_{i,t}$ and $\alpha_{i,t}$ represent the price and the number of i-th stock supplied in equilibrium at time t. We define the *market portfolio* $X_{m,t}$ as

$$X_{m,t} = \sum_{i=1}^{K} \alpha_{i,t} X_{i,t}. \tag{10.8}$$

The relative weight $w_{i,t}$ of the i-th stock in this portfolio is as follows

$$w_{i,t} = \frac{\alpha_{i,t} X_{i,t}}{\sum_k \alpha_{k,t} X_{k,t}}.$$

Most of the well known stock indices are such value weighted indices, nevertheless often only the largest stocks in the market are included in the index (DAX, for example, contains only the 30 largest stocks). As in Definition 10.15, we define the stock return as $R_{i,t} = \ln(X_{i,t}/X_{i,t-1})$ and the market return as $R_{m,t} = \ln(X_{m,t}/X_{m,t-1})$. We assume that the underlying process of the return is covariance stationary. In equilibrium according to the CAPM it holds for every stock i that

$$\mathsf{E}[R_{i,t}] = r + \beta_i(\mathsf{E}[R_{m,t}] - r), \tag{10.9}$$

with the 'beta' factor

$$\beta_i = \frac{\mathrm{Cov}(R_{i,t}, R_{m,t})}{\mathrm{Var}(R_{m,t})}.$$

Equation (10.9) says that in equilibrium the expected return of the i-th stock is comprised of two components: the return of the riskless security and a risk premium which is specifically determined for each stock through the beta factor. Stocks that are positively correlated with the market have a positive risk premium. The larger the correlation of a stock with the market portfolio is, the larger is the premium in CAPM for portfolio risk.

Since the CAPM can be derived using theories on utilities, it is sometimes described as a demand oriented equilibrium model. In contrast to this there are other models that explain the stock returns in terms of various aggregate variables, so called *factors*, and are referred to as being supply oriented. In Section 12.3 we will relax the assumptions of time constant variance and covariance implicit in equation (10.9).

10.4.2 Exchange Rate: Theory of the Interest Rate Parity

For stocks one can find a large variety of econometric models and for exchange rates there are even more. There are two standard and quite simple theories. However they are not sufficient to explain the considerable price movements in currency markets, especially in the short-run. The *purchasing power parity* (PPP) assumes that identical goods in different countries must have the same relative price, i.e., a relative price given in units of currency. It has been empirically determined that in the long-run this theory describes reality well, but in the short-run the price movements could not be explained. The second simple theory, the *theory of interest rate parity*, performs better as capital flows faster than goods. The difference in interest rates can thus resemble the exchange of capital in other currencies. So does the exchange rate. The theory of the interest rate parity assumes that domestic and foreign securities are perfect substitutes with respect to duration and risk structure.

Assume that along with forward and futures markets currency can be traded over time. The *spot price* is calculated by W_t^K, the forward and future price by W_t^T, each is given in units of the foreign currency, i.e., EUR/USD. An internationally acting investor has two choices. Either he holds a domestic capital investment with the domestic interest rate r_t^i or he chooses a foreign investment with the foreign interest rate r_t^a. If he chooses the foreign investment, he must first exchange his capital into foreign currency at the spot price and at the end, exchange back again. The uncertainty about the future developments of the exchange rate can be avoided by purchasing a forward or future contract. In this case the return on the foreign investment is $(1/W_t^K)(1+r_t^a)W_t^T - 1$. If this return is not equal to the domestic interest rate, then an equilibrium has not been reached. Through immediate price adjustments the interest rate arbitrage disappeares and then equilibrium is reached. Thus in equilibrium it must hold that

$$\frac{W_t^T}{W_t^K} = \frac{1+r_t^i}{1+r_t^a}, \tag{10.10}$$

i.e., the relationship between forward and future markets and spot markets corresponds exactly to the relationship between domestic and foreign gross interest rates. The relationship in (10.10) is also called the *covered interest rate parity*, since at the time of investment it deals with riskless exchange and interest rates.

In addition to the interest rate arbitrageur there are the so called forward and future speculators that compare the expected future exchange rate with the forward and future price and the corresponding risk of purchasing (selling) currency below or above the equilibrium. Consider a simple case where forward and future speculators are risk neutral. Then in equilibrium the expected exchange rate is equal to the forward and future price, i.e.,

$$W_t^T = \mathsf{E}[W_{t+1}^K \mid \mathcal{F}_t], \tag{10.11}$$

with the information set $\mathcal{F}_t$ which contains all relevant and available information. Here we assume that the speculators have rational expectations, i.e., the true underlying process is known and is used to build the optimal forecast by the speculators. This can also be written as the relationship

$$W_{t+1}^K = \mathsf{E}[W_{t+1}^K \mid \mathcal{F}_t] + \varepsilon_{t+1} \tag{10.12}$$

which says that the deviations of the speculator's forecast $\mathsf{E}[W_{t+1}^K \mid \mathcal{F}_t]$ from the realized exchange rates is white noise ε_t (see Definition 10.8). The market is inefficient when the speculators actually are risk neutral and ε_t is not white noise. In this case the set $\mathcal{F}_t$ does not reflect all of the relevant information in the expectations of the speculators - they do not have rational expectations. In order to test for market efficiency (that is, in order to test whether ε_t is white noise) we first need a model for $\mathsf{E}[W_{t+1}^K \mid \mathcal{F}_t]$. This can be formulated from (10.11) and (10.10).

Substituting (10.11) into (10.10) we obtain the so called *uncovered interest rate parity*,

$$\frac{\mathsf{E}[W_{t+1}^K \mid \mathcal{F}_t]}{W_t^K} = \frac{1 + r_t^i}{1 + r_t^a}. \tag{10.13}$$

This interest rate parity is risky because the future exchange rates are uncertain and enter the relationship as expectations.

Together with (10.12) the risky interest rate parity (10.13) implies that the following holds

$$W_{t+1}^K = \frac{1 + r_t^i}{1 + r_t^a} W_t^K + \varepsilon_{t+1}. \tag{10.14}$$

When the difference in the long-run interest rates is zero on average, then (10.14) is a random walk (see Definition 10.9). The random walk is the first model to describe exchange rates.

It should be emphasized that the derivation of this simple model occurred under the assumption of risk neutrality of the speculators. In the case of risk aversion a risk premium must be included. If, for example, we want to test the efficiency of the currency markets, we could then test the combined hypothesis of efficiency and uncovered interest rate parity using risk neutrality. A rejection of this hypothesis indicates the market inefficiency or that the interest rate parity model is a poor model for currency markets.

10.4.3 Term Structure: The Cox-Ingersoll-Ross Model

Term structure models are applied to model the chronological development of bond returns with respect to time to maturity. The classical starting point is to identify one or more factors which are believed to determine the term structure. Through specification of the dynamic structure and using specific expectation hypotheses, an explicit solution can be obtained for the returns.

As a typical example we briefly introduce the Cox, Ingersoll and Ross (CIR) model, which has been mentioned in Section 9.2.2. The price of a *Zero*

Coupon Bond with a nominal value of 1 EUR is given by $P_T(t)$ at time t, i.e., a security with no dividend payments that pays exactly one EUR at maturity date T. The log return of the zero coupon bond is given by $Y_T(t)$. We assume that continuous compounding holds. The process $Y_T(t)$ is frequently referred to as the *yield to maturity* . The relationship between the price and the return of the zero coupon bond is

$$P_T(t) = \exp\{-Y_T(t)\tau\}$$

with the remaining time to maturity $\tau = T - t$. This can be easily seen from the definition of a log return (Definition 10.15). For very short time intervals the *short rate* $r(t)$ is defined as

$$r(t) = \lim_{T \to t} Y_T(t).$$

In practice the short rate corresponds to the spot rate, i.e., the interest rate for the shortest possible investment (see Section 9.2.2). Consider, intuitively, the choice between an investment in a zero bond with the return $Y_T(t)$ and repeatedly investing at a (risky) short-term interest rate in future periods. An important expectation hypothesis says that the following holds

$$P_T(t) = \mathsf{E}\left[\exp(-\int_t^T r(s)ds)|\mathcal{F}_t\right] \tag{10.15}$$

(also see equation (9.1) for variable but deterministic interest). The short rate is frequently seen as the most important predicting factor of the term structure. As the CIR model, most one factor models use the short rate as factor. The CIR model specifies the dynamic of the short rate as a continuous stochastic process

$$dr(t) = a\{b - r(t)\}dt + \sigma\sqrt{r(t)}dW_t \tag{10.16}$$

with a Wiener process W_t and constant parameters a, b and σ - see also Section 9.2.2. The process (10.16) has a so called *mean reversion* behavior, i.e., once deviations from the stationary mean b occurs, the process is brought back to the mean value again through a positive a. The volatility, written as $\sigma\sqrt{r(t)}$, is larger whenever the interest level is higher, which can also be shown empirically.

Since in the equation (10.16) $r(t)$ is specified as a Markov process, $P_T(t)$ is, as a consequence of equation (10.15), a function of the actual short rate, i.e.,

$$P_T(t) = V\{r(t), t\}.$$

With Itô's lemma (5.10) and (9.7) we obtain from (10.16) the differential equation

$$a(b-r)\frac{\partial V(r,t)}{\partial r} + \frac{1}{2}\sigma^2 r\frac{\partial^2 V(r,t)}{\partial r^2} + \frac{\partial V(r,t)}{\partial t} - rV(r,t) = 0.$$

With the bounding constraint $V(r,T) = P_T(T) = 1$ the following solution is obtained

$$P_T(t) = V\{r(t),t\} = \exp\{A(T-t) + B(T-t)r(t)\}, \qquad (10.17)$$

where (see Section 9.2.4)

$$\begin{aligned}
A(\tau) &= \frac{2ab}{\sigma^2}\ln\frac{2\psi\exp\{(a+\psi)\tau/2\}}{g(\tau)}, \\
B(\tau) &= \frac{2\{1-\exp(\psi\tau)\}}{g(\tau)} \\
\psi &= \sqrt{a^2 + 2\sigma^2} \\
g(\tau) &= 2\psi + (a+\psi)\{\exp(\psi\tau) - 1\}.
\end{aligned}$$

For increasing time periods $T-t$ the term structure curve $Y_T(t)$ converges to the value

$$Y_{lim} = \frac{2ab}{\psi + a}.$$

If the short-term interest lies above b, then the term structure is decreasing, see Figure 10.1; if it lies below Y_{lim}, then the term structure is increasing, see Figure 10.2. If the short-term interest rate lies between b and Y_{lim}, then the curve could first rise and then fall.

10.4.4 Options: The Black-Scholes Model

Since we have thoroughly covered the Black-Scholes model on option pricing in the first part of this book, here only a brief summary of the model is given. Options are not only theoretically interesting for financial markets, but also from an empirical point of view. Just recently there have been indications of a systematic deviation of actual market prices from the Black-Scholes prices. These deviations will be discussed in more detail in later chapters, specifically in dealing with ARCH models.

As an example let's consider a European call option on a stock which receives no dividends in the considered time periods and has the spot price S_t at time t. $C(S,t)$ is the option price at time t, when the actual price is $S_t = S$. The

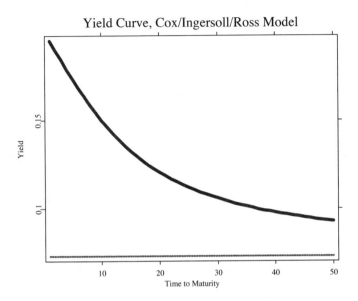

Figure 10.1:   Term structure curve according to the Cox-Ingersoll-Ross model
with a short rate of $r_t{=}0.2$, $a = b = \sigma = 0.1$ and $Y_{lim} = 0.073$
(dotted line).   ☐ SFEcir.xpl

payoff at the time to maturity T is $C(S_T, T) = \max(0, S_T - K)$, where K
is the strike price. The option price is determined from general no arbitrage
conditions as

$$C(S_t, t) = \mathsf{E}[e^{-r\tau} C(S_T, T)|\mathcal{F}_t],$$

where expectations are built on an appropriate risk neutral distribution - see
also (6.23). r is the fixed riskless interest rate.

Special results can only be derived when the dynamics of the stock prices
are known. The assumptions made by Black and Scholes are that the stock
prices S_t are geometric Brownian motion, i.e.,

$$dS_t = \mu S_t dt + \sigma S_t dW_t. \tag{10.18}$$

The option price $C(S, t)$ thus satisfies the Black-Scholes differential equation
(6.3) as a function of time and stock prices

$$\frac{1}{2}\sigma^2 S^2 \frac{\partial^2 C}{\partial S^2} + rS \frac{\partial C}{\partial S} + \frac{\partial C}{\partial t} = rC$$

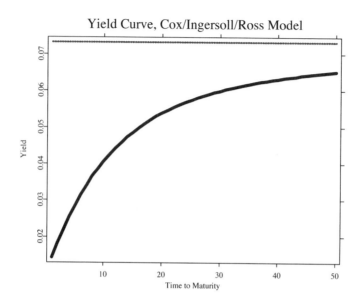

Figure 10.2: Term structure curve according to the Cox-Ingersoll-Ross model
with a short rate of r_t=0.01, $a = b = \sigma = 0.1$ and $Y_{lim} = 0.073$
(dotted line).   **Q** SFEcir.xpl

Black and Scholes derive the following solutions (see Section 6.2):

$$C(S,t) = S\Phi(y + \sigma\sqrt{\tau}) - e^{-r\tau}K\Phi(y), \qquad (10.19)$$

where $\tau = T-t$ is the time to maturity for the option and y is an abbreviation
for

$$y = \frac{\ln\frac{S}{K} + (r - \frac{1}{2}\sigma^2)\tau}{\sigma\sqrt{\tau}}.$$

10.4.5   The Market Price of Risk

In a risk neutral world the market price of risk, see Section 9.2.3, is equal
to zero. In the following section, we will consider the market price of risk
and derive once again the Black-Scholes formula. To do this we will consider
derivatives of financial instruments that are determined by a single random
process θ_t. We will assume that the process θ_t is geometric Brownian motion

:

$$d\theta_t = m\theta_t dt + s\theta_t dW_t \ . \tag{10.20}$$

The variable θ_t does not necessarily represent a financial value. It could be the state of the market, a measure for the popularity of a politician or the frequency of an ad-hoc announcement at time t. Assume that V_{1t} and V_{2t} are the prices for two derivatives of financial instruments that depend only on θ_t and t. As a simplification, no payments are allowed during the observed time period. This process $V_{jt} = V_j(\theta, t)$, $j = 1, 2$ also follows the schema (10.20) with the *same* Wiener process W_t

$$dV_{jt} = \mu_{jt} V_{jt} dt + \sigma_{jt} V_{jt} dW_t, \qquad j = 1, 2 \tag{10.21}$$

where μ_{jt}, σ_{jt} could be functions of θ_t and t. The random process W_t in (10.20) and (10.21) is always the same since we assume that this is the only source that creates uncertainty.

The observation of (10.21) in discrete time leads to:

$$\Delta V_{1t} = \mu_{1t} V_{1t} \Delta t + \sigma_{1t} V_{1t} \Delta W_t \tag{10.22}$$

$$\Delta V_{2t} = \mu_{2t} V_{2t} \Delta t + \sigma_{2t} V_{2t} \Delta W_t \tag{10.23}$$

We could "eliminate the random variable ΔW_t" by constructing a riskless portfolio that continually changes. To do this we take $\sigma_{2t} V_{2t}$ units of the first instrument and $-\sigma_{1t} V_{1t}$ of the second instrument, i.e., we short sell the second instrument. Letting Π_t be the total value of the portfolio at time t we have:

$$\Pi_t = (\sigma_{2t} V_{2t}) V_{1t} - (\sigma_{1t} V_{1t}) V_{2t} \tag{10.24}$$

and

$$\Delta \Pi_t = (\sigma_{2t} V_{2t}) \Delta V_{1t} - (\sigma_{1t} V_{1t}) \Delta V_{2t} \tag{10.25}$$

Substituting in (10.22) and (10.23) we have:

$$\Delta \Pi_t = (\mu_{1t} \sigma_{2t} V_{1t} V_{2t} - \mu_{2t} \sigma_{1t} V_{1t} V_{2t}) \Delta t. \tag{10.26}$$

This portfolio should be riskless, thus in time period Δt it must produce the riskless profit $r\Delta t$:

$$\frac{\Delta \Pi_t}{\Pi_t} = r\Delta t. \tag{10.27}$$

Substituting (10.24) and (10.26) into this equation produces:

$$
\begin{aligned}
(\mu_{1t} \sigma_{2t} V_{1t} V_{2t} - \mu_{2t} \sigma_{1t} V_{1t} V_{2t}) \Delta t &= (\sigma_{2t} V_{1t} V_{2t} - \sigma_{1t} V_{1t} V_{2t}) r \Delta t \\
\mu_{1t} \sigma_{2t} - \mu_{2t} \sigma_{1t} &= r\sigma_{2t} - r\sigma_{1t} \\
\frac{\mu_{1t} - r}{\sigma_{1t}} &= \frac{\mu_{2t} - r}{\sigma_{2t}}
\end{aligned}
$$

Equating this as in (9.2.3) to λ_t we see that the price V_t of a derivative instrument, an instrument that depends only on θ_t and t, follows the dynamics

$$dV_t = \mu_t V_t dt + \sigma_t V_t dW_t, \qquad (10.28)$$

the value

$$\lambda_t = \frac{\mu_t - r}{\sigma_t} = \frac{\mu(\theta_t, t) - r}{\sigma(\theta_t, t)} \qquad (10.29)$$

represents the *market price of risk* . This market price of risk can depend on θ_t (using μ_t, σ_t), but not on the actual price of the instrument V_t! We can rewrite equation (10.29) as:

$$\mu_t - r = \lambda_t \sigma_t \qquad (10.30)$$

Furthermore we can interpret σ_t, which in this interpretation can also be negative, as the level of the θ_t-risk in V_t. Equation (10.30) has strong ties to the CAPM model, which we discussed in Section (10.4.1) - for further details see also Hafner and Herwartz (1998).

Example 10.2 *Assume that there are two objects, both are dependent on a 90 day interest rate. The first instrument has an expected return of 6% per year and a volatility of 20% per year. For the second instrument a volatility of 30% per year is assumed. Furthermore, $r = 3\%$ per year. The market price of risk for the first instrument according to (10.29) is:*

$$\frac{0.06 - 0.03}{0.2} = 0.15 \qquad (10.31)$$

By substituting into equation (10.30) for the second object we obtain:

$$0.03 + 0.15 \cdot 0.3 = 0.075 \qquad (10.32)$$

or 7.5% expected value.

Since V_t is a function of θ_t and t, we can determine the dependence on θ_t using Itô's lemma. The direct application of Itô's lemma (5.10) on $V(\theta, t)$ gives, in comparison to (10.28), the parameters in this equation

$$
\begin{aligned}
\mu_t V_t &= m\theta_t \frac{\partial V_t}{\partial \theta_t} + \frac{\partial V_t}{\partial t} + \frac{1}{2} s^2 \theta_t^2 \frac{\partial^2 V_t}{\partial \theta^2} \\
\sigma_t V_t &= s\theta_t \frac{\partial V_t}{\partial \theta}.
\end{aligned}
$$

Due to equation (10.30) we have $\mu_t V_t - \lambda_t \sigma_t V_t = r V_t$, so that we obtain the following differential equation for V_t:

$$\frac{\partial V_t}{\partial t} + (m - \lambda_t s)\theta_t \frac{\partial V_t}{\partial \theta} + \frac{1}{2} s^2 \theta_t^2 \frac{\partial^2 V_t}{\partial \theta^2} = r \cdot V_t \qquad (10.33)$$

This equation (10.33) is very similar to the Black-Scholes differential equation and is in fact identical to (6.3) for $\theta_t = S_t$, where S_t denotes the stock price with no dividends. In this case θ_t itself is the price of the risk bearing instrument and must therefore satisfy (10.30), like the price V_t of any derivative based on the stock. Thus we obtain

$$m - r = \lambda_t s, \qquad (10.34)$$

so that the second term in (10.33) is equal to

$$r \theta_t \frac{\partial V_t}{\partial \theta}. \qquad (10.35)$$

Thus we have a differential equation:

$$\frac{1}{2} s^2 \theta_t^2 \frac{\partial^2 V_t}{\partial \theta^2} + r \theta_t \frac{\partial V_t}{\partial \theta} - r V_t + \frac{\partial V_t}{\partial t} = 0 \qquad (10.36)$$

which is identical to (6.3) after renaming the variables. More explicitly, let $S_t = \theta_t, b = r$ (since there are no dividends) and let $\sigma = s$ using the notation in Section 6.1.

10.5   The Random Walk Hypothesis

We have seen that econometric models, at least with stock prices and exchange rates, motivate using a random walk as a statistical model. With exchange rates we saw that as a consequence of the uncovered interest rate parity and the assumption of risk neutrality of forward and future speculators the model in (10.14) follows a random walk. Assuming a geometric Brownian motion for stock price as in (10.18), then it follows from Itô's lemma that the log of stock price follows a Wiener process with a constant drift rate:

$$d \ln S_t = \mu^* dt + \sigma dW_t \qquad (10.37)$$

where $\mu^* = \mu - \sigma^2/2$. If one observes (10.37) in time intervals of length $\Delta > 0$, i.e., at discrete points in time $0, \Delta, 2\Delta, ...$, then one obtains

$$\ln S_{t\Delta} = \ln S_{(t-1)\Delta} + \Delta \mu^* + \sqrt{\Delta} \sigma \xi_t \qquad (10.38)$$

with independent, standard normally distributed $\xi_t, t = 1, 2, \ldots$. The process (10.38) is a random walk with a drift for the logged stock prices. The log returns (see Definition 10.15) over the time interval of length Δ are also independently normally distributed with expected value $\Delta\mu^*$ and variance $\Delta\sigma^2$.

With long interest rate time series the random walk appears to be less plausible, since it is assumed that in the long-run there is a stationary level around which interest rates fluctuate in the short run. Let's consider once again the process for the short rate in (10.16), the Cox-Ingersoll-Ross (CIR) model. A discrete approximation is

$$r_t - r_{t-1} = \alpha + \beta r_{t-1} + \sigma\sqrt{r_{t-1}}\xi_t$$

or

$$r_t = \alpha + (1 + \beta)r_{t-1} + \sigma\sqrt{r_{t-1}}\xi_t. \tag{10.39}$$

If β in (10.39) is negative (and larger than -2), then the process is a stationary AR(1) process with heteroscedastic error terms. In Example 10.1 we encountered such a process with heteroscedastic error terms.

There is also the interpretation that interest rates are, at least in the short-run, explained well by a random walk. It is therefore of general interest to test whether a random walk exists. In the following we show the distinguishes through the three versions of the random walk hypothesis. In general we consider a random walk with a drift

$$P_t = \mu + P_{t-1} + \varepsilon_t. \tag{10.40}$$

1. The stochastic errors in (10.40) are independent and identically distributed (i.i.d.) with expectation zero and variance σ^2. This hypothesis has already been tested on multiple data sets in the sixties and was empirically determined to be unsupported. For example, distinct volatility clusters were discovered which under the i.i.d. hypothesis are statistically not expected.

2. The stochastic errors in (10.40) are independent but not necessarily identically distributed with an expectation of zero. This hypothesis is weaker than the first one since, for example, it allows for heteroscedasticity. Nonetheless, even here the empirical discoveries were that a dependence between the error terms must be assumed.

3. The stochastic errors in (10.40) are uncorrelated, i.e., $\gamma_\tau(\varepsilon_t) = 0$ for every $\tau \neq 0$. This is the weakest and most often discussed random walk hypothesis. Empirically it is most often tested through the statistical (in)significance of the estimated autocorrelations of ε_t.

The discussion of the random walk hypotheses deals with, above all, the predicability of financial time series. Another discussion deals with the question of whether the model (10.40) with independent, or as the case may be with uncorrelated, error terms is even a reasonable model for financial time series or whether it would be better to use just a model with a deterministic trend. Such a *trend-stationary* model has the form

$$P_t = \nu + \mu t + \varepsilon_t \qquad (10.41)$$

with constant parameters ν and μ. The process (10.41) is non-stationary since, for example, $\mathsf{E}[P_t] = \nu + \mu t$, the expected value is time dependent. If the linear time trend is filtered from P_t, then the stationary process $P_t - \mu t$ is obtained.

To compare the difference stationary random walk with a drift to the trend stationary process (10.41) we write the random walk from (10.40) through recursive substitution as

$$P_t = P_0 + \mu t + \sum_{i=1}^{t} \varepsilon_i, \qquad (10.42)$$

with a given initial value P_0. One sees that the random walk with a drift also implies a linear time trend, but the cumulative stochastic increments $(\sum_{i=1}^{t} \varepsilon_i)$ in (10.42) are not stationary, unlike the stationary increments (ε_t) in (10.41). Due to the representation (10.42) the random walk with or without a drift will be described as *integrated*, since the deviation from a deterministic trend is the sum of error terms. Moreover, every error term ε_t has a permanent influence on all future values of the process. For the best forecast in the sense of the mean squared error it holds for every $k > 0$,

$$\mathsf{E}[P_{t+k} \mid \mathcal{F}_t] = P_0 + \mu(t + k) + \sum_{i=1}^{t} \varepsilon_i.$$

In contrast, the impact of a shock ε_t on the forecast of the trend-stationary process (10.41) could be zero, i.e.,

$$\mathsf{E}[P_{t+k} \mid \mathcal{F}_t] = \nu + \mu(t + k).$$

It is thus of most importance to distinguish between a difference stationary and a trend-stationary process. Emphasized here is that the random walk is only a special case of a difference stationary process. If, for example, the increasing variables in (10.40) are stationary but autocorrelated, then we have a general difference stationary process. There are many statistical tests which test whether a process is difference stationary or not. Two such tests are discussed in the next section.

10.6   Unit Root Tests

We have discussed in Example 10.1 the AR(1) process is

$$X_t = c + \alpha X_{t-1} + \varepsilon_t. \tag{10.43}$$

Given $|\alpha| < 1$, the process is stationary when $E[X_0] = \frac{c}{1-\alpha}$ or after the "decaying process". The case where $\alpha = 1$ corresponds to the random walk which is non-stationary. The relationship between a stationary AR(1) process and α close to one is so similar to a random walk that it is often tested whether we have the case $\alpha = 1$ or $\alpha < 1$. To do this the so called *unit root tests* have been developed.

10.6.1   Dickey-Fuller Tests

The unit root test developed by Dickey and Fuller tests the null hypothesis of a *unit root*, that is, there is a root for the characteristic equation (11.6) of the AR(1) process with $z = 1$, against the alternative hypothesis that the process has no unit roots. As a basis for the test the following regression used is

$$\Delta X_t = (\alpha - 1)X_{t-1} + \varepsilon_t, \tag{10.44}$$

which is obtained by rearranging (10.43) with $c = 0$. If X_t is a random walk, then the coefficient of X_{t-1} is equal to zero. If, on the other hand, X_t is a stationary AR(1) process, then the coefficient is negative. The standard t-statistic is formed

$$\hat{t}_n = \frac{1 - \hat{\alpha}}{\sqrt{\hat{\sigma}^2 (\sum_{t=2}^n X_{t-1}^2)^{-1}}}, \tag{10.45}$$

where $\hat{\alpha}$ and $\hat{\sigma}^2$ are the least squares estimators for α and the variance σ^2 of ε_t. For increasing n the statistic (10.45) converges not to a standard normal distribution but instead to the distribution of a functional of Wiener process,

$$\hat{t}_n \xrightarrow{\mathcal{L}} \frac{W^2(1) - 1}{2\left\{ \int_0^1 W^2(u)du \right\}^{1/2}},$$

where W is a standard Wiener process. The critical value of the distribution are, for example, at the 1%, 5% and 10% significance levels, -2.58, -1.95, and -1.62 respectively.

A problem with this test is that the normal test significance level (for example 5%) is not reliable when the error terms ε_t in (10.44) are autocorrelated. The larger the autocorrelation of ε_t, the larger the distortion in general will be of the test significance. Ignoring then autocorrelations could lead to rejecting the null hypothesis of a unit root at low significance levels of 5%, when in reality the significance level lies at, for example, 30%. In order to prohibit these negative effects, Dickey and Fuller suggest another regression which contains lagged differences. The regression of this *augmented Dickey Fuller Test* (ADF) is thus

$$\Delta X_t = c + (\alpha - 1)X_{t-1} + \sum_{i=1}^{p} \alpha_i \Delta X_{t-i} + \varepsilon_t \tag{10.46}$$

where as with the simple Dickey-Fuller Test the null hypothesis of a unit root is rejected when the test statistic (10.45) is smaller than the critical value (which have been summarized in a table). Problematic is naturally the choice of p. In general it holds that the size of the test is better when p gets larger, but which causes the test to lose *power*. This is illustrated in a simulated process. The errors ε_t are correlated through the relationship

$$\varepsilon_t = \beta \xi_{t-1} + \xi_t$$

where ξ_t are i.i.d. $(0, \sigma^2)$. In the next chapter these processes will be referred to as *moving average* processes of order 1, MA(1). It holds that $\text{Var}(\varepsilon_t) = \sigma^2(1 + \beta^2)$, $\gamma_1(\varepsilon_t) = \text{Cov}(\varepsilon_t, \varepsilon_{t-1}) = \beta\sigma^2$, and $\gamma_\tau(\varepsilon_t) = 0$ for $\tau \geq 2$. For the ACF of ε_t we then get

$$\rho_\tau(\varepsilon_t) = \left\{ \begin{array}{ll} \frac{\beta}{1+\beta^2} & \text{wenn } \tau = 1 \\ 0 & \text{wenn } \tau \geq 2. \end{array} \right. \tag{10.47}$$

For the process

$$X_t = \alpha X_{t-1} + \beta \xi_{t-1} + \xi_t \tag{10.48}$$

simulations of the ADF Tests were done and are summarized in an abbreviated form in Table 10.3.

As one can see, the nominal significance level of 5% under the null hypothesis ($\alpha = 1$) is held better, if p is larger. However the power of the test decreases, i.e., the test is no longer capable of distinguishing between a process with unit roots and a stationary process with $\alpha = 0.9$. Thus in choosing p there is also the conflict between validity and power of the test.

If X_t is a trend-stationary process as in (10.41), the ADF test likewise does not reject often enough the (false) null hypothesis of a unit root. Asymptotically the probability of rejecting goes to zero. The ADF regression (10.46) can be extended by a linear time trend, i.e., run the regression

$$\Delta X_t = c + \mu t + (\alpha - 1)X_{t-1} + \sum_{i=1}^{p} \alpha_i \Delta X_{t-i} + \varepsilon_t \tag{10.49}$$

α	p	β -0.99	-0.9	0	0.9
1	3	0.995	0.722	0.045	0.034
	11	0.365	0.095	0.041	0.039
0.9	3	1.000	0.996	0.227	0.121
	11	0.667	0.377	0.105	0.086

Table 10.3: ADF-Test: Simulated rejection probabilities for the process (10.48) at a nominal significance level of 5% (according to Friedmann (1992)).

and test the significance of α. The critical values are contained in tables. The ADF test with a time trend (10.49) has power against a trend-stationary process. On the other hand, it loses power as compared to the simple ADF test (10.46), when the true process, for example, is a stationary AR(1) process.

As an empirical example, consider the daily stock prices of the 20 largest German stock companies from Jan. 2, 1974 to Dec. 30, 1996. Table 10.4 displays the ADF test statistics for the logged stock prices for $p = 0$ and $p = 4$. The tests were run with and without a linear time trend. In every regression a constant was included in estimation.

Only for RWE with a linear time trend does the ADF test reject the null hypothesis of a unit root by a significance level of 10%. Since in all other cases no unit root is rejected, it appears that taking differences of stock prices is a necessary operation in order to obtain a stationary process, i.e., to get log returns that can be investigated further. These results will be put into question in the next section using another test.

10.6.2   The KPSS Test of Stationarity

The KPSS Test from Kwiatkowski, Phillips, Schmidt and Shin (1992) tests for stationarity, i.e., for a unit root. The hypotheses are thus exchanged from those of the ADF test. As with the ADF test, there are two cases to distinguish between, whether to estimate with or without a linear time trend. The regression model with a time trend has the form

$$X_t = c + \mu t + k \sum_{i=1}^{t} \xi_i + \eta_t, \qquad (10.50)$$

| | ADF | | | | KPSS | | | |
| | without time trend | | with time trend | | without time trend | | with time trend | |
p and T	0	4	0	4	8	12	8	12
ALLIANZ	-0.68	-0.62	2.44	2.59	24.52**	16.62**	2.36**	1.61**
BASF	0.14	0.34	2.94	3.13	23.71**	16.09**	1.39**	0.95**
BAYER	-0.11	0.08	2.96	3.26	24.04**	16.30**	1.46**	1.00**
BMW	-0.71	-0.66	2.74	2.72	23.92**	16.22**	2.01**	1.37**
COMMERZ-BANK	-0.80	-0.67	1.76	1.76	22.04**	14.96**	1.43**	0.98**
DAIMLER	-1.37	-1.29	2.12	2.13	22.03**	14.94**	3.34**	2.27**
DEUTSCHE BANK	-1.39	-1.27	2.05	1.91	23.62**	16.01**	1.70**	1.16**
DEGUSSA	-0.45	-0.36	1.94	1.88	23.11**	15.68**	1.79**	1.22**
DRESDNER	-0.98	-0.94	1.90	1.77	22.40**	15.20**	1.79**	1.22**
HOECHST	0.36	0.50	3.24	3.37	23.80**	16.15**	1.42**	0.97**
KARSTADT	-1.18	-1.17	1.15	1.15	20.40**	13.84**	3.33**	2.26**
LINDE	-1.69	-1.44	2.74	2.70	24.40**	16.54**	3.14**	2.15**
MAN	-1.78	-1.58	1.66	1.61	21.97**	14.91**	1.59**	1.08**
MANNES-MANN	-0.91	-0.80	2.73	2.55	21.97**	14.93**	1.89**	1.29**
PREUSSAG	-1.40	-1.38	2.21	2.03	23.18**	15.72**	1.53**	1.04**
RWE	-0.09	-0.04	2.95	2.84	24.37**	16.52**	1.66**	1.14**
SCHERING	0.11	0.04	2.37	2.12	24.20**	16.40**	2.35**	1.60**
SIEMENS	-1.35	-1.20	2.13	1.84	23.24**	15.76**	1.69**	1.15**
THYSSEN	-1.45	-1.34	1.92	1.90	21.97**	14.90**	1.98**	1.35**
VOLKS-WAGEN	-0.94	-0.81	1.89	1.73	21.95**	14.89**	1.11**	0.76**

Table 10.4: Unit root tests: ADF Test (Null hypothesis: unit root) and KPSS Test (Null hypothesis: stationary). The augmented portion of the ADF regression as order $p = 0$ and $p = 4$. The KPSS statistic was calculated with the reference point $T = 8$ and $T = 12$. The asterisks indicate significance at the 10% (*) and 1% (**) levels.

Q SFEAdfKpss.xpl

with stationary η_t and i.i.d. ξ_t with an expected value 0 and variance 1. Obviously for $k \neq 0$ the process is integrated and for $k = 0$ trend-stationary. The null hypothesis is $H_0 : k = 0$, and the alternative hypothesis is $H_1 : k \neq 0$.

Under H_0 the regression (10.50) is run with the method of the least squares obtaining the residuals $\hat{\eta}_t$. Using these residuals the partial sum

$$S_t = \sum_{i=1}^{t} \hat{\eta}_i,$$

is built which under H_0 is integrated of order 1, i.e., the variance S_t increases linearly with t. The KPSS test statistic is then

$$KPSS_T = \frac{\sum_{t=1}^{n} S_t^2}{n^2 \hat{\omega}_T^2}, \tag{10.51}$$

where

$$\hat{\omega}_T^2 = \hat{\sigma}_\eta^2 + 2 \sum_{\tau=1}^{T} (1 - \frac{\tau}{T-1}) \hat{\gamma}_\tau$$

is an estimator of the spectral density at a frequency of zero where $\hat{\sigma}_\eta^2$ is the variance estimator of η_t and $\hat{\gamma}_\tau = 1/n \sum_{t=\tau+1}^{n} \hat{\eta}_t \hat{\eta}_{t-\tau}$ is the covariance estimator. The problem again is to determine the reference point T: for T that are too small the test is biased when there is autocorrelation, for T that is too large it loses power.

The results of the KPSS tests in Table 10.4 clearly indicate that the investigated stock prices are not stationary or trend-stationary, since in every case the null hypothesis at a significance level of 1% was rejected. Even RWE, which was significant under the ADF test at a significance level of 10 %, implies a preference of the hypothesis of unit roots here at a lower significance level.

10.6.3 Variance Ratio Tests

If one wants to test whether a time series follows a random walk, one can take advantage of the fact that the variance of a random walk increases linearly with time, see (10.4). Considering the log prices of a financial time series, $\ln S_t$, the null hypothesis would be

$$H_0 : r_t = \mu + \varepsilon_t, \quad \varepsilon_t \sim \mathrm{N}(0, \sigma^2)$$

with log returns $r_t = \ln S_t - \ln S_{t-1}$, constant μ and ε_t white noise. An alternative hypothesis is, for example, that r_t is stationary and autocorrelated. The sum over the returns is formed

$$r_t(q) = r_t + r_{t-1} + \ldots + r_{t-q+1}$$

and the variance of $r_t(q)$ is determined. For $q = 2$ it holds that, for example,

$$
\begin{aligned}
\mathrm{Var}\{r_t(2)\} &= \mathrm{Var}(r_t) + \mathrm{Var}(r_{t-1}) + 2 \, \mathrm{Cov}(r_t, r_{t-1}) \\
&= 2 \, \mathrm{Var}(r_t) + 2\gamma_1 \\
&= 2 \, \mathrm{Var}(r_t)(1 + \rho_1),
\end{aligned}
$$

where taking advantage of the stationarity of r_t, generally

$$\text{Var}\{r_t(q)\} = q\,\text{Var}(r_t)\left(1 + 2\sum_{\tau=1}^{q-1}(1-\frac{\tau}{q})\rho_\tau\right). \qquad (10.52)$$

Under H_0 it holds that $\rho_\tau = 0$ for all $\tau > 0$, so that under H_0

$$\frac{\text{Var}\{r_t(q)\}}{q\,\text{Var}(r_t)} = 1.$$

A test statistic can now be constructed where the consistent estimator

$$\hat{\mu} = \frac{1}{n}(\ln S_n - \ln S_0)$$

for μ,

$$\hat{\gamma}_0 = \frac{1}{n-1}\sum_{t=2}^{n}(\ln S_t - \ln S_{t-1} - \hat{\mu})^2$$

for $\text{Var}(r_t)$ and

$$\hat{\gamma}_0(q) = \frac{n}{q(n-q)(n-q+1)}\sum_{t=q+1}^{n}(\ln S_t - \ln S_{t-q} - q\hat{\mu})^2$$

for $\frac{1}{q}\text{Var}\{r_t(q)\}$ are substituted into (10.52). The test statistic is then

$$VQ(q) = \frac{\hat{\gamma}_0(q)}{\hat{\gamma}_0} - 1.$$

It can be shown that the asymptotic distribution is

$$\sqrt{n}VQ(q) \xrightarrow{\mathcal{L}} \text{N}\left(0, \frac{2(2q-1)(q-1)}{3q}\right).$$

The asymptotic variance can be established through the following approximation: Assume that $\hat{\mu} = 0$ and $n \gg q$. Then we have that $\ln S_t - \ln S_{t-q} = \sum_{j=0}^{q-1} r_{t-j}$ and

$$
\begin{aligned}
VQ(q) &\approx \frac{1}{qn}\sum_{t=q+1}^{n}\left((\sum_{j=0}^{q-1}r_{t-j})^2 - q\hat{\gamma}_0\right)/\hat{\gamma}_0 \\
&= \frac{1}{qn}\sum_{t=q+1}^{n}\frac{1}{\hat{\gamma}_0}\left(\sum_{j=0}^{q-1}r_{t-j}^2 + 2\sum_{j=0}^{q-2}r_{t-j}r_{t-j-1} + \ldots + 2r_t r_{t-q+1} - q\hat{\gamma}_0\right) \\
&\approx \frac{1}{q}\left(q\hat{\gamma}_0 + 2(q-1)\hat{\gamma}_1 + \ldots + 2\hat{\gamma}_{q-1} - q\hat{\gamma}_0\right)/\hat{\gamma}_0 \\
&= 2\sum_{j=1}^{q-1}\frac{q-j}{q}\hat{\rho}_j.
\end{aligned}
$$

Since under H_0 the estimated autocorrelation $\hat{\rho}_j$ scaled with $\sqrt{n}$ is asymptotically standard normal and is independent, see Section 11.5, the asymptotic variance is thus:

$$
\begin{aligned}
\mathrm{Var}_{as}\{\sqrt{n}VQ(q)\} &= \mathrm{Var}_{as}(2\sum_{j=1}^{q-1}\frac{q-j}{q}\sqrt{n}\hat{\rho}_j) \\
&= 4\sum_{j=1}^{q-1}\frac{(q-j)^2}{q^2}\mathrm{Var}_{as}(\sqrt{n}\hat{\rho}_j) \\
&= 4\sum_{j=1}^{q-1}\frac{(q-j)^2}{q^2} \\
&= 4(q-1) - \frac{8}{q}\sum_{j=1}^{q-1}j + \frac{4}{q^2}\sum_{j=1}^{q-1}j^2.
\end{aligned}
$$

With the summation formulas

$$
\sum_{j=1}^{q-1}j = (q-1)q/2
$$

and

$$
\sum_{j=1}^{q-1}j^2 = q(q-1)(2q-1)/6
$$

we finally obtain

$$
\mathrm{Var}_{as}\{\sqrt{n}VQ(q)\} = \frac{2(2q-1)(q-1)}{3q}.
$$

10.7   Recommended Literature

Four current Textbooks in the area of empirical financial market analysis are Mills (1993), Gouriéroux (1997), Campbell, Lo and MacKinlay (1997) and Gouriéroux and Jasiak (2002). The focus of Gouriéroux and Mills is more towards the econometric/time series analysis applications (which will also be followed in this book), whereas Campbell, Lo and MacKinlay discuss many economic applications that do not always end with statistical or econometric models. As an introduction and yet a comprehensive book on time series analysis Schlittgen and Streitberg (1995) is recommended. The same can be found with Copeland and Weston (1992), an introductory book on finance theory.

The experiment of the expectation hypotheses comes from Forsythe, Palfrey and Plott (1982). The definition of expectations and efficient markets is based on Jarrow (1992). The CAPM is developed in Sharpe (1964), Lintner (1965) and Mossin (1966). The discussion on the interest rate parity follows Jarchow and Rühmann (1994)[pp.236] and that of the term structure models of Cox-Ingersoll-Ross follow Ingersoll (1987). The standard option pricing model originated in Black and Scholes (1973). The market price of risk is discussed in Hull (2000),

A good overview of unit root tests is given in Hassler (1994). The ADF test is taken from Dickey and Fuller (1979).

11 ARIMA Time Series Models

In this chapter we will deal with the classical, linear time series analysis. At first we will define the general linear process.

Definition 11.1 (Linear Process)
If the process X_t has the representation

$$X_t = \mu + \sum_{i=-\infty}^{\infty} a_i \varepsilon_{t-i}$$

with white noise ε_t and absolute summability of the filter $(a_i) : \sum_{i=-\infty}^{\infty} |a_i| < \infty$, then it is a linear process.

The linear process X_t is covariance stationary, since $\mathsf{E}(X_t) = \mu$ and

$$\mathrm{Cov}(X_t, X_{t+\tau}) = \sigma^2 \sum_{i=-\infty}^{\infty} \sum_{j=-\infty}^{\infty} a_i a_j \mathbf{1}(\tau = i - j) = \sigma^2 \sum_{i=-\infty}^{\infty} a_i a_{i-\tau}$$

with $\mathrm{Var}(\varepsilon_t) = \sigma^2$.

In general in econometrics, especially in the area of financial markets, series are observed which indicate a non-stationary behavior. In the previous chapter we saw that econometric models, which are based on assumptions of rational expectations, frequently imply that the relevant levels of, for example, prices, follow a random walk. In order to handle these processes within the framework of the classical time series analysis, we must first form the differences in order to get a stationary process. We generalize the definition of a difference stationary process in the following definition.

Definition 11.2 (Integrated process)
We say that the process X_t is integrated of order d, $I(d)$, when $(1 - L)^{d-1} X_t$ is non-stationary and $(1 - L)^d X_t$ is stationary.

White noise is, for example, $I(0)$, a random walk $I(1)$. In only a few cases processes are observed that are $I(d)$ with $d > 1$. This means that in most cases first differences are enough to form a stationary process. In the following we assume that the observed process Y_t is $I(d)$ and we consider the transformed process $X_t = (1 - L)^d Y_t$, i.e., we will concentrate on stationary processes.

11.1   Moving Average Processes

The moving average process of order q, MA(q), is defined as

$$X_t = \beta_1 \varepsilon_{t-1} + \ldots + \beta_q \varepsilon_{t-q} + \varepsilon_t \tag{11.1}$$

with white noise ε_t. With the Lag-Operator L (see Definition 10.13) instead of (11.1) we can write

$$X_t = \beta(L)\varepsilon_t \tag{11.2}$$

with $\beta(L) = 1 + \beta_1 L + \ldots + \beta_q L^q$. The MA$(q)$ process is stationary, since it is formed as the linear combination of a stationary process. The mean function is simply $\mathsf{E}(X_t) = 0$. Let $\beta_0 = 1$, then the covariance structure is

$$
\begin{aligned}
\gamma_\tau &= \operatorname{Cov}(X_t, X_{t+\tau}) \\
&= \operatorname{Cov}(\sum_{i=0}^{q} \beta_i \varepsilon_{t-i}, \sum_{j=0}^{q} \beta_i \varepsilon_{t+\tau-j}) \\
&= \sum_{i=0}^{q} \sum_{j=0}^{q} \beta_i \beta_j \operatorname{Cov}(\varepsilon_{t-i}, \varepsilon_{t+\tau-j}) \\
&= \sum_{i=0}^{q-|\tau|} \beta_i \beta_{i+|\tau|} \sigma^2, \quad |\tau| \leq q.
\end{aligned}
$$

For the ACF we have for $|\tau| \leq q$

$$\rho_\tau = \frac{\sum_{i=0}^{q-|\tau|} \beta_i \beta_{i+|\tau|}}{\sum_{i=0}^{q} \beta_i^2}, \tag{11.3}$$

and $\rho_\tau = 0$ for $|\tau| > q$, i.e., the ACF breaks off after q lags.

As an example consider the MA(1) process

$$X_t = \beta \varepsilon_{t-1} + \varepsilon_t,$$

which according to (11.3) holds that $\rho_1 = \beta/(1 + \beta^2)$ and $\rho_\tau = 0$ for $\tau > 1$. Figure 11.1 shows the correlegram of a MA(1) process.

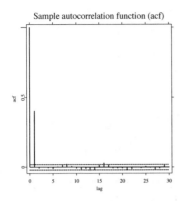
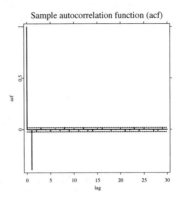

Figure 11.1:   ACF of a MA(1) process with $\beta = 0.5$ (left) and $\beta = -0.5$ (right).   Q SFEacfma1.xpl

Obviously the process

$$X_t = 1/\beta \varepsilon_{t-1} + \varepsilon_t$$

has the same ACF, and it holds that

$$\rho_1 = \frac{1/\beta}{1 + (1/\beta)^2} = \frac{\beta}{1 + \beta^2}.$$

In other words the process with the parameter β has the same stochastic properties as the process with the parameter $1/\beta$. This identification problem can be countered by requiring that the solutions of the characteristic equation

$$1 + \beta_1 z + \ldots + \beta_q z^q = 0 \tag{11.4}$$

lie outside of the complex unit circle. In this case the linear filter $\beta(L)$ is invertible, i.e., there exists a polynomial $\beta^{-1}(L)$ so that $\beta(L)\beta^{-1}(L) = 1$ and

$\beta^{-1}(L) = b_0 + b_1 L + b_2 L^2 + \ldots$. Figure 11.2 displays the correlogram of a MA(2) process $X_t = \beta_1 \varepsilon_{t-1} + \beta_2 \varepsilon_{t-2} + \varepsilon_t$ for some collections of parameters.

11.2   Autoregressive Process

The linear autoregressive process of order p, $(AR(p))$, is defined as

$$X_t = \nu + \alpha_1 X_{t-1} + \ldots + \alpha_p X_{t-p} + \varepsilon_t \tag{11.5}$$

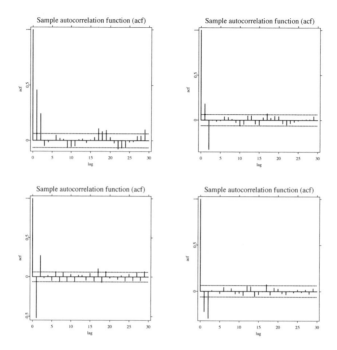

Figure 11.2: ACF of a MA(2) process with $(\beta_1 = 0.5, \beta_2 = 0.4)$ (top left),
$(\beta_1 = 0.5, \beta_2 = -0.4)$ (top right), $(\beta_1 = -0.5, \beta_2 = 0.4)$
(bottom left) and $(\beta_1 = -0.5, \beta_2 = -0.4)$ (bottom right).
                                                         Q SFEacfma2.xpl

Using the definition of the lag-operator L (see Definition 10.13), (11.5) can
also be written as
$$\alpha(L)X_t = \nu + \varepsilon_t,$$
with the lag-polynomial $\alpha(L) = 1 - \alpha_1 L - \ldots - \alpha_p L^p$. The process X_t is
stationary if all roots of the characteristic equation
$$\alpha(z) = 1 - \alpha_1 z - \ldots - \alpha_p z^p = 0. \tag{11.6}$$
lie outside of the complex unit circle, that is, if for all z with $|z| \le 1$ it holds
that
$$\alpha(z) \ne 0. \tag{11.7}$$
In this case there is an inverted filter $\alpha^{-1}(L)$ for the linear filter $\alpha(L)$, such
that the following holds,
$$\alpha(L)\alpha^{-1}(L) = 1$$

and

$$\alpha^{-1}(L) = a_0 + a_1 L + a_2 L^2 + \ldots = \sum_{i=0}^{\infty} a_i L^i.$$

The process (11.5) can also be written under the condition (11.7)

$$
\begin{aligned}
X_t &= \alpha^{-1}(1)\nu + \alpha^{-1}(L)\varepsilon_t \\
&= \sum_{i=0}^{\infty} a_i \nu + \sum_{i=0}^{\infty} a_i L^i \varepsilon_t,
\end{aligned}
$$

as a MA(∞) process.

A simple way to find and invert the autocovariance of an AR(p) process with given parameters is to use the Yule-Walker equations. They are derived from the definition of an AR(p) process in (11.5) by multiplying by $X_{t-\tau}$ and taking expectations.

$$\mathsf{E}[X_t X_{t-\tau}] = \alpha_1 \mathsf{E}[X_{t-1} X_{t-\tau}] + \ldots + \alpha_p \mathsf{E}[X_{t-p} X_{t-\tau}]. \qquad (11.8)$$

Since $\mathsf{E}[X_t X_{t-\tau}]$ is the definition of the autocovariance function γ_τ for $\nu = 0$, it can even be written simpler for $\tau = 1, \ldots, p$

$$
\begin{aligned}
\alpha_1 \gamma_0 &+ \alpha_2 \gamma_1 &+ \cdots &+ \alpha_p \gamma_{p-1} = \gamma_1 \\
\alpha_1 \gamma_1 &+ \alpha_2 \gamma_0 &+ \cdots &+ \alpha_p \gamma_{p-2} = \gamma_2 \\
&\cdots\cdots\cdots\cdots\cdots\cdots\cdots\cdots\cdots\cdots \\
\alpha_1 \gamma_{p-1} &+ \alpha_2 \gamma_{p-2} &+ \cdots &+ \alpha_p \gamma_0 \ = \gamma_p
\end{aligned}
\qquad (11.9)
$$

or by dividing by the variance γ_0

$$\rho = R\alpha \qquad (11.10)$$

with $\rho = (\rho_1 \rho_2 \ldots \rho_p)^\top$, $\alpha = (\alpha_1 \alpha_2 \ldots \alpha_p)^\top$, and the $p \times p$-autocovariance matrix

$$
R = \begin{pmatrix}
1 & \rho_1 & \cdots & \rho_{p-1} \\
\rho_1 & 1 & \cdots & \rho_{p-2} \\
\vdots & \vdots & \ddots & \vdots \\
\rho_{p-1} & \rho_{p-2} & \cdots & 1
\end{pmatrix}.
$$

The Yule-Walker equations are useful in determining the ACF for given parameters or, vice versa, in determining the estimated parameters for the given (empirical) autocorrelation.

Example 11.1 (AR(1))
The AR(1) process from Example 10.1 with $\nu = 0$ has the characteristic

equation $1 - \alpha z = 0$. The explicit solution $z = 1/\alpha$ and $|z| > 1$ occurs exactly when $|\alpha| < 1$. The inverse filter of $\alpha(L) = 1 - \alpha L$ is thus $\alpha^{-1}(L) = \sum_{i=0}^{\infty} \alpha^i L^i$ and the MA(∞) representation of the AR(1) process is

$$X_t = \sum_{i=0}^{\infty} \alpha^i \varepsilon_{t-i}.$$

The ACF of the AR(1) process is $\rho_\tau = \alpha^\tau$. For $\alpha > 0$ all autocorrelations are positive, for $\alpha < 0$ they alternate between positive and negative, see Figure 11.3.

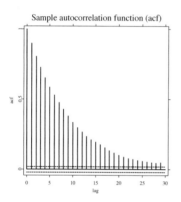 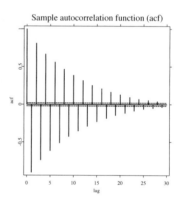

Figure 11.3:   ACF of an AR(1) process with $\alpha = 0.9$ (left) and $\alpha = -0.9$ (right).   ⌕ SFEacfar1.xpl

Example 11.2 (AR(2))
The AR(2) process with $\nu = 0$,

$$X_t = \alpha_1 X_{t-1} + \alpha_2 X_{t-2} + \varepsilon_t$$

is stationary when given the roots z_1 and z_2 of the quadratic equation

$$1 - \alpha_1 z - \alpha_2 z^2 = 0,$$

it holds that $|z_1| > 1$ and $|z_2| > 1$. We obtain solutions as

$$z_{1,2} = -\frac{\alpha_1}{2\alpha_2} \pm \sqrt{\frac{\alpha_1^2}{4\alpha_2^2} + \frac{1}{\alpha_2}}$$

and $z_1 z_2 = -1/\alpha_2$. Due to $|z_1| > 1$ and $|z_2| > 1$ it holds that $|z_1 z_2| = 1/|\alpha_2| > 1$ and

$$|\alpha_2| < 1. \tag{11.11}$$

From the Yule-Walker equations in the case of an AR(2) process

$$\rho_1 = \alpha_1 + \alpha_2 \rho_1 \tag{11.12}$$

$$\rho_2 = \alpha_1 \rho_1 + \alpha_2 \tag{11.13}$$

it follows that $\rho_1 = \alpha_1/(1 - \alpha_2)$. The case $\rho_1 = \pm 1$ is excluded because a root would lie on the unit circle (at 1 or -1). Thus for a stationary AR(2) process it must hold that

$$|\rho_1| = |\alpha_1/(1 - \alpha_2)| < 1,$$

from which, together with (11.11), we obtain the 'stationarity triangle'

$$\alpha_1 + \alpha_2 < 1 \tag{11.14}$$

$$\alpha_2 - \alpha_1 < 1 \tag{11.15}$$

i.e., the region in which the AR(2) process is stationary.

The ACF of the AR(2) process is recursively given with (11.12), (11.13) and $\rho_\tau = \alpha_1 \rho_{\tau-1} + \alpha_2 \rho_{\tau-2}$ for $\tau > 2$. Figure (11.4) displays typical patterns.

11.3 ARMA Models

The ARMA(p, q) model is defined as

$$X_t = \nu + \alpha_1 X_{t-1} + \ldots + \alpha_p X_{t-p} + \beta_1 \varepsilon_{t-1} + \ldots + \beta_q \varepsilon_{t-q} + \varepsilon_t, \tag{11.16}$$

or as

$$\alpha(L) X_t = \nu + \beta(L) \varepsilon_t$$

with the moving average lag-polynomial $\beta(L) = 1 + \beta_1 L + \ldots + \beta_q L^q$ and the autoregressive lag-polynomial $\alpha(L) = 1 - \alpha_1 L - \ldots - \alpha_p L^p$. So that the process (11.16) has an explicit parameterization, it is required that the characteristic polynomials $\alpha(z)$ and $\beta(z)$ do not have any common roots. The process (11.16) is stationary when all the roots of the characteristic equation (11.6) lie outside of the unit circle. In this case (11.16) has the MA(∞) representation

$$X_t = \alpha^{-1}(L) \beta(L) \varepsilon_t.$$

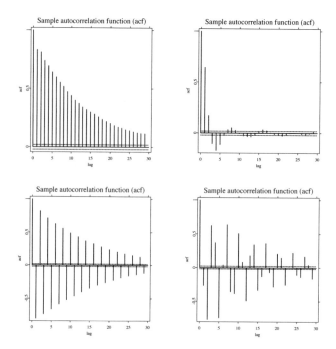

Figure 11.4: ACF of a AR(2) process with ($\alpha_1 = 0.5, \alpha_2 = 0.4$) (top left),
($\alpha_1 = 0.9, \alpha_2 = -0.4$) (top right), ($\alpha_1 = -0.4, \alpha_2 = 0.5$)
(bottom left) and ($\alpha_1 = -0.5, \alpha_2 = -0.9$) (bottom right).
                                                  Q SFEacfar2.xpl

The process X_t in (11.16) is invertible when all the roots of the characteristic
equation (11.4) lie outside of the unit circle. In this case (11.16) can be
written as

$$\beta^{-1}(L)\alpha(L)X_t = \varepsilon_t,$$

that is an AR(∞) process. Thus we can approximate every stationary, invertible ARMA(p, q) process with a pure AR or MA process of sufficiently
large order. Going the other direction, an ARMA(p, q) process offers the
possibility of parsimonious parameterization.

11.4   Partial Autocorrelation

For a given stochastic process one is often interested in the connection between two random variables of a process at different points in time. One way to measure a linear relationship is with the ACF, i.e., the correlation between these two variables. Another way to measure the connection between X_t and $X_{t+\tau}$ is to filter out of X_t and $X_{t+\tau}$ the linear influence of the random variables that lie in between, $X_{t+1}, \ldots, X_{t+\tau-1}$, and then calculate the correlation of the transformed random variables. This is called the *partial autocorrelation*.

Definition 11.3 (Partial autocorrelation)
The partial autocorrelation of k−th order is defined as

$$
\begin{aligned}
\phi_{kk} \;=\; & Corr(X_t - \mathcal{P}(X_t \mid X_{t+1}, \ldots, X_{t+k-1}), \\
& X_{t+k} - \mathcal{P}(X_{t+k} \mid X_{t+1}, \ldots, X_{t+k-1})) \qquad (11.17)
\end{aligned}
$$

where $\mathcal{P}(W \mid Z)$ is the best linear projection of W on Z, i.e., $\mathcal{P}(W \mid Z) = \Sigma_{WZ}\Sigma_{ZZ}^{-1}Z$ with $\Sigma_{ZZ} = Var(Z)$ as the covariance matrix of the regressors and $\Sigma_{WZ} = Cov(W, Z)$ as the matrix of covariances between W and Z.

The 'best linear projection' is understood in the sense of minimizing the mean squared error.

An equivalent definition is the solution to the system of equations

$$
P_k \phi_k = \rho_{(k)}
$$

with

$$
P_k =
\begin{pmatrix}
1 & \rho_1 & \cdots & \rho_{k-1} \\
\rho_1 & 1 & \cdots & \rho_{k-2} \\
\vdots & \vdots & \ddots & \vdots \\
\rho_{k-1} & \rho_{k-2} & \cdots & 1
\end{pmatrix}
$$

$\phi_k = (\phi_{k1}, \ldots, \phi_{kk})^\top$ and $\rho_{(k)} = (\rho_1, \ldots, \rho_k)^\top$. These are the Yule-Walker equations for an AR(k) process. The last coefficient, ϕ_{kk}, is the partial autocorrelation of order k, as defined above. Since only this coefficient is of interest in this context, the system of equations can be solved for ϕ_{kk} using the Cramer-Rule. We get

$$
\phi_{kk} = \frac{|P_k^*|}{|P_k|}
$$

where P_k^* is equal to the matrix P_k, in which the k−th column is replaced with $\rho_{(k)}$. Here $|.|$ indicates the determinant. Since this can be applied for various orders k, in the end we obtain a *partial autocorrelation function* (PACF). The PACF can be graphically displayed for a given stochastic process, similar to the ACF as a function of order k. This is called the partial autocorrelogram.

From the definition of PACF it immediately follows that there is no difference between PACF and ACF of order 1:

$$\phi_{11} = \rho_1.$$

For order 2 we have

$$\phi_{22} = \frac{\begin{vmatrix} 1 & \rho_1 \\ \rho_1 & \rho_2 \end{vmatrix}}{\begin{vmatrix} 1 & \rho_1 \\ \rho_1 & 1 \end{vmatrix}} = \frac{\rho_2 - \rho_1^2}{1 - \rho_1^2} \qquad (11.18)$$

Example 11.3 (AR(1))
The AR(1) process $X_t = \alpha X_{t-1} + \varepsilon_t$ has the ACF $\rho_\tau = \alpha^\tau$. For the PACF we have $\phi_{11} = \rho_1 = \alpha$ and

$$\phi_{22} = \frac{\rho_2 - \rho_1^2}{1 - \rho_1^2} = \frac{\alpha^2 - \alpha^2}{1 - \alpha^2} = 0,$$

and $\phi_{kk} = 0$ for all $k > 1$. This is plausible since the last coefficient of an AR(k) model for this process is zero for all $k > 1$. For $k = 2$ we illustrate the equivalence with Definition 11.3: From $X_t = \alpha X_{t-1} + \varepsilon_t$ we directly obtain $\mathcal{P}(X_{t+2}|X_{t+1}) = \alpha X_{t+1}$ with

$$\alpha = \frac{Cov(X_{t+2}, X_{t+1})}{Var(X_{t+1})}.$$

From the 'backward regression' $X_t = \alpha' X_{t+1} + \eta_t$ with white noise η_t it further follows that $\mathcal{P}(X_t|X_{t+1}) = \alpha' X_{t+1}$ with

$$\alpha' = \frac{Cov(X_t, X_{t+1})}{Var(X_{t+1})}.$$

For $|\alpha| < 1$ the process is covariance-stationary and it holds that $Cov(X_{t+2}, X_{t+1}) = Cov(X_t, X_{t+1}) = \gamma_1$ and $\alpha = \alpha' = \rho_1$. We obtain

$$\begin{aligned} & Cov\{X_t - \mathcal{P}(X_t|X_{t+1}), X_{t+2} - \mathcal{P}(X_{t+2}|X_{t+1})\} \\ = \ & Cov(X_t - \rho_1 X_{t+1}, X_{t+2} - \rho_1 X_{t+1}) \\ = \ & \mathsf{E}[(X_t - \rho_1 X_{t+1})(X_{t+2} - \rho_1 X_{t+1})] \\ = \ & \gamma_2 - 2\rho_1 \gamma_1 + \rho_1^2 \gamma_0 \end{aligned}$$

and

$$
\begin{aligned}
Var\{X_{t+2} - \mathcal{P}(X_{t+2}|X_{t+1})\} &= \mathsf{E}[(X_{t+2} - \rho_1 X_{t+1})^2] \\
&= \gamma_0(1 + \rho_1^2) - 2\rho_1\gamma_1 \\
&= \mathsf{E}[(X_t - \rho_1 X_{t+1})^2] \\
&= Var[X_t - \mathcal{P}(X_t|X_{t+1})].
\end{aligned}
$$

With this we get for the partial autocorrelation of 2nd order

$$
\begin{aligned}
\phi_{22} &= Corr\{X_t - \mathcal{P}(X_t|X_{t+1}), X_{t+2} - \mathcal{P}(X_{t+2}|X_{t+1})\} \\
&= \frac{Cov\{X_t - \mathcal{P}(X_t|X_{t+1}), X_{t+2} - \mathcal{P}(X_{t+2}|X_{t+1})\}}{\sqrt{Var\{X_{t+2} - \mathcal{P}(X_{t+2}|X_{t+1})\}}\sqrt{Var(X_t - \mathcal{P}(X_t|X_{t+1}))}} \\
&= \frac{\gamma_2 - 2\rho_1\gamma_1 + \rho_1^2\gamma_0}{\gamma_0(1 + \rho_1^2) - 2\gamma_1\rho_1} \\
&= \frac{\rho_2 - \rho_1^2}{1 - \rho_1^2}
\end{aligned}
$$

which corresponds to the results in (11.18). For the AR(1) process it holds that $\rho_2 = \rho_1^2$ and thus $\phi_{22} = 0$.

It holds in general for AR(p) processes that $\phi_{kk} = 0$ for all $k > p$. In Figure 11.5 the PACF of an AR(2) process is displayed using the parameters as in Figure 11.4.

Example 11.4 (MA(1))
For a MA(1) process $X_t = \beta\varepsilon_{t-1} + \varepsilon_t$ with $Var(\varepsilon_t) = \sigma^2$ it holds that $\gamma_0 = \sigma^2(1 + \beta^2)$, $\rho_1 = \beta/(1 + \beta^2)$ and $\rho_k = 0$ for all $k > 1$. For the partial autocorrelations we obtain $\phi_{11} = \rho_1$ and

$$
\phi_{22} = \frac{\begin{vmatrix} 1 & \rho_1 \\ \rho_1 & 0 \end{vmatrix}}{\begin{vmatrix} 1 & \rho_1 \\ \rho_1 & 1 \end{vmatrix}} = -\frac{\rho_1^2}{1 - \rho_1^2} \tag{11.19}
$$

For a MA(1) process it strictly holds that $\phi_{22} < 0$. If one were to continue the calculation with $k > 2$, one could determine that the partial autocorrelations will not reach zero.

Figure 11.6 shows the PACF of a MA(2) process. In general for a MA(q) process it holds that the PACF does not decay, in contrast to the autoregressive process. Compare the PACF to the ACF in Figure 11.2. This is thus a possible criterium for the specification of a linear model.

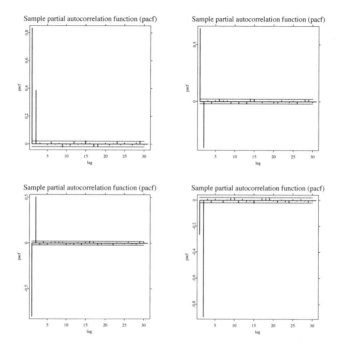

Figure 11.5:   PACF of an AR(2) process with $(\alpha_1 = 0.5, \alpha_2 = 0.4)$ (top
left), $(\alpha_1 = 0.9, \alpha_2 = -0.4)$ (top right), $(\alpha_1 = -0.4, \alpha_2 = 0.5)$
(bottom left) and $(\alpha_1 = -0.5, \alpha_2 = -0.9)$ (bottom right).
Q SFEpacfar2.xpl

11.5   Estimation Moments

In the following we assume a stationary stochastic process X_t, i.e., $\mathsf{E}[X_t] = \mu$
and $\mathrm{Cov}(X_t, X_{t+\tau}) = \gamma_\tau$. In the previous sections, we have assumed that we
knew the process and thus the moment generating function was also known.
In practice one observes only a realization of the process, $X_1, \ldots, X_n$, and
thus there is the problem of estimating the moment generating function.

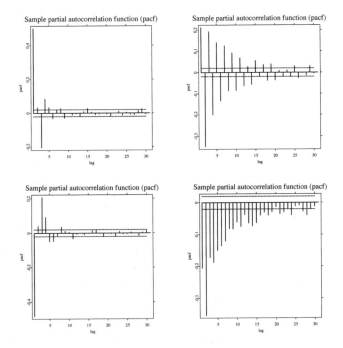

Figure 11.6:   PACF of a MA(2) process with $(\beta_1 = 0.5, \beta_2 = 0.4)$ (top left), $(\beta_1 = 0.5, \beta_2 = -0.4)$ (top right), $(\beta_1 = -0.5, \beta_2 = 0.4)$ (bottom left) and $(\beta_1 = -0.5, \beta_2 = -0.4)$ (bottom right).

Q SFEpacfma2.xpl

11.5.1   Estimation of the Mean Function

The parameter $\mu = \mathsf{E}[X_t]$ can be estimated with the simple arithmetic sample mean:

$$\bar{X}_n = 1/n \sum_{i=1}^{n} X_i. \qquad (11.20)$$

The estimator $\bar{X}_n$ is unbiased since it holds that $\mathsf{E}[\bar{X}_n] = \mu$, and its variance is

$$
\begin{aligned}
\mathrm{Var}(\bar{X}_n) &= \mathrm{Var}(1/n \sum_{i=1}^{n} X_i) \\
&= 1/n^2 \sum_{t=1}^{n} \sum_{s=1}^{n} \mathrm{Cov}(X_t, X_s) \\
&= 1/n^2 \sum_{t=1}^{n} \sum_{s=1}^{n} \gamma_{t-s} \\
&= 1/n \sum_{\tau=-(n-1)}^{n-1} \frac{n - |\tau|}{n} \gamma_\tau
\end{aligned}
$$

When the autocovariance function γ_τ is absolutely summable, it holds that $\mathrm{Var}(\bar{X}_n) < \infty$ and $\lim_{n\to\infty} \mathrm{Var}(\bar{X}_n) = 0$. The estimator X is then also a consistent estimator for μ. In many cases there are more efficient estimators which take advantage of the correlation structure of the process.

The asymptotic variance

$$
\lim_{n\to\infty} n\,\mathrm{Var}(\bar{X}_n) = \gamma_0 + 2\sum_{\tau=1}^{\infty} \gamma_\tau
$$

is denoted as $f(0)$, since this is exactly the spectral density at frequency zero. Under the absolute summability of γ_τ the following asymptotic distribution for the estimator holds:

$$
\sqrt{n}(\bar{X}_n - \mu) \xrightarrow{\mathcal{L}} \mathrm{N}(0, f(0)). \tag{11.21}
$$

11.5.2   Estimation of the Covariance Function

A possible estimator of the covariance function γ_τ is

$$
\hat{\gamma}_{\tau,n} = \frac{1}{n} \sum_{t=1}^{n-\tau} (X_t - \bar{X}_n)(X_{t+\tau} - \bar{X}_n) \tag{11.22}
$$

with the mean estimator $\bar{X}_n$ from (11.20). Instead of dividing by n in (11.22) one could also divide by $n - \tau$, although the estimator would then have less favorable properties. The estimator $\hat{\gamma}_{\tau,n}$ is no longer unbiased, since the following can be shown.

$$
\mathsf{E}[\hat{\gamma}_{\tau,n}] = \left(1 - \frac{\tau}{n}\right)\gamma_\tau - \left(1 - \frac{\tau}{n}\right)\mathrm{Var}(\bar{X}_n) + \mathcal{O}(n^{-2}).
$$

Positive autocovariances are in general underestimated with $\hat{\gamma}_{\tau,n}$. Asymptotically $\hat{\gamma}_{\tau,n}$ is nevertheless unbiased: $\lim_{n\to\infty} E[\hat{\gamma}_{\tau,n}] = \gamma_{\tau}$. For the variance when terms of higher order are ignored it holds that

$$\text{Var}(\hat{\gamma}_{\tau,n}) = \frac{1}{n}\sum_{j=-\infty}^{\infty}(\gamma_j^2 + \gamma_{j-\tau}\gamma_{j+\tau}) + \mathcal{O}(n^{-1}) = \frac{1}{n}\sigma_{\tau,\infty}^2 + \mathcal{O}(n^{-1})$$

and since $\lim_{n\to\infty}\text{Var}(\hat{\gamma}_{\tau,n}) = 0$ holds, $\hat{\gamma}_{\tau,n}$ is a consistent estimator for γ_{τ}. Furthermore, it can be shown that the covariance estimator behaves asymptotically like a normally distributed random variable:

$$\sqrt{n}(\hat{\gamma}_{\tau,n} - \gamma_{\tau}) \xrightarrow{\mathcal{L}} N(0, \sigma_{\tau,\infty}^2).$$

11.5.3 Estimation of the ACF

An obvious estimator for the ACF ρ_{τ} is

$$\hat{\rho}_{\tau,n} = \frac{\hat{\gamma}_{\tau,n}}{\hat{\gamma}_{0,n}}. \tag{11.23}$$

Once again we have a bias of order $1/n$, i.e.,

$$E(\hat{\rho}_{\tau,n}) = \rho_{\tau} + \mathcal{O}(n^{-1})$$

and $\hat{\rho}_{\tau,n}$ is asymptotically unbiased. For the variance it holds that

$$\text{Var}(\hat{\rho}_{\tau,n}) = \frac{1}{n}\Sigma_{\rho,\tau\tau} + \mathcal{O}(n^{-2}).$$

The estimator $\hat{\rho}_{\tau,n}$ is consistent, since $\lim_{n\to\infty}\text{Var}(\hat{\rho}_{\tau,n}) = 0$. For the asymptotic distribution of the vector $\hat{\rho}_{(k),n} = (\hat{\rho}_{1,n}, \ldots, \hat{\rho}_{k,n})^{\top}$ it can be shown that

$$\sqrt{n}(\hat{\rho}_{(k),n} - \rho_{(k)}) \xrightarrow{\mathcal{L}} N(0, \Sigma_{\rho})$$

with the covariance matrix Σ_{ρ} with the typical element

$$\begin{aligned}
\Sigma_{\rho,kl} &= \sum_{j=-\infty}^{\infty}\rho_j\rho_{j+k+l} + \sum_{j=-\infty}^{\infty}\rho_j\rho_{j+k-l} \\
&+ 2\rho_k\rho_l\sum_{j=-\infty}^{\infty}\rho_j^2 - 2\rho_l\sum_{j=-\infty}^{\infty}\rho_j\rho_{j+k} - 2\rho_k\sum_{j=-\infty}^{\infty}\rho_j\rho_{j+l}.
\end{aligned}$$

In particular for the asymptotic variance of $\sqrt{n}(\hat{\rho}_{\tau,n} - \rho_\tau)$, it holds that

$$
\begin{aligned}
\Sigma_{\rho,\tau\tau} &= \sum_{j=-\infty}^{\infty} \rho_j \rho_{j+2\tau} + \sum_{j=-\infty}^{\infty} \rho_j^2 \\
&+ 2\rho_\tau^2 \sum_{j=-\infty}^{\infty} \rho_j^2 - 4\rho_\tau \sum_{j=-\infty}^{\infty} \rho_j \rho_{j+\tau}.
\end{aligned}
$$

Example 11.5 (MA(q))

For the MA(q) process in (11.1) we know that $\rho_\tau = 0$ for all $\tau > q$. Thus the asymptotic variance can be simplified from $\sqrt{n}(\hat{\rho}_{\tau,n} - \rho_\tau)$ for $\tau > q$ to

$$
\Sigma_{\rho,\tau\tau} = 1 + 2 \sum_{i=1}^{q} \rho_i^2.
$$

Example 11.6 (white noise)

If X_t is white noise, it holds that

$$
\mathsf{E}(\hat{\rho}_{\tau,n}) = -\frac{1}{n} + \mathcal{O}(n^{-2})
$$

and

$$
Var(\hat{\rho}_{\tau,n}) = \frac{1}{n} + \mathcal{O}(n^{-2})
$$

for $\tau \neq 0$. The asymptotic covariance matrix of $\sqrt{n}(\hat{\rho}_{(k),n} - \rho_{(k)})$ is the identity matrix. Using this we can build approximately 95% confidence intervals for the ACF: $[-\frac{1}{n} \pm \frac{2}{\sqrt{n}}]$.

11.6   Portmanteau Statistics

With the help of the knowledge about the asymptotic distribution of the autocorrelations we can derive a statistic to test the hypothesis of white noise. One can either test the original series X_t or the residuals of an ARMA(p,q) process. The number of estimated parameters is in the first case $k = 0$ and in the second case $k = p + q$.

Under the null hypothesis it holds for every m

$$
\rho_1 = 0, \ldots, \rho_m = 0.
$$

The alternative hypothesis is accordingly, that at least one ρ_i, $1 \leq i \leq m$ is not equal to zero. Under the null hypothesis $\sqrt{n}\hat{\rho}_{\tau,n}$ is asymptotically standard normally distributed. The statistic

$$Q_m = n \sum_{j=1}^{m} \hat{\rho}_{j,n}^2$$

has an asymptotic χ^2 distribution with $m - k$ degrees of freedom. One would reject the null hypothesis at a significance level of α, as long as $Q_m > \chi^2_{m-k;\alpha}$, the $(1 - \alpha)$-quantile of the Chi-squared distribution with $m - k$ degrees of freedom.

Studies show that Q_m in small samples poorly approximates the asymptotic distribution. This results from the fact that $\hat{\rho}_{\tau,n}$ is a biased estimator for ρ_τ. The bias is stronger for small τ, and thus an asymptotically equivalent statistic can be defined as

$$Q_m^* = n(n+2) \sum_{j=1}^{m} \frac{1}{n-j} \hat{\rho}_{j,n}^2$$

which weights the empirical autocorrelations of smaller order less than those of larger order. The modified Portmanteau statistic Q_m^* is therefore in small samples frequently closer to the asymptotic χ^2 distribution. For large n, both statistics performs equally well.

11.7   Estimation of AR(p) Models

A simple way to estimate the parameters of the autoregressive model

$$X_t = \alpha_1 X_{t-1} + \ldots + \alpha_p X_{t-p} + \varepsilon_t$$

with $\text{Var}(\varepsilon_t) = \sigma^2$, is to use the Yule-Walker equations from (11.10), where the theoretical autocorrelation is replaced with the empirical:

$$\begin{pmatrix} 1 & \hat{\rho}_1 & \cdots & \hat{\rho}_{p-1} \\ \hat{\rho}_1 & 1 & \cdots & \hat{\rho}_{p-2} \\ \vdots & \vdots & \ddots & \vdots \\ \hat{\rho}_{p-1} & \hat{\rho}_{p-2} & \cdots & 1 \end{pmatrix} \begin{pmatrix} \hat{\alpha}_1 \\ \hat{\alpha}_2 \\ \vdots \\ \hat{\alpha}_p \end{pmatrix} = \begin{pmatrix} \hat{\rho}_1 \\ \hat{\rho}_2 \\ \vdots \\ \hat{\rho}_p \end{pmatrix}.$$

Solving for $\hat{\alpha}$ gives the Yule-Walker estimator. It is consistent and has an asymptotic normal distribution with covariance matrix $\sigma^2\Gamma^{-1}$,

$$
\Gamma = \begin{pmatrix}
\gamma_0 & \gamma_1 & \cdots & \gamma_{p-1} \\
\gamma_1 & \gamma_0 & \cdots & \gamma_{p-2} \\
\vdots & \vdots & \ddots & \vdots \\
\gamma_{p-1} & \gamma_{p-2} & \cdots & \gamma_0
\end{pmatrix}, \tag{11.24}
$$

The Yule-Walker estimators are asymptotically equivalent to other estimators such as the least squares estimator, in the special case of normally distributed ε_t and the maximum likelihood estimator for the normally distributed X_t. In this case, these estimators are also asymptotically efficient.

11.8   Estimation of MA(q) and ARMA(p, q) Models

As soon as *moving average* coefficients are included in an estimated model, the estimation turns out to be more difficult. Consider the example of a simple MA(1) model

$$
X_t = \beta\varepsilon_{t-1} + \varepsilon_t \tag{11.25}
$$

with $|\beta| < 1$ and $\mathrm{Var}(\varepsilon_t) = \sigma^2$. A simple estimator for the parameter β is obtained from the Yule-Walker equations $\gamma_0 = \sigma^2(1 + \beta^2)$ and $\gamma_1 = \beta\sigma^2$. By dividing both equations we get $\rho_1 = \gamma_1/\gamma_0 = \beta/(1 + \beta^2)$ and the solution to the quadratic equation is

$$
\beta = \frac{1}{2\rho_1} \pm \sqrt{\frac{1}{4\rho_1^2} - 1}. \tag{11.26}
$$

The Yule-Walker estimator replaces in (11.26) the theoretical autocorrelation of 1st order ρ_1 with the estimator $\hat{\rho}_1$. The estimator is quite simple, but has the disadvantage that it is asymptotically inefficient.

The least squares estimator leads to non-linear systems of equations, that can only be solved with iterative numerical algorithms. Using the example of a MA(1) process (11.25) this is illustrated: The LS estimator is defined by

$$
\hat{\beta} = \arg\min_{\beta} \sum_{t=2}^{n} \varepsilon_t^2 = \arg\min_{\beta} \sum_{t=2}^{n} (X_t - \beta\varepsilon_{t-1})^2 \tag{11.27}
$$

Given that ε_t is not observed, one must turn to the $\mathrm{AR}(\infty)$ representation
of the MA(1) process in order to find the solution, i.e.,

$$\varepsilon_t = X_t + \sum_{k=1}^{\infty} (-\beta)^k X_{t-k}. \tag{11.28}$$

Given $X_1, \ldots, X_n$, (11.28) can be approximated by

$$\varepsilon_t = X_t + \sum_{k=1}^{t-1} (-\beta)^k X_{t-k}.$$

Solving the first order conditions

$$\frac{\partial}{\partial \beta} \sum_{t=2}^{n} \varepsilon_t^2 = 0,$$

we obtain a non-linear equation for β, which cannot be explicitly solved.
For the minimization problem (11.27) one usually implements numerical optimization methods. The least squares estimator is asymptotically efficient
and has asymptotically the same properties as the maximum likelihood (ML)
estimator.

In the following we assume a stationary and invertible $\mathrm{ARMA}(p, q)$ process
with the $\mathrm{AR}(\infty)$ representation

$$X_t = \sum_{j=1}^{\infty} \pi_j X_{t-j} + \varepsilon_t.$$

Maximum likelihood estimation allude to the distribution assumptions

$$\varepsilon_t \sim \mathrm{N}(0, \sigma^2),$$

under which $X = (X_1, \ldots, X_n)^\top$ have multivariate normal distributions with
a density

$$p(x \mid \theta) = (2\pi\sigma^2)^{-n/2} |\Gamma|^{-1/2} \exp\left(-\frac{1}{2\sigma^2} x^\top \Gamma^{-1} x\right)$$

with covariance matrix Γ, which is given in (11.24), and the parameter vector

$$\theta = (\alpha_1, \ldots, \alpha_p, \beta_1, \ldots, \beta_q; \sigma^2)^\top.$$

The likelihood function L is then a density function interpreted as a function
of the parameter vector θ for given observations, i.e., $L(\theta \mid x) = p(x \mid \theta)$.

One chooses the respective parameter vector that maximizes the likelihood function for the given observations, i.e., the ML estimator is defined by

$$\hat{\theta} = \arg\max_{\theta \in \Theta} L(\theta \mid x).$$

Under the assumption of the normal distribution the logarithm of the likelihood function

$$\log L(\theta \mid x) = -\frac{n}{2}\log(2\pi\sigma^2) - \frac{1}{2}\log|\Gamma| - \frac{1}{2\sigma^2}x^\top\Gamma^{-1}x \qquad (11.29)$$

takes on a simple form without changing the maximizer $\hat{\theta}$. The log-likelihood function (11.29) is also called the *exact* log-likelihood function. One notices that, in particular, the calculation of the inverse and the determinant of the $(n \times n)$ matrix Γ is quite involved for long time series. Therefore one often forms an approximation to the exact likelihood, which are good for long time series. One possibility is use the *conditional* distribution $p(X_t \mid X_{t-1}, \ldots, X_1; \theta)$:

$$L(\theta \mid x) = \prod_{t=1}^{n} p(X_t \mid X_{t-1}, \ldots, X_1; \theta)$$

Under the assumption of normal distributions the conditional distributions are normal with an expected value

$$\mathsf{E}[X_t \mid X_{t-1}, \ldots, X_1]$$

and variance

$$\mathrm{Var}(X_t \mid X_{t-1}, \ldots, X_1).$$

The larger t is, the better the approximation of

$$\mathsf{E}[X_t \mid X_{t-1}, \ldots, X_1, \ldots] = \sum_{j=1}^{\infty} \pi_j X_{t-j}$$

by $\sum_{j=1}^{t-1} \pi_j X_{t-j}$ becomes. The conditional log-likelihood function

$$\log L^b(\theta \mid x) = -\frac{n}{2}\log(2\pi\sigma^2) - \frac{1}{2}\log\sigma^2 - \frac{1}{2\sigma^2}\sum_{t=1}^{n}\left(X_t - \sum_{j=1}^{t-1}\pi_j X_{t-j}\right)^2 \quad (11.30)$$

can be calculated from the data $X_1, \ldots, X_n$ and optimized with respect to the parameter θ. As an initial value for the numerical optimization algorithm the Yule-Walker estimators, for example, can be used (except in specific cases of asymptotic inefficiency).

To compare the exact and the conditional likelihood estimators consider a MA(1) process (11.25) with $\beta = 0.5$ and $\varepsilon_t \sim N(0,1)$. The matrix Γ is band diagonal with elements $1 + \beta^2$ on the main diagonal and β on diagonals both above and below it. Two realizations of the process with $n = 10$ and $n = 20$ are shown in Figure 11.7. Since the process has only one parameter, one can simply search in the region (-1,1). This is shown for both estimators in Figure 11.8 ($n = 10$) and 11.9 ($n = 20$). For the process with $n = 10$ one still sees a clear discrepancy between both likelihood functions, which for $n = 20$ can be ignored. Both estimators are in this case quite close to the true parameter 0.5.

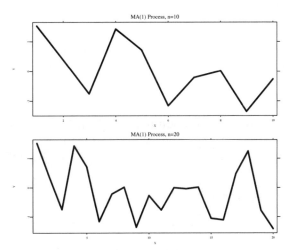

Figure 11.7: Two realizations of a MA(1) process with $\beta = 0.5$, $\varepsilon_t \sim N(0,1)$, $n = 10$ (above) and $n = 20$ (below). **Q** SFEplotma1.xpl

Under some technical assumptions the ML estimators are consistent, asymptotically efficient and have an asymptotic normal distribution:

$$\sqrt{n}(\hat{\theta} - \theta) \xrightarrow{\mathcal{L}} N(0, J^{-1})$$

with the Fisher Information matrix

$$J = \mathsf{E}\left[-\frac{\partial^2 \log L(\theta, x)}{\partial\theta\partial\theta^\top}\right]. \qquad (11.31)$$

For the optimization of the likelihood function one frequently uses numerical

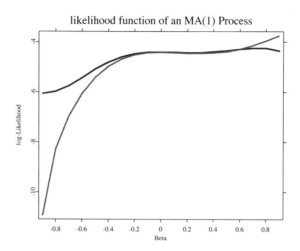

Figure 11.8: Exact (solid) and conditional (dashed) likelihood functions for the MA(1) process from figure 11.7 with $n = 10$. The true parameter is $\beta = 0.5$.   Q SFElikma1.xpl

methods. The necessary condition for a maximum is

$$\text{grad } l^b(\theta) = 0$$

with $l^b = \log L(\theta \mid x)$. By choosing an initial value θ_0 (for example, the Yule-Walker estimator), and the Taylor approximation

$$\text{grad } l^b(\theta) \approx \text{grad } l^b(\theta_0) + \text{Hess } l^b(\theta_0)(\theta - \theta_0)$$

one obtains the following relation:

$$\theta = \theta_0 - \text{Hess } l^b(\theta_0)^{-1}\text{grad } l^b(\theta_0).$$

Since generally one does not immediately hit the maximizing parameter, one builds the iteration

$$\theta_{j+1} = \theta_j - \text{Hess } l^b(\theta_j)^{-1}\text{grad } l^b(\theta_j)$$

with $j = 1, 2, \ldots$ until a convergence is reached, i.e., $\theta_{j+1} \approx \theta_j$. Often it is easier to use the expectation of the Hessian matrix, that is, the information matrix from (11.31):

$$\theta_{j+1} = \theta_j + J(\theta_j)^{-1}\text{grad } l^b(\theta_j). \tag{11.32}$$

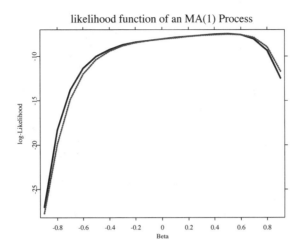

Figure 11.9: Exact (solid) and conditional (dashed) likelihood functions for
the MA(1) process from figure 11.7 with $n = 20$. The true
parameter is $\beta = 0.5$.   **Q** SFElikma1.xpl

The notation $J(\theta_j)$ here means that (11.31) is evaluated at θ_j. The iteration
(11.32) is called the *score*-algorithm or Fisher scoring.

11.9 Recommended Literature

Comprehensive textbooks on classical time series analysis are, for example,
Schlittgen and Streitberg (1995), Brockwell and Davis (1991), Gouriéroux
and Monfort (1996). In addition, classical books are Box and Jenkins (1976)
and Hamilton (1994).

12 Time Series with Stochastic Volatility

In the previous chapters we have already indicated that volatility plays an important role in modelling financial systems and time series. Unlike the term structure, volatility is unobservable and thus must be estimated from the data.

Reliable estimation and forecast of volatility are important for large credit institutes where volatility is directly used to measure risk. The risk premium for example is often specified as a function of volatility. It is interesting to find an appropriate model for volatility. In the literature, the capability of macroeconomic factors to forecast volatility has been examined. Although macroeconomic factors have some forecasting capabilities, the most important factor seems to be the lagged endogenous return. As a result recent studies are mainly concentrated on time series models.

Stock, exchange rate, interest rate and other financial time series have *stylized facts* that are different from other time series. A good candidate for modelling financial time series should represent the properties of the stochastic processes. Neither the classical linear AR or ARMA processes nor the nonlinear generalizations can fulfil the task. In this chapter we will describe the most popular volatility class of models: the ARCH (*autoregressive conditional heteroscedasticity*) model that can replicate these stylized facts appropriately.

Stylized fact 1: *Time series of share prices X_t and other basic financial instruments are not stationary time series and possess at least a local trend.*

Similar to the ARIMA model in Chapter 11, we transform the original data by taking first differences to get a stationary time series. Here we consider the log return (see Definition 10.15) instead of the original share prices. We simply call it *return* in this chapter. One could consider the simple return R_t as well (see Definition 10.14).

Stylized fact 2: *Returns r_t have a leptokurtic distribution. The empirically estimated kurtosis is mostly greater than 3.*

We have discussed the properties of the return's distribution in Section 3.3 and Section 10.2. The leptokurtosis can be illustrated in a comparison of the density of a normal distribution and a kernel estimator of the adjusted data (see Figure 14.1). We can see in Theorem 12.3 that an ARCH process has a kurtosis greater than 3 even if the innovation of the process itself is normally distributed.

Stylized fact 3: *The return process is white noise (Definition 10.8) since the sample autocorrelation $\hat{\rho}_{\tau,n}, k \neq 0$ (11.23) is not significantly different from 0. Furthermore the white noise is not independent since the sample autocorrelations of squared and absolute returns are clearly greater than 0.*

ARCH models possess the characteristic (Theorem 12.1) that we have already described in Section 10.2. A stronger condition than pairwise uncorrelation of returns is that returns are unpredictable, which is connected to the no arbitrage condition. As in Section 10.3 $\mathcal{F}_t$ denotes the information set at time t. The best prediction of return r_{t+1} at day t for day $t + 1$ is the conditional expectation $r_{t+1|t} = \mathsf{E}[r_{t+1}|\mathcal{F}_t]$ (Theorem 10.1) based on the information set $\mathcal{F}_t$. The time series of the return is called unpredictable if

$$r_{t+1|t} = \mathsf{E}[r_{t+1}|\mathcal{F}_t] = \mathsf{E}[r_{t+1}],$$

i.e. the best prediction of the next return is simply its unconditional mean. The information set $\mathcal{F}_t$ gives no hints for predicting future prices. ARCH processes are automatically unpredictable (Definition 12.1).

An unpredictable time series is always white noise because the autocorrelation is equal to 0. It is even possible that a linear prediction is better than the expectation estimated only by the unpredictable time series (see the proof of Theorem 12.1). The condition of unpredictability is actually stronger than pairwise uncorrelation. A predictable white noise is for example $\varepsilon_t = \eta_t + \gamma\eta_{t-1}\eta_{t-2}$, where η_t is independent white noise with expectation of 0. This bilinear process has vanishing autocorrelations but $\mathsf{E}[\varepsilon_{t+1}|\mathcal{F}_t] = \gamma\eta_t\eta_{t-1} \neq 0 = \mathsf{E}[\varepsilon_{t+1}]$.

If the returns were predictable we could develop a trading strategy based on the resulting predictions of price, which would give us a positive profit. The existence of a stochastic arbitrage probability obviously contradicts the assumption of a perfect financial market (Section 2.1).

Stylized fact 4: *Volatility tends to form cluster: After a large (small) price change (positive or negative) a large (small) price change tends to occur. This effect is called volatility clustering.*

We will consider the properties of financial time series in more detail in the following section. According to the stylized fact 4, the squared returns are positively correlated. Thus returns are conditionally heteroscedastic i.e.

$$\text{Var}[r_{t+1}|\mathcal{F}_t] \neq \text{Var}[r_{t+1}].$$

The returns r_t are not independent but their variability depends on recent changes of price.

12.1 ARCH and GARCH Models

After the introduction of ARCH models there were enormous theoretical and practical developments in financial econometrics in the eighties. It became clear that ARCH models could efficiently and quite easily represent the typical empirical findings in financial time series, e.g. the conditional heteroscedasticity. In particular after the collapse of the Bretton Woods system and the implementation of flexible exchange rates in the seventies ARCH models are increasingly used by researchers and practitioners.

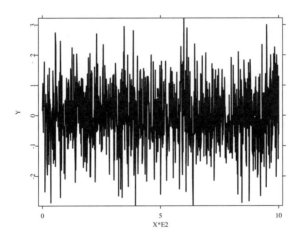

Figure 12.1: Normally distributed white noise. Q SFEtimewr.xpl

In addition a far-reaching agreement has been formed that returns cannot be regarded as i.i.d. and at most as being uncorrelated. This argument

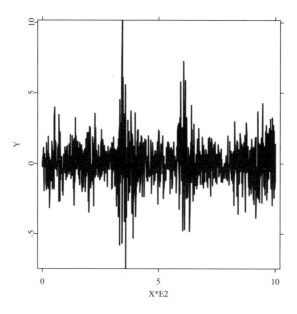

Figure 12.2: A GARCH(1,1) process ($\alpha = 0.15$, $\beta = 0.8$).

Q SFEtimegarc.xpl

holds at least for financial time series of relatively high frequency, for example for daily data. In Figure 12.1 we show a normally distributed white noise, a GARCH(1,1) process in Figure 12.2 and the DAFOX index (1993-96) in Figure 12.3, see http://finance.wiwi.uni-karlsruhe.de/Forschung/dafox.html. It can be seen from the figure that the GARCH process is obviously more appropriate for modelling stock returns than white noise.

However the ARCH model is only the starting point of the empirical study and relies on a wide range of specification tests. Some practically relevant disadvantages of the ARCH model have been discovered recently, for example, the definition and modelling of the persistence of shocks and the problem of modelling asymmetries. Thus a large number of extensions of the standard ARCH model have been suggested. We will discuss them in detail later.

Let X_t be a discrete stochastic process and from Definition 10.15 $r_t = \log X_t / X_{t-1}$ the relative increase or the *return* of the process X_t. If

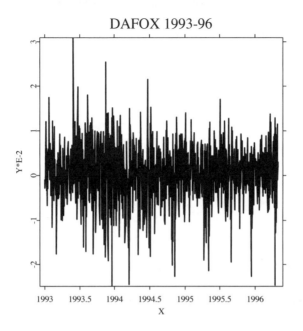

Figure 12.3: DAFOX returns from 1993 to 1996.   Q SFEtimedax.xpl

the returns are independent and identically distributed, then X_t follows a geometric random walk. It is assumed in ARCH models that the returns depend on past information with a specific form.

As mentioned before $\mathcal{F}_t$ denotes the information set at time t, which encompasses X_t and all the past realizations of the process X_t. This means in a general model

$$r_t = \mu_t + \varepsilon_t \qquad (12.1)$$

with $\mathsf{E}[\varepsilon_t \mid \mathcal{F}_{t-1}] = 0$. Here μ_t can represent the risk premium which results from the econometric models and is time dependent. The stochastic error term ε_t is no longer independent but centered and uncorrelated. In ARCH models the conditional variance of ε_t is a linear function of the lagged squared error terms.

12.1.1   ARCH(1): Definition and Properties

The ARCH model of order 1, ARCH(1), is defined as follows:

Definition 12.1 (ARCH(1))
The process ε_t, $t \in \mathbb{Z}$, is ARCH(1), if $\mathsf{E}[\varepsilon_t \mid \mathcal{F}_{t-1}] = 0$,

$$\sigma_t^2 = \omega + \alpha \varepsilon_{t-1}^2 \tag{12.2}$$

with $\omega > 0$, $\alpha \geq 0$ and

- *$Var(\varepsilon_t \mid \mathcal{F}_{t-1}) = \sigma_t^2$ and $Z_t = \varepsilon_t / \sigma_t$ is i.i.d. (strong ARCH)*

- *$Var(\varepsilon_t \mid \mathcal{F}_{t-1}) = \sigma_t^2$ (semi-strong ARCH),*

- *$\mathcal{P}(\varepsilon_t^2 \mid 1, \varepsilon_{t-1}, \varepsilon_{t-2}, \dots, \varepsilon_{t-1}^2, \varepsilon_{t-2}^2, \dots) = \sigma_t^2$ (weak ARCH),*

where $\mathcal{P}$ is the best linear projection described in Section 11.4. Obviously a strong ARCH(1) process is also semi-strong and a semi-strong also weak. On the other hand the conditional variance of a weak ARCH(1) process can be non-linear (unequal to σ_t^2). In this case it can not be a semi-strong ARCH process.

Setting $Z_t = \varepsilon_t / \sigma_t$, it holds for the semi-strong and the strong ARCH models that $\mathsf{E}[Z_t] = 0$ and $Var(Z_t) = 1$. In strong ARCH models Z_t is i.i.d. so that no dependence can be modelled in higher moments than the second moment. It is frequently assumed that Z_t is normally distributed, which means ε_t is conditionally normally distributed:

$$\varepsilon_t | \mathcal{F}_{t-1} \sim \mathrm{N}(0, \sigma_t^2). \tag{12.3}$$

Under (12.3) the difference between the strong and the semi-strong ARCH models disappears.

Originally only strong and semi-strong ARCH models are discussed in the literature. Weak ARCH models are important because they are closed under temporal aggregation. If, for example, daily returns follow a weak ARCH process, then the weekly and monthly returns are also weak ARCH with corresponding parameter adjustments. This phenomenon holds in general for strong and semi-strong models.

According to Definition 12.1 the process ε_t is a martingale difference and therefore white noise.

Theorem 12.1
*Assume that the process ε_t is a weak ARCH(1) process with $\text{Var}(\varepsilon_t) = \sigma^2 <$
∞. Then it follows that ε_t is white noise.*

Proof:
From $\mathsf{E}[\varepsilon_t \mid \mathcal{F}_{t-1}] = 0$ it follows that $\mathsf{E}[\varepsilon_t] = 0$ and $\text{Cov}(\varepsilon_t, \varepsilon_{t-k}) = \mathsf{E}[\varepsilon_t \varepsilon_{t-k}] =$
$\mathsf{E}[\mathsf{E}(\varepsilon_t \varepsilon_{t-k} \mid \mathcal{F}_{t-1})] = \mathsf{E}[\varepsilon_{t-k} \mathsf{E}(\varepsilon_t \mid \mathcal{F}_{t-1})] = 0.$ □
Note that ε_t is not an independent white noise.

Theorem 12.2 (Unconditional variance of the ARCH(1))
*Assume the process ε_t is a semi-strong ARCH(1) process with $\text{Var}(\varepsilon_t) = \sigma^2 <$
∞. Then it holds that*

$$\sigma^2 = \frac{\omega}{1 - \alpha}.$$

Proof:
$\sigma^2 = \mathsf{E}[\varepsilon_t^2] = \mathsf{E}[\mathsf{E}(\varepsilon_t^2 \mid \mathcal{F}_{t-1})] = \mathsf{E}[\sigma_t^2] = \omega + \alpha\,\mathsf{E}[\varepsilon_{t-1}^2] = \omega + \alpha\sigma^2$. It holds
then $\sigma^2 = \omega/(1 - \alpha)$ when $\alpha < 1$.   □
$\alpha < 1$ is the necessary and sufficient condition for a weak stationarity of a
semi-strong process.

If the innovation $Z_t = \varepsilon_t/\sigma_t$ is symmetrically distributed around zero, then
all odd moments of ε_t are equal to zero. Under the assumption of normal
distribution (12.3) the conditions for the existence of higher even moments
can be derived.

Theorem 12.3 (Fourth Moment)
Let ε_t be a strong ARCH(1) process, $Z_t \sim N(0,1)$ and $\mathsf{E}[\varepsilon_t^4] = c < \infty$. Then

1.

$$\mathsf{E}[\varepsilon_t^4] = \frac{3\omega^2}{(1 - \alpha)^2} \frac{1 - \alpha^2}{1 - 3\alpha^2}$$

   with $3\alpha^2 < 1$.

2. *the unconditional distribution of ε_t is leptokurtic.*

Proof:

1. $c = \mathsf{E}[\varepsilon_t^4] = \mathsf{E}[\mathsf{E}(\varepsilon_t^4 \mid \mathcal{F}_{t-1})] = \mathsf{E}[\sigma_t^4\,\mathsf{E}(Z_t^4 \mid \mathcal{F}_{t-1})] = \mathsf{E}[Z_t^4]\,\mathsf{E}[(\omega + \alpha_1\varepsilon_{t-1}^2)^2] = 3(\omega^2 + 2\omega\alpha\,\mathsf{E}[\varepsilon_{t-1}^2] + \alpha^2\,\mathsf{E}[\varepsilon_{t-1}^4])$. Since $\mathsf{E}[\varepsilon_{t-1}^2] = \omega/(1-\alpha)$ and $\mathsf{E}[\varepsilon_{t-1}^4] = c$, after rearranging the claim follows.

2.

$$\text{Kurt}(\varepsilon_t) = \frac{\mathsf{E}[\varepsilon_t^4]}{\mathsf{E}[\varepsilon_t^2]^2} = 3\frac{1-\alpha^2}{1-3\alpha^2} \geq 3.$$

□

For the boundary case $\alpha = 0$ and the normally distributed innovations $\text{Kurt}(\varepsilon_t) = 3$, while for $\alpha > 0$ it holds that $\text{Kurt}(\varepsilon_t) > 3$. The unconditional distribution is also leptokurtic under conditional heteroscedasticity, i.e., the curvature is high in the middle of the distribution and the tails are fatter than those of a normal distribution, which is frequently observed in financial markets.

The thickness of the tails and thus the existence of moments depend on the parameters of the ARCH models. The variance of the ARCH(1) process is finite when $\alpha < 1$ (Theorem 12.2), while the fourth moment in the case of normally distributed error terms exists when $3\alpha^2 < 1$ (Theorem 12.3). Already in the sixties Mandelbrot had questioned the existence of the variance of several financial time series. Frequently empirical distributions have so fat tails that one can not conclude a finite variance. In order to make empirical conclusions on the degree of the tail's thickness of the unconditional distribution, one can assume, for example, that the distribution is a Pareto type, i.e., for large x:

$$P(x) = P(X_t > x) \sim kx^{-a}$$

for $a > 0$. When $a > c$, it holds that $\mathsf{E}[|X_t|^c] < \infty$. The question is, how can we estimate the tail index a? A simple method follows from the conclusion that for large x the log function $P(x)$ is linear, i.e.,

$$\log P(x) \approx \log k - a \log x. \tag{12.4}$$

Therefore we can build the order statistics $X_{(1)} > X_{(2)} > \ldots > X_{(n)}$ and estimate the probability $P(x)$ for $x = X_{(i)}$ using the relative frequency

$$\frac{\#\{t; X_t \geq X_{(i)}\}}{n} = \frac{i}{n}.$$

In (12.4) $P(X_{(i)})$ is replaced with the estimator i/n:

$$\log\frac{i}{n} \approx \log k - a \log X_{(i)}, \tag{12.5}$$

from which a can be estimated from the regression of i/n on $X_{(i)}, i = 1, ..., n$, using the least squares method. In general only a small part of the data will be used for the regression, since the linear approximation of $\log P(x)$ is only appropriate in the tail. Thus only the largest order statistics are used to estimate the regression (12.5). Figure 12.4 shows the regression (12.5) for the DAFOX from 1974 to 1996 with $m = 20$, i.e. we choose the 20 largest observations. The slope of the least squares (LS) line is -3.25. It indicates that the variance and the third moment of this time series are finite whereas the fourth moment and the kurtosis are not finite.

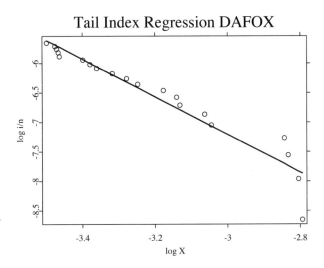

Figure 12.4:   The right side of the logged empirical distribution of the DAFOX returns from 1974 to 1996.   **Q** SFEtaildax.xpl

Hill (1975) has suggested an estimator using the maximum likelihood method:

$$\hat{a} = \left(\frac{1}{m-1} \sum_{i=1}^{m} \log X_{(i)} - \log X_{(m)} \right)^{-1}, \qquad (12.6)$$

where m is the number of observations taken from the tail and used in the estimation. How to choose m obviously raises a problem. When m is too large, the approximation of the distribution is no longer good; when m is too small, the bias and the variance of the estimator could increase. A simple rule of thumb says that m/n should be around 0.5% or 1%. Clearly one requires a large amount of data in order to estimate a well. As an example we consider again the daily returns of German stocks from 1974 to 1996, a total of 5747 observations per stock. The results of the ordinary least squares estimator and the Hill estimator with $m = 20$ and $m = 50$ are given in Table 12.1. In every case the estimators are larger than 2, which indicates the existence of variances. The third moment may not exist in some cases, for example, for Allianz and Daimler.

Theorem 12.4 (Representation of an ARCH(1) process)
Let ε_t be a strong ARCH(1) process with $Var(\varepsilon_t) = \sigma^2 < \infty$. It holds that

$$\varepsilon_t^2 = \omega \sum_{k=0}^{\infty} \alpha^k \prod_{j=0}^{k} Z_{t-j}^2$$

and the sum converges in L_1.

Proof:
Through the recursive substitution of $\varepsilon_s^2 = \sigma_s^2 Z_s^2$ and $\sigma_s^2 = \omega + \alpha \varepsilon_{s-1}^2$. The convergence follows from

$$
\begin{aligned}
\mathsf{E}[\varepsilon_t^2 - \omega \sum_{k=0}^{m} \alpha^k \prod_{j=0}^{k} Z_{t-j}^2] &= \alpha^{m+1} \mathsf{E}[\varepsilon_{t-m-1}^2 \prod_{j=0}^{m} Z_{t-j}^2] \\
&= \alpha^{m+1} \mathsf{E}[\varepsilon_{t-m-1}^2] \longrightarrow 0
\end{aligned}
$$

for $m \longrightarrow \infty$, since Z_t is independent with $\mathsf{E}(Z_t^2) = 1$.   □

Theorem 12.5
Let ε_t be a stationary strong ARCH(1) process with $\mathsf{E}(\varepsilon_t^4) = c < \infty$ and $Z_t \sim N(0,1)$. It holds that

1.

$$\varepsilon_t^2 = \omega \sum_{k=0}^{\infty} \alpha^k \prod_{j=0}^{k} Z_{t-j}^2$$

   and the sum converges in L_2.

2. $\eta_t = \sigma_t^2(Z_t^2 - 1)$ *is white noise.*

3. ε_t^2 *is an AR(1) process with $\varepsilon_t^2 = \omega + \alpha \varepsilon_{t-1}^2 + \eta_t$.*

Proof:

	LS		Hill	
m	20	50	20	50
DAFOX	3.25	2.94	3.17	2.88
ALLIANZ	2.29	2.44	2.28	2.26
BASF	4.19	4.29	4.58	4.01
BAYER	3.32	3.20	3.90	3.23
BMW	3.42	3.05	3.05	2.89
COMMERZBANK	6.58	4.67	7.14	5.19
DAIMLER	2.85	2.85	2.43	2.56
DEUTSCHE BANK	3.40	3.26	3.41	3.29
DEGUSSA	3.03	4.16	2.93	3.30
DRESDNER	5.76	4.08	4.20	4.32
HOECHST	4.77	3.68	5.66	4.05
KARSTADT	3.56	3.42	3.11	3.16
LINDE	3.30	3.35	3.87	3.37
MAN	3.83	3.66	3.17	3.45
MANNESMANN	3.19	3.85	2.84	3.22
PREUSSAG	3.52	4.11	3.57	3.68
RWE	3.87	3.78	3.51	3.54
SCHERING	3.34	4.82	3.22	3.64
SIEMENS	6.06	4.50	5.96	5.23
THYSSEN	5.31	5.36	4.67	4.97
VOLKSWAGEN	4.59	3.31	4.86	4.00

Table 12.1:   Least Square (LS) and Hill estimators of the tail index a with m observations used for the estimation.

1. As in Theorem 12.4. The convergence is L_2 follows from

$$
\begin{aligned}
\mathsf{E}[(\varepsilon_t^2 - \omega \sum_{k=0}^{m} \alpha^k \prod_{j=0}^{k} Z_{t-j}^2)^2] &= \mathsf{E}[(\alpha^{m+1}\varepsilon_{t-m-1}^2 \prod_{j=0}^{m} Z_{t-j}^2)^2] \\
&= \alpha^{2(m+1)}3^{m+1}\,\mathsf{E}[\varepsilon_{t-m-1}^4] \\
&= \alpha^{2(m+1)}3^{m+1}c \longrightarrow 0
\end{aligned}
$$

for $m \longrightarrow \infty$, since $3\alpha^2 < 1$ due to the assumption that $\mathsf{E}(\varepsilon_t^4)$ is finite and since Z_t is independent with $\mathrm{Kurt}(Z_t) = 3$.

2.   a) $\mathsf{E}[\eta_t] = \mathsf{E}[\sigma_t^2]\,\mathsf{E}[Z_t^2 - 1] = 0$

   b)

$$
\begin{aligned}
\mathrm{Var}(\eta_t) &= \mathsf{E}[\sigma_t^4]\,\mathsf{E}[(Z_t^2 - 1)^2] = 2\,\mathsf{E}[(\omega + \alpha\varepsilon_{t-1}^2)^2] \\
&= 2(\omega^2 + 2\alpha\omega\,\mathsf{E}[\varepsilon_{t-1}^2] + \alpha^2\,\mathsf{E}[\varepsilon_{t-1}^4]) = \mathrm{const}.
\end{aligned}
$$

   is independent of t.

c)

$$
\begin{aligned}
\mathrm{Cov}(\eta_t, \eta_{t+s}) &= \mathsf{E}[\sigma_t^2(Z_t^2 - 1)\sigma_{t+s}^2(Z_{t+s}^2 - 1)] \\
&= \mathsf{E}[\sigma_t^2(Z_t^2 - 1)\sigma_{t+s}^2]\,\mathsf{E}[(Z_{t+s}^2 - 1)] \\
&= 0 \qquad \text{for } s \neq 0.
\end{aligned}
$$

3. It follows from rearranging: $\varepsilon_t^2 = \sigma_t^2 Z_t^2 = \sigma_t^2 + \sigma_t^2(Z_t^2 - 1) = \omega + \alpha\varepsilon_{t-1}^2 + \eta_t$.

$\qquad\qquad\qquad\qquad\qquad\qquad\qquad\qquad\qquad\qquad\qquad\qquad\qquad\qquad\qquad$ $\square$

Remark 12.1
Nelson (1990a) shows that the strong ARCH(1) process ε_t is strictly stationary when $\mathsf{E}[\log(\alpha Z_t^2)] < 0$. If, for example, $Z_t \sim N(0,1)$, then the condition for strict stationarity is $\alpha < 3.5622$, which is weaker than the condition for covariance-stationarity with $\alpha < 1$ due to the assumption that the variance is finite.

The dynamics of the volatility process in the case of ARCH(1) is essentially determined by the parameter α. In Theorem 12.5 it was shown that the square of an ARCH(1) process follows an AR(1) process. The correlation structure of the empirical squared observations of returns are frequently more complicated than a simple AR(1) process. In Section 12.1.3 we will consider an ARCH model of order q with $q > 1$, which allows a more flexible modelling of the correlation structure.

The volatility is a function of the past squared observations in ARCH models in a narrow sense. In the more general GARCH models (Section 12.1.5) it may depend on the past squared volatilities in addition. These models belong to the large group of unpredictable time series with *stochastic volatility*. In the strong form, they have $\varepsilon_t = \sigma_t Z_t$ where σ_t is $\mathcal{F}_{t-1}$-measurable, i.e. the volatility σ_t depends only on the information to the time point $t-1$ and the i.i.d. innovations Z_t with $\mathsf{E}[Z_t] = 0, \mathrm{Var}(Z_t) = 1$. For such a time series it holds $\mathsf{E}[\varepsilon_t|\mathcal{F}_{t-1}] = 0, \mathrm{Var}(\varepsilon_t|\mathcal{F}_{t-1}) = \sigma_t^2$, i.e. ε_t is unpredictable and, except in the special case that $\sigma_t \overset{\text{def}}{=}$ const., conditionally heteroscedastic. The stylized facts 2-4 are only fulfilled under certain qualitative assumptions. For example, in order to produce volatility cluster σ_t must tend to be large when the squared observations or volatilities of the recent past observations are large. The generalizations of the ARCH models observed in this section fulfill the corresponding conditions.

Remark 12.2

At first glance stochastic volatility models in discrete time deliver a different approach in modelling the financial data compared with diffusion processes, on which the Black-Schole model and its generalization are based (Section 5.4). Nelson (1990b) has however shown that ARCH and also the more general GARCH processes converge in the limit to a diffusion process in continuous time when the difference of the time points of the successive observations goes against zero.

This result is often used reversely in order to estimate the parameter of financial models in the continuous time where one approximates the corresponding diffusion processes through discrete GARCH time series and estimates its parameter. Nelson (1990b) shows only the convergence of GARCH processes against diffusion processes in a weak sense (convergence on the distribution). A recent work of Wang (2002) shows however that the approximation does not hold in a stronger sense, especially the likelihood process is not asymptotically equivalent. In this sense the maximum likelihood estimators for the discrete time series do not converge against the parameters of the diffusion limit process.

12.1.2   Estimation of ARCH(1) Models

Theorem 12.5 says that an ARCH(1) process can be represented as an AR(1) process in X_t^2. A simple Yule-Walker estimator uses this property:

$$\hat{\alpha}^{(0)} = \frac{\sum_{t=2}^{n}(\varepsilon_t^2 - \hat{\omega}^{(0)})(\varepsilon_{t-1}^2 - \hat{\omega}^{(0)})}{\sum_{t=2}^{n}(\varepsilon_t^2 - \hat{\omega}^{(0)})^2}$$

with $\hat{\omega}^{(0)} = n^{-1}\sum_{t=1}^{n}\varepsilon_t^2$. Since the distribution of ε_t^2 is naturally not normal, the Yule-Walker estimator is inefficient. However it can be used as an initial value for iterative estimation methods.

The estimation of ARCH models is normally done using the maximum likelihood (ML) method. Assuming that the returns ε_t have a conditionally normal distribution, we have:

$$p(\varepsilon_t \mid \mathcal{F}_{t-1}) = \frac{1}{\sqrt{2\pi}\sigma_t}\exp\left\{-\frac{1}{2}\frac{\varepsilon_t^2}{\sigma_t^2}\right\}, \qquad (12.7)$$

The log-likelihood function $l(\omega, \alpha)$ can be written as a function of the parameters ω and α:

$$l(\omega, \alpha) \;=\; \sum_{t=2}^{n} l_t(\omega, \alpha) + \log p_\varepsilon(\varepsilon_1) \tag{12.8}$$

$$= \sum_{t=2}^{n} \log p(\varepsilon_t \mid \mathcal{F}_{t-1}) + \log p_\varepsilon(\varepsilon_1)$$

$$= -\frac{n-1}{2} \log(2\pi) - \frac{1}{2} \sum_{t=2}^{n} \log(\omega + \alpha \varepsilon_{t-1}^2)$$

$$-\frac{1}{2} \sum_{t=2}^{n} \frac{\varepsilon_t^2}{\omega + \alpha \varepsilon_{t-1}^2} + \log p_\varepsilon(\varepsilon_1),$$

where p_ε is the stationary marginal density of ε_t. A problem is that the analytical expression for p_ε is unknown in ARCH models thus (12.8) can not be calculated. In the conditional likelihood function $l^b = \log p(\varepsilon_n, \dots, \varepsilon_2 \mid \varepsilon_1)$ the expression $\log p_\varepsilon(\varepsilon_1)$ disappears:

$$l^b(\omega, \alpha) \;=\; \sum_{t=2}^{n} l_t(\omega, \alpha) \tag{12.9}$$

$$= \sum_{t=2}^{n} \log p(\varepsilon_t \mid \mathcal{F}_{t-1})$$

$$= -\frac{n-1}{2} \log(2\pi) - 1/2 \sum_{t=2}^{n} \log(\omega + \alpha \varepsilon_{t-1}^2) - 1/2 \sum_{t=2}^{n} \frac{\varepsilon_t^2}{\omega + \alpha \varepsilon_{t-1}^2}.$$

For large n the difference $l - l^b$ is negligible.

Figure 12.5 shows the conditional likelihood of a generated ARCH(1) process with $n = 100$. The parameter ω is chosen so that the unconditional variance is everywhere constant, i.e., with a variance of σ^2, $\omega = (1 - \alpha)\sigma^2$. The optimization of the likelihood of an ARCH(1) model can be found by analyzing the graph. Most often we would like to know the precision of the estimator as well. Essentially it is determined by the second derivative of the likelihood at the optimization point by the asymptotic properties of the ML estimator (see Section 12.1.6). Furthermore one has to use numerical methods such as the score algorithm introduced in Section 11.8 to estimate the parameters of the models with a larger order. In this case the first and second partial derivatives of the likelihood must be calculated.

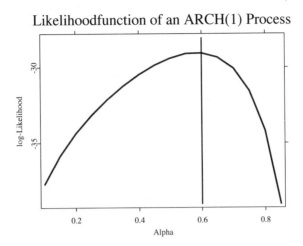

Figure 12.5: Conditional likelihood function of a generated ARCH(1) process with $n = 100$.   The true parameter is $\alpha = 0.5$.
Q SFElikarch1.xpl

With the ARCH(1) model these are

$$\frac{\partial l_t^b}{\partial \omega} = \frac{1}{2\sigma_t^2}\left(\frac{\varepsilon_t^2}{\sigma_t^2} - 1\right) \tag{12.10}$$

$$\frac{\partial l_t^b}{\partial \alpha} = \frac{1}{2\sigma_t^2}\varepsilon_{t-1}^2\left(\frac{\varepsilon_t^2}{\sigma_t^2} - 1\right) \tag{12.11}$$

$$\frac{\partial^2 l_t^b}{\partial \omega^2} = -\frac{1}{2\sigma_t^4}\left(2\frac{\varepsilon_t^2}{\sigma_t^2} - 1\right) \tag{12.12}$$

$$\frac{\partial^2 l_t^b}{\partial \alpha^2} = -\frac{1}{2\sigma_t^4}\varepsilon_{t-1}^4\left(2\frac{\varepsilon_t^2}{\sigma_t^2} - 1\right) \tag{12.13}$$

$$\frac{\partial^2 l_t^b}{\partial \omega \partial \alpha} = -\frac{1}{2\sigma_t^4}\varepsilon_{t-1}^2\left(2\frac{\varepsilon_t^2}{\sigma_t^2} - 1\right). \tag{12.14}$$

The fist order conditions are $\sum_{t=2}^{n} \partial l_t^b/\partial \omega = 0$ and $\sum_{t=2}^{n} \partial l_t^b/\partial \alpha = 0$. For the score algorithm the expected value of the second derivative has to be calculated. It is assumed that $\mathsf{E}[Z_t^2] = \mathsf{E}[(\varepsilon_t/\sigma_t)^2] = 1$, so that the expression in the parentheses $(2\varepsilon_t^2/\sigma_t^2 - 1)$ has an expected value of one. From this it follows that

$$\mathsf{E}\left[\frac{\partial^2 l_t^b}{\partial \omega^2}\right] = -\frac{1}{2}\mathsf{E}\left[\frac{1}{\sigma_t^4}\right].$$

The expectation of σ_t^{-4} is consistently estimated by $(n-1)^{-1}\sum_{t=2}^n (\omega + \alpha\varepsilon_{t-1}^2)^{-2}$, so that for the estimator of the expected value of the second derivative we have:

$$\hat{\mathsf{E}}\frac{\partial^2 l_t^b}{\partial \omega^2} = -\frac{1}{2(n-1)}\sum_{t=2}^n \frac{1}{\sigma_t^4}.$$

Similarly the expected value of the second derivative with respect to α follows with

$$\mathsf{E}\left[\frac{\partial^2 l_t^b}{\partial \alpha^2}\right] = -\frac{1}{2}\mathsf{E}\left[\frac{\varepsilon_{t-1}^4}{\sigma_t^4}\right]$$

and the estimator is

$$\hat{\mathsf{E}}\frac{\partial^2 l_t^b}{\partial \alpha^2} = -\frac{1}{2(n-1)}\sum_{t=2}^n \frac{\varepsilon_{t-1}^4}{\sigma_t^4}.$$

Theorem 12.6
Given $Z_t \sim N(0,1)$, it holds that

$$\mathsf{E}\left[\left(\frac{\partial l_t^b}{\partial \omega}\right)^2\right] = -\mathsf{E}\left[\frac{\partial^2 l_t^b}{\partial \omega^2}\right]$$

Proof:
This follows immediately from $\mathsf{E}\left[\left(\frac{\partial l_t^b}{\partial \omega}\right)^2\right] = \mathsf{E}\left[\frac{1}{4\sigma_t^4}(Z_t^4 - 2Z_t^2 + 1)\right]$
$= \mathsf{E}\left[\frac{1}{4\sigma_t^4}\right](3 - 2 + 1).$ □

Obviously Theorem 12.6 also holds for the parameter α in place of ω. In addition it essentially holds for more general models, for example the estimation of GARCH models in Section 12.1.6. In more complicated models one can replace the second derivative with the square of the first derivative, which is easier to calculate. It is assumed, however, that the likelihood function is correctly specified, i.e., the true distribution of the error terms is normal.

Under the two conditions

1. $\mathsf{E}[Z_t \mid \mathcal{F}_{t-1}] = 0$ and $\mathsf{E}[Z_t^2 \mid \mathcal{F}_{t-1}] = 1$

2. $\mathsf{E}[\log(\alpha Z_t^2) \mid \mathcal{F}_{t-1}] < 0$ (strict stationarity)

n	$k^{-1}\sum_{j=1}^{k}\hat{\alpha}_j$	$\sqrt{k^{-1}\sum_{j=1}^{k}(\hat{\alpha}_j - \alpha)^2}$	$\#(\alpha_j \geq 1)$
100	0.852	0.257	27%
250	0.884	0.164	24%
500	0.893	0.107	15%
1000	0.898	0.081	10%

Table 12.2: Monte Carlo simulation results for QML estimates of the parameter $\alpha = 0.9$ from an ARCH(1) model with $k = 1000$ replications. The last column gives the proportion of the estimator that are larger than 1 (according to Shephard (1996)).

and under certain technical conditions, the ML estimators are consistent. If $\mathsf{E}[Z_t^4 \mid \mathcal{F}_{t-1}] < \infty$ and $\omega > 0$, $\alpha > 0$ hold in addition, then $\hat{\theta} = (\hat{\omega}, \hat{\alpha})^\top$ is asymptotically normally distributed:

$$\sqrt{n}(\hat{\theta} - \theta) \xrightarrow{\mathcal{L}} \mathrm{N}(0, J^{-1}IJ^{-1}) \qquad (12.15)$$

with

$$I = \mathsf{E}\left(\frac{\partial l_t(\theta)}{\partial \theta}\frac{\partial l_t(\theta)}{\partial \theta^\top}\right)$$

and

$$J = -\mathsf{E}\left(\frac{\partial^2 l_t(\theta)}{\partial \theta \partial \theta^\top}\right).$$

If the true distribution of Z_t is normal, then $I = J$ and the asymptotic covariance matrix is simplified to J^{-1}, i.e., the inverse of the Fischer Information matrix. If the true distribution is instead leptokurtic, then the maximum of (12.9) is still consistent, but no longer efficient. In this case the ML method is interpreted as the 'Quasi Maximum Likelihood' (QML) method.

In a Monte Carlo simulation study in Shephard (1996) 1000 ARCH(1) processes with $\omega = 0.2$ and $\alpha = 0.9$ were generated and the parameters were estimated using QML. The results are given in Table 12.2. Obviously with the moderate sample sizes ($n = 500$) the bias is negligible. The variance, however, is still so large that a relatively large proportion (10%) of the estimators are larger than one, which would imply covariance nonstationarity. This, in turn, has a considerable influence on the volatility prediction.

12.1.3 ARCH(q): Definition and Properties

The definition of an ARCH(1) model will be extended for the case that $q > 1$ lags, on which the conditional variance depends.

Definition 12.2 (ARCH(q))
The process (ε_t), $t \in \mathbb{Z}$, is ARCH(q), when $\mathsf{E}[\varepsilon_t \mid \mathcal{F}_{t-1}] = 0$,

$$\sigma_t^2 = \omega + \alpha_1 \varepsilon_{t-1}^2 + \ldots + \alpha_q \varepsilon_{t-q}^2 \tag{12.16}$$

with $\omega > 0$, $\alpha_1 \geq 0, \ldots, \alpha_q \geq 0$ and

- $Var(\varepsilon_t \mid \mathcal{F}_{t-1}) = \sigma_t^2$ *and $Z_t = \varepsilon_t / \sigma_t$ is i.i.d. (strong ARCH)*
- $Var(\varepsilon_t \mid \mathcal{F}_{t-1}) = \sigma_t^2$ *(semi-strong ARCH), or*
- $\mathcal{P}(\varepsilon_t^2 \mid 1, \varepsilon_{t-1}, \varepsilon_{t-2}, \ldots, \varepsilon_{t-1}^2, \varepsilon_{t-2}^2, \ldots) = \sigma_t^2$ *(weak ARCH)*

The conditional variance σ_t^2 in an ARCH(q) model is also a linear function of the q squared lags.

Theorem 12.7
Let ε_t be a semi-strong ARCH(q) process with $Var(\varepsilon_t) = \sigma^2 < \infty$. Then

$$\sigma^2 = \frac{\omega}{1 - \alpha_1 - \ldots - \alpha_q}$$

with $\alpha_1 + \cdots + \alpha_q < 1$.

Proof:
as in Theorem 12.2.   □

If instead $\alpha_1 + \cdots + \alpha_q \geq 1$, then the unconditional variance does not exist and the process is not covariance-stationary.

Theorem 12.8 (Representation of an ARCH(q) Process)
Let ε_t be a (semi-)strong ARCH(q) process with $\mathsf{E}[\varepsilon_t^4] = c < \infty$. Then

1. $\eta_t = \sigma_t^2 (Z_t^2 - 1)$ *is white noise.*

2. ε_t^2 *is an AR(q) process with $\varepsilon_t^2 = \omega + \sum_{i=1}^{q} \alpha_i \varepsilon_{t-i}^2 + \eta_t$.*

Proof:
as in Theorem 12.5.   □

It is problematic with the ARCH(q) model that for some applications a larger order q must be used, since large lags only lose their influence on the volatility slowly. It is suggested as an empirical rule of thumb to use a minimum order of $q = 14$. The disadvantage of a large order is that many parameters have to be estimated under restrictions. The restrictions can be categorized as conditions for stationarity and the strictly positive parameters. If efficient estimation methods are to be used, for example, the maximum likelihood method, the estimation of large dimensional parameter spaces can be numerically quite complicated to obtain.

One possibility of reducing the number of parameters while including a long history is to assume linearly decreasing weights on the lags, i.e.,

$$\sigma_t^2 = \omega + \alpha \sum_{i=1}^{q} w_i \varepsilon_{t-i}^2,$$

with

$$w_i = \frac{2(q+1-i)}{q(q+1)},$$

so that only two parameters have to be estimated. In Section 12.1.5 we describe a generalized ARCH model, which on the one hand, has a parsimonious parameterization, and on the other hand a flexible lag structure.

12.1.4 Estimation of an ARCH(q) Model

For the general ARCH(q) model from (12.16) the conditional likelihood is

$$
\begin{aligned}
l^b(\theta) &= \sum_{t=q+1}^{n} l_t(\theta) \\
&= -\frac{n-1}{2} \log(2\pi) - 1/2 \sum_{t=2}^{n} \log \sigma_t^2 - 1/2 \sum_{t=q+1}^{n} \frac{\varepsilon_t^q + 1}{\sigma_t^2} \quad (12.17)
\end{aligned}
$$

with the parameter vector $\theta = (\omega, \alpha_1, \ldots, \alpha_q)^\top$. Although one can find the optimum of ARCH(1) models by analyzing the graph such as Figure 12.5, it is complicated and impractical for a high dimensional parameter space. The maximization of (12.17) with respect to θ is a non-linear optimization problem, which can be solved numerically. The *score algorithm* is used empirically not only in ARMA models (see Section 11.8) but also in ARCH models. In order to implement this approach the first and second derivatives of the (conditional) likelihood with respect to the parameters need to be formed. For the ARCH(q) model the first derivative is

$$\frac{\partial l_t^b}{\partial \theta} = \frac{1}{2\sigma_t^2} \frac{\partial \sigma_t^2}{\partial \theta} \left(\frac{\varepsilon_t^2}{\sigma_t^2} - 1 \right) \quad (12.18)$$

with

$$\frac{\partial \sigma_t^2}{\partial \theta} = (1, \varepsilon_{t-1}^2, \dots, \varepsilon_{t-q}^2)^\top.$$

The first order condition is $\sum_{t=q+1}^{n} \partial l_t / \partial \theta = 0$. For the second derivative and the asymptotic properties of the QML estimator see Section 12.1.6.

12.1.5   Generalized ARCH (GARCH)

The ARCH(q) model can be generalized by extending it with autoregressive terms of the volatility.

Definition 12.3 (GARCH(p, q)) *The process* (ε_t), $t \in \mathbb{Z}$, *is GARCH(p, q),* *if* $\mathsf{E}[\varepsilon_t \mid \mathcal{F}_{t-1}] = 0$,

$$\sigma_t^2 = \omega + \sum_{i=1}^{q} \alpha_i \varepsilon_{t-i}^2 + \sum_{j=1}^{p} \beta_j \sigma_{t-j}^2, \tag{12.19}$$

and

- *$Var(\varepsilon_t \mid \mathcal{F}_{t-1}) = \sigma_t^2$ and $Z_t = \varepsilon_t / \sigma_t$ is i.i.d. (strong GARCH)*
- *$Var(\varepsilon_t \mid \mathcal{F}_{t-1}) = \sigma_t^2$ (semi-strong GARCH), or*
- *$\mathcal{P}(\varepsilon_t^2 \mid 1, \varepsilon_{t-1}, \varepsilon_{t-2}, \dots, \varepsilon_{t-1}^2, \varepsilon_{t-2}^2, \dots) = \sigma_t^2$ (weak GARCH).*

The sufficient but not necessary conditions for

$$\sigma_t^2 > 0 \quad a.s., \qquad (\; \mathsf{P}[\sigma_t^2 > 0] = 1 \;) \tag{12.20}$$

are $\omega > 0$, $\alpha_i \geq 0$, $i = 1, \dots, q$ and $\beta_j \geq 0$, $j = 1, \dots, p$. In the case of the GARCH(1,2) model

$$\begin{aligned}
\sigma_t^2 &= \omega + \alpha_1 \varepsilon_{t-1}^2 + \alpha_2 \varepsilon_{t-2}^2 + \beta_1 \sigma_{t-1}^2 \\
&= \frac{\omega}{1 - \beta} + \alpha_1 \sum_{j=0}^{\infty} \beta_1^j \varepsilon_{t-j-1}^2 + \alpha_2 \sum_{j=0}^{\infty} \beta_1^j \varepsilon_{t-j-2}^2 \\
&= \frac{\omega}{1 - \beta} + \alpha_1 \varepsilon_{t-1}^2 + (\alpha_1 \beta_1 + \alpha_2) \sum_{j=0}^{\infty} \beta_1^j \varepsilon_{t-j-2}^2
\end{aligned}$$

with $0 \leq \beta_1 < 1$. $\omega > 0$, $\alpha_1 \geq 0$ and $\alpha_1\beta_1 + \alpha_2 \geq 0$ are necessary and sufficient conditions for (12.20) assuming that the sum $\sum_{j=0}^{\infty} \beta_1^j \varepsilon_{t-j-2}^2$ converges.

Theorem 12.9 (Representation of a GARCH(p, q) process)
Let ε_t be a (semi-)strong GARCH(p,q) process with $\mathsf{E}[\varepsilon_t^4] = c < \infty$. Then

1. $\eta_t = \sigma_t^2(Z_t^2 - 1)$ is white noise.

2. ε_t^2 is an ARMA(m,p) process with

$$\varepsilon_t^2 = \omega + \sum_{i=1}^{m} \gamma_i \varepsilon_{t-i}^2 - \sum_{j=1}^{p} \beta_j \eta_{t-j} + \eta_t, \qquad (12.21)$$

with $m = \max(p, q)$, $\gamma_i = \alpha_i + \beta_i$. $\alpha_i = 0$ when $i > q$, and $\beta_i = 0$ when $i > p$.

Proof:
as in Theorem 12.5.   □

If ε_t follows a GARCH process, then from Theorem 12.9 we can see that ε_t^2 follows an ARMA model with conditional heteroscedastic error terms η_t. As we know if all the roots of the polynomial $(1 - \beta_1 z - \ldots - \beta_p z^p)$ lie outside the unit circle, then the ARMA process (12.21) is invertible and can be written as an AR(∞) process. Moveover it follows from Theorem 12.8 that the GARCH(p, q) model can be represented as an ARCH(∞) model. Thus one can deduce analogous conclusions from the ARMA models in determining the order (p, q) of the model. There are however essential differences in the definition of the persistence of shocks.

Theorem 12.10 (Unconditional variance of a GARCH(p, q) process)

Let ε_t be a semi-strong GARCH(p,q) process with $Var(\varepsilon_t) = \sigma^2 < \infty$. Then

$$\sigma^2 = \frac{\omega}{1 - \sum_{i=1}^{q} \alpha_i - \sum_{j=1}^{p} \beta_j},$$

with $\sum_{i=1}^{q} \alpha_i + \sum_{j=1}^{p} \beta_j < 1$.

Proof:
as in Theorem 12.2.   □

General conditions for the existence of higher moments of the GARCH(p, q) models are given in He and Teräsvirta (1999). For the smaller order models and under the assumption of distribution we can derive:

Theorem 12.11 (Fourth moment of a GARCH(1,1) process)
Let ε_t be a (semi-)strong GARCH(1,1) process with $Var(\varepsilon_t) = \sigma^2 < \infty$ and $Z_t \sim N(0,1)$. Then $E[\varepsilon_t^4] < \infty$ holds if and only if $3\alpha_1^2 + 2\alpha_1\beta_1 + \beta_1^2 < 1$. The Kurtosis $Kurt(\varepsilon_t)$ is given as

$$Kurt[\varepsilon_t] = \frac{E[\varepsilon_t^4]}{(E[\varepsilon_t^2])^2} = 3 + \frac{6\alpha_1^2}{1 - \beta_1^2 - 2\alpha_1\beta_1 - 3\alpha_1^2}. \tag{12.22}$$

Proof:
It can be proved that $E[\varepsilon_t^4] = 3\,E[(\omega + \alpha_1\varepsilon_{t-1}^2 + \beta_1\sigma_{t-1}^2)^2]$ and the stationarity of ε_t. $\qquad\qquad\square$

The function (12.22) is illustrated in Figure 12.6 for all $\alpha_1 > 0$, $Kurt[\varepsilon_t] > 3$, i.e., the distribution of ε_t is leptokurtic. We can observe that the kurtosis equals 3 only in the case of the boundary value $\alpha_1 = 0$ where the conditional heteroscedasticity disappears and a Gaussian white noise takes place. In addition it can be seen in the figure that the kurtosis increases in β_1 slowly for a given α_1. On the contrary it increases in α_1 much faster for a given β_1.

Remark 12.3
Nelson (1990a) shows that the strong GARCH(1,1) process X_t is strictly stationary when $E[\log(\alpha_1 Z_t^2 + \beta_1)] < 0$. If $Z_t \sim N(0,1)$, then the conditions for strict stationarity are weaker than those for covariance-stationarity: $\alpha_1 + \beta_1 < 1$.

In practical applications it is frequently shown that models with smaller order sufficiently describe the data. In most cases GARCH(1,1) is sufficient.

A substantial disadvantage of the standard ARCH and GARCH models exists since they can not model asymmetries of the volatility with respect to the sign of past shocks. This results from the squared form of the lagged shocks in (12.16) and (12.19). Therefore they have an effect on the level but no effect on the sign. In other words, bad news (identified by a negative sign) has the same influence on the volatility as good news (positive sign) if the absolute values are the same. Empirically it is observed that bad news has a larger effect on the volatility than good news. In Section 12.2 and 13.1 we will take a closer look at the extensions of the standard models which can be used to calculate these observations.

Kurtosis of a GARCH(1,1) Process

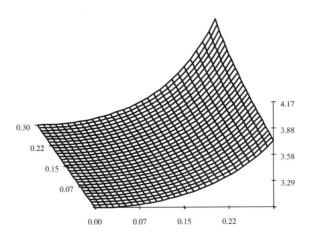

Figure 12.6:   Kurtosis of a GARCH(1,1) process according to (12.22).
The left axis shows the parameter β_1, the right α_1.
◘ SFEkurgarch.xpl

12.1.6   Estimation of GARCH(p, q) Models

Based on the ARMA representation of GARCH processes (see Theorem
12.9) Yule-Walker estimators $\tilde{\theta}$ are considered once again. These estimators
are, as can be shown, consistent and asymptotically normally distributed,
$\sqrt{n}(\tilde{\theta} - \theta) \overset{\mathcal{L}}{\longrightarrow} N(0, \tilde{\Sigma})$. However in the case of GARCH models they are
not efficient in the sense that the matrix $\tilde{\Sigma} - J^{-1}IJ^{-1}$ is positively definite,
where $J^{-1}IJ^{-1}$ is the asymptotic covariance matrix of the QML estimator,
see (12.25). In the literature there are several experiments on the efficiency
of the Yule-Walker and QML estimators in finite samples, see Section 12.4.
In most cases maximum likelihood methods are chosen in order to get the
efficiency.

The likelihood function of the general GARCH(p, q) model (12.19) is identical to (12.17) with the extended parameter vector $\theta = (\omega, \alpha_1, \ldots, \alpha_q, \beta_1, \ldots, \beta_p)^\top$. Figure 12.7 displays the likelihood function of a generated GARCH(1,1) process with $\omega = 0.1$, $\alpha = 0.1$, $\beta = 0.8$ and $n = 500$. The parameter ω was chosen so that the unconditional variance is everywhere constant, i.e., with a variance of σ^2, $\omega = (1 - \alpha - \beta)\sigma^2$. As one can see, the function is flat on the right, close to the optimum, thus the estimation will be relatively imprecise, i.e., it will have a larger variance. In addition, Figure 12.8 displays the contour plot of the likelihood function.

Likelihood function of a GARCH (1,1) Process

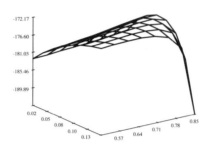

Figure 12.7:   Likelihood function of a generated GARCH(1,1) process with $n = 500$. The left axis shows the parameter β, the right α. The true parameters are $\omega = 0.1$, $\alpha = 0.1$ and $\beta = 0.8$.

Q SFElikgarch.xpl

The first partial derivatives of (12.17) are

$$\frac{\partial l_t}{\partial \theta} = \frac{1}{2\sigma_t^2} \frac{\partial \sigma_t^2}{\partial \theta} \left(\frac{\varepsilon_t^2}{\sigma_t^2} - 1 \right) \tag{12.23}$$

with

$$\frac{\partial \sigma_t^2}{\partial \theta} = \vartheta_t + \sum_{j=1}^{p} \frac{\partial \sigma_{t-j}^2}{\partial \theta}.$$

and $\vartheta_t = (1, \varepsilon_{t-1}^2, \ldots, \varepsilon_{t-q}^2, \sigma_{t-1}^2, \ldots, \sigma_{t-p}^2)^\top$. The first order conditions are $\sum_{t=q+1}^{n} \partial l_t / \partial \theta = 0$. The matrix of the second derivatives takes the following

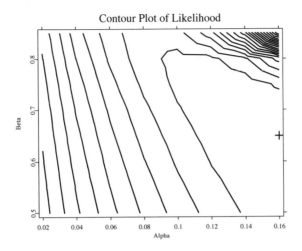

Figure 12.8:   Contour plot of the likelihood function of a generated
GARCH(1,1) process with $n = 500$. The perpendicular axis displays the parameter β, the horizontal α. The true parameters
are $\omega = 0.1$, $\alpha = 0.1$ and $\beta = 0.8$.   ⬛ SFElikgarch.xpl

form:

$$\frac{\partial^2 l_t(\theta)}{\partial\theta\partial\theta^\top} = \frac{1}{2\sigma_t^4}\frac{\partial\sigma_t^2}{\partial\theta}\frac{\partial\sigma_t^2}{\partial\theta^\top} - \frac{1}{2\sigma_t^2}\frac{\partial^2\sigma_t^2(\theta)}{\partial\theta\partial\theta^\top}$$
$$- \frac{\varepsilon_t^2}{\sigma_t^6}\frac{\partial\sigma_t^2}{\partial\theta}\frac{\partial\sigma_t^2}{\partial\theta^\top} + \frac{\varepsilon_t^2}{2\sigma_t^4}\frac{\partial^2\sigma_t^2(\theta)}{\partial\theta\partial\theta^\top} \tag{12.24}$$

Under the conditions

1. $\mathsf{E}[Z_t \mid \mathcal{F}_{t-1}] = 0$ and $\mathsf{E}[Z_t^2 \mid \mathcal{F}_{t-1}] = 1$,

2. strict stationarity of ε_t

and under some technical conditions the ML estimator is consistent. If in
addition it holds that $\mathsf{E}[Z_t^4 \mid \mathcal{F}_{t-1}] < \infty$, then $\hat{\theta}$ is asymptotically normally
distributed:

$$\sqrt{n}(\hat{\theta} - \theta) \xrightarrow{\mathcal{L}} \mathrm{N}_{p+q+1}(0, J^{-1}IJ^{-1}) \tag{12.25}$$

with

$$I = \mathsf{E}\left(\frac{\partial l_t(\theta)}{\partial\theta}\frac{\partial l_t(\theta)}{\partial\theta^\top}\right)$$

and

$$J = - \mathsf{E} \left(\frac{\partial^2 l_t(\theta)}{\partial \theta \partial \theta^T} \right).$$

Theorem 12.12 (Equivalence of I and J)
If $Z_t \sim N(0, 1)$, then it holds that $I = J$.

Proof:
Building the expectations of (12.24) one obtains

$$\mathsf{E} \left[\frac{\partial^2 l_t(\theta)}{\partial \theta \partial \theta^\top} \right] = - \mathsf{E} \frac{1}{2\sigma_t^4} \frac{\partial \sigma_t^2}{\partial \theta} \frac{\partial \sigma_t^2}{\partial \theta^\top}.$$

For I we have

$$
\begin{aligned}
\mathsf{E} \left[\frac{\partial l_t(\theta)}{\partial \theta} \frac{\partial l_t(\theta)}{\partial \theta^T} \right] &= \mathsf{E} \left[\frac{1}{4\sigma_t^4} \frac{\partial \sigma_t^2}{\partial \theta} \frac{\partial \sigma_t^2}{\partial \theta^T} (Z_t^4 - 2Z_t^2 + 1) \right] \qquad (12.26) \\
&= \mathsf{E} \left[\frac{1}{4\sigma_t^4} \frac{\partial \sigma_t^2}{\partial \theta} \frac{\partial \sigma_t^2}{\partial \theta^\top} \right] \{ \mathrm{Kurt}(Z_t \mid \mathcal{F}_{t-1}) - 1 \}
\end{aligned}
$$

From the assumption $Z_t \sim N(0, 1)$ it follows that $\mathrm{Kurt}(Z_t \mid \mathcal{F}_{t-1}) = 3$ and thus the claim. □

If the distribution of Z_t is specified correctly, then $I = J$ and the asymptotic variance can be simplified to J^{-1}, i.e., the inverse of the Fisher Information matrix. If this is not the case and it is instead leptokurtic, for example, the maximum of (12.9) is still consistent but no longer efficient. In this case the ML method is interpreted as the 'Quasi Maximum Likelihood' (QML) method.

Consistent estimators for the matrices I and J can be obtained by replacing the expectation with the simple average.

12.2 Extensions of the GARCH Model

Standard GARCH models assume that positive and negative error terms have a symmetric effect on the volatility. In other words, good and bad news have the same effect on the volatility in this model. In practice this assumption is frequently violated, in particular by stock returns, in that the volatility increases more after bad news than after good news. This so called *Leverage Effect* appears firstly in Black (1976), who noted that:

> *"a drop in the value of the firm will cause a negative return on its stock, and will usually increase the leverage of the stock. [...] That rise in the debt-equity ratio will surely mean a rise in the volatility of the stock".*

A very simple but plausible explanation for the leverage effect: Negative returns imply a larger proportion of debt through a reduced market value of the firm, which leads to a higher volatility. The risk, i.e. the volatility reacts first to larger changes of the market value, nevertheless it is empirically shown that there is a high volatility after smaller changes. On the other hand, Black said nothing about the effect of positive returns on the volatility. Although the positive returns cause smaller increases, they do cause an increase in the volatility. From an empirical point of view the volatility reacts asymmetrically to the sign of the shocks and therefore a number of parameterized extensions of the standard GARCH model have been suggested recently. In the following we will discuss two of the most important ones: the exponential GARCH (EGARCH) and the threshold GARCH (TGARCH) model.

12.2.1   Exponential GARCH

Let Z_t further denote a series of *i.i.d.* standardized random variables with expectation 0 and variance 1. The general exponential GARCH (EGARCH) model is given by Nelson (1991):

$$\log \sigma_t^2 = \omega_t + \sum_{k=1}^{\infty} \beta_k g(Z_{t-k}), \tag{12.27}$$

where ω_t, β_k are deterministic coefficients and

$$g(Z_t) = \theta Z_t + \gamma(|Z_t| - E|Z_t|). \tag{12.28}$$

It can be directly seen that $E\left[g(Z_t)\right] = 0$.

The EGARCH model in (12.27) shows some differences from the standard GARCH model:

- Volatility of the EGARCH model, which is measured by the conditional variance σ_t^2, is an explicit multiplicative function of lagged innovations. On the contrary, volatility of the standard GARCH model is an additive function of the lagged error terms ε_t, which causes a complicated functional dependency on the innovations; for example the ARCH(1) in Theorem 12.4.

- Volatility can react asymmetrically to the good and bad news.

- For the general distributions of Z_t the parameter restrictions for strong and covariance-stationarity coincide.

- The parameters in (12.27) and (12.28) are not restricted to positive values.

The function $g(\cdot)$ in (12.28) is piecewise linear. It contains two parameters which define the 'size effect' and the 'sign effect' of the shocks on volatility. The first is a typical ARCH effect while the second is an asymmetrical effect, for example, the leverage effect. The term $\gamma(|Z_t| - E|Z_t|)$ determines the size effect and the term θZ_t determines the sign effect. The parameter γ is thus typically positive and θ is negative.

To estimate EGARCH models instead of the general MA(∞) representation (12.27), an ARMA(p, q) model is applied, i.e.,

$$\Delta(L) \log \sigma_t^2 = \omega + \Psi(L) g(Z_t), \qquad (12.29)$$

with lag-polynomial $\Delta(L)$ and $\Psi(L)$ of order p and q respectively.

EGARCH models benefit from no parameter restrictions, thus the possible instabilities of optimization routines are reduced. On the other hand the theoretical properties of QML estimators of EGARCH models are not clarified to a great extent.

Let $\omega_t = \omega = 0$ and $\sum_{k=1}^{\infty} \beta_k^2 < \infty$. Then σ_t^2 is strictly stationary and ergodic, see Theorem 2.1 in Nelson (1991). Furthermore, under these conditions the unconditional variance exists when Z_t has a *generalized error distribution* (GED) with parameter $\zeta > 1$, which determines the thickness of the tails, see Theorem 2.2 in Nelson (1991). The GED is leptokurtic when $\zeta < 2$.

The normal distribution is a special case of the GED ($\zeta = 2$). Nelson gives in addition complicated formulas of the unconditional moments. One problem is that under other leptokurtic distributions such as the Student-t, the unconditional variance does not exist. The reason is that exponential growth of the conditional variance changes with the level of the shocks, which leads to the explosion of the unconditional variance when the probability for extreme shocks is sufficiently large. Therefore the existence of the unconditional moments depends on the choice of the distribution of the innovations, which is an undesirable property of the EGARCH models. In empirical studies it has been found that EGARCH often overweighs the effects of larger shocks on volatility and thus results in poorer fits than standard GARCH models, see the empirical studies of Engle and Ng (1993).

12.2.2 Threshold ARCH Models

The idea of the Threshold ARCH (TARCH) models is to divide the distribution of the innovations into disjoint intervals and then approximate a piecewise linear function for the conditional standard deviation, see Zakoian (1991), and the conditional variance respectively, see Glosten, Jagannathan and Runkle (1993). If there are only two intervals, the division is normally at zero, i.e., the influence of positive and negative innovations on the volatility is differentiated. In this case the TARCH model of order q can be written as

$$\sigma_t^\delta = \omega + \sum_{i=1}^{q} \alpha_i \varepsilon_{t-i}^\delta + \sum_{i=1}^{q} \alpha_i^- \varepsilon_{t-i}^\delta I(\varepsilon_{t-i} < 0), \qquad (12.30)$$

with the indicator function $I(\cdot)$ and $\delta = 1$ as in Zakoian (1991) or $\delta = 2$ as in Glosten et al. (1993).

Rabemananjara and Zakoian (1993) extend this model by including the lagged conditional standard deviations (variance respectively) as a regressor, which is known as the TGARCH model. They also give conditions for covariance-stationarity in their study.

Instead of a piecewise linear function Gouriéroux and Monfort (1992) use a stepwise function (piecewise constant) as a model for the volatility. Let $A_j, j = 1, \ldots, J$ be a partition of the distribution of the innovation. Then a *qualitative threshold ARCH* model (QTARCH) of order 1 is given by:

$$y_t = \sum_{j=1}^{J} m_j I(y_{t-1} \in A_j) + \sum_{j=1}^{J} s_j I(y_{t-1} \in A_j) Z_t, \qquad (12.31)$$

where m_j and s_j are scalars. In (12.31) conditional expectations and conditional standard deviations are modelled as stepwise functions. One notices that (12.31) is a homogenous Markov Chain of order one. Models of higher order can be easily derived. Gouriéroux and Monfort (1992) give a detailed discussion of the statistical properties of (12.31). Moreover the consistency and asymptotic normal distribution of the QML estimators are also discussed by them.

The threshold models are identified by an abrupt transition between two regimes when the generating innovation crosses a threshold value. If a smooth transition is preferred in the model, then the indicator function in (12.30) can be replaced with the desired continuous function, which tends to zero if the values are close to ε_{t-i} and tends to one for the values further away.

Frequently, the logistic function is chosen. The model is thus

$$\sigma_t^\delta = \omega + \sum_{i=1}^{q} \alpha_i \varepsilon_{t-i}^\delta + \sum_{i=1}^{q} \alpha_i^- \varepsilon_{t-i}^\delta F_\gamma(\varepsilon_{t-i}) \qquad (12.32)$$

$$F_\gamma(u) = \frac{1}{1 + \exp(-\gamma u)}, \qquad (12.33)$$

with the parameter $\gamma > 0$. The indicator function is a limiting case of the logistic function for $\gamma \longrightarrow \infty$.

Finally, another model class needs to be mentioned, which is very general and can replicate the asymmetries: the Asymmetric Power ARCH (APARCH) model from Ding, Granger and Engle (1993),

$$\sigma_t^\delta = \omega + \sum_{i=1}^{q} \alpha_i (|\varepsilon_{t-i}| - \gamma_i \varepsilon_{t-i})^\delta + \sum_{j=1}^{p} \beta_j \sigma_{t-j}^\delta, \qquad (12.34)$$

where $\delta > 0$ is a parameter to be estimated. However note that the EGARCH model is not included in this model class, a direct test between GARCH and EGARCH models is thus impossible. A very general ARCH model, the *augmented GARCH* model from Duan (1997), also includes the EGARCH model.

12.2.3   Risk and Returns

In finance theory the relationship between risk and returns plays an important role. Many theoretical models such as CAPM, imply a linear relationship between the expected returns of a market portfolio and the variance. If the risk (i.e. the variance) is not constant over time, then the conditional expectation of the market returns is a linear function of the conditional variance. The idea from Engle, Lilien and Robins (1987) was consequently used to estimate the conditional variances in GARCH and then the estimations will be used in the conditional expectations' estimation. This is the so called *ARCH in Mean* (ARCH–M) model.

Let y_t be a covariance-stationary return process of a broad market index and σ_t^2 be the conditional variance specified in an ARCH(1) model. The ARCH-M model is

$$y_t = \nu + \lambda g(\sigma_t^2) + \varepsilon_t \qquad (12.35)$$

$$\sigma_t^2 = \omega + \alpha \varepsilon_{t-1}^2,$$

where $g(\cdot)$ is a known parameter function. The CAPM implies that $g(x) = x$, although in most empirical applications the square root or the logarithm is used. The expression $\lambda g(\sigma_t^2)$ can be interpreted as the risk premium.

12.2.4 Estimation Results for the DAX Returns

We applied various ARCH models discussed before to the returns of the German stock index (DAX). Here we didn't use the DAX as quoted on the stock exchange, but instead the DAFOX from the capital market database in Karlsruhe, which has been created for analysis purposes and is adjusted for dividends and inflation. We consider daily returns from 1974 to 1996 (5748 observations).

The returns indicate a clear autocorrelation of first order. There are various possibilities to model these autocorrelations. Two most important models, which we have discussed, are the AR models and the ARCH-M models. The latter is easy to be interpreted economically, i.e., a time dependent risk premium implying an autocorrelation of the returns. This economic motivation is missing for the AR models: the AR term cannot be interpreted as the risk premium, since it can be negative, which contradicts the usual assumption of a risk averse agent. However the AR models offer frequently a better fit to the data than ARCH-M model. The basic model is thus

$$y_t = \mu_t + \sigma_t Z_t$$

with $\mu_t = \nu + \phi y_{t-1}$ (AR(1)) respectively $\mu_t = \nu + \lambda \sigma_t$ (ARCH-M), and σ_t can be GARCH, TGARCH or EGARCH.

The estimation results are given in Table 12.3. They can be summarized as follows:

- The parameter ν is significantly positive for all AR models, which is reflected in the long-run increasing trend of the stock price. For the ARCH-M model the sign of the trends is not only given in ν but also in λ. The effect of a negative ν can be dominated by a positive λ, which is the case in the GARCH-M and the EGARCH-M models.

- The ARCH effects are very pronounced, i.e., the parameter α in the GARCH model is significant.

- There is a high persistence of shocks in the volatility. This persistence is measured in the GARCH case by the sum of α and β and is in each case close to 1.

	AR-G	AR-TG	AR-EG	GARCH-M	TGARCH-M	EGARCH-M
λ				0.107	0.051	0.338
				(2.14)	(1.09)	(3.31)
ν	3.75E-04	3.03E-04	2.57E-04	-2.84E-04	4.71E-05	-0.002
	(4.414)	(3.290)	(2.608)	(-0.79)	(0.14)	(-2.72)
ϕ	0.131	0.137	0.136			
	(6.808)	(8.079)	(5.940)			
ω	8.42E-07	8.22E-07	-5.259	8.81E-07	8.78E-07	-3.086
	(5.312)	(5.444)	(-3.692)	(5.28)	(5.45)	(-4.79)
α	0.079	0.045		0.076	0.049	
	(3.004)	(2.073)		(2.74)	(1.94)	
α^-		0.058			0.044	
		(1.752)			(1.77)	
β	0.914	0.918	0.490	0.917	0.919	0.711
	(44.07)	(38.18)	(3.41)	(41.43)	(36.57)	(10.87)
γ			0.431			0.388
			(13.95)			(11.25)
θ			-0.171			-0.085
			(-3.65)			(-1.97)
logL	20030.86	20049.18	19713.81	19996.19	20008.22	19827.41

Table 12.3: Estimation results of various ARCH models, applied to DAFOX returns 1974–1996. In the parenthesis is the t-statistic based on the QML asymptotic standard error.

- Except for the EGARCH specification of the volatility the AR(1) model describes the data better than the ARCH-M models.

- There exists a leverage effect: the corresponding parameters in the TGARCH and the EGARCH models have the appropriate signs. In the TGARCH case the t-statistic for α^- is 1.75 and 1.77 respectively, and in the EGARCH case the t-statistic for θ is -3.65 and -1.97 respectively. Negative shocks increase the volatility more than positive shocks.

- The TGARCH and the EGARCH models have a priority for asymmetry, since they have a better fit to the data when the same number of parameters are considered.

12.3   Multivariate GARCH models

The generalization of univariate GARCH models to the multivariate case is straightforward. For the error term ε_t of a d-dimensional time series model we assume that the conditional mean is zero and the conditional covariance matrix is given by the positive definite $(d \times d)$ matrix H_t, i.e.,

$$\varepsilon_t = H_t^{1/2} \xi_t \tag{12.36}$$

with i.i.d. innovation vector ξ_t, whose mean is zero and covariance matrix equals the identity matrix I_d. As in the univariate case, H_t depends on lagged error terms ε_{t-i}, $i = 1, \ldots, q$, and on lagged conditional covariance matrices H_{t-i}, $i = 1, \ldots, p,$. As we will see shortly, the general case with arbitrary dependencies can lead to very complex structures that may be too difficult to deal with in practice. It is therefore often tried to reduce the dimension of the parameter space. In the following, we first discuss a general specification and then a popular restriction, the BEKK model. We will also briefly sketch a model that assumes constant conditional correlations.

12.3.1   The Vec Specification

Let vech$(\cdot)$ denote the operator that stacks the lower triangular part of a symmetric $d \times d$ matrix into a $d^* = d(d+1)/2$ dimensional vector. Furthermore we use the notation $h_t = \text{vech}(H_t)$ and $\eta_t = \text{vech}(\varepsilon_t \varepsilon_t^\top)$. The *Vec specification* of a multivariate GARCH(p,q) model is then given by

$$h_t = \omega + \sum_{i=1}^{q} A_i \eta_{t-i} + \sum_{j=1}^{p} B_j h_{t-j}, \tag{12.37}$$

where A_i and B_j are parameter matrices with each one containing $(d^*)^2$ parameters. The vector ω represents constant components of the covariances and contains d^* parameters.

For the bivariate case and $p = q = 1$ we can write the model explicitly as

$$
\begin{pmatrix} h_{11,t} \\ h_{12,t} \\ h_{22,t} \end{pmatrix} = \begin{pmatrix} \omega_1 \\ \omega_2 \\ \omega_3 \end{pmatrix} + \begin{pmatrix} a_{11} & a_{12} & a_{13} \\ a_{21} & a_{22} & a_{23} \\ a_{31} & a_{32} & a_{33} \end{pmatrix} \begin{pmatrix} \varepsilon_{1,t-1}^2 \\ \varepsilon_{1,t-1}\varepsilon_{2,t-1} \\ \varepsilon_{2,t-1}^2 \end{pmatrix}
$$
$$
+ \begin{pmatrix} b_{11} & b_{12} & b_{13} \\ b_{21} & b_{22} & b_{23} \\ b_{31} & b_{32} & b_{33} \end{pmatrix} \begin{pmatrix} h_{11,t-1} \\ h_{12,t-1} \\ h_{22,t-1} \end{pmatrix}
$$

By rearranging terms, we can write the second order process η_t as a vector autoregressive moving average (VARMA) process of order $(\max(p,q), p)$,

$$\eta_t = \omega + \sum_{i=1}^{\max(p,q)} (A_i + B_i) \eta_{t-i} - \sum_{j=1}^{p} B_j u_{t-j} + u_t, \tag{12.38}$$

where $u_t = \eta_t - h_t$ is a vector white noise process, i.e., $\mathsf{E}[u_t] = 0$, $\mathsf{E}[u_t u_t^\top] = \Sigma_u$ und $\mathsf{E}[u_t u_s^\top] = 0$, $s \neq t$. In (12.38) we set $A_{q+1} = \ldots = A_p = 0$ if $p > q$ and $B_{p+1} = \ldots = B_q = 0$ if $q > p$. Often the VARMA representation of multivariate GARCH models simplifies the derivation of stochastic properties, as one can refer to known results of the VARMA literature.

In the Vec representation (12.37), the multivariate GARCH(p,q) process ε_t is covariance stationary if and only if all eigenvalues of the matrix

$$\sum_{i=1}^{\max(p,q)} (A_i + B_i)$$

are smaller than one in modulus, see Engle and Kroner (1995). In that case, the unconditional covariance matrix is given by

$$\sigma = \mathrm{vech}(\Sigma) = \left(I_{d^*} - \sum_{i=1}^{\max(p,q)} (A_i + B_i) \right)^{-1} \omega. \qquad (12.39)$$

In order to illustrate the prediction of volatility, let us consider in the following the often used GARCH(1,1) model. The optimal prediction with respect to the mean squared prediction error is the conditional expectation of volatility. Due to the law of iterated expectations, the k-step prediction of η_{t+k} is identical to the k-step prediction of h_{t+k}, that is,

$$\mathsf{E}[\eta_{t+k} \mid \mathcal{F}_t] = \mathsf{E}[\mathsf{E}(\eta_{t+k} \mid \mathcal{F}_{t+k-1}) \mid \mathcal{F}_t] = \mathsf{E}[h_{t+k} \mid \mathcal{F}_t].$$

Having information up to time t, the predictions for the next three time periods are given by

$$\begin{aligned}
\mathsf{E}[\eta_{t+1} \mid \mathcal{F}_t] &= h_{t+1} \\
\mathsf{E}[\eta_{t+2} \mid \mathcal{F}_t] &= \omega + (A + B)h_{t+1} \\
\mathsf{E}[\eta_{t+3} \mid \mathcal{F}_t] &= (I_{d^*} + A + B)\omega + (A + B)^2 h_{t+1},
\end{aligned}$$

and it can be seen that in general, the k-step prediction with $k \geq 2$ is given by

$$\mathsf{E}[\eta_{t+k} \mid \mathcal{F}_t] = \left\{ I_{d^*} + (A + B) + \ldots + (A + B)^{k-2} \right\} \omega + (A + B)^{k-1} h_{t+1}.$$

This converges to the unconditional covariance matrix $\sigma = (I_{d^*} - A - B)^{-1}\omega$ if and only if the process is covariance stationary.

In the bivariate case ($d = 2$) and with $p = q = 1$, there are already 21 parameters that characterize the dynamics of volatility. In order to obtain a feasible model for empirical work, one often imposes restrictions on the parameter matrices of the Vec model. Bollerslev, Engle and Wooldridge (1988) propose to use diagonal parameter matrices such that the conditional variance of one variable only depends on lagged squared values of the same variable, and the conditional covariances between two variables only depend on lagged values of cross-products of these variables. This model reduces substantially the number of parameters (in the above case from 21 to 9), but potentially important causalities are excluded.

For parameter estimation the Quasi Maximum Likelihood Method (QML) is suitable. The conditional likelihood function for a sample time series of n observations is given by $\log L = \sum_{t=1}^{n} l_t$ with

$$l_t = -\frac{d}{2}\log(2\pi) - \frac{1}{2}\log\{\det(H_t)\} - \frac{1}{2}\varepsilon_t^\top H_t^{-1}\varepsilon_t. \qquad (12.40)$$

If the conditional distribution of ε_t is not normal, then (12.40) is interpreted as quasi likelihood function, which serves merely as target function in the numerical optimization, but which does not say anything about the true distribution. In the multivariate case, the QML estimator is consistent and asymptotically normal under the main assumptions that the considered process is strictly stationary and ergodic with finite eighth moment. Writing all parameters in one vector, θ, we obtain the following standard result.

$$\sqrt{n}(\hat{\theta} - \theta) \xrightarrow{\mathcal{L}} N(0, J^{-1}IJ^{-1}), \qquad (12.41)$$

where I is the expectation of outer product of the score vector (i.e., the vector $\partial l_t/\partial\theta$), and J the negative expectation of the Hessian (i.e., the matrix of second derivatives). In the case of a normal distribution, we have $I = J$ and the asymptotic distribution simplifies to

$$\sqrt{n}(\hat{\theta} - \theta) \xrightarrow{\mathcal{L}} N(0, J^{-1}). \qquad (12.42)$$

In other words, these results are completely analogous to the univariate case, but the analytical expressions for I and J become much more complicated. Of course one can also determine I and J numerically, but this can lead to unreliable results, especially for J, in the multivariate case.

In empirical work one often finds that estimated standardized residuals are not normally distributed. In this case the QML likelihood function would be misspecified and provides only consistent, not efficient parameter estimators. Alternatively, one can assume that the true innovation distribution is given by some specific non-normal parametric distribution, but in general this does not guarantee that parameter estimates are consistent in the case that the assumption is wrong.

12.3.2   Die BEKK Spezifikation

Engle and Kroner (1995) discuss the following specification of a multivariate
GARCH model.

$$H_t = C_0 C_0^\top + \sum_{k=1}^{K}\sum_{i=1}^{q} A_{ki}^\top \varepsilon_{t-i}\varepsilon_{t-i}^\top A_{ki} + \sum_{k=1}^{K}\sum_{j=1}^{p} B_{kj}^\top H_{t-j}B_{kj}. \qquad (12.43)$$

In (12.43), C_0 is a lower triangular matrix and A_{ki} and B_{ki} are $d{\times}d$ parameter
matrices. For example, in the bivariate case with $K = 1$, $p = 1$ and $q = 0$,
the conditional variance of ε_{1t} can be written as

$$h_{11,t} = c_{11}^2 + a_{11}^2\varepsilon_{1t}^2 + a_{12}^2\varepsilon_{2t}^2 + 2a_{11}a_{12}\varepsilon_{1t}\varepsilon_{2t}$$

and the conditional covariance as

$$h_{12,t} = c_{11}c_{21} + a_{11}a_{21}\varepsilon_{1t}^2 + a_{12}a_{22}\varepsilon_{2t}^2 + (a_{12}a_{21} + a_{11}a_{22})\varepsilon_{1t}\varepsilon_{2t}$$

The so-called BEKK specification in (12.43) guarantees under weak assumptions that H_t is positive definite. A sufficient condition for positivity is for
example that at least one of the matrices C_0 or B_{ki} have full rank and the
matrices $H_0, \ldots, H_{1-p}$ are positive definite. The BEKK model allows for
dependence of conditional variances of one variable on the lagged values of
another variable, so that causalities in variances can be modelled. For the
case of diagonal parameter matrices A_{ki} and B_{ki}, the BEKK model is a
restricted version of the Vec model with diagonal matrices.

Due to the quadratic form of the BEKK model, the parameters are not
identifiable without further restriction. However, simple sign restrictions will
give identifiability. For example, in the often used model $K = 1$ and $p =
q = 1$, it suffices to assume that the upper left elements of A_{11} and B_{11}
are positive. The number of parameters reduces typically strongly when
compared to the Vec model. For the above mentioned case, the number of
parameters reduces from 21 to 11.

For each BEKK model there is an equivalent Vec representation, but not vice
versa, so that the BEKK model is a special case of the Vec model. To see this,
just apply the vech operator to both sides of (12.43) and define $\omega = L_d(C_0 \otimes C_0)^\top D_d \text{vech}(I_d)$, $A_i = \sum_{k=1}^{K} L_d(A_{ki} \otimes A_{ki})^\top D_d$, and $B_j = \sum_{k=1}^{K} L_d(B_{kj} \otimes B_{kj})^\top D_d$. Here $\otimes$ denotes the Kronecker matrix product, and L_d and D_d
are the elementary elimination and duplication matrices. Therefore, one can
derive the stochastic properties of the BEKK model by those of the Vec
model. For the empirical work, the BEKK model will be preferable, because
it is much easier to estimate while being sufficiently general.

	Min.	Max.	Mean	Median	Std.Error
DEM/USD	−0.040	0.032	$-4.718e - 06$	0	0.0071
GBP/USD	−0.047	0.039	0.000110	0	0.0070

Table 12.4:   **Q** `SFEmvol01.xpl`

12.3.3   The CCC model

Bollerslev (1990) suggested a multivariate GARCH model in which all conditional correlation are constant and the conditional variances are modelled by univariate GARCH models. This so-called CCC model (constant conditional correlation) is not a special case of the Vec model, but belongs to another, nonlinear model class. For example, the CCC(1,1) model is given by

$$h_{ii,t} = \omega_i + \alpha_i \varepsilon_{t-1}^2 + \beta_i h_{ii,t-1},$$

$$h_{ij,t} = \rho_{ij} \sqrt{h_{ii,t} h_{jj,t}}$$

for $i, j = 1 \ldots, d$, and ρ_{ij} equal to the constant correlation between ε_{it} and ε_{jt}, which can be estimated separately from the conditional variances. The advantage of the CCC model is in the unrestricted applicability for large systems of time series. On the other hand, the assumption of constant correlation is possibly quite restrictive. For example, in the empirical analysis of financial markets one typically observes increasing correlation in times of crisis or in crash situations.

12.3.4   An empirical illustration

We consider a bivariate exchange rates example, two European currencies, DEM and GBP, with respect to the US Dollar. The sample period is 01/01/1980 to 04/01/1994 with altogether $n = 3720$ observations. Figure 12.9 shows the time series of returns on both exchange rates. Table 12.4 provides some simple descriptive statistics of returns ε_t. Apparently, the empirical mean of both processes is close to zero.

As can be seen in Figure 12.9, the exchange rate returns follow a pattern that resembles a GARCH process: there is a clustering of volatilities in both series, and the cluster tend to occur simultaneously. This motivates an application of a bivariate GARCH model.

A first simple method to estimated the parameters of a BEKK model is the BHHH algorithm. This algorithm uses the first derivatives of the QML

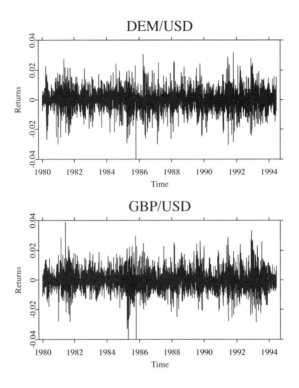

Figure 12.9: Exchange rate returns. **Q** SFEmvol01.xpl

likelihood with respect to the 11 parameters that are contained in C_0, A_{11} and G_{11}, recalling equation (12.43). As this is an iterative procedure, the BHHH algorithm needs suitable initial parameters. For the diagonal elements of the matrices A_{11} and B_{11}, values between 0.3 and 0.9 are sensible, because this is the range often obtained in estimations. For the off-diagonal elements there is no rule of thumb, so one can try different starting values or just set them to zero. The starting values for C_0 can be obtained by the starting values for A_{11} and B_{11} using the formula for the unconditional covariance matrix and matching the sample covariance matrix with the theoretical version.

For the bivariate exchange rate example, we obtain the following estimates:

$$\hat{\theta} = \begin{pmatrix} 0.00115 \\ 0.00031 \\ 0.00076 \\ 0.28185 \\ -0.05719 \\ -0.05045 \\ 0.29344 \\ 0.93878 \\ 0.02512 \\ 0.02750 \\ 0.93910 \end{pmatrix}$$

$$l_t = -28599$$

Q SFEmvol02.xpl

the previous value represents the computed minimum of the negative log likelihood function. The displayed vector contains in the first three components the parameters in C_0, the next four components are the parameters in A_{11}, and the last four components are the parameters in B_{11}.

In this example we thus obtain as estimated parameters of the BEKK model:

$$C_0 = 10^{-3} \begin{pmatrix} 1.15 & 0.31 \\ 0.00 & 0.76 \end{pmatrix},$$

$$A_{11} = \begin{pmatrix} 0.282 & -0.050 \\ -0.057 & 0.293 \end{pmatrix}, \; B_{11} = \begin{pmatrix} 0.939 & 0.028 \\ 0.025 & 0.939 \end{pmatrix}. \tag{12.44}$$

Estimates for the conditional covariances are obtained by applying successively the difference equation (12.43), where the empirical covariance matrix

$$\hat{H}_0 = \frac{1}{n} \sum_{t=1}^{n} \varepsilon_t \varepsilon_t^\top$$

of the observations ε_t is taken as initial value.

In Figure 12.10 estimated conditional variance and covariance processes are compared. The upper and lower plots show the variance of the DEM/USD and GBP/USD returns and the plot in the middle shows the estimated conditional covariance process. Apart from a very short period at the beginning of the sample, the covariance is positive and of not negligible magnitude.

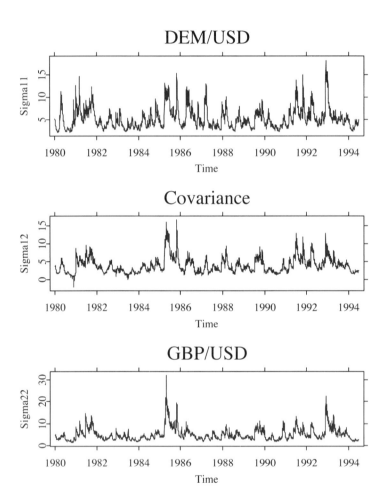

Figure 12.10: Estimated variance and covariance processes, $10^5 \hat{H}_t$.

Q SFEmvol02.xpl

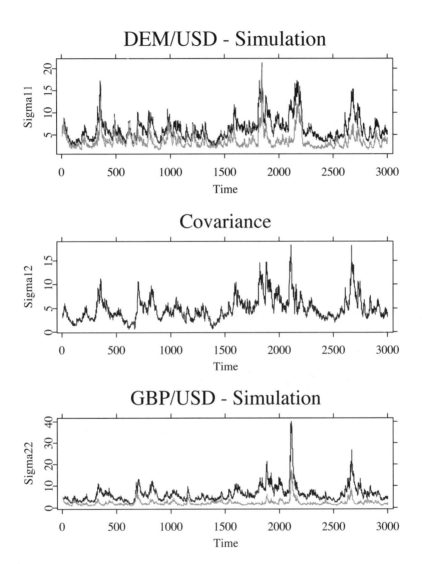

Figure 12.11: Simulated variance and covariance processes with a bivariate (blue) and two univariate (green) GARCH processes,
$10^5 \hat{H}_t$.   Q SFEmvol03.xpl

This confirms our intuition of mutual dependence in exchange markets which motivated the use of the bivariate GARCH model.

Q SFEmvol03.xpl

The estimated parameters can also be used to simulate volatility. This can be done by drawing at every time step one realization of a multivariate normal distribution with mean zero and variance $\hat{H}_t$. With these realizations one updates $\hat{H}_t$ according to equation (12.43). Next, a new realization is obtained by drawing from $N(0, \hat{H}_{t+1})$, and so on. We will now apply this method with $n = 3000$. The results of the simulation in Figure 12.11 show similar patterns as in the original process (Figure 12.10). For a further comparison, we include two independent univariate GARCH processes fitted to the two exchange rate return series. This corresponds to a bivariate Vec representation with diagonal parameter matrices. Obviously, both methods capture the clustering of volatilities. However, the more general bivariate model also captures spill over effect, that is, the increased uncertainty in one of the returns due to increased volatility in the other returns. This has an important impact on the amplitude of volatility.

12.4   Recommended Literature

The empirical properties of financial market data, in particular the leptokurtosis and clustering of volatilities, have been investigated systematically by Mandelbrot (1963) and Fama (1965). ARCH Models were introduced by Engle (1982) and generalized to GARCH by Bollerslev (1986). For an excellent overview of ARCH models we refer to Gouriéroux (1997). An extensive discussion of the estimation of the tail exponent and the Hill estimator can be found in Embrechts, Klüppelberg and Mikosch (1997). A comparison of the efficiency of the Yule Walker estimator with ML estimators of ARCH and GARCH models is given in Maercker (1997).

The theory of QML estimation was developed by White (1982) and Gouriéroux, Monfort and Trognon (1984). Weiss (1986) applied the theory to ARCH models, Lee and Hansen (1994) and Lumsdaine (1996) to GARCH models. Bollerslev and Wooldridge (1992) considered QML estimation for general conditionally heteroscedastic models. The idea of the *smooth transition* specification stems from Teräsvirta (1994) who used it for AR models. It was applied to GARCH models by Lubrano (1998). Hafner and Herwartz (2000) discussed various methods to test for significance of the AR parameter under conditional heteroscedasticity. Moreover, they compare empirical results of AR models versus ARCH-M models, applied to several German stock returns.

In the multivariate case, Jeantheau (1998) has shown the consistency of the QML estimator, and Comte and Lieberman (2003) derived asymptotic normality. Analytical expressions for the score and Hessian matrices are provided by Hafner and Herwatz (2003).

13 Non-parametric Concepts for Financial Time Series

With the analysis of (financial) time series one of the most important goals is to produce forecasts. Using past observed data one would like to make some statements about the future mean, the future volatility, etc., i.e., one would like to estimate the expectation and variance of the underlying process conditional on the past. One method to produce such estimates will be introduced in this chapter.

Let (Y_t), $t = 0, 1, 2, \ldots$, be a time series. We consider a nonlinear autoregressive heteroscedastic model of the form

$$Y_t = f(Y_{t-1}) + s(Y_{t-1})\xi_t, \quad t = 1, 2, \ldots \tag{13.1}$$

Here the innovations ξ_t are i.i.d. random variables with $\mathsf{E}[\xi_t] = 0$ and $\mathsf{E}[\xi_t^2] = 1$, $f : \mathbb{R} \longrightarrow \mathbb{R}$ and $s : \mathbb{R} \longrightarrow (0, \infty)$ are unknown functions, and Y_0 is independent of (ξ_t). Under these assumptions and according to Theorem 3.1 it holds that

$$\mathsf{E}[Y_t \mid Y_{t-1} = x] = f(x) + \mathsf{E}[s(Y_{t-1})\xi_t \mid Y_{t-1} = x] = f(x) + s(x)\mathsf{E}[\xi_t] = f(x),$$

where in the second to last equation the independence of ξ_t and Y_{t-1} is used. A similar calculation gives $s^2(x) = \mathrm{Var}[Y_t \mid Y_{t-1} = x]$. The unknown functions f and s describe the conditional mean and the conditional volatility of the process, which we want to estimate.

With the specific choice $f(x) = \alpha x$ and $s = \sigma > 0$ the process Y_t is an AR(1) process. Every strong ARCH(1) process (Y_i) satisfies the model (13.1). In this case $f = 0$, and it holds that $s(x) = \sqrt{\omega + \alpha x^2}$ with the parameters $\omega > 0$ and $\alpha \geq 0$, compare Definition 12.1. With respect to the structure of the conditional mean and the conditional variance, the model above is another broad generalization of the (strong) ARCH models. The advantage of this *nonparametric* Ansatz is that the model contains no structural assumptions about the functions f and s, since such assumptions are often not supported by observations in the data.

Closely related to our model is the Qualitative Threshold ARCH model (QTARCH) studied in Gouriéroux and Monfort (1992), which for the case of one lag (QTARCH(1)) is a special case of (13.1), where the unknown functions $f : \mathbb{R} \longrightarrow \mathbb{R}$ and $s : \mathbb{R} \longrightarrow (0, \infty)$ take the form of step functions - see (12.31). On the other hand (13.1) can also be described under certain regularity assumptions on f and s as a limit model of the QTARCH(1) models when $J \to \infty$, in that f and s are approximated with elementary functions.

The work of Gouriéroux and Monfort is the first to consider the conditional mean and the conditional variance *together* in a nonparametric model. The applications of this idea introduced here are taken from Härdle and Tsybakov (1997), and are also considered independently in Franke, Kreiss and Mammen (2002). In the following we will construct a class of estimators based on the local polynomial regression for the conditional volatility $v(x) = s^2(x)$ and the conditional mean $f(x)$ of the time series (Y_i) under the model assumptions (13.1).

In addition to the model assumptions (13.1) certain regularity assumptions, although no structural assumptions, on f and s will be made. As the main result of this chapter we will show that this combined estimation of the conditional expectation and the conditional volatility is asymptotically normally distributed.

13.1   Nonparametric Regression

In this section we introduce several basic terms and ideas from the theory of nonparametric regressions and explain in particular the method of local polynomial regression. To conclude we explain how this can be applied to (financial) time series. A detailed representation can be found in Härdle, Müller, Sperlich and Werwatz (2004).

In nonparametric regression one is interested in the (functional) relationship between an explanatory variable X and a dependent variable Y, i.e., one is interested in obtaining an estimation for the unknown function $m(x) = \mathsf{E}[Y \mid X = x]$. In doing this, in contrast to parametric statistics, no special assumptions on the form of the function m is made. Only certain regularity and smoothing assumptions are made about m.

One way to estimate m is to use the method of local polynomial regression (LP Method). The idea is based on the fact that the function m can be locally approximated with a Taylor polynomial, i.e., in a neighborhood around a given point x_0 it holds that

$$m(x) \approx \sum_{k=0}^{p} \frac{m^{(k)}(x_0)}{k!}(x - x_0)^k. \tag{13.2}$$

In order to find an estimate for m at point x_0, one therefore tries to find a polynomial based on observations $(X_1, Y_1), \ldots, (X_n, Y_n)$ that is a good approximation of m around x_0. As a measure of the quality of the approximation one usually chooses a LS criterion, i.e., one wants to minimize the expression

$$\sum_{i=1}^{n} \left\{ Y_i - \sum_{j=0}^{p} \beta_j (X_i - x_0)^j \right\}^2 \tag{13.3}$$

with respect to $\beta = (\beta_0, \ldots, \beta_p)^\top$. Since the representation (13.2) holds only locally, one still has to take into consideration that some of the observations X_i may not lie close enough to x_0 and thus (13.2) no longer applies to them. One must then sufficiently localize the observations, i.e., only consider those observations that lie close enough to x_0.

One of the classical methods for localization is based on weighting the data with the help of a kernel. A kernel is a function $K : \mathbb{R} \longrightarrow [0, \infty)$ with $\int K(u)\, du = 1$. The most useful kernels are also symmetric and disappear outside of a suitable interval around the zero point.

If K is a kernel and $h > 0$, then the kernel K_h

$$K_h(u) = \frac{1}{h} K\left(\frac{u}{h}\right)$$

is re-scaled with the *bandwidth* h, which again integrates to 1. If, for example, the initial kernel K disappears outside of the interval $[-1, 1]$, then K_h is zero outside of the interval $[-h, h]$. By weighting the i-th term in (13.3) with $K_h(x - X_i)$, one has a minimization problem which, due to the applied localization, can be formulated to be independent of the point x_0. The coefficient vector $\hat{\beta} = \hat{\beta}(x) = (\hat{\beta}_0(x), \ldots, \hat{\beta}_p(x))^\top$ that determines the polynomial of the point x is thus given by

$$\hat{\beta} = \arg\min_{\beta} \sum_{i=1}^{n} \left\{ Y_i - \sum_{j=0}^{p} \beta_j (x - X_i)^j \right\}^2 K_h(x - X_i). \tag{13.4}$$

It is obvious that $\hat{\beta}$ depends heavily on the choice of kernel and the bandwidth. Different methods for determining K and h are introduced in Härdle et al. (2004).

With the representation

$$\mathbf{X} = \begin{pmatrix} 1 & X_1 - x & (X_1 - x)^2 & \cdots & (X_1 - x)^p \\ \vdots & \vdots & \vdots & \ddots & \vdots \\ 1 & X_n - x & (X_n - x)^2 & \cdots & (X_n - x)^p \end{pmatrix}, \mathbf{Y} = \begin{pmatrix} Y_1 \\ \vdots \\ Y_n \end{pmatrix},$$

$$\mathbf{W} = \begin{pmatrix} K_h(x - X_1) & & 0 \\ & \ddots & \\ 0 & & K_h(x - X_n) \end{pmatrix}$$

the solution $\hat{\beta}$ to the weighted least squares problem (13.4) can be explicitly written as

$$\hat{\beta}(x) = \left(\mathbf{X}^\top \mathbf{W} \mathbf{X}\right)^{-1} \mathbf{X}^\top \mathbf{W} \mathbf{Y} \tag{13.5}$$

The estimation $\hat{m}(x)$ for $m(x)$ can be obtained only by calculating the approximating polynomial at x:

$$\hat{m}(x) = \hat{\beta}_0(x). \tag{13.6}$$

The remaining components of $\hat{\beta}(x)$, due to equations (13.2) and (13.3) deliver estimators for the derivatives of m: $\hat{m}^{(j)}(x) = j! \, \hat{\beta}_j(x), j = 1, ..., p$, which will not be discussed in further detail here. In the special case where $p = 0$, $\hat{m}(x)$ is a typical kernel estimator of Nadaraya-Watson type, see Härdle (1990).

The similarly derived method of local polynomial approximation, or LP method for short, will now be applied to a time series (Y_i). As mentioned before, one is most interested in creating forecasts.

For the simplest case a one-step-ahead forecast means that the functional relationship between Y_{i-1} and a function $\lambda(Y_i)$ of Y_i will be analyzed, i.e., we want to obtain an estimate for the unknown function

$$m(x) = \mathsf{E}\big[\lambda(Y_i) \,|\, Y_{i-1} = x\big].$$

In order to apply the LP Method mentioned above, consider a given sample $Y_0, \ldots, Y_n$ as observations of the form $(Y_0, Y_1), \ldots, (Y_{n-1}, Y_n)$. The process (Y_i) must fulfil certain conditions, so that these observations are identically distributed and in particular so that the function m is independent of the time index i. Such is the case when (Y_i) is stationary. By substituting $X_i = Y_{i-1}$ into (13.4) and replacing Y_i with $\lambda(Y_i)$, we obtain in this situation

$$\hat{\beta} = \arg\min_\beta \sum_{i=1}^n \left\{ \lambda(Y_i) - \sum_{j=0}^p \beta_j (x - Y_{i-1})^j \right\}^2 K_h(x - Y_{i-1}), \tag{13.7}$$

and the estimate for $m(x)$ is again given by $\hat{\beta}_0(x)$.

13.2   Construction of the Estimator

The LP method introduced in the previous section will now be applied under the assumption of a nonparametric autoregressive model of the form (13.1) to estimate the volatility function $s(x)$ of the process (Y_i) based on the observations $Y_0, \ldots, Y_n$.

The conditional volatility $s_i(x)$ and the conditional variance $v_i(x)$ respectively at time i is defined by

$$v_i(x) = s_i^2(x) = \mathsf{E}[Y_i^2 \mid Y_{i-1} = x] - \mathsf{E}^2[Y_i \mid Y_{i-1} = x]. \qquad (13.8)$$

Included in the assumptions of the model (13.1) is the independence from the time index i. An estimate for $v(x) = s^2(x)$ using the LP Method is based on the fact that the two dimensional marginal distribution (Y_{i-1}, Y_i) is independent of i. In the following we will see that (Y_i) approach is a stationary process, with which the following application is justified.

Referring back to the representation (13.8) of the conditional variance $v(x)$ we search for an estimator $\hat{v}_n$ for v with the form

$$\hat{v}_n(x) = \hat{g}_n(x) - \hat{f}_n^2(x), \qquad (13.9)$$

i.e., we are looking for an estimator $\hat{g}_n(x)$ for $g(x) = f^2(x) + s^2(x)$ and an estimator $\hat{f}_n(x)$ for $f(x)$.

In order to define these two estimators with the LP Method, after applying the steps discussed in the previous section we have to solve both of the following minimization problems:

$$\begin{aligned} \bar{c}_n(x) &= \arg\min_{c \in \mathbb{R}^{p+1}} \sum_{i=1}^{n} (Y_i^2 - c^\top U_{in})^2 K\left(\frac{Y_{i-1}-x}{h_n}\right), \\ c_n(x) &= \arg\min_{c \in \mathbb{R}^{p+1}} \sum_{i=1}^{n} (Y_i - c^\top U_{in})^2 K\left(\frac{Y_{i-1}-x}{h_n}\right). \end{aligned} \qquad (13.10)$$

Here $K : \mathbb{R} \longrightarrow \mathbb{R}$ is a kernel and $\{h_n\}$ a series of positive numbers (bandwidth) with $\lim_{n \to \infty} h_n = 0$. The vectors U_{in} from (13.10) are defined by

$$U_{in} = F(u_{in}), \quad u_{in} = \frac{Y_{i-1} - x}{h_n}. \qquad (13.11)$$

with $\mathbb{R}^{p+1}$ valued function $F(u) = \{F_0(u), \ldots, F_p(u)\}^\top$ given by

$$F_k(u) = \frac{u^k}{k!}.$$

According to the LP Method we define $\hat{g}_n$ and $\hat{f}_n$ with

$$\hat{g}_n(x) = \bar{c}_n(x)^\top F(0) \quad \text{and} \quad \hat{f}_n(x) = c_n(x)^\top F(0),$$

which the above mentioned application ensures that

$$\hat{v}_n(x) = \bar{c}_n(x)^\top F(0) - \left\{ c_n(x)^\top F(0) \right\}^2. \qquad (13.12)$$

This estimate is a direct modification of the estimator from the local polynomial, nonparametric regression in Tsybakov (1986).

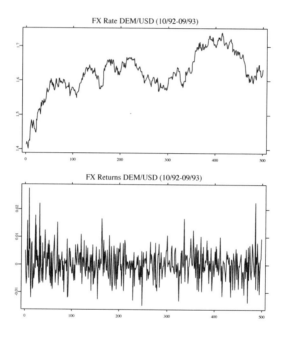

Figure 13.1: DEM/USD Exchange rate and its returns   Q SFEdmusrate.xpl

To illustrate the estimator we consider an example. Figure 13.1 above displays the DEM/USD exchange rate from October 1, 1992 to September 30, 1993 in 20 minute intervals (volatility time scale). There are $n = 25434$ observations. We have calculated the returns of this series (see Figure 13.1 below) and applied the estimator (13.12) to the time series of the returns. Under the model for the geometric Brownian motion for the price, which is based on the Black-Scholes method (see Section 6.1), the returns must follow an ordinary Brownian motion. Their volatilities $v(x)$ are thus constant and independent of x. The estimated conditional variance functions (see Figure 13.2) show a U shaped structure, which is called a "smiling face" structure or *smile.* The estimated volatility functions $\hat{s}(x) = \sqrt{\hat{v}(x)}$ appear to be qualitatively analogous. This means that the expected risk of the returns is significantly higher when extreme values were observed the period before.

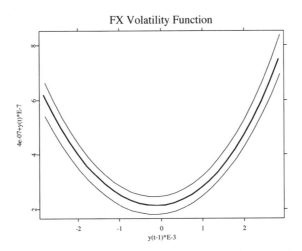

FX Volatility Function

Figure 13.2:   The estimated conditional variance function $\hat{v}(x)$ of the DEM/USD returns   ⬛ SFEdmusvol.xpl

As an alternative to equation (13.9) it is also possible to first determine the sample residuals

$$\hat{Z}_i = Y_i - \hat{f}_n(Y_{i-1}), \quad i = 1, ..., n, .$$

They approximate the true residuals $Z_i = Y_i - f(Y_{i-1})$, which under the assumptions of model (13.1) satisfy

$$E[Z_i|Y_{i-1} = x] = 0, \quad E[Z_i^2|Y_{i-1} = x] = v(x).$$

The volatility can be estimated as in the previous section directly from the nonparametric regression of $\hat{Z}_i^2$ on Y_{i-1}. Fan and Yao (1998) have shown that this process has advantages in heteroscedastic regression models. In estimating $f(x)$ and $v(x) = s^2(x)$, various bandwidths may be used that do not encounter the danger of the variance estimator taking on negative values. This makes sense when it is expected that the local fluctuations of f and s are of very different proportions.

13.3   Asymptotic Normality

We will now show that the estimator $\hat{v}_n(x)$ defined by (13.12) is asymptotically normally distributed. For this we will assume several technical conditions for the model. These will ensure, among other things, that the process (Y_i) is ergodic. It holds that:

(A1) $\mathsf{E}[\xi_1^2] = 1$, $\mathsf{E}[\xi_1] = \mathsf{E}[\xi_1^3] = 0$, and

$$m_4 = \mathsf{E}\big[(\xi_1^2 - 1)^2\big] < \infty.$$

(A2) ξ_1 has a probability density p, that

$$\inf_{x \in \mathcal{K}} p(x) > 0$$

for every compact subset $\mathcal{K} \subset \mathbb{R}$.

(A3) There exist constants C_1, $C_2 > 0$, such that

$$
\begin{aligned}
|f(y)| &\leq & C_1(1 + |y|), && (13.13) \\
|s(y)| &\leq & C_2(1 + |y|), \quad y \in \mathbb{R}. && (13.14)
\end{aligned}
$$

(A4) For the function s it holds that

$$\inf_{y \in \mathcal{K}} s(y) > 0,$$

for every compact subset $\mathcal{K} \subset \mathbb{R}$.

(A5) $C_1 + C_2 E|\xi_1| < 1$.

With (A2) and (A4) it is certain that the process (Y_i) does not die out, whereas conditions (A3) and (A5) ensure that (Y_i) does not explode. These simply formed conditions can be relaxed at a large technical cost as in Franke, Kreiss, Mammen and Neumann (2003). In particular the linear growth condition (A3) must only hold asymptotically for $|y| \to \infty$.

The model (13.1) implies that (Y_i) is a Markov chain. From the following lemma from Ango Nze (1992) it follows that the chain is ergodic. It is based on applications of the results given in Nummelin and Tuominen (1982) and Tweedie (1975).

Lemma 13.1 *Under conditions (A1) - (A5) the Markov chain* (Y_i) *is geometrically ergodic, i.e.,* (Y_i) *is ergodic with a stationary probability density* π, *and there exists a* $\rho \in [0,1)$, *so that for almost all* y *it holds that*

$$\| P^n(\,\cdot\,|y) - \pi \|_{TV} = \mathcal{O}(\rho^n).$$

Here

$$P^n(B\,|\,y) = P(Y_n \in B\,|\,Y_0 = y), \quad B \in \mathcal{B},$$

represents the conditional distribution of Y_n *given* $Y_0 = y$, *and*

$$\| \nu \|_{TV} = \sup \left\{ \sum_{i=1}^{k} |\nu(B_i)| \,;\, k \in \mathbb{N}, \ B_1, \ldots, B_k \in \mathcal{B} \ pairwise \ disjunct \right\}$$

is the total variation of a signed measure ν *of the Borel* σ*-Algebra* $\mathcal{B}$ *on* $\mathbb{R}$.

To derive the asymptotic normality from $\hat{v}_n(x)$ at a fixed point $x \in \mathbb{R}$ we require additional conditions. To simplify notation $l = p + 1$.

(A6) The functions f and s are at the point x $(l-1)$-times continuously differentiable, and the one sided derivative $f_{\pm}^l(x)$, $s_{\pm}^l(x)$ of l-th order exists.

(A7) The stationary distribution π has a bounded, continuous probability density γ, which is strictly positive in a small region around x.

(A8) The kernel $K : \mathbb{R} \longrightarrow \mathbb{R}^+$ is bounded with compact support and it holds that $K > 0$ for a set of positive Lebesgue measures.

(A9) The bandwidth h_n is of the form $h_n = \beta n^{-1/(2l+1)}$, where $\beta > 0$.

(A10) The initial value Y_0 is a real number and is constant.

According to lemma 1 in Tsybakov (1986) it follows from (A8), that the matrices

$$A = \int F(u)\, F(u)^{\top}\, K(u)\, du \quad \text{and}$$

$$Q = \int F(u)\, F(u)^{\top}\, K^2(u)\, du$$

are positive definite. Let

$$\mathcal{D} = A^{-1} Q A^{-1} \quad \text{and}$$

$$f^{(l)}(x; u) = \begin{cases} f_+^{(l)}(x), & u \geq 0, \\ f_-^{(l)}(x), & u < 0, \end{cases}$$

With this we define the asymptotic errors

$$b_f(x) \;=\; A^{-1}\frac{\beta^l}{l!}\int F(u)\,u^l\,K(u)\,f^{(l)}(x;u)\,du \quad \text{and}$$

$$b_g(x) \;=\; A^{-1}\frac{\beta^l}{l!}\int F(u)\,u^l\,K(u)\,g^{(l)}(x;u)\,du.$$

Furthermore, let

$$c(x) = \begin{pmatrix} f(x) \\ f'(x)h_n \\ \vdots \\ f^{(l-1)}(x)\frac{h_n^{l-1}}{(l-1)!} \end{pmatrix} \quad \text{and} \quad \bar{c}(x) = \begin{pmatrix} g(x) \\ g'(x)h_n \\ \vdots \\ g^{(l-1)}(x)\frac{h_n^{l-1}}{(l-1)!} \end{pmatrix}.$$

The assertions of the following theorem is the central result of this chapter.

Theorem 13.1 *Under assumptions (A1) - (A10) it holds that*

$$\left\{\bar{c}_n(x) - \bar{c}(x)\right\}^\top F(0) \xrightarrow{\;P\;} 0, \qquad \left\{c_n(x) - c(x)\right\}^\top F(0) \xrightarrow{\;P\;} 0 \qquad (13.15)$$

and

$$n^{l/(2l+1)}\begin{pmatrix} \bar{c}_n(x) - \bar{c}(x) \\ c_n(x) - c(x) \end{pmatrix} \xrightarrow{\;\mathcal{L}\;} N(b(x), \Sigma(x)) \qquad (13.16)$$

for $n \to \infty$, where

$$b(x) = \begin{pmatrix} b_g(x) \\ b_f(x) \end{pmatrix}$$

and

$$\Sigma(x) = \frac{s^2(x)}{\beta\gamma(x)}\begin{pmatrix} 4f^2(x) + s^2(x)m_4 & 2f(x) \\ 2f(x) & 1 \end{pmatrix} \otimes \mathcal{D}.$$

Here $\mathcal{D}' \otimes \mathcal{D}$ represents the Kronecker product of matrices $\mathcal{D}'$ and $\mathcal{D}$.

Proof:
The normal equation for the first least squares problem in (13.10) is given by

$$n^{\frac{l}{2l+1}} B_n \bar{c}_n(x) = n^{-\frac{l}{2l+1}} \sum_{i=1}^{n} Y_i^2 \, U_{in}\, K(u_{in}) \qquad (13.17)$$

with the matrix

$$B_n = n^{-\frac{2l}{2l+1}} \sum_{i=1}^{n} U_{in}\, U_{in}^\top\, K(u_{in}).$$

On the other hand it holds under the definition of B_n

$$n^{\frac{l}{2l+1}} B_n \bar{c}(x) = n^{-\frac{l}{2l+1}} \sum_{i=1}^{n} U_{in} U_{in}^{\top} \bar{c}(x) K(u_{in}), \qquad (13.18)$$

from which together with (13.17) we get

$$n^{\frac{l}{2l+1}} B_n \left\{ \bar{c}_n(x) - \bar{c}(x) \right\} = n^{-\frac{l}{2l+1}} \sum_{i=1}^{n} \left\{ Y_i^2 - U_{in}^{\top} \bar{c}(x) \right\} U_{in} K(u_{in}). \quad (13.19)$$

From the model assumptions (13.1) it follows that

$$
\begin{aligned}
Y_i^2 &= \left(f(Y_{i-1}) + s(Y_{i-1}) \xi_i \right)^2 \\
&= f^2(Y_{i-1}) + 2f(Y_{i-1}) s(Y_{i-1}) \xi_i + (\xi_i^2 - 1) s^2(Y_{i-1}) + s^2(Y_{i-1}) \\
&= g(Y_{i-1}) + \alpha_i
\end{aligned}
$$

$$(13.20)$$

with

$$\alpha_i = 2f(Y_{i-1}) s(Y_{i-1}) \xi_i + s^2(Y_{i-1})(\xi_i^2 - 1).$$

According to the definition of U_{in} and $\bar{c}(x)$ it holds that $U_{in}^{\top} \bar{c}(x) = \sum_{j=0}^{l-1} \frac{1}{j!} g^{(j)}(x) (Y_{i-1} - x)^j$. Through a Taylor expansion of $g = f^2 + s^2$ we obtain by using the integral representation of the remainder

$$
\begin{aligned}
g(Y_{i-1}) - U_{in}^{\top} \bar{c}(x) &= \frac{(Y_{i-1} - x)^l}{(l-1)!} \int_0^1 g^{(l)} \left(x + t(Y_{i-1} - x) \right) (1-t)^{l-1} \, dt \\
&= r_g(Y_{i-1}, x).
\end{aligned}
$$

$$(13.21)$$

From (13.19), (13.20) and (13.21) we obtain

$$
\begin{aligned}
& n^{\frac{l}{2l+1}} B_n \left(\bar{c}_n(x) - \bar{c}(x) \right) \\
&= n^{-\frac{l}{2l+1}} \sum_{i=1}^{n} \left(g(Y_{i-1}) - U_{in}^{\top} \bar{c}(x) \right) U_{in} K(u_{in}) \\
&\quad + n^{-\frac{l}{2l+1}} \sum_{i=1}^{n} \left\{ 2f(Y_{i-1}) s(Y_{i-1}) \xi_i + (\xi_i^2 - 1) s^2(Y_{i-1}) \right\} U_{in} K(u_{in}) \\
&= \bar{b}_n(x) + \bar{q}_n(x)
\end{aligned}
$$

$$(13.22)$$

with

$$\bar{b}_n(x) = n^{-\frac{l}{2l+1}} \sum_{i=1}^{n} r_g(Y_{i-1}, x) \, U_{in} \, K(u_{in})$$

and

$$\bar{q}_n(x) = n^{-\frac{l}{2l+1}} \sum_{i=1}^{n} \alpha_i \, U_{in} \, K(u_{in}),$$

In an analogous fashion one obtains

$$n^{\frac{l}{2l+1}} B_n \left\{ c_n(x) - c(x) \right\} = b_n(x) + q_n(x) \qquad (13.23)$$

with

$$b_n(x) = n^{-\frac{l}{2l+1}} \sum_{i=1}^{n} r_f(Y_{i-1}, x) \, U_{in} \, K(u_{in})$$

and

$$q_n(x) = n^{-\frac{l}{2l+1}} \sum_{i=1}^{n} \beta_i \, U_{in} \, K(u_{in}),$$

where $\beta_i = s(Y_{i-1})\xi_i$ has been substituted in.

Referring back to the representations (13.22) and (13.23) the remaining steps of the proof of Theorem 13.1 are as follows:

a) First we show that

$$B_n \xrightarrow{\text{P}} B \quad \text{for } n \to \infty \qquad (13.24)$$

is fulfilled for each element. Here the matrix $B = \beta \, \gamma(x) \, A$ is positive definite.

b) Next we prove the relationships

$$\bar{b}_n(x) \xrightarrow{\text{P}} B \, b_g(x) \quad \text{for } n \to \infty \qquad (13.25)$$

and

$$b_n(x) \xrightarrow{\text{P}} B \, b_f(x) \quad \text{for } n \to \infty. \qquad (13.26)$$

c) The common random vector $(\bar{q}_n(x), q_n(x))^{\top}$ is asymptotically normally distributed:

$$\begin{pmatrix} \bar{q}_n(x) \\ q_n(x) \end{pmatrix} \xrightarrow{\mathcal{L}} \mathrm{N}(0, \Sigma_0) \quad \text{for } n \to \infty \qquad (13.27)$$

with the covariance matrix

$$\Sigma_0 = s^2(x)\beta\gamma(x) \begin{pmatrix} 4f^2(x) + s^2(x)m_4 & 2f(x) \\ 2f(x) & 1 \end{pmatrix} \otimes Q.$$

d) It holds that

$$n^{-l/(2l+1)}q_n^\top(x)\,F(0) \xrightarrow{P} 0 \quad \text{and}$$
$$n^{-l/(2l+1)}\bar{q}_n^\top(x)\,F(0) \xrightarrow{P} 0 \tag{13.28}$$

for $n \to \infty$.

With statements a) to d) proven, the statement of the theorem can be shown in the following way:
from b) and d) it follows that

$$B_n \left\{\bar{c}_n(x) - \bar{c}(x)\right\}^\top F(0) \tag{13.29}$$
$$= n^{-l/(2l+1)}\bar{b}_n(x)\,F(0) + n^{-l/(2l+1)}\bar{q}_n(x)\,F(0) \xrightarrow{P} 0$$

for $n \to \infty$. Because of a) and the definite results of the boundary matrix this implies that $\left\{\bar{c}_n(x) - \bar{c}(x)\right\}^\top F(0) \xrightarrow{P} 0$. Similarly one can show that $\left\{c_n(x) - c(x)\right\}^\top F(0) \xrightarrow{P} 0$.

The asymptotic Normality (13.16) can be seen in a similar way:
because of b) and c) it holds that

$$n^{\frac{l}{2l+1}} B_n \begin{pmatrix} \bar{c}_n(x) - \bar{c}(x) \\ c_n(x) - c(x) \end{pmatrix} = \begin{pmatrix} \bar{b}_n(x) \\ b_n(x) \end{pmatrix} + \begin{pmatrix} \bar{q}_n(x) \\ q_n(x) \end{pmatrix}$$
$$\xrightarrow{\mathcal{L}} N\left(\begin{pmatrix} B\,b_g(x) \\ B\,b_f(x) \end{pmatrix}, \Sigma_0\right),$$

from which, according to a) the validity of (13.16) follows. $\square$

It remains to prove a) to d). To do this we need a couple of helpful results.

Lemma 13.2 (Davydov (1973))

Let (Y_i) be a geometric ergodic Markov chain, so that Y_0 is distributed according to the stationary measures π of the chain. Then the chain is geometric strongly mixed, i.e., it is strongly mixing (α-mixing) with mixing coefficients $\alpha(n)$, where $\alpha(n) \leq c_0\,\rho_0^n$ for particular $0 < \rho_0 < 1$ and $c_0 > 0$ is fulfilled.

Let $(\mathcal{F}_k)$ be the canonical filter of the process (Y_k), i.e. $\mathcal{F}_k = \sigma(Y_k, Y_{k-1}, \ldots, Y_0)$ represents the generated σ-algebra from $Y_0, \ldots, Y_k$.

Lemma 13.3 (Liptser and Shirjaev (1980), Corollary 6)

For every $n > 0$ the series $(\eta_{nk}, \mathcal{F}_k)$ is a quadratic integrable Martingale difference, i.e.,

$$\mathsf{E}[\eta_{nk} \mid \mathcal{F}_{k-1}] = 0, \quad \mathsf{E}[\eta_{nk}^2] < \infty, \quad 1 \le k \le n, \tag{13.30}$$

and it holds that

$$\sum_{k=1}^{n} \mathsf{E}[\eta_{nk}^2] = 1, \quad \forall\, n \ge n_0 > 0. \tag{13.31}$$

Then the conditions

$$\sum_{k=1}^{n} \mathsf{E}[\eta_{nk}^2 \mid \mathcal{F}_{k-1}] \xrightarrow{\mathrm{P}} 1 \quad for\ n \to \infty, \tag{13.32}$$

$$\sum_{k=1}^{n} \mathsf{E}\left[\eta_{nk}^2 \mathbf{1}(|\eta_{nk}| > \varepsilon) \mid \mathcal{F}_{k-1}\right] \xrightarrow{\mathrm{P}} 0 \quad for\ n \to \infty,\ \forall \varepsilon > 0 \tag{13.33}$$

are sufficient for the distribution convergence

$$\sum_{k=1}^{n} \eta_{nk} \xrightarrow{\mathcal{L}} N(0,1) \quad for\ n \to \infty.$$

Lemma 13.4 *Let ϕ_1 be a continuous, bounded function and let ϕ_2 be a bounded function. Under conditions (A1) through (A10) it holds for every process $Y_i, i \ge 0$, which fulfils (13.1)*

$$n^{-\frac{2l}{2l+1}} \sum_{i=1}^{n} \phi_1(Y_{i-1})\, \phi_2(u_{in})\, K(u_{in})$$

$$\xrightarrow{\mathrm{P}} \beta\gamma(x)\, \phi_1(x) \int \phi_2(u)\, K(u)\, du \tag{13.34}$$

$$n^{-\frac{2l}{2l+1}} \sum_{i=1}^{n} \mathsf{E}\left[\phi_1(Y_{i-1})\, \phi_2(u_{in})\, K(u_{in})\right]$$

$$\longrightarrow \beta\gamma(x)\, \phi_1(x) \int \phi_2(u)\, K(u)\, du$$

for $n \to \infty$.

Proof:

We will first prove this for the case where the Markov chain begin in equilibrium and then work our way back to the general case.

For this let (Y_i^*) be a Markov chain, which fulfils (13.1) and which for Y_0^* has the stationary distribution π of (Y_i) introduced in Lemma 13.1. This chain is constructed to be stationary, and by applying Lemma 13.2 we get that (Y_i^*) is a geometric strong mixing process. From this it follows that

$$n^{-\frac{2l}{2l+1}} \sum_{i=1}^{n} \phi_1(Y_{i-1}^*) \, \phi_2(u_{in}^*) \, K(u_{in}^*) - n^{\frac{1}{2l+1}} \, \mathsf{E}\big[\phi_1(Y_1^*) \, \phi_2(u_{1n}^*) \, K(u_{1n}^*)\big] \xrightarrow{\mathrm{P}} 0$$
(13.35)

for $n \to \infty$, where $u_{in}^* = (Y_{i-1}^* - x)/h_n$ was substituted in. For the second term in (13.35) it holds that

$$n^{\frac{1}{2l+1}} \, \mathsf{E}\big[\phi_1(Y_1^*) \, \phi_2(u_{1n}^*) \, K(u_{1n}^*)\big]$$

$$= \beta \frac{1}{h_n} \int \phi_1(y) \, \phi_2\left(\frac{y-x}{h_n}\right) K\left(\frac{y-x}{h_n}\right) \gamma(y) \, dy$$

$$= \beta\gamma(x) \, \phi_1(x) \int \phi_2(u) \, K(u) \, du \, (1 + o(1))$$
(13.36)

for $n \to \infty$. Together with (13.35) it follows that for (Y_i^*) (13.34) is fulfilled. Define

$$\zeta_i = \phi_1(Y_{i-1}) \, \phi_2(u_{in}) \, K(u_{in}), \quad \zeta_i^* = \phi_1(Y_{i-1}^*) \, \phi_2(u_{in}^*) \, K(u_{in}^*),$$

and choose a series $\{\delta_n\}$ with $\delta_n = o(n^{\frac{2l}{2l+1}})$ and $\lim_{n\to\infty} \delta_n = \infty$. It follows that

$$n^{-\frac{2l}{2l+1}} \sum_{i=1}^{n} \big|\mathsf{E}[\zeta_i - \zeta_i^*]\big| \;\leq\; n^{-\frac{2l}{2l+1}} \left[\sum_{i=1}^{\delta_n-1} \big|\mathsf{E}[\zeta_i - \zeta_i^*]\big| + \sum_{i=\delta_n}^{n} \big|\mathsf{E}[\zeta_i - \zeta_i^*]\big|\right]$$

$$\leq\; 2n^{-\frac{2l}{2l+1}} \delta_n \, \|\phi_1\phi_2 \, K\|_\infty + n^{-\frac{2l}{2l+1}} \sum_{i=\delta_n}^{n} \big|\mathsf{E}[\zeta_i - \zeta_i^*]\big|$$

$$=\; n^{-\frac{2l}{2l+1}} \sum_{i=\delta_n}^{n} \big|\mathsf{E}[\zeta_i - \zeta_i^*]\big| + o(1)$$
(13.37)

for $n \to \infty$. From the geometric ergodicity of (Y_i), according to Lemma 13.1 we obtain for the left hand side of the last expression

$$
n^{-\frac{2l}{2l+1}} \sum_{i=\delta_n}^{n} \left| E[\zeta_i - \zeta_i^*] \right| \quad = \quad n^{-\frac{2l}{2l+1}} \sum_{i=\delta_n}^{n} \left| E\left[\phi_1(Y_{i-1}) \phi_2(u_{in}) K(u_{in}) \right. \right.
$$

$$
\left. \left. - \phi_1(Y_{i-1}^*) \phi_2(u_{in}^*) K(u_{in}^*) \right] \right|
$$

$$
\leq \quad n^{-\frac{2l}{2l+1}} \sum_{i=\delta_n}^{n} \|\phi_1 \phi_2 K\|_\infty \int \left| \gamma_i(y) - \gamma(y) \right| dy
$$

$$
= \quad \mathcal{O}\left(n^{-\frac{2l}{2l+1}} \sum_{i=\delta_n}^{n} \rho^i \right) = o(1) \tag{13.38}
$$

for $n \to \infty$, where γ_i represents the density of Y_{i-1}. Thus is holds that

$$
\lim_{n \to \infty} n^{-\frac{2l}{2l+1}} \sum_{i=1}^{n} \left| E[\zeta_i - \zeta_i^*] \right| = 0.
$$

From this it follows with the help of the Markov inequality that (13.34) also applies to (Y_i). □

Proof:
(for Theorem 13.1, continuation)
If remains to prove conditions a) to d).

a) Using the definition of B_n it holds for the elements of this matrix

$$
(B_n)_{j,\,k} = n^{-\frac{2l}{2l+1}} \sum_{i=1}^{n} \frac{u_{in}^{k+j-2}}{(k-1)!(j-1)!} K(u_{in}).
$$

These take on the form defined in Lemma 13.4, and it follows

$$
(B_n)_{j,k} \xrightarrow{\text{P}} \frac{\beta \gamma(x)}{(k-1)!(j-1)!} \int u^{k+j-2} K(u) \, du,
$$

according to the definition of matrix A this is the same as $B_n \xrightarrow{\text{P}} \beta\gamma(x)A = B$. The definiteness of A carries over to B.

b) With f and s fulfilled, $g = f^2 + s^2$ holds, condition (A6). For the remainder from the Taylor expansion of g it holds that

$$
r_g(Y_{i-1}, x) \quad = \quad u_{in}^l h_n^l \frac{1}{(l-1)!} \int_0^1 g^{(l)}\big(x + t(Y_{i-1} - x)\big)(1-t)^{l-1} \, dt
$$

$$
= \quad u_{in}^l \, n^{-\frac{l}{2l+1}} \, \phi_3(Y_{i-1})
$$

with

$$\phi_3(Y_{i-1}) = \frac{\beta^l}{(l-1)!} \int_0^1 g^{(l)}\big(x + t(Y_{i-1} - x)\big)(1-t)^{l-1}\, dt.$$

With this $\bar{b}_n(x)$ can be rewritten as

$$\bar{b}_n(x) = n^{-\frac{2l}{2l+1}} \sum_{i=1}^{n} \phi_3(Y_{i-1})\, u_{in}^l\, U_{in}\, K(u_{in}),$$

i.e., the elements of $\bar{b}_n(x)$ fulfil the requirements of Lemma 13.4.

Once again we choose (Y_i^*) as in the proof to Lemma 13.4 and set $U_{in}^* = F(u_{in}^*)$. From (13.37) and (13.38) we obtain

$$\bar{b}_n(x) - n^{-\frac{2l}{2l+1}} \sum_{i=1}^{n} \phi_3(Y_{i-1}^*)\, (u_{in}^*)^l\, U_{in}^*\, K(u_{in}^*) \xrightarrow{\mathrm{P}} 0 \qquad (13.39)$$

for $n \to \infty$. Since (Y_i^*) is α-mixing, as in (13.35) we get

$$n^{-\frac{2l}{2l+1}} \sum_{i=1}^{n} \phi_3(Y_{i-1}^*)\, (u_{in}^*)^l\, U_{in}^*\, K(u_{in}^*) -$$

$$n^{\frac{1}{2l+1}}\, \mathsf{E}\Big[\phi_3(Y_1^*)\, (u_{1n}^*)^l\, U_{1n}^*\, K(u_{1n}^*)\Big] \xrightarrow{\mathrm{P}} 0$$

for $n \to \infty$. The right term of this expression can be rewritten as

$$n^{\frac{1}{2l+1}}\, \mathsf{E}\Big[\phi_3(Y_1^*)\, (u_{1n}^*)^l\, U_{in}^*\, K(u_{in}^*)\Big]$$

$$= \beta \int \phi_3(x + uh_n)\, u^l\, F(u)\, K(u)\, \gamma(x + uh_n)\, du.$$

Furthermore, it holds that

$$\lim_{n\to\infty} \phi_3(x + uh_n) = \beta^l\, g^{(l)}(x; u)/l \qquad (13.40)$$

for every $u \in \mathbb{R}$. Together with (13.40) and (A7), it follows that

$$\lim_{n\to\infty} \beta \int \phi_3(x + uh_n)\, u^l\, F(u)\, K(u)\, \gamma(x + uh_n)\, du$$

$$= \frac{\beta^{l+1}}{l!}\left(\int F(u)\, u^l\, K(u)\, g^{(l)}(x; u)\, du \right) \gamma(x)$$

$$= A\, \gamma(x)\, \beta\, b_g(x) = B\, b_g(x).$$

With this (13.25) has been shown. The proof for (13.26) follows analogously.

c) We define the matrices

$$
\Sigma_n^{11} = n^{-\frac{2l}{2l+1}} \sum_{i=1}^{n} \mathsf{E}[\alpha_i^2 \mid \mathcal{F}_{i-1}] \, U_{in} \, U_{in}^{\top} \, K^2(u_{in}),
$$

$$
\Sigma_n^{12} = n^{-\frac{2l}{2l+1}} \sum_{i=1}^{n} \mathsf{E}[\alpha_i \beta_i \mid \mathcal{F}_{i-1}] \, U_{in} \, U_{in}^{\top} \, K^2(u_{in}),
$$

$$
\Sigma_n^{22} = n^{-\frac{2l}{2l+1}} \sum_{i=1}^{n} \mathsf{E}[\beta_i^2 \mid \mathcal{F}_{i-1}] \, U_{in} \, U_{in}^{\top} \, K^2(u_{in})
$$

and construct the block matrix

$$
\Sigma_n = \begin{pmatrix} \Sigma_n^{11} & \Sigma_n^{12} \\ \Sigma_n^{12} & \Sigma_n^{22} \end{pmatrix}.
$$

The elements of Σ_n^{11}, Σ_n^{12} and Σ_n^{22} fulfil the requirements of Lemma 13.4. In particular, the combined functions $\phi_1(Y_{i-1})$ that appear there are in this case given by

$$
\begin{aligned}
\mathsf{E}[\alpha_i^2 \mid \mathcal{F}_{i-1}] &= 4f^2(Y_{i-1})\, s^2(Y_{i-1}) + s^4(Y_{i-1}) m_4, \\
\mathsf{E}[\alpha_i \beta_i \mid \mathcal{F}_{i-1}] &= 2f(Y_{i-1})\, s^2(Y_{i-1}) \quad \text{respectively} \\
\mathsf{E}[\beta_i^2 \mid \mathcal{F}_{i-1}] &= s^2(Y_{i-1}),
\end{aligned}
$$

for which (A1) has been used. One observes that the corresponding functions ϕ_1 are, due to (A6), in a small region around x continuous and restricted. Since K disappears outside of a compact set, this is sufficient for Lemma 13.4. With this we obtain

$$
\Sigma_n \xrightarrow{\mathrm{P}} \Sigma_0 \quad \text{and} \quad \mathsf{E}[\Sigma_n] \longrightarrow \Sigma_0 \tag{13.41}
$$

for $n \to \infty$.

To prove (13.27) it is sufficient to show using the theorem from Cramér-Wold that

$$
a^{\top} \begin{pmatrix} \bar{q}_n(x) \\ q_n(x) \end{pmatrix} \xrightarrow{\mathcal{L}} \mathrm{N}(0, a^{\top} \Sigma_0 a) \quad \text{for } n \to \infty \tag{13.42}
$$

for every vector $a \in \mathbb{R}^{2l}$ with a Euclidian norm $\|a\| = 1$ is fulfilled. In addition we choose according to (13.41) a $n_0 \in \mathbb{N}$, so that $\mathsf{E}[\Sigma_n] > \frac{1}{2}\Sigma_0$ holds for all $n \geq n_0$, and substitute in for $n \geq n_0$,

$$
\eta_{ni} = \frac{n^{-\frac{l}{2l+1}}}{\sqrt{a^{\top} \mathsf{E}[\Sigma_n] a}} \, a^{\top} \begin{pmatrix} \alpha_i \, U_{in} \\ \beta_i \, U_{in} \end{pmatrix} K(u_{in}).
$$

Then

$$\sum_{i=1}^{n} \eta_{ni} = \frac{1}{\sqrt{a^\top \mathsf{E}[\Sigma_n]a}} \, a^\top \begin{pmatrix} \bar{q}_n(x) \\ q_n(x) \end{pmatrix},$$

and (13.42) is equivalent to

$$\sum_{k=1}^{n} \eta_{nk} \xrightarrow{\mathcal{L}} \mathrm{N}(0,1) \quad \text{for } n \to \infty. \tag{13.43}$$

We will now show that (η_{nk}) fulfills the requirements (13.30) to (13.33) from Lemma 13.3, from which (13.43) follows.

First notice that $\mathsf{E}[\alpha_i \,|\, \mathcal{F}_{i-1}] = 0$ a.s. and $\mathsf{E}[\beta_i \,|\, \mathcal{F}_{i-1}] = 0$ a.s. hold, from which (13.30) follows. Furthermore, one can easily show that

$$\sum_{k=1}^{n} \mathsf{E}[\eta_{nk}^2 \,|\, \mathcal{F}_{k-1}] = \frac{a^\top \Sigma_n a}{a^\top \mathsf{E}[\Sigma_n]a}.$$

Therefore (13.31) if fulfilled and from (13.41) we obtain (13.32).

We still have to show (13.33). For $n \geq n_0$,

$$\eta_{nk}^2 \leq \frac{n^{-\frac{2l}{2l+1}}}{a^\top \mathsf{E}[\Sigma_n]a} (a^\top Z_{nk})^2 \leq \frac{2n^{-\frac{2l}{2l+1}}}{a^\top \Sigma_0 a} (a^\top Z_{nk})^2 \leq \kappa_1 n^{-\frac{2l}{2l+1}} |Z_{nk}|^2,$$

with an appropriate constant $\kappa_1 > 0$ and

$$Z_{nk} = \begin{pmatrix} \alpha_k U_{kn} \\ \beta_k U_{kn} \end{pmatrix} K(u_{kn}).$$

Since K is restricted and has compact support, and since f and s are locally bounded, there exists a constant $\kappa_2 > 0$, so that

$$\begin{aligned} \eta_{nk}^2 &\leq \kappa_1 n^{-\frac{2l}{2l+1}} (\alpha_k^2 + \beta_k^2) |U_{kn}|^2 K^2(u_{kn}) \\ &\leq \kappa_2 n^{-\frac{2l}{2l+1}} (1 + |\xi_k|^4) K(u_{kn}). \end{aligned}$$

From this it follows that

$$\begin{aligned} \mathsf{E}[\eta_{nk}^2 \, \mathbf{1}(|\eta_{nk}| \geq \varepsilon) \,|\, \mathcal{F}_{k-1}] \\ &\leq \kappa_2 n^{-\frac{2l}{2l+1}} K(u_{kn}) \\ &\qquad E\left[(1 + |\xi_1|^4) \, \mathbf{1}\left(\sqrt{1 + |\xi_1|^4} \geq \varepsilon \, n^{\frac{l}{2l+1}} \kappa_2^{-1} \|K\|_\infty^{-1}\right) \right] \\ &= \kappa_2 n^{-\frac{2l}{2l+1}} K(u_{kn}) \cdot o(1) \end{aligned}$$

for $n \to \infty$, where $o(1)$ is independent of k. With this we have

$$\sum_{k=1}^{n} \mathsf{E}[\eta_{nk}^2 \, \mathbf{1}(|\eta_{nk}| \geq \varepsilon) \,|\, \mathcal{F}_{k-1}] \leq o(1) \sum_{k=1}^{n} n^{-\frac{2l}{2l+1}} K(u_{kn}) \quad \text{for } n \to \infty.$$

(13.44)

According to Lemma 13.4 it holds for the last term that

$$n^{-\frac{2l}{2l+1}} \sum_{k=1}^{n} K(u_{kn}) \xrightarrow{\mathrm{P}} \beta\gamma(x) \int K(u)\, du \quad \text{for } n \to \infty. \qquad (13.45)$$

From (13.44) and (13.45), (13.33) follows, i.e., the requirements of Lemma 13.3 are actually fulfilled, and thus (13.42) is also shown.

d) It is

$$
\begin{aligned}
n^{-l/(2l+1)} q_n^\top(x)\, F(0) &= n^{-2l/(2l+1)} \sum_{i=1}^{n} \beta_i\, U_{in}^\top\, F(0)\, K(u_{in}) \\
&= n^{-2l/(2l+1)} \sum_{i=1}^{n} \beta_i\, u_{in}\, K(u_{in}) \\
&= n^{-2l/(2l+1)} \sum_{i=1}^{n} \left(\beta_i - \mathsf{E}[\beta_i \,|\, \mathcal{F}_{i-1}] \right) u_{in}\, K(u_{in}).
\end{aligned}
$$

According to (A8) the kernel K is bounded, and it holds that $d^* = \max\{|u| : u \in \operatorname{supp} K\} < \infty$. Thus there exists a constant $\kappa_0 > 0$, such that

$$
\begin{aligned}
&\mathsf{E}\big[(n^{-l/(2l+1)} q_n^\top(x)\, F(0))^2\big] \\
&= n^{-\frac{4l}{2l+1}}\, \mathsf{E}\Big[\Big(\sum_{i=1}^{n} (\beta_i - \mathsf{E}[\beta_i \,|\, \mathcal{F}_{i-1}])\, u_{in} K(u_{in})\Big)^2\Big] \\
&\leq \kappa_0 n^{-\frac{4l}{2l+1}} \sum_{i=1}^{n} \mathsf{E}\Big[(\beta_i - \mathsf{E}[\beta_i \,|\, \mathcal{F}_{i-1}])^2\, \mathbf{1}(|u_{in}| \leq d^*)\Big].
\end{aligned}
$$

If n is sufficiently large, then for the last term in the last sum it holds that

$$
\begin{aligned}
&\mathsf{E}\Big[(\beta_i - \mathsf{E}[\beta_i \,|\, \mathcal{F}_{i-1}])^2\, \mathbf{1}(|u_{in}| \leq d^*)\Big] \\
&= \mathsf{E}\Big[s^2(Y_{i-1})\, \xi_i^2\, \mathbf{1}\Big(\frac{|Y_{i-1} - x|}{h_n} \leq d^*\Big)\Big] \\
&= \mathsf{E}\Big[s^2(Y_{i-1})\, \mathbf{1}\Big(\frac{|Y_{i-1} - x|}{h_n} \leq d^*\Big)\Big] \\
&\leq \sup_{|y-x| \leq h_n d^*} s^2(y) \quad < \infty.
\end{aligned}
$$

Thus $n^{-l/(2l+1)} q_n^\top(x) F(0) \xrightarrow{\text{P}} 0$ is shown. Similarly it can be shown that

$$n^{-l/(2l+1)} \bar{q}_n^\top(x) F(0) \xrightarrow{\text{P}} 0.$$

$\square$

As a direct consequence of Theorem 13.1 we have:

Theorem 13.2 *Under conditions (A1) through (A10) it holds that*

$$n^{l/(2l+1)} \{\hat{v}_n(x) - v(x)\} \xrightarrow{\mathcal{L}} N(b_v(x), \sigma_v^2(x)) \quad \text{for } n \to \infty,$$

where

$$
\begin{aligned}
b_v(x) &= F^\top(0) (b_g(x) - 2f(x) b_f(x)) \quad \text{and} \\
\sigma_v^2(x) &= \frac{s^4(x) m_4}{\beta \gamma(x)} F^\top(0) \mathcal{D} F(0).
\end{aligned}
$$

Proof:
From $g(x) = \bar{c}(x)^\top F(0)$, $f(x) = c(x)^\top F(0)$, $v(x) = g(x) - f^2(x)$ and the construction of $\hat{v}_n$ we obtain

$$
\begin{aligned}
\hat{v}_n(x) - v(x) &= \{\bar{c}_n(x) - \bar{c}(x)\}^\top F(0) \\
&\quad - \left[2c(x)^\top F(0) + \{c_n(x) - c(x)\}^\top F(0) \right] \\
&\quad \left[\{c_n(x) - c(x)\}^\top F(0) \right].
\end{aligned}
$$

It also holds that

$$
n^{l/(2l+1)} (\hat{v}_n(x) - v(x)) = n^{l/(2l+1)} \Psi(x) \begin{pmatrix} \bar{c}_n(x) - \bar{c}(x) \\ c_n(x) - c(x) \end{pmatrix} \quad (13.46)
$$

$$
+ n^{l/(2l+1)} \left((c_n(x) - c(x))^\top F(0) \right)^2
$$

with the transformations matrix

$$
\Psi(x) = \begin{pmatrix} F(0) \\ -2f(x) F(0) \end{pmatrix}^\top.
$$

According to (13.15) it holds that $\{c_n(x) - c(x)\}^\top F(0) \xrightarrow{\text{P}} 0$ for $n \to \infty$, from which together with (13.16) $n^{l/(2l+1)} \{[c_n(x) - c(x)]^\top F(0)\}^2 \xrightarrow{\text{P}} 0$ follows.

The limiting distribution of $n^{l/(2l+1)}\{\hat{v}_n(x) - v(x)\}$ is thus given by the first term of the right side of (13.46). For this we get using (13.16) that

$$n^{l/(2l+1)}\{\hat{v}_n(x) - v(x)\} \xrightarrow{\mathcal{L}} \mathrm{N}\{\Psi(x)b(x), \Psi(x)\Sigma(x)\Psi(x)^\top\}$$

for $n \to \infty$. A simple calculation gives $\Psi(x)b(x) = b_v(x)$ as well as $\Psi(x)\Sigma(x)\Psi(x)^\top = \sigma_v^2(x)$, with which the claim is shown. $\qquad\square$

Going beyond the asymptotic normality shown in Theorem 13.2, Franke et al. (2002) have shown that bootstrap methods for nonparametric volatility estimators can also be used. They consider routine kernel estimators, i.e., the special case LP estimator with $p = 0$ in (13.4), but the results can be directly applied to the general LP estimators, see also Kreiss (2000).

To illustrate consider the case where $l = 2$. We assume that f and s are twice differentiable and that the kernel K satisfies the condition

$$\int K(u)\,du = 1 \quad\text{and}\quad K(u) = K(-u).$$

Then it holds that

$$A = \begin{pmatrix} 1 & 0 \\ 0 & \sigma_K^2 \end{pmatrix} \quad\text{mit } \sigma_K^2 = \int u^2\,K(u)\,du,$$

$$Q = \begin{pmatrix} \int K^2(u)\,du & 0 \\ 0 & \int u^2\,K^2(u)\,du \end{pmatrix},$$

$$b_f(x) = A^{-1}\frac{\beta^2\,f''(x)}{2}\begin{pmatrix} \sigma_K^2 \\ 0 \end{pmatrix} = \begin{pmatrix} \sigma_K^2\beta^2 f''(x)/2 \\ 0 \end{pmatrix},$$

$$b_g(x) = A^{-1}\frac{\beta^2\,g''(x)}{2}\begin{pmatrix} \sigma_K^2 \\ 0 \end{pmatrix} = \begin{pmatrix} \sigma_K^2\beta^2 g''(x)/2 \\ 0 \end{pmatrix},$$

$$\mathcal{D} = \begin{pmatrix} \int K^2(u)\,du & 0 \\ 0 & \frac{1}{\sigma_K^4}\int u^2\,K^2(u)\,du \end{pmatrix},$$

and thus

$$b_v(x) = \frac{\sigma_K^2\beta^2}{2}\left\{\left(f^2(x)+s^2(x)\right)'' - 2f(x)\,f''(x)\right\} = \frac{\sigma_K^2\beta^2}{2}\left[v''(x)+2\{f'(x)\}^2\right]$$

and

$$\sigma_v^2(x) = \frac{s^4(x)m_4}{\beta\gamma(x)}\int K^2(u)\,du = \frac{v^2(x)m_4}{\beta\gamma(x)}\int K^2(u)\,du.$$

In particular, from the normalized quadratic errors of $\hat{v}_n$ that is calculated from the asymptotic distribution, we have that

$$
\begin{aligned}
\mathsf{E}\left[n^{2l/2l+1}\left(\hat{v}_n(x) - v(x)\right)^2\right] &\approx b_v^2(x) + \sigma_v^2(x) \\
&= \frac{v^2(x)m_4}{\beta\gamma(x)} \int K^2(u)\,du \\
&\quad + \frac{\sigma_K^4\beta^4}{4}\left\{v''(x) + 2\left(f'(x)\right)^2\right\}^2.
\end{aligned}
$$

Minimizing these expressions with respect to K and β results in the Epanechnikov-Kernel

$$
K(u) = K^*(u) = \frac{3}{4}\mathbf{1}(1 - u^2 > 0)
$$

and the following values for β:

$$
\beta(K) = \left(\frac{v^2(x)\,m_4 \int K^2(u)\,du}{\gamma(x)\,\sigma_K^4\left[v''(x) + 2\{f'(x)\}^2\right]^2}\right)^{1/5}.
$$

With this we obtain

$$
\beta^* = \beta(K^*) = \left(\frac{125\,v^2(x)\,m_4}{4\gamma(x)\left[v''(x) + 2\{f'(x)\}^2\right]^2}\right)^{1/5}.
$$

13.4   Recommended Literature

The model (13.1) is thoroughly studied together with financial time series, in particular under the assumptions of the ARCH structure, in Engle (1982). Until recently academic research focused mainly on the (linear) conditional mean, or it was assumed that the conditional variance was constant or, as in the ARCH models, that it had a special form. At the beginning of the eighties this deficit in the literature was corrected by Engle (1982), and Robinson (1983; 1984) and in the statistic literature by Collomb (1984) and Vieu (1995). There have also been nonparametric and semi-parametric approximations suggested in Gregory (1989), Engle and Gonzalez-Rivera (1991). Since then the interest in the nonparametric situation discussed here, in which the form of the functions f and s is not identified ahead of time, has clearly grown in the economics and statistics literature, see Fan and Yao (2003).

The QTARCH models (12.31) in Gouriéroux and Monfort (1992) create a generalization of the threshold models for the conditional mean in Tong (1983). The methods from Gouriéroux and Monfort (1992) and McKeague and Zhang

(1994) are based on histogram estimations of the volatility. The works from Chen and Tsay (1993a; 1993b) concentrate on additive modelling of the the mean function f. Additive or multiplicative structures of volatility are considered in Härdle, Lütkepohl and Chen (1997), Yang, Härdle and Nielsen (1999) and Hafner (1998). The general nonparametric ARCH model is handled in Härdle, Tsybakov and Yang (1996). Franke (1999) discusses the connection between the nonparametric AR-ARCH model and the discrete version of geometric Brownian motion which is used as a foundation for the Black-Scholes applications. Franke, Härdle and Kreiss (2003) study in connection to a special stochastic volatility model a nonparametric de-convolution estimator for the volatility function as the first step towards the nonparametric handling of general GARCH models.

The idea of the local polynomial estimation originates in Stone (1977), Cleveland (1979) and Katkovnik (1979; 1985), who have used it on nonparametric regression models. Statistical properties of LP estimators by nonparametric regression models (convergence, convergence rate and pointwise asymptotic normality) are derived in Tsybakov (1986). References to more recent studies in this area can be found in Fan and Gijbels (1996).

Apart from the statistical studies of the model (13.1), the utilized theoretical probability properties of the constructed process (Y_i) are also of importance. This is studied in the works of Doukhan and Ghindès (1981), Chan and Tong (1985), Mokkadem (1987), Diebolt and Guégan (1990) and Ango Nze (1992). In these articles the ergodicity, geometric ergodicity and mixture properties of the process (Y_i) are derived.

Part III

Selected Financial Applications

14 Valuing Options with Flexible Volatility Estimators

Since their introduction by Engle and Bollerslev models with autoregressive, conditional heteroscedasticity (*autoregressive conditional heteroscedasticity models* or ARCH) have been successfully applied to financial market data. Thus it is natural to discuss option pricing models where the underlying instrument follows an ARCH process. From an empirical point of view the form of the *news impact curve*, which is defined as a function of the current volatility dependent on yesterday's returns, is the dominant factor in determining the price. It is important, for example, to know whether the news impact curve is symmetric or asymmetric. In order to avoid inaccurate pricing due to asymmetries it is necessary to use flexible volatility models. In this way EGARCH models (see Section 12.2) can be used when stock prices and volatility are correlated. This model however has a weakness that the problem of the stationarity conditions and the asymptotic of the Quasi-Maximum-Likelihood-Estimator (QMLE) is not yet completely solved. Another Ansatz, as in the Threshold GARCH-Models, is to introduce thresholds in the news impact curve to create flexible asymmetry.

In this chapter we would like to concentrate on the specification of the volatility. We will concentrate on a TGARCH process and produce extensive Monte Carlo simulations for three typical parameter groups. In particular we will compare the simulated GARCH option prices with option prices based on the simulations from TGARCH and Black-Scholes models. In the empirical section of the chapter we will show that the market price of call options indeed reflect the asymmetries that were discovered in the news impact curve of the DAX time series.

14.1   Valuing Options with ARCH-Models

Consider an economy in discrete time in which interest and proceeds are paid out at the end of every constant, equally long time interval. Let $S_t, t = 0, 1, 2, \ldots$ be the price of the stock at time t and $Y_t = (S_t - S_{t-1})/S_{t-1}$ the corresponding one period return without dividends. Assume that a price for risk exists in the form of a risk premium which is added to the risk free interest rate r to obtain the expected return of the next period. It seems reasonable to model the risk premium dependent on the conditional variance. As a basis we assume an ARCH-M-Model (see Section 12.2.3) with a risk premium, which is a linear function of the conditional standard deviation:

$$Y_t \quad = \quad r + \lambda \sigma_t + \varepsilon_t \qquad (14.1)$$

$$\mathcal{L}(\varepsilon_t \mid \mathcal{F}_{t-1}) \quad = \quad \mathrm{N}(0, \sigma_t^2) \qquad (14.2)$$

$$\sigma_t^2 \quad = \quad \omega + \alpha \varepsilon_{t-1}^2 + \beta \sigma_{t-1}^2. \qquad (14.3)$$

In (14.3) ω, α and β are constant parameters that satisfy the stationarity and non-negativity conditions. The constant parameter λ can be understood as the price of one unit of risk. $\mathcal{F}_t$ indicates, as usual, the set of information available up to and including time t. In order to simplify the notation our discuss will be limited to the GARCH(1,1) case.

The above model is estimated under the empirical measure P. In order to deal with a valuation under no arbitrage, similar to Black-Scholes in continuous time (see Section 6.1), assumptions on the valuation of risk must be met. Many studies have researched option pricing with stochastic volatility under the assumption that the volatility has a systematic risk of zero, that is, the risk premium for volatility is zero. Duan (1995) has identified an equivalent martingale measure Q for P under the assumption that the conditional distribution of the returns are normal and in addition it holds that

$$\mathrm{Var}^P(Y_t \mid \mathcal{F}_{t-1}) = \mathrm{Var}^Q(Y_t \mid \mathcal{F}_{t-1}) \qquad (14.4)$$

P a.s.. He shows that under this assumption a representative agent with, for example, constant relative risk aversion and a normally distributed relative change of aggregate consumption maximizes his expected utility. The assumption (14.4) contains a constant risk premium for the volatility that directly enters its mean.

In order to obtain a martingale under the new measure a new error term, η_t, needs to be introduced that captures the effect of the time varying risk premium. When we define $\eta_t = \varepsilon_t + \lambda \sigma_t$, (14.4) leads to the following model under the new measure Q:

$$
\begin{aligned}
Y_t &= r + \eta_t & (14.5)\\
\mathcal{L}(\eta_t \mid \mathcal{F}_{t-1}) &= N(0, \sigma_t^2) & (14.6)\\
\sigma_t^2 &= \omega + \alpha(\eta_{t-1} - \lambda\sigma_{t-1})^2 + \beta\sigma_{t-1}^2. & (14.7)
\end{aligned}
$$

In the case of a GARCH(1,1) model according to Theorem 12.10 the variance of the stationary distribution under the empirical measure P is $\mathrm{Var}^P(\varepsilon_t) = \omega/(1 - \alpha - \beta)$. For the Duan measure Q the variance of the stationary distribution increases to $\mathrm{Var}^Q(\eta_t) = \omega/\{1 - \alpha(1 + \lambda^2) - \beta\}$, because the volatility process under the new measure is determined by the innovations from an asymmetric and not a symmetric Chi squared distribution. Later on we will see that changes in the unconditional variance depend in a critical way on the specification of the news impact curve.

The restriction to a quadratic or symmetric news impact curve is not always optimal, as many empirical studies of stock returns have indicated. Within the framework of the above mentioned model these assumptions can lead to a non-linear news impact function $g(\cdot)$. The following model is a semi-parametric analogue to the GARCH model. Under the empirical measure P we obtain

$$
\begin{aligned}
Y_t &= r + \lambda\sigma_t + \varepsilon_t\\
\mathcal{L}_P(\varepsilon_t \mid \mathcal{F}_{t-1}) &= N(0, \sigma_t^2)\\
\sigma_t^2 &= g(\varepsilon_{t-1}) + \beta\sigma_{t-1}^2.
\end{aligned}
$$

Under the Duan martingale measure Q the model changes to

$$
\begin{aligned}
Y_t &= r + \eta_t\\
\mathcal{L}_Q(\eta_t \mid \mathcal{F}_{t-1}) &= N(0, \sigma_t^2)\\
\sigma_t^2 &= g(\eta_{t-1} - \lambda\sigma_{t-1}) + \beta\sigma_{t-1}^2.
\end{aligned}
$$

One notices that as soon as an estimator of $g(\cdot)$ under P is known it can immediately be substituted under the measure Q.

In this general specification the estimation without additional information on $g(\cdot)$ is a difficult matter, since iterative estimation procedures would be necessary in order to estimate the parameters λ, β and the non-parametric function g at the same time. Therefore we will consider a specific, flexible parametric model: the Threshold GARCH Model, see Section 12.2. With this model the news impact function can be written as:

$$
g(x) = \omega + \alpha_1 x^2 \mathbf{1}(x < 0) + \alpha_2 x^2 \mathbf{1}(x \geq 0)
$$

To motivate this model consider fitting a very simple non-parametric model $Y_t = \sigma(Y_{t-1})\xi_t$ to the returns of a German stock index, the DAX, where ξ_t is independent and identically distributed with mean 0 and variance 1. The estimator of the news impact curve $\sigma^2(\cdot)$ is given in Figure 14.2. To get an idea of the underlying distribution of the returns a non-parametric estimator of the return distribution has been added in Figure 14.1 over a smoothed normal distribution. Obviously $g(\cdot)$ is not symmetric around zero. The TGARCH model captures this phenomenon when $\alpha_1 > \alpha_2$. Other parametric models can describe these properties as well but the TGARCH model in the case of stock returns has proven to be extremely flexible and technically manageable as claimed, for example, in Rabemananjara and Zakoian (1993).

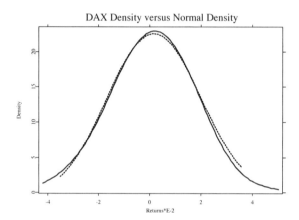

Figure 14.1: Kernel estimation of the density of DAX returns (solid line) against a kernel estimation of a normal distribution (dotted line) with the same mean and variance. A bandwidth of 0.03 is used and a quadratic kernel function $K(u) = 15/16(1 - u^2)^2 \mathbf{1}(|u| < 1)$. The tails have been eliminated from the figure.

Q SFEDaxReturnDistribution.xpl

Remember that the innovations are normally distributed. Thus it follows for the TGARCH model that the unconditional variance, similar to Theorem 12.10, under the measure P is $\mathrm{Var}^P(\varepsilon_t) = \omega/(1 - \bar{\alpha} - \beta)$, where $\bar{\alpha} = (\alpha_1 + \alpha_2)/2$. The following theorem gives the unconditional variance for $\eta_t = \varepsilon_t + \lambda\sigma_t$ under Q.

Theorem 14.1 *The unconditional variance of the TGARCH(1,1) model un-*

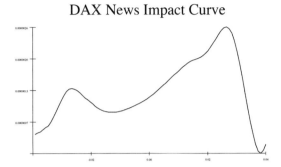

Figure 14.2: Local linear estimation of the news impact curve for the DAX.
The model is $Y_t = \sigma(Y_{t-1})\xi_t$. Shown is the estimator of the
function $\sigma^2(y)$ with a bandwidth of 0.03. The tails have been
eliminated from the figure.

Q SFENewsImpactCurve.xpl

der the equivalent martingale measure Q from Duan is

$$Var^Q(\eta_t) = \frac{\omega}{1 - \psi(\lambda)(\alpha_1 - \alpha_2) - \alpha_2(1 + \lambda^2) - \beta} \qquad (14.8)$$

where

$$\psi(u) = u\varphi(u) + (1 + u^2)\Phi(u)$$

*and $\varphi(u), \Phi(u)$ are the density and the distribution function of the standard
normal distribution.*

Proof:
Let $Z_t = \eta_t/\sigma_t - \lambda$. Under measure Q it holds that $\mathcal{L}(Z_t \mid \mathcal{F}_{t-1}) = \mathrm{N}(-\lambda, 1)$.
The conditional variance σ_t^2 can be written as

$$\sigma_t^2 = \omega + \alpha_1\sigma_{t-1}^2 Z_{t-1}^2 \mathbf{1}(Z_{t-1} < 0) + \alpha_2\sigma_{t-1}^2 Z_{t-1}^2 \mathbf{1}(Z_{t-1} \geq 0) + \beta\sigma_{t-1}^2.$$

By calculating the expected value it can be shown that for the integral over the negative values it follows that:

$$
\begin{aligned}
\mathsf{E}^Q[Z_t^2\mathbf{1}(Z_t<0)\mid\mathcal{F}_{t-1}] &= \frac{1}{\sqrt{2\pi}}\int_{-\infty}^{0} z^2 e^{-\frac{1}{2}(z+\lambda)^2}\,dz \\
&= \frac{1}{\sqrt{2\pi}}\int_{-\infty}^{\lambda}(u-\lambda)^2 e^{-\frac{1}{2}u^2}\,du \\
&= \frac{\lambda}{\sqrt{2\pi}}e^{-\frac{1}{2}\lambda^2}+(1+\lambda^2)\Phi(\lambda) \\
&\stackrel{\text{def}}{=} \psi(\lambda).
\end{aligned}
\tag{14.9}
$$

Because of

$$
\mathsf{E}^Q[Z_t^2\mid\mathcal{F}_{t-1}]=\frac{1}{\sqrt{2\pi}}\int_{-\infty}^{\infty}z^2 e^{-\frac{1}{2}(z+\lambda)^2}\,dz=1+\lambda^2
$$

it follows for the positive values that

$$
\mathsf{E}^Q[Z_t^2\mathbf{1}(Z_t\geq 0)\mid\mathcal{F}_{t-1}]=1+\lambda^2-\psi(\lambda).
\tag{14.10}
$$

Thus we obtain

$$
\mathsf{E}^Q[\sigma_t^2]=\omega+\alpha_1\psi(\lambda)\mathsf{E}^Q[\sigma_{t-1}^2]+\alpha_2[1+\lambda^2-\psi(\lambda)]\mathsf{E}^Q[\sigma_{t-1}^2]+\beta\mathsf{E}^Q[\sigma_{t-1}^2].
\tag{14.11}
$$

Since the unconditional variance is independent of t, the theorem follows. $\square$

The function ψ is positive and $\psi(\lambda)>1/2$ for the realistic case $\lambda>0$. We can make the following statement about the changes in the unconditional variance: for $\alpha_1=\alpha_2$ in (14.8), one obtains the GARCH(1,1) results. For $\alpha_1>\alpha_2$ (the case of the leverage effect) the increase in the unconditional variance is even stronger than the symmetric GARCH case. For $\alpha_1<\alpha_2$, the unconditional variance is smaller as in the leverage case, and we can distinguish between two cases: when the inequality

$$
\alpha_1<\alpha_2\frac{2\psi(\lambda)-1-2\lambda^2}{2\psi(\lambda)-1}
\tag{14.12}
$$

is fulfilled then the unconditional variance under Q is actually smaller than under P. If (14.12) is not fulfilled, then we obtain as above $\operatorname{Var}^P(\varepsilon_t)\leq\operatorname{Var}^Q(\eta_t)$. Indeed the quotient on the right hand side of (14.12) takes on negative values for realistic values of a unit of the risk premium, (for example for small positive values), so that in most empirical studies (14.12) can not be fulfilled.

Naturally the stationary variance has an effect on an option's price: the larger (smaller) the variance is, the higher (lower) is the option price. This holds in particular for options with longer time to maturity where the long-run average of the volatility is the most important determinant of the option's price. Therefore, an option can be undervalued when a GARCH model is used and at the same time a leverage effect is present.

A second feature of the Duan approach is that under Q and with positive risk premia the current innovation is negatively correlated with the next period's conditional variance of the GARCH risk premium, whereas under P the correlation is zero. More precisely, we obtain $\text{Cov}^Q(\eta_t/\sigma_t, \sigma_{t+1}^2) = -2\lambda\alpha\text{Var}^Q(\eta_t)$ with the GARCH parameter α. It is obvious that small forecasts of the volatility under Q (that influences the option's price) depend not only on the past squared innovations, but also on their sign. In particular a negative (positive) past innovation for $\lambda > 0$ leads to the fact that the volatility increases (falls) and with it, the option price. The following theorem claims that the covariance is dependent on the asymmetry of the news impact function when a TGARCH instead of a GARCH model is used.

Theorem 14.2 *For the TGARCH(1,1) model the covariance between the innovation in t and the conditional variance in $t+1$ under the equivalent martingale measure Q from Duan is given by*

$$Cov^Q(\frac{\eta_t}{\sigma_t}, \sigma_{t+1}^2) = -2\,Var^Q(\eta_t)[\lambda\alpha_2 + \{\varphi(\lambda) + \lambda\Phi(\lambda)\}(\alpha_1 - \alpha_2)], \quad (14.13)$$

where $Var^Q(\eta_t)$ follows from the previous theorem.

Proof:
First the conditional covariance is determined:

$$\begin{aligned}
\text{Cov}_{t-1}^Q(\frac{\eta_t}{\sigma_t}, \sigma_{t+1}^2) &= \mathsf{E}_{t-1}^Q\left[\frac{\eta_t}{\sigma_t}\sigma_{t+1}^2\right] = \omega\mathsf{E}_{t-1}^Q\left[\frac{\eta_t}{\sigma_t}\right] \\
&+ \alpha_1\mathsf{E}_{t-1}^Q\left[\frac{\eta_t}{\sigma_t}(\eta_t - \lambda\sigma_t)^2\mathbf{1}(\eta_t - \lambda\sigma_t < 0)\right] \\
&+ \alpha_2\mathsf{E}_{t-1}^Q\left[\frac{\eta_t}{\sigma_t}(\eta_t - \lambda\sigma_t)^2\mathbf{1}(\eta_t - \lambda\sigma_t \geq 0)\right] \\
&+ \beta\sigma_t\mathsf{E}_{t-1}^Q[\eta_t], \quad\quad\quad\quad (14.14)
\end{aligned}$$

where $\mathsf{E}_t(\cdot)$ and $\text{Cov}_t(\cdot)$ are abbreviations of $\mathsf{E}(\cdot \mid \mathcal{F}_t)$ and $\text{Cov}(\cdot \mid \mathcal{F}_t)$ respectively. Due to (14.6) the first and the fourth expectation values on the right side of (14.14) are zero. The second conditional expected value is

$$\mathsf{E}_{t-1}^Q \left[\tfrac{\eta_t}{\sigma_t} (\eta_t - \lambda\sigma_t)^2 \mathbf{1}(\eta_t - \lambda\sigma_t < 0) \right]$$

$$= -2\sigma_t^2 \left[\tfrac{1}{\sqrt{2\pi}} \exp(-\tfrac{1}{2}\lambda^2) + \lambda\Phi(\lambda) \right]. \tag{14.15}$$

Since $\mathsf{E}_{t-1}^Q \left[\tfrac{\eta_t}{\sigma_t} (\eta_t - \lambda\sigma_t)^2 \right] = -2\lambda\sigma_t^2$, we can write for the third conditional expected value in (14.14):

$$\mathsf{E}_{t-1}^Q \left[\tfrac{\eta_t}{\sigma_t} (\eta_t - \lambda\sigma_t)^2 \mathbf{1}(\eta_t - \lambda\sigma_t \geq 0) \right]$$

$$= -2\sigma_t^2 \left[\lambda - \tfrac{1}{\sqrt{2\pi}} \exp(-\tfrac{1}{2}\lambda^2) - \lambda\Phi(\lambda) \right]. \tag{14.16}$$

Inserting (14.15) and (14.16) into (14.14), it follows that

$$\mathrm{Cov}_{t-1}^Q(\tfrac{\eta_t}{\sigma_t}, \sigma_{t+1}^2) = -2\sigma_t^2 [\lambda\alpha_2 + \{\varphi(\lambda) + \lambda\Phi(\lambda)\}(\alpha_1 - \alpha_2)]. \tag{14.17}$$

One notices that $\mathrm{Cov}^Q(\eta_t/\sigma_t, \sigma_{t+1}^2) = \mathsf{E}^Q[\mathrm{Cov}_{t-1}^Q(\eta_t/\sigma_t, \sigma_{t+1}^2)]$, thus the claim follows immediately. $\qquad\square$

In the following we assume that a positive risk premium λ exists per unit. Three cases can be identified: for $\alpha_1 = \alpha_2$ (in the symmetric case) we obtain $\mathrm{Cov}^Q(\eta_t/\sigma_t, \sigma_{t+1}^2) = -2\lambda\alpha_2 \mathrm{Var}^Q(\eta_t)$, i.e., the GARCH(1,1) result. For $\alpha_1 < \alpha_2$ (the case of the reverse leverage effect) the covariance increases, and when

$$\lambda\alpha_2 + \left[\frac{1}{\sqrt{2\pi}} \exp(-\frac{1}{2}\lambda^2) + \lambda\Phi(\lambda) \right](\alpha_1 - \alpha_2) < 0, \tag{14.18}$$

the correlation is positive. In the last case, $\alpha_1 > \alpha_2$ (the leverage case), the covariance is negative and increases with the total.

This also shows that the return of the volatility to a stationary variance under Q is different from the symmetric GARCH case. The negative covariance in the leverage case is actually larger. This could indicate that options are over (under) valued when for positive (negative) past innovation a TGARCH process with $\alpha_1 > \alpha_2$ is used for the price process and then mistakenly a GARCH model ($\alpha_1 = \alpha_2$) is used for the volatility forecast.

14.2   A Monte Carlo Study

Since the discounted price process is a martingale under the equivalent martingale measure Q, we can utilize the method of risk neutral valuation according to Cox and Ross (1976). The Q price, C_t, of a call at time t is given

by the discounted conditional expectation of the payments due at maturity,
see (6.23)

$$C_t = (1+r)^{-\tau} \mathsf{E}^Q[\max(S_T - K, 0) \mid \mathcal{F}_t] \qquad (14.19)$$

where T is the maturity date, $\tau = T - t$ is the time to maturity and K is the
strike price. For European options the arbitrage free price P_t of a put follows
from the Put-Call-Parity (Theorem 2.3), i.e., $P_t = C_t - S_t + (1+r)^{-\tau} K$. Since
there is no analytical expression in a GARCH or TGARCH model for the
expectation in (14.19), we have to calculate the option price numerically. The
distribution of the payment function $\max(S_T - K, 0)$ at maturity is simulated
in that m stock processes

$$S_{T,i} = S_t \prod_{s=t+1}^{T} (1 + Y_{s,i}), \quad i = 1, \ldots, m, \qquad (14.20)$$

are generated, where $Y_{s,i}$ is the return of the i-th replication at time s. Finally the mean of the payment function is discounted by the risk free interest
rate

$$C_t = (1+r)^{-\tau} \frac{1}{m} \sum_{i=1}^{m} \max(S_{T,i} - K, 0). \qquad (14.21)$$

In the simulation study we used the following parameters: $r = 0$, $S_0 = 100$,
$\tau = 30$ days, $m = 400\,000$, $\lambda = 0.01$. The *Moneyness* S_0/K varies between
0.85 and 1.15, which corresponds to the usual bandwidth of the traded option.
We are not comparing here the effect of various maturity dates, T, since many
characteristics such as the smile in the stochastic volatility disappear with
increasing time periods. In general the effects remain qualitatively equal,
but become from a quantitative point of view less important. This has been
shown in numerous experiments; thus we will concentrate on shorter time
periods.

The effect of an asymmetric news impact function on the price of an option
is studied in three different situations which are characterized by the degree
of the short-run autocorrelation of the squared returns and the persistence,
i.e., the value from $\alpha + \beta$. For the GARCH(1,1) process it can be shown that
the autocorrelation ρ_1 of first order of the squared residuals is given by

$$\rho_1 = \alpha(1 - \alpha\beta - \beta^2)/(1 - 2\alpha\beta - \beta^2), \qquad (14.22)$$

and $\rho_j = (\alpha + \beta)\rho_{j-1}$, $j \geq 2$. These are the autocorrelations of an ARMA(1,1)
process, since the quadratic GARCH(1,1) process satisfy a ARMA(1,1) model
(see Theorem 12.9). Table 14.1 lists the parameter groups and characteristics
of the three types.

Type	α	β	$\alpha + \beta$	ρ_1
1	0.1	0.85	0.95	0.1791
2	0.5	0.45	0.95	0.8237
3	0.1	0.5	0.6	0.1077

Table 14.1: Characterization of the types of GARCH(1,1) models

Type 1 is characterized by a high persistence and a low first order correlation; type 2 is characterized by a high persistence and a high first order autocorrelation and type 3 has a low persistence and a small first order autocorrelation. Type 1 is typical for financial time series (for daily as well as intra day data), since one usually observes that the autocorrelation function of the squared returns diminishes quickly in the first few lags and then slowly after that. Type 2 describes a situation with a very strong ARCH effect, and type 3 is similar to the behavior of heavily aggregated data such as monthly or quarterly. In every case the parameter ω is set so that $\sigma^2 = 0.0002$, i.e. the unconditional variance remains constant.

In view of the non-linear news impact function $g(\cdot)$ we choose the Threshold ARCH model with two asymmetrical cases. In the first case, which we call the leverage case,

$$g_1(x) = \omega + 1.2\alpha x^2 \mathbf{1}(x < 0) + 0.8\alpha x^2 \mathbf{1}(x \geq 0)$$

and in the second case, that of the inverse leverage effect,

$$g_2(x) = \omega + 0.8\alpha x^2 \mathbf{1}(x < 0) + 1.2\alpha x^2 \mathbf{1}(x \geq 0).$$

For type 1 and the leverage effect case the simulation results are given in Figure 14.3. We have removed the absolute and the relative difference of the GARCH and the TGARCH prices from the corresponding Black-Scholes price. The relative difference is defined as the absolute difference divided by the Black-Scholes price. Because of the small step length (we assume a step length of 0.01 for moneyness) the functions appear quite smooth. For the GARCH case we obtain the well known result that the price difference to the Black-Scholes displays a U-shape with respect to moneyness. Due to the monotone increase in moneyness of the call price, the relative difference is the largest for options out of the money. The relative difference becomes insignificantly smaller, the more it is in the money. This could explain the frequently observed skewness of the smile effect. For the TGARCH option

Type	Moneyness	GARCH		TGARCH Leverage Effect		TGARCH Inv. Lev. Eff.	
		% diff	SE	% diff	SE	% diff	SE
Type 1	0.85	35.947	1.697	0.746	1.359	75.769	2.069
	0.90	-0.550	0.563	-12.779	0.498	11.606	0.631
	0.95	-6.302	0.261	-9.786	0.245	-3.153	0.278
	1.00	-3.850	0.132	-4.061	0.125	-3.806	0.139
	1.05	-1.138	0.057	-0.651	0.052	-1.692	0.061
	1.10	-0.020	0.025	0.347	0.022	-0.400	0.028
	1.15	0.162	0.012	0.347	0.010	-0.013	0.014
Type 2	0.85	199.068	5.847	104.619	4.433	293.704	7.884
	0.90	0.489	1.136	-23.964	0.891	22.140	1.469
	0.95	-30.759	0.370	-39.316	0.305	-24.518	0.454
	1.00	-20.975	0.167	-22.362	0.141	-20.804	0.198
	1.05	-6.038	0.077	-5.427	0.063	-7.148	0.095
	1.10	-0.302	0.042	0.202	0.033	-0.966	0.054
	1.15	0.695	0.027	0.991	0.021	0.351	0.037
Type 3	0.85	-2.899	1.209	-11.898	1.125	6.687	1.297
	0.90	-5.439	0.496	-8.886	0.479	-1.982	0.513
	0.95	-4.027	0.249	-4.970	0.245	-3.114	0.254
	1.00	-2.042	0.128	-2.077	0.126	-2.025	0.130
	1.05	-0.710	0.055	-0.559	0.053	-0.867	0.056
	1.10	-0.157	0.023	-0.047	0.022	-0.267	0.023
	1.15	-0.009	0.010	0.042	0.010	-0.059	0.011

Table 14.2: Simulation results for selected values of moneyness. Shown are the proportional differences between the GARCH and TGARCH option prices and the Black-Scholes price and the corresponding standard error (SE) of the simulation.

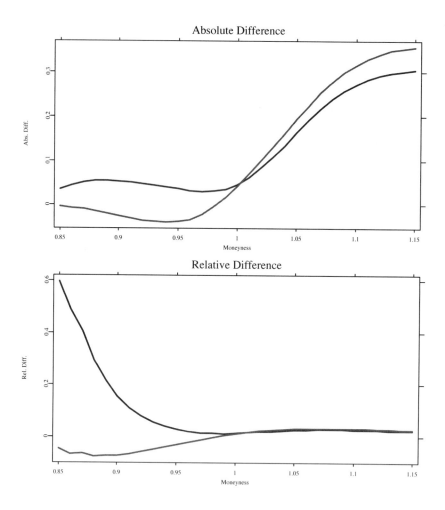

Figure 14.3: The difference between the simulated GARCH (solid line) and
              TGARCH (dotted line) option prices from the BS prices is given
              as a function of the moneyness for type 1 and the leverage case.
              The figure above shows the absolute differences, the figure below
              shows the absolute differences divided by the BS price.

Q SFEoptpricesim.xpl

price we observe in principle a similar deviation from Black-Scholes, although with an important difference: in the case of the leverage effect the price of the out of the money options is lower and the price of those in the money is higher than in the GARCH model. This is also plausible: when an option is way out of the money and the maturity date is close, the only way to achieve a positive payment at maturity is when the price of the underlying instrument consecutively increases in value in large jumps. This is, however, less likely in the leverage case, since positive returns have a smaller effect on the volatility than they do in the symmetric case, assuming that the parameter groups named above hold.

Table 14.2 shows the results for the type 2 and 3 and the case of the inverse leverage effect and for chosen values of moneyness. For the leverage effect case the described deviation of the TGARCH price from each GARCH price is visible even for type 2 and 3. In the case of the inverse leverage effect the arguments are reverse: it is more probable that an out of the money option can still end up in the money so that TGARCH prices of out of the money options are higher than the GARCH prices. As one would expect, the deviations of the simulated GARCH and TGARCH prices from the Black-Schole prices are the largest for type 2, i.e., for strong short-run ARCH effects, and are the smallest for the type with the lowest persistence, type 3. This last statement is to be expected, since the differences should disappear the closer we get to the homoscedastic case.

14.3   Application to the Valuation of DAX Calls

The valuation method with GARCH is applied to the German stock index and options data. For the stock index we use the daily closing values of the DAX from January 1, 1988 to March 31, 1992. The closing values are usually set at 13:30 (Frankfurt time). For the options data on this index we have taken the recorded values of the transaction prices from the German derivative exchange (DTB) from January to March 1992. In order to synchronize the observation time periods of the index and options we interpolate between the last option price before 13:30 and the first price after, as long as the difference is no more than two hours.

No evidence for autocorrelated DAX returns was found but the squared and absolute returns are highly autocorrelated. We estimate a GARCH(1,1)-M

	GARCH	TGARCH
ω	1.66E-05 (1.04E-06)	1.91E-05 (1.359E-06)
α	0.144 (0.006)	
α_1		0.201 (0.008)
α_2		0.045 (0.011)
β	0.776 (0.012)	0.774 (0.016)
λ	0.069 (0.018)	0.039 (0.018)
$-2logL$	-7698	-7719

Table 14.3: The GARCH and TGARCH estimation results for DAX returns, January 1, 1988 to December 30, 1991 (QMLE standard error in parentheses)

model

$$Y_t = \lambda\sigma_t + \varepsilon_t \tag{14.23}$$
$$\mathcal{L}(\varepsilon_t \mid \mathcal{F}_{t-1}) = N(0, \sigma_t^2) \tag{14.24}$$
$$\sigma_t^2 = \omega + \alpha\varepsilon_{t-1}^2 + \beta\sigma_{t-1}^2 \tag{14.25}$$

for the DAX with the Quasi-Maximum-Likelihood-Method - see Section 12.1.6. A possible constant in (14.23) is not significant and is thus ignored from the very beginning. Table 14.3 shows the results of the estimation. All parameters are significantly different from zero. The degree of persistence $\alpha + \beta = 0.9194$ is significantly smaller than 1 and thus the unconditional variance is finite, see Theorem 12.10. The parameter of the risk premium λ is positive, as is expected from economic theory.

The Quasi-Maximum-Likelihood-Estimator of the TGARCH model

$$\sigma_t^2 = \omega + \alpha_1\varepsilon_{t-1}^2\mathbf{1}(\varepsilon_{t-1} < 0) + \alpha_2\varepsilon_{t-1}^2\mathbf{1}(\varepsilon_{t-1} \geq 0) + \beta\sigma_{t-1}^2 \tag{14.26}$$

is also given in Table 14.3. Taking the value of the log-likelihood into consideration, the ability of the TGARCH model is better than that of GARCH model. A likelihood-quotient test rejects the GARCH model at every rational confidence level. α_1 and α_2 are significantly different; thus the asymmetry of the news impact function is significant. Since $\alpha_1 > \alpha_2$ we observe the usual leverage effect for financial time series.

After the model was fitted to the data from 1988 to 1991, the next step in calculating the option price for the observed time period from January to March 1992 is to use the simulation method described above and then compare this to the market prices. Here we will concentrate on call options.

Since the DAX option, which is traded on the DTB, is a European option, the results for put options can be calculated as usual from the put-call-parity. We consider nine call options with maturity dates January 17, March 20, and June 19, 1992. In order to distinguish the case of in, out and at the money, we have chosen the strike prices 1550, 1600 and 1650 for the January option 1600, 1650 and 1700 for the March and June options. We simulate the price of the January option from January 3rd to the 16th (10 days), for the March option from January 3rd to the 19th (57 days) and for the June option from January 3rd to the 31st of March (64 days). The June option with a strike price of 1700 began on January 16th so that there are no observations for the first 10 trading days. Due to low trading volume not all market prices are available thus we reduced the number of observations, k in Table 14.4, even further.

A remaining question is how to choose the starting value of the volatility process. We set the starting value equal to the running estimator of the volatility (GARCH or TGARCH), in which the volatility process is extrapolated and the parameters are held constant. Alternatively one can use the implied volatility, see Section 6.3.4.

To calculate the Black-Scholes price at time t the implied volatility at time $t-1$ is used. To obtain a measure of the quality of the estimate, we define the relative residuals as

$$u_t \stackrel{\text{def}}{=} \frac{C_t - C_{Market,t}}{C_{Market,t}}$$

where C_t is either the Black-Scholes or the GARCH or the TGARCH price and $C_{Market,t}$ is the price observed on the market. Residuals should be considered as relative values, since a trader would always prefer the cheaper option, which is undervalued by the same amount as a more expensive option, simply because he can multiply his position in the cheaper option. A similar argument holds for the sale of an overvalued option. For reasons of symmetry we use a squared loss criterion, i.e.,

$$U = \sum_{t=1}^{k} u_t^2.$$

The results for the three models are given in Table 14.4.

Overall the GARCH as well as the TGARCH options valuation model performs substantially better than the Black-Scholes model. For options in and at the money the improvement of the TGARCH forecast compared to the GARCH model is small. When the option, however, is out of the money there is a large reduction of the loss criterion. In the simulation study out

T	K	k	BS	GARCH	TGARCH
	1550	10	0.017	0.014	0.014
Jan	1600	10	0.099	0.029	0.028
	1650	10	4.231	1.626	1.314
	1600	47	1.112	0.961	0.954
Mar	1650	53	1.347	1.283	1.173
	1700	56	1.827	1.701	1.649
	1600	53	1.385	1.381	1.373
Jun	1650	56	2.023	1.678	1.562
	1700	51	2.460	2.053	1.913
Sum		346	14.500	10.725	9.980

Table 14.4: The loss criterium U for the DAX calls with maturity at T and a strike price K using BS, GARCH and TGARCH option prices. The number of observations is given by k.

of the money options react the most sensitive to stochastic volatility and the leverage effect. In the situation with real data this is most obvious for the January-1650 option, where Black-Scholes performs poorly and TGARCH performs better than GARCH. For the March and June options the difference is not so obvious. This can be explained by the fact that the index increased to a level of 1736 points on March 20th of 1717 points on March 30th, so that the option with a strike price of 1700 became in the money. This is also the explanation for the fact that U is the highest for the January-1650 option. There were only 10 trading days, but the option was out of the money for several days. For example, the DAX closed on January 8th at 1578 points.

Since in every case TGARCH performs better than GARCH, we conclude that the market follows the asymmetry of the volatility. Therefore, specifying the volatility model correctly plays an important role in determining option prices.

14.4   Recommended Literature

The presentation of this chapter closely follows the work of Härdle and Hafner (2000). The standard ARCH model originated in Engle (1982), the development of EGARCH in Nelson (1991) and TGARCH in Zakoian (1994) (for the standard deviation) and Glosten et al. (1993) (for the variance). Nonparametric and semi-parametric variants of the ARCH model were suggested and studied by Carroll, Härdle and Mammen (2002) and Hafner (1998). The classical option pricing model with stochastic volatility originated in Hull and White (1987). Hull and White implicitly assume that the market price of the risk of the volatility is zero, whereas in Melino and Turnbull (1990) it is different from zero, constant and exogenous. Empirical evidence for the valuation of risk of the volatility is given in Wiggins (1987). Renault and Touzi (1996) generalize the model from Hull and White (1987), in that they allow a market price of the risk for the volatility, which itself can vary over time. The concept of minimizing the quadratic loss of a hedge portfolio is given in Föllmer and Sondermann (1991) and Föllmer and Schweizer (1991). The practical procedure to implement "15 minutes old" implied volatility into the Black/Scholes formula, was successfully used in Bossaerts and Hillion (1993).

15 Value at Risk and Backtesting

The Value-at-Risk (VaR) is probably the most known measure for quantifying and controlling the risk of a portfolio. The establishment of the VaR is of central importance for a credit institute, since it is the basis for a regulatory notification technique and for required equity investments. The description of risk is done with the help of an "internal model", whose job is to reflect the market risk of portfolios and similar risky investments over time. This often occurs though the choice of suitable portfolios of a specific risk factor, i.e., through principal components analysis (Chapter 19). With risks from option trading a linear transformation is often applied using the "Greeks" (Chapter 6).

The objective parameter in the model is the probability forecasts of portfolio changes over a given time horizon. Whether the model and its technical application correctly identify the essential aspects of the risk, remains to be checked. The backtesting procedure serves to evaluate the quality of the forecast of a risk model in that it compares the actual results to those generated with the VaR model. For this the daily VaR estimates are compared to the results from hypothetical trading that are holden from the end-of-day position to the end of the next day, the so called "clean backtesting". The concept of clean backtesting is differentiated from that of "mark-to-market" profit and loss ("dirty $P\&L$") analyzes in which intra-day changes are also observed. In judging the quality of the forecast of a risk model it is advisable to concentrate on the clean backtesting.

The interest of an institute in a correct VaR calculation can be traced back to a rule of equity investing, which we will briefly describe here. Since 1997 (modification of the Basle market risk paper) institutes have been allowed to replicate specific risks using internal models. Included here under specific risks are those associated with daily price developments ("residual risks") and others realized from rare occurrences ("event risks" such as rating changes). Models that only consider residual risks are called "surcharge model", and those that consider event risks are called "non-surcharge model". For calculating capital investments the institutes have to use the following formula,

Graumert and Stahl (2001):

$$EMU_t = max\{VaR_{t-1} + d \cdot SR_{t-1}; M \cdot \frac{1}{60} \sum_{i=1}^{60} VaR_{t-i} + d \cdot \frac{1}{60} \sum_{i=1}^{60} SR_{t-i}\}$$

$$(15.1)$$

- EMU_t = Capital investment for the price risks determined by the risk model at day t

- VaR_{t-i} = VaR estimation at day $t-i$ for the general and the specific price risk

- d = Indicator variable with $d = 1$ for surcharge models and $d = 0$ for non-surcharge models and for models that only model general risk

- M = Multiplier with $M = 3 + ZBT + ZQM$

- ZBT = Backtesting surcharge factor according to § 37 II GI ($0 \leq ZBT \leq 1$)

- ZQM = Surcharge factor for qualitative deficiencies ($0 \leq ZQM \leq 1$)

- SR_{t-i} = Surcharge for not modelling event risk in surcharge models on day $t-i$

The multiplier M in (15.1) contains the backtesting surcharge factor which is calculated from the so called "traffic light". According to the "traffic light" the value M increases with the number of years the VaR values exceeds the actual loss. Table 15.1 explains the "traffic light" zones.

15.1   Forecast and VaR Models

Value at Risk (VaR) models are used in many financial applications. Their goal is to quantify the profit or loss of a portfolio which could occur in the near future. The uncertainty of the development of a portfolio is expressed in a "forecast distribution" P_{t+1} for period $t + 1$.

$$P_{t+1} = \mathcal{L}(L_{t+1}|\mathcal{F}_t)$$

is the conditional distribution of the random variable L_{t+1}, which represents the possible profits and losses of a portfolio in the following periods up to

Exceedances	Increase of M	Zone
0 bis 4	0	**green**
5	0.4	yellow
6	0.5	yellow
7	0.65	yellow
8	0.75	yellow
9	0.85	yellow
More than 9	1	**red**

Table 15.1: Traffic light as a factor of the exceeding amount.

date $t+1$, and $\mathcal{F}_t$ stands for the information in the available historical data up to date t. An estimator for this distribution is given by the forecast model. Consequently the possible conditional distributions of L_{t+1} come from a parameter class $\mathcal{P}_{t+1} = \{P_{t+1}^{\theta(t)} \,|\, \theta(t) \in \Theta\}$. The finite-dimensional parameter $\theta(t)$ is typically estimated from $n = 250$ historical return observations at time t, that is approximately the trading days in a year. Letting $\hat{\theta}(t)$ stand for this estimator then $\mathcal{L}(L_{t+1}|\mathcal{F}_t)$ can be approximated with $P_{t+1}^{\hat{\theta}(t)}$.

An important example of $\mathcal{P}_{t+1}$ is the Delta-Normal Model, RiskMetrics (1996). In this model we assume that the portfolio is made up of d linear (or linearized) instruments with market values $X_{k,t}, k = 1,...,d$, and that the combined conditional distribution of the log returns of the underlying

$$Y_{t+1} \in \mathbb{R}^d, Y_{k,t+1} = \ln X_{k,t+1} - \ln X_{k,t}, k = 1, ..., d,$$

given the information up to time t is a multivariate normal distribution, i.e.,

$$\mathcal{L}(Y_{t+1}|\mathcal{F}_t) = N_d(0, \Sigma_t) \qquad (15.2)$$

where Σ_t is the (conditional) covariance matrix of the random vector Y_{t+1}. We consider first a single position $(d = 1)$, which is made up of λ_t shares of a single security with an actual market price $X_t = x$. With $w_t = \lambda_t x$ we represent the *exposure* of this position at time t, that is its value given $X_t = x$. The conditional distribution of the changes to the security's value $L_{t+1} = \lambda_t(X_{t+1} - X_t)$ is approximately:

$$
\begin{aligned}
\mathcal{L}(L_{t+1}|\mathcal{F}_t) &= \mathcal{L}(\lambda_t(X_{t+1} - x) \,|\, \mathcal{F}_t) \\
&= \mathcal{L}(w_t \frac{X_{t+1} - x}{x} \,|\, \mathcal{F}_t) \\
&\approx \mathcal{L}(w_t Y_{t+1} \,|\, \mathcal{F}_t) = N(0, w_t^2 \sigma_t^2) \qquad (15.3)
\end{aligned}
$$

with $\sigma_t^2 = \mathrm{Var}(Y_{t+1} \mid \mathcal{F}_t)$. Here we have used the Taylor approximation

$$\ln X_{t+1} - \ln x = \frac{X_{t+1} - x}{x} + o(X_{t+1} - x). \tag{15.4}$$

The generalization to a portfolio that is made up of $\lambda_t^1, \cdots, \lambda_t^d$ shares of d (linear) instruments is quite obvious. Let w_t be the d-dimensional exposure vector at time t

$$w_t = (w_t^1, \cdots, w_t^d)^\top = (\lambda_t^1 x^1, \cdots, \lambda_t^d x^d)^\top. \tag{15.5}$$

$$L_{t+1} = \sum_{k=1}^{d} \lambda_t^k (X_{k,t+1} - X_{k,t})$$

is the change in the value of the portfolio. For a single position the conditional distribution of L_{t+1} given the information $\mathcal{F}_t$ is approximately equal to the conditional distribution of

$$w_t^\top Y_{t+1} = \sum_{k=1}^{d} w_t^k Y_{k,t+1}.$$

In the framework of Delta-Normal models this distribution belongs to the family
$$\mathcal{P}_{t+1} = \{ N(0, \sigma_t^2) : \sigma_t^2 \in [0, \infty) \}, \tag{15.6}$$
with $\sigma_t^2 = w_t^\top \Sigma_t w_t$. The goal of the VaR analysis is to approximate the parameter $\theta(t) = \sigma_t$ and thus to approximate the forecast distribution of $\mathcal{P}_{t+1}$.

Now consider the problem of estimating the forecast distribution from the view point of the following model's assumptions. The change in the value of the portfolio is assumed to be of the form

$$\begin{aligned} L_{t+1} &= \sigma_t \, Z_{t+1} & (15.7) \\ \sigma_t^2 &= w_t^\top \Sigma_t w_t, & (15.8) \end{aligned}$$

where Z_t is i.i.d. $N(0,1)$ distributed random variable, w_t is the exposure vector at time t and Σ_t is the (conditional) covariance matrix of the vector Y_{t+1} of the log returns. We combine the last n realizations of $Y_t = y_t, \ldots, Y_{t-n+1} = y_{t-n+1}$ from the log return vector with a $(n \times d)$ matrix $\mathcal{Y}_t = (y_i^\top)_{i=t-n+1,\ldots,t}$. From these observations we calculate two estimators from Σ_t; first the naive RMA, i.e., *rectangular moving average*:

$$\hat{\Sigma}_t = \frac{1}{n} \mathcal{Y}_t^\top \mathcal{Y}_t. \tag{15.9}$$

Since the expected value of the vector of returns Y_t is zero according to the Delta-Normal model, this is exactly the empirical covariance matrix. The second so called EMA estimator, i.e., *exponentially moving average*, is based on an idea from Taylor (1986) and uses an exponential weighting scheme. Define for γ, $0 < \gamma < 1$

$$\tilde{y}_{t-k} = \gamma^k y_{t-k}, k = 0, ..., n - 1, \quad \tilde{\mathcal{Y}}_t = (\tilde{y}_i^\top)_{i=t-n+1,...,t}$$

a log return vector is exponentially weighted over time and a $(n \times d)$ matrix is constructed from this, then Σ_t is estimated with

$$\hat{\Sigma}_t = (1 - \gamma)^{-1} \tilde{\mathcal{Y}}_t^\top \tilde{\mathcal{Y}}_t. \tag{15.10}$$

This normalization makes sense, since the sum $\sum_{i=1}^n \gamma^{i-1} = \frac{1-\gamma^n}{1-\gamma}$ for $\gamma \to 1$ converges to n, thus the RMA estimator is the boundary case of the EMA estimator. Both estimators can be substituted in (15.7) and (15.8), and we obtain with

$$\hat{P}_{t+1} = \mathrm{N}(0, \hat{\sigma}_t^2), \quad \hat{\sigma}_t^2 = w_t^\top \hat{\Sigma}_t w_t$$

an approximation of the forecast distribution, i.e., the conditional distribution of L_{t+1}. It should be noted that the Bundesanstalt für Finanzdienstleistungsaufsicht (www.bafin.de) currently dictates the RMA technique.

The *Value at Risk* VaR is determined for a given level α by

$$VaR_t = F_{t+1}^{-1}(\alpha) \stackrel{\text{def}}{=} inf\{x; F_{t+1}(x) \ge \alpha\} \tag{15.11}$$

and estimated with

$$\widehat{VaR}_t = \hat{F}_{t+1}^{-1}(\alpha) \stackrel{\text{def}}{=} inf\{x; \hat{F}_{t+1}(x) \ge \alpha\}. \tag{15.12}$$

Here $F_{t+1}, \hat{F}_{t+1}$ represent the distribution function of $P_{t+1}, \hat{P}_{t+1}$. The quality of the forecast is of particular interest in judging the VaR technique. It can be empirically checked using the realized values $(\hat{P}_t, L_t), t = 1, ..., N,$. In the event that the model assumptions, for example, (15.7) and (15.8), are correct for the form of the forecast's distribution, then the sample $U_t = F_t(L_t), t = 1, ..., N$, should have independent uniformly distributed random values over the interval $[0, 1]$ and $\hat{U}_t = \hat{F}_t(L_t), t = 1, ..., N$, approximately independent identically uniformly distributed random values. Then the ability of the forecasts distribution to fit the data is satisfied.

15.2 Backtesting with Expected Shortfall

In the following we consider the expected shortfall from L_{t+1} as an alternative to the VaR and develop a backtesting method for this risk measurement. The *expected shortfall*, also called the *Tail-VaR*, is in the Delta-Normal Model, i.e. under the assumptions from (15.7) and (15.8), defined by

$$
\begin{aligned}
E(L_{t+1} \mid L_{t+1} > VaR_t) &= E(L_{t+1} \mid L_{t+1} > z_\alpha \, \sigma_t) \\
&= \sigma_t \, E(L_{t+1}/\sigma_t \mid L_{t+1}/\sigma_t > z_\alpha). \quad (15.13)
\end{aligned}
$$

Here $z_\alpha = \Phi^{-1}(\alpha)$ represents the α quantile of the standard normal distribution, where Φ is the standard normal distribution function.

Under this model (15.7) and (15.8) $Z_{t+1} = L_{t+1}/\sigma_t$ has a standard normal distribution. For a defined threshold value u we obtain

$$
\vartheta = E(Z_{t+1} \mid Z_{t+1} > u) = \frac{\varphi(u)}{1 - \Phi(u)} \quad (15.14)
$$

$$
\varsigma^2 = Var(Z_{t+1} \mid Z_{t+1} > u) = 1 + u \cdot \vartheta - \vartheta^2, \quad (15.15)
$$

where φ is the standard normal density. For given observations from a forecast distribution and its realizations $(\hat{F}_{t+1}(\cdot/\hat{\sigma}_t), L_{t+1}/\hat{\sigma}_t)$ we consider (15.14) as the parameter of interest. Replacing the expected value with a sample mean and the unobservable Z_{t+1} with

$$
\hat{Z}_{t+1} = \frac{L_{t+1}}{\hat{\sigma}_t}, \quad (15.16)
$$

where σ_t in (15.8) is estimated with (15.9) or (15.10), we obtain an estimator for ϑ

$$
\hat{\vartheta} = \frac{1}{N(u)} \sum_{t=0}^{n} \hat{Z}_{t+1} \, \mathbf{1}(\hat{Z}_{t+1} > u). \quad (15.17)
$$

$N(u)$ is the random number of times that the threshold value u is exceeded:

$$
N(u) = \sum_{t=1}^{n} \mathbf{1}(\hat{Z}_{t+1} > u).
$$

Inferencing on the expected shortfall, i.e., on the difference $\hat{\vartheta} - \vartheta$, we obtain the following asymptotical result:

$$
\sqrt{N(u)} \left(\frac{\hat{\vartheta} - \vartheta}{\hat{\varsigma}} \right) \xrightarrow{\mathcal{L}} N(0,1) \quad (15.18)
$$

(15.18) can be used to check the adequacy of the Delta-Normal model.

15.3 Backtesting in Action

The data used in this section is a bond portfolio of a German bank from 1994 to 1995. The portfolio is not adjusted so that the exposure vector $w_t = w$ is time dependent. We assume that (15.7) and (15.8) hold. The VaR forecast is based on both prediction rules introduced in Section 15.1 that are used to estimate the parameters σ_t of the forecast distribution in RMA and EMA given $\gamma = 0.94$. In light of the bond crisis in 1994 it is interesting how both techniques respond to this stress factor.

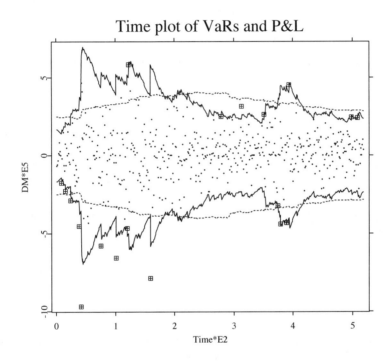

Figure 15.1: The dots show the observed changes L_t in the value of the portfolio. The dashed line represents the forecasted VaRs based on RMA (99% and 1%). The solid line represents the same for EMA.   Q SFEVaRbank.xpl Q SFEVaRtimeplot.xpl

The significance level under consideration is $\alpha = 1\%$ for large losses and $\alpha = 99\%$ for large profits. To investigate we include plots of time series from the realized P/L (i.e., profit-loss) data L_t as compared to the respective VaR estimator $\widehat{VaR}_t$ calculated with (15.12). If the model and the estimation of the parameter σ_t based on forecast distribution are adequate, then approximately 1% of the data should lie below the 1% and above the 99% VaR Estimators. In addition in Figure 15.1 the crossings for the case where VaR is estimated with EMA are marked. We recognize that in 1994 (1995) there were a total of 10 (9) crossings determined for the EMA method. This strongly contrasts the 17 (3) observed values for the RMA Method. It is clear that the RMA technique leads to, above all during the bond crisis in 1994, too many crossings for the 1% VaR estimator, which means that the probability of larger losses is underestimated. This tendency to underestimate the risk is produced from the observation width of 250 days, when the market is moving towards a more volatile phase. The opposite is true when moving in the other direction; RMA overestimates risk. The EMA adapts more quickly to market phases since data in the past has less of influence on the estimator due to the exponentially deteriorating weights. With **Q** SFEVaRtimeplot.xpl we have calculated the estimated VaRs for another bank using the EMA and RMA respectively.

The poor forecast quality of the RMA, in particular for the left side of the distribution, can also be seen in that for a particular day the VaR was exceeded by 400%. If the model (15.7) - (15.8) is correct, then the variable (15.19) must have a standard deviation of about 0.41. The empirical standard deviation calculated from the data is about 0.62. According to the volatility scale of the RMA the risk is underestimated on average by $\frac{0.62-0.41}{0.41} \approx 50\%$. The EMA plot in Figure 15.1 shows a better calibration. The empirical standard deviation of (15.19) is in this case around 0.5, which corresponds to an underestimation of risk by approximately 25%.

All other diagnostic measurements are entered into the QQ plot of the variable

$$\frac{L_{t+1}}{\widehat{VaR}_t} = \frac{L_{t+1}}{2.33\hat{\sigma}_t}, \tag{15.19}$$

see Figure 15.2 and Figure 15.3. If the VaR forecast $\widehat{VaR}_t$ was perfect, the QQ plot would produce a straight line and fill out the area in $[-1, 1]$.

A comparison of the graphs in Figure 15.2 and Figure 15.3 show that the EMA method is calibrated better than the RMA method. The RMA method clearly shows outliers at both ends. The interval boundaries of $[-1, 1]$ are in both cases clearly exceeded. This indicates a possible inadequacy of an assumed normal distribution. QQ plots for the year 1995 are not shown, which also clearly show the dominance of EMA over RMA.

Another important assumption of our model is the independence of the rescaled random variable Z_t. Figure 15.4 shows the outliers of another bank

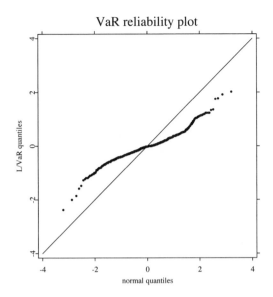

Figure 15.2: QQ plot of $L_{t+1}/\widehat{VaR}_t$ for RMA in 1994.

Q SFEVaRqqplot.xpl

$$\{t, \mathbf{1}(L_{t+1} > \widehat{VaR}_t)\}, \ t = 1, ..., 750, \tag{15.20}$$

as a function of t. The contradictory temporal non-uniform distribution of the outliers from the independence of Z_t is clearer to see by the RMA method than by the EMA method.

The exploratory analysis clearly shows the differences between RMA and EMA. As a supplement we now compare both estimation techniques with an appropriate test within the framework of the model (15.7) - (15.8). We again consider the sample residuals $\hat{Z}_{t+1}$ from (15.16) and set the threshold value in (15.14) to $u = 0.8416$, i.e., to the 80% quantile of the distribution of $Z_{t+1} = \frac{L_{t+1}}{\sigma_t}$. From this we obtain $\vartheta = 1.4$ according to (15.14). Due to the asymptotic distribution (15.18) we can check the significance of the hypothesis

$$H_0 \ : \vartheta \stackrel{(\leq)}{=} 1.4. \tag{15.21}$$

A better approximation than the standard normal distribution for the sample

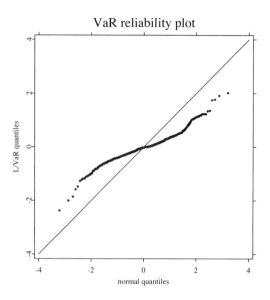

Figure 15.3: QQ plot of $L_{t+1}/\widehat{VaR}_t$ for EMA in 1994.

Q SFEVaRqqplot.xpl

is the Student $t(20)$ distribution, if we generalize the degrees of freedom.

$$\mathcal{L}(\hat{Z}_{t+1}) = \mathcal{L}(\frac{L_{t+1}}{\hat{\sigma}_t}) \approx t(20). \tag{15.22}$$

The value of ϑ obtained differs from the value given above by 5%, the corresponding variances ς^2 by 18%. Therefore, we also consider the hypothesis

$$H_0 : \vartheta \overset{(\leq)}{=} 1.47. \tag{15.23}$$

The following Table 15.2 to Table 15.5 summarizes our results.

From Table 15.2 and Table 15.3 it is obvious that the observed outliers for EMA are calibrated better than for the RMA method. For a random sample of 260 values we expect 52 outliers (standard deviation 6.45). For EMA we observe 61 ($61 - 52 \approx 1.5 \cdot$ standard deviation) outliers and for RMA 68 ($68 - 52 \approx 2.5 \cdot$ standard deviation). Naturally the outliers influence the test considerably. Therefore, we repeat the analysis excluding the outliers and obtain (15.4) and (15.5).

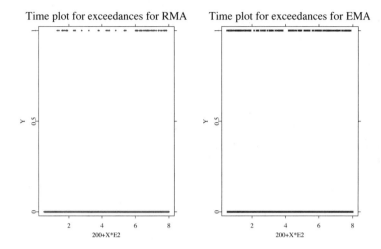

Figure 15.4: Time diagram of the exceedances at the 80% significance level
from VaR for RMA (left) and EMA. The superiority of EMA is
obvious.   🔲 SFEVaRtimeplot2.xpl

Concluding we can say that the EMA method gives better calibrated results
than the RMA method. Both methods are extremely sensitive to outliers and
should both be considered. Even the EMA method suffers from the assumptions (15.7) - (15.8), which are based on the Delta-Normal Model, can only
be approximately fulfilled. The residuals Z_t are neither normally distributed
nor independent, although the EMA method is not strongly effected by the
independence assumption due to its exponentially decreasing memory.

Method	$\vartheta = 1.4$	$\varsigma = 0.46$	$\sqrt{N(u)}\frac{\hat{\vartheta}-\vartheta}{\hat{\varsigma}}$	significance	$N(u)$
EMA	$\hat{\vartheta} = 1.72$	$\hat{\varsigma} = 1.01$	2.44	0.75%	61
RMA	$\hat{\vartheta} = 1.94$	$\hat{\varsigma} = 1.3$	3.42	0.03%	68

Table 15.2: $H_0 \; : \vartheta \stackrel{(\leq)}{=} 1.4$

Method	$\vartheta = 1.47$	$\varsigma = 0.546$	$\sqrt{N(u)}\frac{\hat{\vartheta}-\vartheta}{\hat{\varsigma}}$	significance	$N(u)$
EMA	$\hat{\vartheta} = 1.72$	$\hat{\varsigma} = 1.01$	2.01	2.3%	61
RMA	$\hat{\vartheta} = 1.94$	$\hat{\varsigma} = 1.3$	3.04	0.14%	68

Table 15.3: $H_0 : \vartheta \overset{(\leq)}{=} 1.47$

Method	$\vartheta = 1.4$	$\varsigma = 0.46$	$\sqrt{N(u)}\frac{\hat{\vartheta}-\vartheta}{\hat{\varsigma}}$	significance	$N(u)$
EMA	$\hat{\vartheta} = 1.645$	$\hat{\varsigma} = 0.82$	2.31	1%	60
RMA	$\hat{\vartheta} = 1.83$	$\hat{\varsigma} = 0.93$	3.78	0.00%	67

Table 15.4: $H_0 : \vartheta \overset{(\leq)}{=} 1.4$ largest outlier excluded

15.4   Recommended Literature

The classical start to Value at Risk (VaR) estimation lies in the consideration of linear or linearized portfolios, see RiskMetrics (1996). The linear structure transforms the multidimensional normally distributed random variables into one dimensional Gaussian values whose quantile can be estimated. An introduction to the asymptotic distributions of extreme values can be found in Leadbetter, Lindgren and Rootzen (1983) and Embrechts et al. (1997). McAllister and Mingo (1996) describe the advantages from (15.13) in a RAROC (risk-adjusted return on capital) setup. Artzner, Delbaen, Eber and Heath (1997) claim that the expected shortfall is a coherent measurement of risk. Jaschke and Küchler (1999) show that (15.13) is a reasonable approximation for a worst case scenario. Leadbetter et al. (1983) show how (15.13) can be used in the context of the theory of extreme values. A good overview of the VaR problems is given in Jorion (2000). The majority of the German laws can be found under www.bafin.de. Taleb (2001) is a critic of specific VaR definitions and gives several examples in which Value at Risk definitions can

Method	$\vartheta = 1.47$	$\varsigma = 0.546$	$\sqrt{N(u)}\frac{\hat{\vartheta}-\vartheta}{\hat{\varsigma}}$	significance	$N(u)$
EMA	$\hat{\vartheta} = 1.645$	$\hat{\varsigma} = 0.82$	1.65	5%	60
RMA	$\hat{\vartheta} = 1.83$	$\hat{\varsigma} = 0.93$	3.1	0.15%	67

Table 15.5: $H_0 : \vartheta \overset{(\leq)}{=} 1.47$ largest outlier excluded

be "blinding" given certain trading strategies ("Peso Problem Traders"). A complete literture review can be found in Franke, Härdle and Stahl (2000). There VaR calculations from Overbeck (2000) based on the ability to pay process are discussed and country risk is evaluated in Lehrbass (2000).

16 Copulas and Value-at-Risk

The conventional procedure of approximating risk factors with multivariate normal distributions implies that the risk's dependence structure is reduced to a fixed, predetermined type. Even if the autocorrelation structure of the risk factors is neglected, stipulating a multivariate normal distribution means that the following assumptions hold:

1. symmetric distribution of returns

2. the tails of the distribution are not too heavy

3. linear dependence

The first point is discussed in Chapter 3. The second point is not empirically proven, since in general the tails of the distribution display leptokurtic. The third point deals with the properties of the covariance (correlation): high correlation means that there is almost a linear relationship among the risk factors. Although there are many reasons against this procrustes type assumption of a normal distribution, there are a number of practical reasons, which in particular are associated with performing the calculations, Embrechts, McNeil and Straumann (1999a) and Embrechts, McNeil and Straumann (1999b).

A generalized representation of the dependence of the risk factors can be obtained using a *Copula*. Nelsen (1999) gives a good overview of this mathematical concept. In this chapter we will concentrate on the representation of two-dimensional copulas and we will discuss their application in calculating the Value-at-Risk (VaR).

A copula is a function $C : [0,1]^p \to [0,1]$ with particular properties. The basic idea is to describe the joint distribution of a random variable $X = (X_1, \ldots, X_p)^\top$ using a copula C:

$$
\begin{aligned}
\mathrm{P}(X_1 \leq x_1, \ldots, X_p \leq x_p) &= C\left(\mathrm{P}(X_1 \leq x_1), \ldots, \mathrm{P}(X_p \leq x_p)\right) \\
&= C\left(F_1(x_1), \ldots, F_p(x_p)\right),
\end{aligned}
$$

where $F_1, \ldots, F_p$ represent the cumulative distributions function of the variables X_j, $j = 1, \cdots, p$. A copula C is in general dependent on parameters that determine the respective form of the dependence. The correlation of two variables represents a special dependence structure which can be described with the help of the Gaussian copula (which will be introduced shortly).

This chapter introduces how to calculate the VaR with the help of the copula technique. For clarity of presentation we will first focus on cases with two risk factors: the FX time series USD/EUR and GBP/EUR, see also Rank and Siegl (2002).

16.1   Copulas

Definition 16.1
A two-dimensional copula is a function $C : [0,1]^2 \to [0,1]$ with the following properties:

 1. For every $u \in [0,1]$

$$C(0, u) = C(u, 0) = 0 \, . \tag{16.1}$$

 2. For every $u \in [0,1]$

$$C(u, 1) = u \quad and \quad C(1, u) = u \, . \tag{16.2}$$

 3. For every $(u_1, u_2), (v_1, v_2) \in [0,1] \times [0,1]$ with $u_1 \leq v_1$ and $u_2 \leq v_2$:

$$C(v_1, v_2) - C(v_1, u_2) - C(u_1, v_2) + C(u_1, u_2) \geq 0 \, . \tag{16.3}$$

A function that satisfies the first property is called *grounded*. The third property describes the analog of a non-decreasing, one-dimensional function. A function with this property is thus called *2-increasing*. An example of a non-decreasing function is $\max(u, v)$. It is easy to see that for $u_1 = u_2 = 0$, $v_1 = v_2 = 1$ the third property is not satisfied; thus this function is not 2-increasing. The function $(u, v) \to (2u - 1)(2v - 1)$ is, on the other hand, 2-increasing, yet decreasing for $v \in (0, \frac{1}{2})$.

The notation "copula" becomes clear in the following theorem from Sklar (1959).

Theorem 16.1 (Sklar's theorem)
Let H be a joint distribution function with marginal distributions F_1 and F_2.

A copula C exists if:

$$H(x_1, x_2) = C(F_1(x_1), F_2(x_2)) \tag{16.4}$$

C is unique when F_1 and F_2 are continuous. Conversely for a given copula C and marginal distributions F_1 and F_2 the function H defined by (16.4) is the joint distribution function.

A particular example is the *product copula* Π: two random variables X_1 and X_2 are independent if and only if

$$H(x_1, x_2) = F_1(x_1) \cdot F_2(x_2) \tag{16.5}$$

The product copula $C = \Pi$ is given by:

$$\Pi(u_1, \cdots, u_p) = \prod_{j=1}^{p} u_p \tag{16.6}$$

Another important example of a copula is the *Gaussian* or *normal copula*:

$$C_\rho^{\text{Gauss}}(u_1, u_2) \stackrel{\text{def}}{=} \int_{-\infty}^{\Phi_1^{-1}(u_1)} \int_{-\infty}^{\Phi_2^{-1}(u_2)} f_\rho(r_1, r_2) dr_2 dr_1 \,, \tag{16.7}$$

Here f_ρ denotes the bivariate normal density function with correlation ρ and Φ_j, $j = 1, 2$ represents the gaussian marginal distribution. In the case $\rho = 0$ we obtain:

$$
\begin{aligned}
C_0^{\text{Gauss}}(u_1, u_2) &= \int_{-\infty}^{\Phi_1^{-1}(u_1)} f_1(r_1) dr_1 \int_{-\infty}^{\Phi_2^{-1}(u_2)} f_2(r_2) dr_2 \\
&= u_1 u_2 \\
&= \Pi(u_1, u_2) \quad \text{if} \quad \rho = 0 \,.
\end{aligned}
\tag{16.8}
$$

An important class of copulas is the Gumbel-Hougaard Family, Hutchinson and Lai (1990), Nelsen (1999). This class is parameterized by

$$C_\theta(u_1, u_2) \stackrel{\text{def}}{=} \exp\left\{ -\left[(-\ln u_1)^\theta + (-\ln u_2)^\theta \right]^{1/\theta} \right\} \,. \tag{16.9}$$

For $\theta = 1$ we obtain the product copula: $C_1(u_1, u_2) = \Pi(u_1, u_2) = u_1 u_2$. For $\theta \to \infty$ we obtain the minimum copula:

$$C_\theta(u_1, u_2) \longrightarrow \min(u_1, u_2) \stackrel{\text{def}}{=} M(u_1, u_2).$$

M is also a copula which dominates every other copula C:

$$C(u_1, u_2) \leq M(u_1, u_2).$$

M is therefore referred to as the *Fréchet-Hoeffding upper bound*. The two-dimensional function $W(u_1, u_2) \overset{\text{def}}{=} \max(u_1 + u_2 - 1, 0)$ satisfies:

$$W(u_1, u_2) \leq C(u_1, u_2)$$

for all copulas. W is therefore called the *Fréchet-Hoeffding lower bound*.

Theorem 16.2
Let C be a copula. Then for every $u_1, u_2, v_1, v_2 \in [0, 1]$ the following Lipschitz conditions hold:

$$|C(u_2, v_2) - C(u_1, v_1)| \leq |u_2 - u_1| + |v_2 - v_1|. \tag{16.10}$$

Moreover the differentiability of the copulas can be shown.

Theorem 16.3
Let C be a copula. For every $u \in [0, 1]$, the partial derivative $\partial C/\partial v$ exists almost everywhere in $[0, 1]$. In addition it holds that:

$$0 \leq \frac{\partial}{\partial v} C(u, v) \leq 1. \tag{16.11}$$

A similar statement for the partial derivative $\partial C/\partial u$ can be made. The function $C_v(u) \overset{\text{def}}{=} \partial C(u, v)/\partial v$ of u and $C_u(v) \overset{\text{def}}{=} \partial C(u, v)/\partial u$ of v are non-decreasing almost everywhere in $[0,1]$.

To illustrate this theorem we consider the Gumbel-Hougaard copula (16.9):

$$\begin{aligned}
C_{\theta,u}(v) &= \frac{\partial}{\partial u} C_\theta(u, v) = \exp\left\{-\left[(-\ln u)^\theta + (-\ln v)^\theta\right]^{1/\theta}\right\} \times \\
&\quad \left[(-\ln u)^\theta + (-\ln v)^\theta\right]^{-\frac{\theta-1}{\theta}} \frac{(-\ln u)^{\theta-1}}{u}.
\end{aligned} \tag{16.12}$$

It is easy to see that $C_{\theta,u}$ is a strictly monotone increasing function of v. The inverse $C_{\theta,u}^{-1}$ is therefore well defined. How do copulas behave under transformations? The next theorem gives some information on this.

Theorem 16.4
Let X_1 and X_2 be random variables with continuous density functions and the copula $C_{X_1 X_2}$. If T_1, T_2 are strictly, monotone increasing transformations in the region of X_1 and X_2, then it holds that $C_{T_1(X_1) T_2(X_2)} = C_{X_1 X_2}$. In other words: $C_{X_1 X_2}$ is invariant under strictly, monotone increasing transformations of X_1 and X_2.

16.2   The Calculation of VaR and Copulas

The copula method can be employed with every given marginal distribution. In order to make a comparison with the classical VaR procedure, we will concentrate on Gaussian marginal densities. Numerous copulas exist in the two-dimensional case, Nelsen (1999). A selection is given in Table 16.1.

After choosing the copula, the parameter θ needs to be determined. This occurs on the basis of a given financial time series $\{S_t\}_{t=1}^T$, $S_t \in \mathbb{R}^p$ and log-returns $X_{tj} = \log(S_{tj}/S_{t-1,j})$ $j = 1, \cdots, p$. The time series S_{tj} represent the p risk factors and under the assumption that X_j is normal, they are themselves log-normally distributed. The variance of the Gaussian distribution is estimated using the method shown in Section 3.2, $\hat{\sigma}_j^2 = \frac{1}{T-1}\sum_{t=2}^T X_{tj}^2$.

A very simple method for estimating the parameter θ is the least-squares method. In the case of determining the density functions this means that the distance between the empirical density function of the log-returns and the chosen parameterized function from Table 16.1 is minimized. This can, for example, be done using the Newton method, with however the disadvantage that the estimation is concentrated on the region containing the most data points. In risk management this is the least interesting region.

The maximum likelihood method corrects this characteristic by maximizing the likelihood function

$$L(\theta) = \prod_{t=2}^T f_\theta(x_t).$$

Here f_θ represents one of the densities resulting from the combination of the marginal Gaussian distribution with a copula from Table 16.1.

Assume that a copula C has been selected. Analytical methods to calculate the VaR only exist in a few cases, e.g., for the Gaussian copula. Therefore, one has to rely on Monte Carlo simulations, for generating the random variables according to the density schema $F_{\hat{\theta}}$ (after estimating θ with $\hat{\theta}$). Such simulations create scenarios for the VaR analysis.

From Theorem 16.3 we know that the partial derivative $C_u(v)$ exists and

#	$C_\theta(u,v) =$	$\theta \in$
1	$\max\left([u^{-\theta} + v^{-\theta} - 1]^{-1/\theta}, 0\right)$	$[-1, \infty)\backslash\{0\}$
2	$\max\left(1 - [(1-u)^\theta + (1-v)^\theta - 1]^{1/\theta}, 0\right)$	$[1, \infty)$
3	$\frac{uv}{1 - \theta(1-u)(1-v)}$	$[-1, 1)$
4	$\exp\left(-[(-\ln u)^\theta + (-\ln v)^\theta]^{1/\theta}\right)$	$[1, \infty)$
5	$-\frac{1}{\theta}\ln\left(1 + \frac{(e^{-\theta u}-1)(e^{-\theta v}-1)}{e^{-\theta}-1}\right)$	$(-\infty, \infty)\backslash\{0\}$
6	$1 - \left[(1-u)^\theta + (1-v)^\theta - (1-u)^\theta(1-v)^\theta\right]^{1/\theta}$	$[1, \infty)$
7	$\max\left[\theta uv + (1-\theta)(u+v-1), 0\right]$	$(0, 1]$
8	$\max\left[\frac{\theta^2 uv - (1-u)(1-v)}{\theta^2 - (\theta-1)^2(1-u)(1-v)}, 0\right]$	$(0, 1]$
9	$uv\exp(-\theta\ln u\ln v)$	$(0, 1]$
10	$uv/\left[1 + (1-u^\theta)(1-v^\theta)\right]^{1/\theta}$	$(0, 1]$
11	$\max\left(\left[u^\theta v^\theta - 2(1-u^\theta)(1-v^\theta)\right]^{1/\theta}, 0\right)$	$(0, 1/2]$
12	$\left(1 + \left[(u^{-1}-1)^\theta + (v^{-1}-1)^\theta\right]^{1/\theta}\right)^{-1}$	$[1, \infty)$
13	$\exp\left(1 - \left[(1-\ln u)^\theta + (1-\ln v)^\theta - 1\right]^{1/\theta}\right)$	$(0, \infty)$
14	$\left(1 + \left[(u^{-1/\theta}-1)^\theta + (v^{-1/\theta}-1)^\theta\right]^{1/\theta}\right)^{-\theta}$	$[1, \infty)$
15	$\max\left(\left\{1 - \left[(1-u^{1/\theta})^\theta + (1-v^{1/\theta})^\theta\right]^{1/\theta}\right\}^\theta, 0\right)$	$[1, \infty)$
16	$\frac{1}{2}\left(S + \sqrt{S^2 + 4\theta}\right)$	$[0, \infty)$
	$\hookrightarrow S = u + v - 1 - \theta\left(\frac{1}{u} + \frac{1}{v} - 1\right)$	
21	$1 - \left(1 - \left\{\max(S(u) + S(v) - 1, 0)\right\}^\theta\right)^{\frac{1}{\theta}}$	$[1, \infty)$
	$\hookrightarrow S(u) = \left[1 - (1-u)^\theta\right]^{1/\theta}$	

Table 16.1: A Selection of Copulas.

is strictly monotone increasing. Now we can generate the desired dependence
structure using the following steps:

1. Generate 2 independent uniformly distributed (pseudo) random numbers $u, w \in [0, 1]$. Fix u.

2. Calculate the inverse of C_u, which in general is dependent on the copula
   and the parameter θ. Set $v = C_u^{-1}(w)$. The pair (u, v) has the desired
   joint density.

Here we show possible applications of the Gumbel-Hougaard copula. The
form of this copula for $\theta = 3$ is sketched in Figure 16.1. Selecting from Table

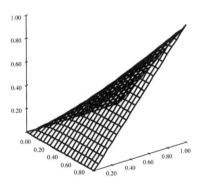

Figure 16.1: $C_4(u, v)$ für $\theta = 3$ ⎗ SFEaccvar1.xpl

16.1 copulas 4, 5, 6 and 12 and setting the parameters $\sigma_1 = 1$, $\sigma_2 = 1$, $\theta = 3$,
the varying dependency structures in Figure 16.2 are created. The parameter
θ controls the form of the copula and thus the dependency. Figure 16.3
displays the connection between θ (for C_4) and the correlation for normally
distributed, two-dimensional variables. One can clearly see the extent of

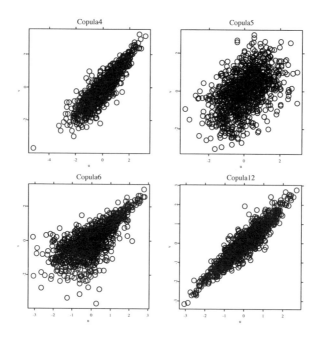

Figure 16.2: 10000 Simulations with σ_1 = 1, σ_2 = 1, θ =
       3   Q SFEaccvar2.xpl

the variation relative to ρ. The parameter θ parameterizes the non-linear
dependence structure.

An application of the method on FX rates USD/EUR and GBP/EUR (time
period: Jan. 2, 1991 through Mar. 9, 2000) and a simple linear portfolio is
described in the following. The portfolio has the structure:

$$\text{Value}(a_i, t)[EUR] = a_{i,1} \times \text{USD}_t - a_{i,2} \times \text{GBP}_t . \qquad (16.13)$$

with $a_1 = (-3, -2)$, $a_2 = (3, -2)$, $a_3 = (-3, 2)$, $a_4 = (3, 2)$. The VaR is
calculated with a confidence level of $1 - \alpha_i$, $\alpha_1 = 0.1$, $\alpha_2 = 0.05$, $\alpha_3 = 0.01$
and $T = 250$ trading days. Within the framework of backtesting one is
interested in the number of outliers crossing the barriers. The results are
given in Table 16.2.

As a benchmark the variance-covariance method from Deutsch and Eller
(1999) is used. This is based on the multivariate normal distribution. In

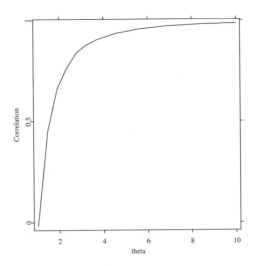

Figure 16.3: Plot of θ against ρ for C_4 ▣ SFEaccvar3.xpl

the last row the ranking of the weighted error is given: $|\hat{\alpha}_1 - \alpha_1| + 5|\hat{\alpha}_2 - \alpha_2| + 10|\hat{\alpha}_3 - \alpha_3|$. According to this ranking the historical simulation method (based on an empirical density function) performs quite well. The copulas 5, 12, 13 and 14, however, lie altogether in front of the variance-covariance method.

16.3 Recommended Literature

The term copula goes back to the works of Sklar (1959) and Sklar (1996). A detailed discussion can be found in Nelsen (1999).

Nelsen (1999) features a theoretical introduction to copulas. A practical introduction is given in Deutsch and Eller (1999). Embrechts et al. (1999b) discuss restrictions of the copula technique and their relation to the classical correlation analysis.

310   16   *Copulas and Value-at-Risk*

α=	a=	his	vcv	1	2	3	4	5	6	7	8	9	10	11	12	13	14	15	16	21
										Copula in Table 16.1										
.10	a_1	.103	.084	.111	.074	.100	.086	.080	.086	.129	.101	.128	.129	.249	.090	.087	.084	.073	.104	.080
.05	a_1	.053	.045	.066	.037	.059	.041	.044	.040	.079	.062	.076	.079	.171	.052	.051	.046	.038	.061	.041
.01	a_1	.015	.019	.027	.013	.027	.017	.020	.016	.032	.027	.033	.034	.075	.020	.022	.018	.015	.027	.018
.10	a_2	.092	.078	.066	.064	.057	.076	.086	.062	.031	.049	.031	.031	.011	.086	.080	.092	.085	.065	.070
.05	a_2	.052	.044	.045	.023	.033	.041	.049	.031	.012	.024	.012	.013	.003	.051	.046	.054	.049	.039	.032
.01	a_2	.010	.011	.016	.002	.007	.008	.009	.006	.002	.002	.002	.002	.001	.015	.010	.018	.025	.011	.005
.10	a_3	.099	.086	.126	.086	.064	.088	.096	.073	.032	.054	.033	.031	.016	.094	.086	.105	.133	.070	.086
.05	a_3	.045	.048	.093	.047	.032	.052	.050	.040	.017	.026	.017	.016	.009	.049	.047	.058	.101	.034	.050
.01	a_3	.009	.018	.069	.018	.012	.018	.016	.012	.007	.009	.006	.006	.002	.018	.015	.018	.073	.013	.020
.10	a_4	.103	.090	.174	.147	.094	.095	.086	.103	.127	.094	.129	.127	.257	.085	.085	.085	.136	.088	.111
.05	a_4	.052	.058	.139	.131	.056	.060	.058	.071	.084	.068	.084	.085	.228	.053	.054	.051	.114	.053	.098
.01	a_4	.011	.020	.098	.108	.017	.025	.025	.035	.042	.056	.041	.042	.176	.016	.017	.016	.087	.015	.071
.10	Avg	.014	.062	.145	.123	.085	.055	.052	.082	.193	.104	.194	.194	.478	.045	.061	.045	.110	.082	.075
.05	Avg	.011	.021	.154	.124	.051	.030	.016	.060	.134	.080	.132	.136	.387	.006	.012	.017	.127	.041	.075
.01	Avg	.007	.029	.169	.117	.028	.031	.032	.036	.065	.071	.065	.067	.249	.029	.025	.029	.160	.026	.083
Avg	Avg	.009	.028	.163	.120	.039	.032	.028	.047	.095	.076	.094	.096	.306	.022	.023	.026	.147	.034	.080
Rank		1	6	18	16	9	7	5	10	14	11	13	15	19	2	3	4	17	8	12

Table 16.2: Number of outliers in backtesting for the VaR with a confidence level of $1 - \alpha_i$, $i = 1, \cdots, 3$ **Q** SFMaccvar4.xpl

17 Statistics of Extreme Risks

When we model returns using a GARCH process with normally distributed innovations, we have already taken into account the second *stylized fact* (see Chapter 12). The distribution of the random returns automatically has a leptokurtosis and larger losses occurring more frequently than under the assumption that the returns are normally distributed. If one is interested in the 95%-VaR of liquid assets, this approach produces the most useful results. For the extreme risk quantiles such as the 99%-VaR and for riskier types of investments the risk is often underestimated when the innovations are assumed to be normally distributed, since a higher probability of particularly extreme losses than a GARCH process ε_t with normally distributed Z_t can produce.

Thus procedures have been developed which assume that the tails of the innovation's distribution are heavier. The probability of extreme values largely depends on how slowly the probability density function $f_Z(x)$ of the innovations goes to 0 as $|x| \to \infty$. The rate at which it diminishes must be estimated from the data. Since extreme observations are rare, this produces a difficult estimation problem. Even large data sets contain only limited information on the true probability of an extreme loss (profit). In such a situation methods from extreme value statistics produce a more realistic estimate of the risk. In this chapter a short overview of the basic ideas and several of the latest applications are given.

17.1 Limit Behavior of Maxima

Consider the stochastic behavior of the maximum $M_n = \max(X_1, \ldots, X_n)$ of n identically distributed random variables $X_1, \ldots, X_n$ with cumulative distribution function (cdf) $F(x)$. From a risk management perspective $X_t =$

$-Z_t$ is the negative return at day t. The cdf of M_n is

$$P(M_n \leq x) = P(X_1 \leq x, \ldots, X_n \leq x) = \prod_{t=1}^{n} P(X_t \leq x) = F^n(x). \quad (17.1)$$

We are only considering unbounded random variables X_t, i.e. $F(x) < 1$ for all $x < \infty$. Obviously it holds that $F^n(x) \to 0$ for all x, when $n \to \infty$, and thus $M_n \xrightarrow{P} \infty$. The maximum of n unbounded random variables increases over all boundaries. In order to achieve a non-degenerate behavior limit, M_n has to be standardized in a suitable fashion.

Definition 17.1 (Maximum Domain of Attraction)
The random variable X_t belongs to the maximum domain of attraction *(MDA) of a non-degenerate distribution G, if for suitable sequences $c_n > 0, d_n$ it holds that:*

$$\frac{M_n - d_n}{c_n} \xrightarrow{\mathcal{L}} G \quad for \ n \to \infty,$$

i.e. $F^n(c_n x + d_n) \to G(x)$ at all continuity points x of the cdf $G(x)$.

It turns out that only a few distributions G can be considered as the asymptotic limit distribution of the standardized maximum M_n. They are referred to as the *extreme value distriubtions*. These are the following three distribution functions:

   Fréchet: $G_{1,\alpha}(x) = \exp\{-x^{-\alpha}\}$, $x \geq 0$, for $\alpha > 0$,

   Gumbel: $G_0(x) = \exp\{-e^{-x}\}$, $x \in \mathbb{R}$,

   Weibull: $G_{2,\alpha}(x) = \exp\{-|x|^{-\alpha}\}$, $x \leq 0$, for $\alpha < 0$.

The Fréchet distributions are concentrated on the non-negative real numbers $[0, \infty)$, while the Weibull distribution, on the other hand, on $(-\infty, 0]$, whereas the Gumbel distributed random variables can attain any real number. Figure 17.1 displays the density function of the Gumbel distribution, the Fréchet distribution with parameter $\alpha = 2$ and the Weibull distribution with parameter $\alpha = -2$. All three distributions types can be displayed in a single Mises form:

Definition 17.2 (Extreme Value Distributions)
The generalized extreme value distribution *(GEV = generalized extreme value) with the* form parameter $\gamma \in \mathbb{R}$ *has the distribution function:*

$$G_\gamma(x) = \exp\{-(1 + \gamma x)^{-1/\gamma}\}, \ 1 + \gamma x > 0 \ for \ \gamma \neq 0$$
$$G_0(x) = \exp\{-e^{-x}\}, \ x \in \mathbb{R}$$

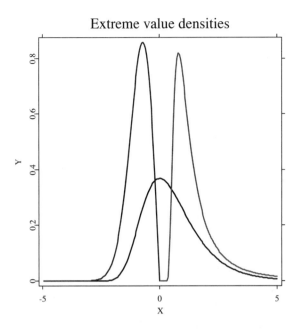

Figure 17.1: Fréchet (red), Gumbel (black) and Weibull distributions (blue).   Q SFEevt1.xpl

G_0 is the Gumbel distribution, whereas $G_\gamma, \gamma \neq 0$ is linked to the Fréchet- and Weibull distributions by the following relationships:

$$G_\gamma(\frac{x-1}{\gamma}) = G_{1,1/\gamma}(x) \text{ for } \gamma > 0,$$

$$G_\gamma(-\frac{x+1}{\gamma}) = G_{2,-1/\gamma}(x) \text{ for } \gamma < 0.$$

This definition describes the standard form of the GEV distributions. In general we can change the center and the scale to obtain other GEV distributions: $G(x) = G_\gamma(\frac{x-\mu}{\sigma})$ with the form parameter γ, the location parameter $\mu \in \mathbb{R}$ and the scale parameter $\sigma > 0$. For asymptotic theory this does not matter since the standardized sequences c_n, d_n can be always chosen so that the asymptotic distribution G has the standard form ($\mu = 0, \sigma = 1$). An important result of the asymptotic distribution of the maximum M_n is the *Fisher-Tippett theorem*:

Theorem 17.1

If there exists sequences $c_n > 0, d_n$ and a non-degenerate distribution G, so that

$$\frac{M_n - d_n}{c_n} \xrightarrow{\mathcal{L}} G \quad \text{for } n \to \infty,$$

then G is a GEV distribution.

Proof:

As a form of clarification the basic ideas used to prove this central result are outlined. Let $t > 0$, and $[z]$ represent the integer part of z. Since $F^{[nt]}$ is the distribution function of $M_{[nt]}$, due to our assumptions on the asymptotic distribution of M_n it holds that

$$F^{[nt]}(c_{[nt]}x + d_{[nt]}) \longrightarrow G(x) \quad \text{for } [nt] \to \infty, \quad \text{i.e. } n \to \infty.$$

On the other hand it also holds that

$$F^{[nt]}(c_n x + d_n) = \{F^n(c_n x + d_n)\}^{\frac{[nt]}{n}} \longrightarrow G^t(x) \quad \text{for } n \to \infty.$$

In other words this means that

$$\frac{M_{[nt]} - d_{[nt]}}{c_{[nt]}} \xrightarrow{\mathcal{L}} G , \qquad \frac{M_{[nt]} - d_n}{c_n} \xrightarrow{\mathcal{L}} G^t$$

for $n \to \infty$. According to the Lemma, which is stated below, this is only possible when

$$\frac{c_n}{c_{[nt]}} \longrightarrow b(t) \geq 0, \qquad \frac{d_n - d_{[nt]}}{c_{[nt]}} \longrightarrow a(t)$$

and

$$G^t(x) = G(b(t)x + a(t)), \ t > 0, \ x \in \mathbb{R}. \tag{17.2}$$

This relationship holds for arbitrary values t. We use it in particular for arbitrary t, s and $s \cdot t$ and obtain

$$b(st) = b(s) \, b(t), \ a(st) = b(t)a(s) + a(t). \tag{17.3}$$

The functional equations (17.2), (17.3) for $G(x), b(t), a(t)$ have only one solution, when G is one of the distributions $G_0, G_{1,\alpha}$ or $G_{2,\alpha}$, that is, G must be a GEV distribution.

$\square$

Lemma 17.1 (Convergence Type Theorem)
Let $U_1, U_2, \ldots, V, W$ be random variables, $b_n, \beta_n > 0$, $a_n, \alpha_n \in \mathbb{R}$. If

$$\frac{U_n - a_n}{b_n} \xrightarrow{\mathcal{L}} V$$

in distribution for $n \to \infty$, then it holds that:

$$\frac{U_n - \alpha_n}{\beta_n} \xrightarrow{\mathcal{L}} W \quad \text{if and only if} \quad \frac{b_n}{\beta_n} \longrightarrow b \geq 0, \quad \frac{a_n - \alpha_n}{\beta_n} \longrightarrow a \in \mathbb{R}.$$

In this case W has the same distribution as $bV + a$.

Notice that the GEV distributions are identical to the so called *max-stable* distributions, by which for all $n \geq 1$ the maximum M_n of n i.i.d. random variables $X_1, \ldots, X_n$ have the same distribution as $c_n X_1 + d_n$ for appropriately chosen $c_n > 0, d_n$.

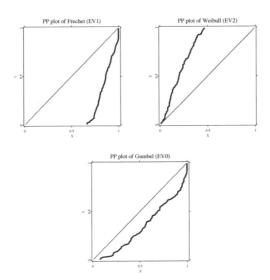

Figure 17.2: PP plot for the normal distribution and pseudo random variables with extreme value distributions. Fr'echet (upper left), Weibull (upper right) and Gumbel (below).   **Q** SFEevt2.xpl

Figure 17.2 shows the so called normal plot, i.e., it compares the graph of the cdf of the normal distribution with the one in Section 17.2 for the special case

$F(x) = \Phi(x)$ with computer generated random variables that have a Gumbel distribution, Fréchet distribution with parameter $\alpha = 2$ and a Weibull distribution with parameter $\alpha = -2$ respectively. The differences with the normally distributed random variables, which would have approximately a straight line in a normal plot, can be clearly seen.

If the maximum of i.i.d. random variables converges in distribution after being appropriately standardized, then the question arises which of the three GEV distributions is the asymptotic distribution. The deciding factor is how fast the probability for extremely large observations decreases beyond a threshold x, when x increases. Since this exceedance probability plays an important role in extreme value theory, we will introduce some more notations:

$$\overline{F}(x) = \mathrm{P}(X_1 > x) = 1 - F(x).$$

The relationship between the exceedance probability $\overline{F}(x)$ and the distribution of the maxima M_n will become clear with the following theorem.

Theorem 17.2
a) For $0 \le \tau \le \infty$ and every sequence of real numbers $u_n, n \ge 1$, it holds for $n \to \infty$ that

$$n\overline{F}(u_n) \to \tau \quad \text{if and only if} \quad \mathrm{P}(M_n \le u_n) \to e^{-\tau}.$$

b) F belongs to the maximum domain of attraction of the GEV distribution G with the standardized sequences c_n, d_n exactly when $n \to \infty$

$$n\overline{F}(c_n x + d_n) \to -\log G(x) \quad \text{for all } x \in \mathbb{R}.$$

The exceedance probability of the Fréchet distribution $G_{1,\alpha}$ behaves like $1/x^\alpha$ for $x \to \infty$, because the exponential function around 0 is approximately linear, i.e.,

$$\overline{G}_{1,\alpha}(x) = \frac{1}{x^\alpha}\{1 + o(1)\} \qquad \text{for} \quad x \to \infty.$$

Essentially all of the distributions that belong to the MDA of this Fréchet distribution show the same behavior; $x^\alpha \overline{F}(x)$ is almost constant for $x \to \infty$, or more specifically: a slowly varying function.

Definition 17.3
A positive measurable function L in $(0, \infty)$ is called slowly varying, *if for all $t > 0$*

$$\frac{L(tx)}{L(x)} \to 1 \qquad \text{for} \quad x \to \infty.$$

Typical slowly varying functions are, in addition to constants, logarithmic growth rates, for example $L(x) = \log(1 + x), x > 0$.

Theorem 17.3
F belongs to the maximum domain of attraction of the Fréchet distribution $G_{1,\alpha}$ for some $\alpha > 0$, if and only if $x^{\alpha}\overline{F}(x) = L(x)$ is a slowly varying function. The random variables X_t with the distribution function F are unbounded, i.e., $F(x) < 1$ for all $x < \infty$, and it holds that

$$\frac{M_n}{c_n} \xrightarrow{\mathcal{L}} G_{1,\alpha}$$

with $c_n = F^{-1}(1 - \frac{1}{n})$.

For the description of the standardized sequence c_n we have used the following notation. c_n is an extreme quantile of the distribution F, and it holds that $\overline{F}(c_n) = \mathrm{P}(X_t > c_n) = 1/n$.

Definition 17.4 (Quantile Function)
If F is a distribution function, we call the generalized inverse

$$F^{-1}(\gamma) = \inf\{x \in \mathbb{R}; \ F(x) \geq \gamma\}, \ 0 < \gamma < 1,$$

the quantile function. *It then holds that $\mathrm{P}(X_1 \leq F^{-1}(\gamma)) = \gamma$, i.e., $F^{-1}(\gamma)$ is the γ-quantile of the distribution F.*

If F is strictly monotonic increasing and continuous, then F^{-1} is the generalized inverse of F.

There is a corresponding criterion for the Weibull distribution that can be shown using the relationship $G_{2,\alpha}(-x^{-1}) = G_{1,\alpha}(x)$, $x > 0$,. Random variables, whose maxima are asymptotically Weibull distributed, are by all means bounded, i.e., there exists a constant $c < \infty$, such that $X_t \leq c$ with probability 1. Therefore, in financial applications they are only interesting in special situations where using a type of hedging strategy, the loss, which can result from an investment, is limited. In order to prohibit continuous differentiations in various cases, in the following we will mainly discuss the case where the losses are unbounded. The cases in which losses are limited can be dealt with in a similar fashion.

Fréchet distributions appear as asymptotic distributions of the maxima of those random variables whose probability of values beyond x only slowly decreases with x, whereas only bounded random variables belong to the maximum domain of attraction of Weibull distributions. Many known distributions such as the exponential or the normal distribution do not belong to either one of the groups. It is likely that in such cases the distribution of the appropriate standardized maxima converges to a Gumbel distribution. The general conditions need for this are however more complicated and more difficult to prove than they were for the Fréchet distribution.

Theorem 17.4
The distribution function F of the unbounded random variables X_t belongs to the maximum domain of attraction of the Gumbel distribution if measurable scaling functions $c(x), g(x) > 0$ as well as an absolute continuous function $e(x) > 0$ exist with $c(x) \to c > 0$, $g(x) \to 1, e'(x) \to 0$ for $x \to \infty$ so that for $z < \infty$

$$\overline{F}(x) = c(x)\exp\{-\int_z^x \frac{g(y)}{e(y)}dy\}, \quad z < x < \infty.$$

In this case it holds that

$$\frac{M_n - d_n}{c_n} \xrightarrow{\mathcal{L}} G_0$$

with $d_n = F^{-1}(1 - \frac{1}{n})$ and $c_n = e(d_n)$.

As a function $e(x)$, the *average excess function* can be used:

$$e(x) = \frac{1}{\overline{F}(x)} \int_x^\infty \overline{F}(y)\, dy, \quad x < \infty,$$

which will be considered in more detail in the following.

The exponential distribution with parameter λ has the distribution function $F(x) = 1 - e^{-\lambda x}, x \geq 0$, so that $\overline{F}(x) = e^{-\lambda x}$ fulfills the conditions stipulated in the theorem with $c(x) = 1$, $g(x) = 1$, $z = 0$ and $e(x) = 1/\lambda$. The maximum M_n of n independent exponentially distributed random variables with parameter λ thus converges in distribution to the Gumbel distribution:

$$\lambda(M_n - \frac{1}{\lambda}\log n) \xrightarrow{\mathcal{L}} G_0 \quad \text{for} \quad n \to \infty.$$

In general, however, the conditions are not so easy to check. There are other simple sufficient conditions with which it can be shown, for example, that also the normal distribution belongs to the maximum domain of attraction of the Gumbel distribution. If, for example, M_n is the maximum of n independent standard normally distributed random variables, then it holds that

$$\sqrt{2\log n}(M_n - d_n) \xrightarrow{\mathcal{L}} G_0 \quad \text{for} \quad n \to \infty$$

$$\text{with} \qquad d_n = \sqrt{2\log n} - \frac{\log\log n + \log(4\pi)}{2\sqrt{2\log n}}.$$

Another member of the distributions in the maximum domain of attraction of the Fréchet distribution $G_{1,\alpha}$ is the *Pareto distribution* with the distribution function

$$W_{1,\alpha}(x) = 1 - \frac{1}{x^{\alpha}}, x \geq 1, \alpha > 0,$$

as well as all other distributions with *Pareto tails*, i.e., with

$$\overline{F}(x) = \frac{\kappa}{x^{\alpha}}\{1 + o(1)\} \quad \text{for} \quad x \to \infty.$$

Since $\overline{F}^{-1}(\gamma)$ for $\gamma \approx 1$ behaves here like $(\kappa/\gamma)^{1/\alpha}$, c_n for $n \to \infty$ is identical to $(\kappa n)^{1/\alpha}$, and

$$\frac{M_n}{(\kappa n)^{1/\alpha}} \xrightarrow{\mathcal{L}} G_{1,\alpha} \quad \text{for} \quad n \to \infty.$$

There is a tight relationship between the asymptotic behavior of the maxima of random variables and the distribution of the corresponding excesses which builds the foundation for an important estimation method in the extreme value statistic, which is defined in the next section. In general it deals with observations crossing a specified threshold u. Their distribution F_u is defined as follows:

Definition 17.5 (Excess Distribution)
Let u be an arbitrary threshold and F a distribution function of an unbounded random variable X.

a) $F_u(x) = P\{X - u \leq x \mid X > u\} = \{F(u+x) - F(u)\}/\overline{F}(u), \; 0 \leq x < \infty$
   is called the excess distribution *beyond the threshold u.*

b) $e(u) = \mathsf{E}\{X - u \mid X > u\}, \; 0 < u < \infty,$ *is the* average excess function.

With partial integration it follows that this definition of the average excess function together with the following Theorem 17.4 agrees with:

$$e(u) = \int_u^{\infty} \frac{\overline{F}(y)}{\overline{F}(u)} dy.$$

If Δ_u is a random variable with the distribution function F_u, then its expectation is $\mathsf{E}\Delta_u = e(u)$.

Theorem 17.5

X is a positive, unbounded random variable with an absolutely continuous distribution function F.

a) The average excess function $e(u)$ identifies F exactly:

$$\overline{F}(x) = \frac{e(0)}{e(x)} \exp\{-\int_0^x \frac{1}{e(u)} du\}, \quad x > 0.$$

b) If F is contained in the MDA of the Fréchet distribution $G_{1,\alpha}$, then $e(u)$ is approximately linear for $u \to \infty$: $e(u) = \frac{1}{\alpha-1} u\{1 + o(1)\}$.

Definition 17.6 (Pareto Distribution)

The generalized Pareto distribution (GP = generalized Pareto) with parameters $\beta > 0$, γ has the distribution function

$$W_{\gamma,\beta}(x) = 1 - (1 + \frac{\gamma x}{\beta})^{-\frac{1}{\gamma}} \quad for \quad \left\{ \begin{array}{ll} x \geq 0 & if \quad \gamma > 0 \\ 0 \leq x \leq \frac{-\beta}{\gamma} & if \quad \gamma < 0, \end{array} \right.$$

and

$$W_{0,\beta}(x) = 1 - e^{-\frac{1}{\beta}x}, \quad x \geq 0.$$

$W_\gamma(x) = W_{\gamma,1}(x)$ is called the generalized standard Pareto distribution or standardized GP distribution.

Figure 17.3 shows the generalized standard Pareto distribution with parameters $\gamma = 0.5, 0$ and -0.5 respectively.

For $\gamma = 0$ the standardized GP distribution is an exponential distribution with parameter 1. For $\gamma > 0$ it is a Pareto distribution $W_{1,\alpha}$ with the parameter $\alpha = 1/\gamma$. For $\gamma < 0$ the GP distribution is also referred to as a *Beta distribution* and has the distribution function $W_{2,\alpha} = 1 - (-x)^{-\alpha}, -1 \leq x \leq 0, \alpha < 0$.

Theorem 17.6

The distribution F is contained in the MDA of the GEV distribution G_γ with the form parameter $\gamma \geq 0$, exactly when for a measurable function $\beta(u) > 0$ and the GP distribution $W_{\gamma,\beta}$ it holds that:

$$\sup_{x \geq 0} |F_u(x) - W_{\gamma,\beta(u)}(x)| \to 0 \, for \, u \to \infty.$$

A corresponding result also holds for the case when $\gamma < 0$, in which case the supremum of x must be taken for those $0 < W_{\gamma,\beta(u)}(x) < 1$.

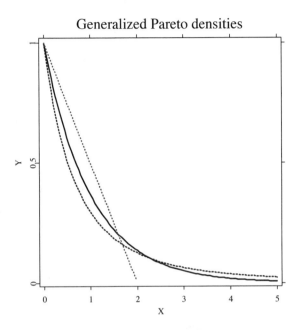

Figure 17.3: Standard pareto distribution ($\beta = 1$) with parameter $\gamma = 0.5$ (red), 0 (black) and -0.5 (blue).   Q `SFEgpdist.xpl`

For the generalized Pareto distribution $F = W_{\gamma,\beta}$ it holds for every finite threshold $u > 0$

$$F_u(x) = W_{\gamma,\beta+\gamma u}(x) \quad \text{for} \quad \begin{cases} x \geq 0 & \text{if } \gamma \geq 0 \\ 0 \leq x < -\frac{\beta}{\gamma} - u & \text{if } \gamma < 0, \end{cases}$$

In this case $\beta(u) = \beta + \gamma\, u$.

17.2   Statistics of Extreme Events

Throughout the entire section $X, X_1, \ldots, X_n$ are unbounded, i.i.d. random variables with distribution function F.

Notation: $X_{(1)} \leq \ldots \leq X_{(n)}$ and $X^{(1)} \geq \ldots \geq X^{(n)}$ represent the *order statistics*, that is, the data is sorted according to increasing or decreasing size. Obviously then $X_{(1)} = X^{(n)}$, $X_{(n)} = X^{(1)}$ etc.

Definition 17.7 (Empirical Average Excess Function)
Let $K_n(u) = \{j \leq n;\ X_j > u\}$ be the index of the observations outside of the threshold u, and let $N(u) = \#K_n(u)$ be their total number and

$$\hat{F}_n(x) = \frac{1}{n} \sum_{j=1}^{n} \mathbf{1}(X_j \leq x)$$

the empirical distribution function, $\overline{\hat{F}_n} = 1 - \hat{F}_n$.

$$e_n(u) = \int_u^\infty \overline{\hat{F}_n}(y)dy / \overline{\hat{F}_n}(u) \quad = \quad \frac{1}{N(u)} \sum_{j \in K_n(u)} (X_j - u)$$

$$= \quad \frac{1}{N(u)} \sum_{j=1}^{n} max\{(X_j - u), 0\}$$

is called the empirical average excess function.

$e_n(u)$ estimates the average excess function $e(u)$ from Section 17.1.

As an explorative data analysis the following graphs will be considered:

Plot of the probability distribution function $\quad \left\{ F(X^{(k)}),\ \frac{n-k+1}{n+1} \right\}_{k=1}^{n}$,

Quantile plot $\quad \left\{ X^{(k)},\ F^{-1}\left(\frac{n-k+1}{n+1}\right) \right\}_{k=1}^{n}$,

Average excess plot $\quad \left\{ X^{(k)}, e_n(X^{(k)}) \right\}_{k=1}^{n}$.

If the original model assumptions, that F is the distribution of the data, is correct, then the first two graphs should be approximately linear. If this is not the case, then the distribution assumptions must be changed. On the other hand, due to Theorem 17.5, b) the average excess plot is for size k approximately linear with a slope $1/(\alpha - 1)$ if F belongs to the maximum domain of attraction of a Fréchet distribution $G_{1,\alpha}$ for $\alpha > 1$, i.e. with a finite expectation.

As an example consider the daily returns of the exchange rate between the Yen and the U.S. dollar from December 1, 1978 to January 31, 1991 in Figure 17.4. Figure 17.5 shows the plot of the probability distribution function and the quantile plot for the pdf $F(x) = \Phi(x)$ of the standard normal. The deviations from the straight line clearly shows that the data is not normally distributed. Figure 17.6 shows again the average excess plot of the data.

17.2.1   The POT (peaks-over-threshold) Method

In this section and the following we will take a look at estimators for extreme value characteristics such as the exceedance probabilities $\overline{F}(x) = 1 - F(x)$

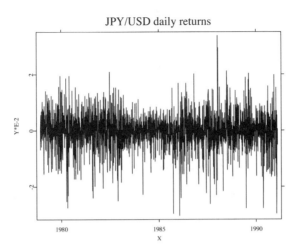

Figure 17.4: Daily log-return of JPY/USD exchange rate. ⊙ SFEjpyusd.xpl

for values x or the extreme quantile $F^{-1}(q)$ for $q \approx 1$.

First, we only consider distributions F that are contained in the MDA of a GEV distribution G_γ, $\gamma \geq 0$,. The corresponding random variables are thus unbounded.

Definition 17.8 (Excess)
Let $K_n(u)$ and $N(u)$ be, as before, the index and total number of observations beyond the threshold u respectively. The excess *beyond the threshold u is defined as the random variables $Y_l, l = 1, \ldots, N(u)$, with*

$$\{Y_1, \ldots, Y_{N(u)}\} = \{X_j - u;\ j \in K_n(u)\} = \{X^{(1)} - u, \ldots, X^{(N(u))} - u\}.$$

The excesses Y_l, $l \leq N(u)$ describe by how much the observations, which are larger than u, go beyond the threshold u. The POT method (*peaks-over-threshold method*) assumes that these excesses are the basic information source for the initial data. From the definition it immediately follows that $Y_1, \ldots, Y_{N(u)}$ are i.i.d. random variables with distribution F_u given their random total number $N(u)$, i.e., the excess distribution from Definition 17.5 is the actual distribution of the excesses. Due to Theorem 17.6 it also holds that $F_u(y) \approx W_{\gamma, \beta(u)}(y)$ for a GP distribution $W_{\gamma, \beta(u)}$ and all sufficiently large u.

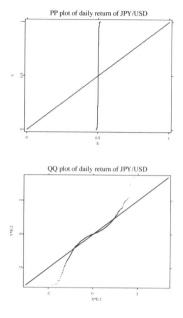

Figure 17.5: PP plot and QQ plot. ⍰ SFEjpyusd.xpl

Let's first consider the problem of estimating the exceedance probability $\overline{F}(x)$ for large x. A natural estimator is $\hat{\overline{F}}_n(x)$, the cdf at x is replaced with the empirical distribution function. For large x, however, the empirical distribution function varies a lot, because it is determined by the few extreme observations which are located around x. The effective size of the sub-sample of extreme, large observations is too small to use a pure non-parametric estimator such as the empirical distribution function. Therefore, we use the following relationship among the extreme exceedance probability $\overline{F}(x)$, the exceedance probability $\overline{F}(u)$ for a large, but not extremely large threshold and the excess distribution. Due to Definition 17.5 the excess distribution is

$$\overline{F}_u(y) = P(X - u > y \mid X > u) = \overline{F}(y + u)/\overline{F}(u), \qquad \text{i.e.}$$
$$\overline{F}(x) = \overline{F}(u) \cdot \overline{F}_u(x - u), \quad u < x < \infty. \qquad (17.4)$$

For large u and using Theorem 17.6 we can approximate F_u with $W_{\gamma,\beta}$ for appropriately chosen γ, β. $F(u)$ is replaced with the empirical distribution function $\hat{F}_n(u)$ at the threshold u, for which due to the definition of $N(u)$ it

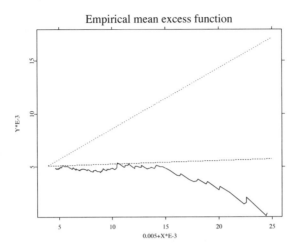

Figure 17.6: Empirical mean excess function (solid line), GP mean excess function for Hill estimator (dotted line) and moment estimator (broken line). **Q** SFEjpyusd.xpl

holds that

$$\hat{F}_n(u) = \frac{n - N(u)}{n} = 1 - \frac{N(u)}{n}.$$

For u itself this is a useful approximation, but not for the values x, which are clearly larger than the average sized threshold u. The estimator $1 - \hat{F}_n(x)$ of $\overline{F}(x)$ for extreme x only depends on a few observations and is therefore too unreliable. For this reason the POT method uses the identity (17.4) for $\overline{F}(x)$ and replaces both factors on the right hand side with their corresponding approximations, whereby the unknown parameter of the generalized Pareto distribution is replaced with a suitable estimator.

Definition 17.9 (POT Estimator)
The POT estimator $\overline{F}^{\wedge}(x)$ for the exceedance probability $\overline{F}(x)$, for large x, is

$$\overline{F}^{\wedge}(x) = \frac{N(u)}{n}\,\overline{W}_{\hat{\gamma},\hat{\beta}}(x - u) = \frac{N(u)}{n}\left\{1 + \frac{\hat{\gamma}(x - u)}{\hat{\beta}}\right\}^{-1/\hat{\gamma}}, \quad u < x < \infty,$$

whereby $\hat{\gamma}, \hat{\beta}$ are suitable estimators for γ and β respectively.

$\hat{\gamma}, \hat{\beta}$ can be, for example, calculated as maximum likelihood estimators from the excesses $Y_1, \ldots, Y_{N(u)}$. First let's consider the case where $N(u) = m$ is a constant and where $Y_1, \ldots, Y_m$ is a sample of i.i.d. random variables with the distribution $W_{\gamma,\beta}, \gamma > 0,$. Thus $W_{\gamma,\beta}$ is literally a Pareto distribution and has the probability density

$$p(y) = \frac{1}{\beta}(1 + \frac{\gamma y}{\beta})^{-\frac{1}{\gamma}-1}, \quad x \ge 0.$$

Therefore, the log likelihood function is

$$\ell(\gamma, \beta \mid Y_1, \ldots, Y_m) = -m \log \beta - (\frac{1}{\gamma} + 1) \sum_{j=1}^{m} \log(1 + \frac{\gamma}{\beta} Y_j).$$

By maximizing this function with respect to γ, β we obtain the maximum likelihood (ML) estimator $\hat{\gamma}, \hat{\beta}$. Analogously we could also define the ML estimator for the parameter of the generalized Pareto distribution using $\gamma \le 0$.

Theorem 17.7
For all $\gamma > -\frac{1}{2}$ it holds for $m \to \infty$

$$\sqrt{m}(\hat{\gamma} - \gamma, \frac{\hat{\beta}}{\beta} - 1) \xrightarrow{\mathcal{L}} N_2(0, D^{-1}),$$

with $D = (1 + \gamma) \begin{pmatrix} 1+\gamma & -1 \\ -1 & 2 \end{pmatrix}$, i.e. $(\hat{\gamma}, \hat{\beta})$ are asymptotically normally distributed. In addition they are asymptotically efficient estimators.

In our initial problem $m = N(u)$ was random. Here the estimators we just defined, $\hat{\gamma}$ and $\hat{\beta}$, are the conditional ML estimators given $N(u)$. The asymptotic distribution theory is also known in this case; in order to avoid an asymptotic bias, $\overline{F}$ must fulfill an additional regularity condition. After we find an estimator for the exceedance probability and thus a cdf for large x, we immediately obtain an estimator for the extreme quantile.

Definition 17.10 (POT Quantile Estimator)
The POT Quantile estimator $\hat{x}_q$ for the q-quantile $x_q = F^{-1}(q)$ is the solution to $\overline{F}^{\wedge}(\hat{x}_q) = 1 - q$, i.e.

$$\hat{x}_q = u + \frac{\hat{\beta}}{\hat{\gamma}} \left[\left\{ \frac{n}{N(u)}(1-q) \right\}^{-\hat{\gamma}} - 1 \right].$$

Q SFEpotquantile.xpl

We can compare these estimators with the usual sample quantiles. To do this we select a threshold value u so that exactly k excesses lie beyond u, that is $N(u) = k > n(1 - q)$ and thus $u = X^{(k+1)}$. The POT quantile estimator that is dependent on the choice of u respectively k is

$$\hat{x}_{q,k} = X^{(k+1)} + \frac{\hat{\beta}_k}{\hat{\gamma}_k} \left[\left\{ \frac{n}{k}(1 - q) \right\}^{-\hat{\gamma}_k} - 1 \right],$$

where $\hat{\gamma}_k, \hat{\beta}_k$ is the ML estimator, dependent on the choice of k, for γ and β. The corresponding sample quantile is

$$\hat{x}_q^s = X^{([n(1-q)]+1)}.$$

This is in approximate agreement with $\hat{x}_{q,k}$ when the minimal value $k = [n(1 - q)] + 1$ is chosen for k. Simulation studies show that the value k_0 of k, which minimizes the mean squared error $\mathrm{MSE}(\hat{x}_{q,k}) = \mathsf{E}(\hat{x}_{q,k} - x_q)^2$, is much larger than $[n(1 - q)] + 1$, i.e., the POT estimator for x_q differs distinctly from the sample quantile $\hat{x}_q^s$ and is superior to it with respect to the mean squared error when the threshold u respectively k is cleverly chosen.

We are interested in a threshold u, for which the mean squared error of $\hat{x}_q$ is as small as possible. The error can be split up into the variance and the squared bias of $\hat{x}_q$:

$$\mathrm{MSE}(\hat{x}_q) = \mathsf{E}(\hat{x}_q - x_q)^2 = \mathrm{Var}(\hat{x}_q) + \{\mathsf{E}(\hat{x}_q) - x_q\}^2.$$

Unfortunately the two components of the mean squared error move in opposite directions when we vary the threshold u used in calculating the POT quantile estimators. We are therefore confronted with the following bias variance dilemma:

- when u is too large, there are few excesses Y_l, $l \le N(u)$, and the estimator's variance is too large,

- when u is too small, the approximation of the excess distribution using a generalized Pareto distribution is not good enough, and the bias $\mathsf{E}(\hat{x}_q) - x_q$ is no longer reliable.

An essential aid in selecting an appropriate threshold u is the average excess plot, which is approximately linear beyond the appropriate threshold. This has already been discussed in Theorem 17.5, when one considers the relationship between the Fréchet distribution as the asymptotic distribution of the maxima and the Pareto distribution as the asymptotic distribution of the excesses. It is supported by the following result for the Pareto and exponential distributions $W_{\gamma,\beta}, \gamma \ge 0,$.

Theorem 17.8
Let Z be a $W_{\gamma,\beta}$ distributed random variable with $0 \leq \gamma < 1$. The average excess function is linear:

$$e(u) = \mathsf{E}\{Z - u | Z > u\} = \frac{\beta + \gamma u}{1 + \gamma}, \quad u \geq 0, \quad \text{for } 0 \leq \gamma < 1.$$

With the usual parametrization of the Pareto distribution $\gamma = \frac{1}{\alpha}$, i.e., the condition $\gamma < 1$ means that $\alpha > 1$ and thus $\mathsf{E}|Z| < \infty$.

This result motivates the following application in choosing the threshold: select the threshold u of the POT estimator so that the empirical average excess function $e_n(v)$ for values $v \geq u$ is approximately linear. An appropriate u is chosen by considering the average excess plots, where it is recommended that the largest points $(X_{(k)}, e_n(X_{(k)}))$, $k \approx n$, along the righthand edge of the plot be excluded, since their large variability for the most part distorts the optical impression.

17.2.2 The Hill Estimator

The POT method for estimating the exceedance probability and the extreme quantiles can be used on data with cdf that is in the MDA of a Gumbel or a Fréchet distribution, as long as the expected value is finite. Even for extreme financial data, this estimator seems reasonable based on empirical evidence. A classic alternative to the POT method is the Hill estimator, which was already discussed in Chapter 12 in connection with the estimation of the tail exponents of the DAX stocks. It is of course only useful for distributions with slowly decaying tails, such as those in the MDA of the Fréchet distribution, and performs in simulations more often worse in comparison to the POT estimator. The details are briefly introduced in this section.

In this section we will always assume that the data $X_1, \ldots, X_n$ are i.i.d. with a distribution function F in the MDA of $G_{1,\alpha}$ for some $\alpha > 0$. Due to Theorem 17.3 this is the case when $\overline{F}(x) = x^{-\alpha} L(x)$ with a slowly varying function L. The tapering behavior of $\overline{F}(x) = \mathsf{P}(X_t > x)$ for increasing x is mainly determined by the so called *tail exponents* α. The starting point of the Hill method is the following estimator for α.

Definition 17.11 (Hill estimator)
$X^{(1)} \geq X^{(2)} \geq \ldots \geq X^{(n)}$ *are the order statistics in decreasing order. The*

Hill estimator $\hat{\alpha}_H$ *of the tail exponents* α *for a suitable* $k = k(n)$ *is*

$$\hat{\alpha}_H = \{\frac{1}{k} \sum_{j=1}^{k} \log \ X^{(j)} - \log \ X^{(k)}\}^{-1}.$$

The form of the estimator can be seen from the following simple special case. In general it holds that $\overline{F}(x) = L(x)/(x^\alpha)$, but we now assume that with a fixed $c > 0$ $L(x) = c^\alpha$ is constant. Set $V_j = \log(X_j/c)$, it holds that

$$P(V_j > v) = P(X_j > ce^v) = \overline{F}(ce^v) = \frac{c^\alpha}{(ce^v)^\alpha} = e^{-\alpha v}, \ y \geq 0,$$

$V_1, \ldots, V_n$ are therefore independent exponentially distributed random variables with parameter α. As is well known it holds that $\alpha = (\mathsf{E}V_j)^{-1}$, and the ML estimator $\hat{\alpha}$ for α is $1/\overline{V}_n$, where $\overline{V}_n$ stands for the sample average of $V_1, \ldots, V_n$, thus,

$$\hat{\alpha} = \frac{1}{\overline{V}_n} = \{\frac{1}{n} \sum_{j=1}^{n} \log(X_j/c)\}^{-1} = \{\frac{1}{n} \sum_{j=1}^{n} \log \ X^{(j)} - \log \ c\}^{-1},$$

where for the last equation only the order of addition was changed. $\hat{\alpha}$ is already similar to the Hill estimator. In general it of course only holds that $\overline{F}(x) \approx \frac{c^\alpha}{x^\alpha}$ for sufficiently large x. The argument for the special case is similar for the largest observations $X^{(1)} \geq X^{(2)} \geq \ldots \geq X^{(k)} \geq u$ beyond the threshold u, so that only the k largest order statistics enter the definition of the Hill estimator.

The Hill estimator is consistent, that is it converges in probability to α when $n, k \to \infty$ such that $k/n \to 0$. Under an additional condition it can also be shown that $\sqrt{k}(\hat{\alpha}_H - \alpha) \xrightarrow{\mathcal{L}} N(0, \alpha^2)$, i.e., $\hat{\alpha}_H$ is asymptotically normally distributed.

Similar to the POT estimator when considering the Hill estimator the question regarding the choice of the threshold $u = X^{(k)}$ comes into play, since the observations located beyond it enter the estimation. Once again we have a bias variance dilemma:

- When k is too small, only a few observations influence $\hat{\alpha}_H$, and the variance of the estimator, which is α^2/k asymptotically, is too large,

- when k is too large, the assumption underlying the derivation of the estimator, i.e., that $L(x)$ is approximately constant for all $x \geq X^{(k)}$, is in general not well met and the bias $\mathsf{E}\hat{\alpha}_H - \alpha$ becomes too large.

Based on the fundamentals of the Hill estimator for the tail exponents α we obtain direct estimators for the exceedance probability $\overline{F}(x)$ and for the quantiles of F. Since $\overline{F}(x) = x^{-\alpha}L(x)$ with a slowly varying function L, it holds for large $x \geq X^{(k)}$ that:

$$\frac{\overline{F}(x)}{\overline{F}(X^{(k)})} = \frac{L(x)}{L(X^{(k)})} \left(\frac{X^{(k)}}{x}\right)^{\alpha} \approx \left(\frac{X^{(k)}}{x}\right)^{\alpha}, \qquad (17.5)$$

Because exactly one portion k/n of the data is larger or equal to the order statistic $X^{(k)}$, this is the $(1 - k/n)$ sample quantile. Therefore, the empirical distribution function takes on the value $1 - k/n$ at $X^{(k)}$, since it uniformly converges to the distribution function F, for sufficiently large n, a k that is not too large in comparison to n yields: $F(X^{(k)}) \approx 1 - k/n$, i.e., $\overline{F}(X^{(k)}) \approx k/n$. Substituting this into (17.5), we obtain a *Hill esitmator for the exceedance probability* $\overline{F}(x)$:

$$\widehat{\overline{F}}_H(x) = \frac{k}{n} \left(\frac{X^{(k)}}{x}\right)^{\hat{\alpha}_H}$$

By inverting this estimator we have the *Hill quantile estimator* for the $q-$ quantile x_q with $q \approx 1$:

$$\begin{aligned} \hat{x}_{q,H} &= X^{(k)} \left\{\frac{n}{k}(1 - q)\right\}^{-1/\hat{\alpha}_H} \\ &= X^{(k)} + X^{(k)} \left[\left\{\frac{n}{k}(1 - q)\right\}^{-\hat{\gamma}_H} - 1\right] \end{aligned}$$

with $\hat{\gamma}_H = 1/\hat{\alpha}_H$, where the second representation clearly shows the similarities and differences to the POT quantile estimator.

Q SFEhillquantile.xpl

17.3   Estimators for Risk Measurements

The value at risk discussed in the previous chapter is not the single measure of the market risk. In this section we introduce an alternative risk measure. In addition we discuss how to estimate the measure given extremely high loss.

Definition 17.12 (Value-at-Risk and Expected Shortfall)
Let $0 < q < 1$, and let F be the distribution of the loss X of a financial investment within a given time period, for example, one day or 10 trading

days. Typical values for q are q = 0.95 and q = 0.99.
a) The Value-at-Risk *(VaR) is the q-quantile*

$$VaR_q(X) = x_q = F^{-1}(q).$$

b) The expected shortfall *is defined as*

$$S_q = \mathsf{E}\{X|X > x_q\}.$$

Value-at-Risk is today still the most commonly used measurement, which can quantify the market risk. It can be assumed, however, that in the future the expected shortfall will play at least an equal role.

Definition 17.13 (Coherent Risk Measure)
A coherent risk measure *is a real-valued function* $\rho : \mathbb{R} \to \mathbb{R}$ *of real-valued random variables, which model the losses, with the following characteristics:*

(A1) $X \geq Y$ *a.s.* $\implies \rho(X) \geq \rho(Y)$ *(Monotonicity)*

(A2) $\rho(X + Y) \leq \rho(X) + \rho(Y)$ *(Subadditivity)*

(A3) $\rho(\lambda X) = \lambda \rho(X)$ *for* $\lambda \geq 0$ *(Positive homogeneity)*

(A4) $\rho(X + a) = \rho(X) + a$ *(Translation equivariance)*

These conditions correspond to intuitive obvious requirements of a market risk measurement:
(A1) When the loss from investment X is always larger than that from investment Y, then the risk from investment X is also larger.
(A2) The risk of a portfolio consisting of investments in X and Y is at most as large as the sum of the individual risks (diversification of the risk).
(A3) When an investment is multiplied, then the risk is also multiplied accordingly.
(A4) By adding a risk free investment, i.e., a non-random investment with known losses a ($a < 0$, when the investment has fixed payments), to a portfolio, the risk changes by exactly a.

The VaR does not meet condition (A2) in certain situations. Let X and Y, for example, be i.i.d. and both can take on the value 0 or 100 with probability $P(X = 0) = P(Y = 0) = p$ and $P(X = 100) = P(Y = 100) = 1 - p$. Then $X + Y$ can be 0, 100 and 200 with probability $P(X + Y = 0) = p^2$, $P(X + Y = 100) = 2p(1 - p)$ and $P(X + Y = 200) = (1 - p)^2$ respectively. For $p^2 < q < p$ and $q < 1 - (1 - p)^2$, for example, for $p = 0.96, q = 0.95$, it holds that

$$VaR_q(X) = VaR_q(Y) = 0, \quad \text{but} \ \ VaR_q(X + Y) = 100.$$

The expected shortfall, on the other hand, is a coherent risk measure that always fulfills all four conditions. It also gives a more intuitive view of the actual risk of extreme losses than the Value-at-Risk. The VaR only depends on the probability of losses above the q-quantile x_q, but it doesn't say anything about whether these losses are always just a little above the threshold x_q or whether there are also losses that are much larger than x_q that need to be taken into account. In contrast the expected shortfall is the expected value of the potential losses from x_q and depends on the actual size of the losses.

The Value-at-Risk is simply a quantile and can be, for example, estimated as a sample quantile $\hat{F}_n^{-1}(q)$, where $\hat{F}_n(x)$ is the empirical distribution of a sample of negative values, i.e., losses, from the past. As was discussed at the beginning of the chapter, this particular estimator of $q \approx 1$, which is for the typical VaR-level of 0.95 and 0.99, is often too optimistic. An alternative VaR estimator, which has the possibility of reflecting extreme losses better, is the POT or the Hill quantile estimator.

Analogous estimators for the expected shortfall are easy to derive. This risk measure is closely related to the average excess function when $u = x_q$, as immediately can be seen from the definition:

$$S_q = e(x_q) + x_q.$$

Here we only consider the POT estimator for S_q. Since $F_u(x) \approx W_{\gamma,\beta}(x)$ for a sufficiently large threshold u, it holds from Theorem 17.5, b) with $\alpha = 1/\gamma$

$$e(v) \approx \frac{\beta + (v - u)\gamma}{1 - \gamma} \quad \text{for} \ \ v > u.$$

Therefore, for $x_q > u$ we have

$$\frac{S_q}{x_q} = 1 + \frac{e(x_q)}{x_q} \approx \frac{1}{1 - \gamma} + \frac{\beta - \gamma u}{x_q(1 - \gamma)}.$$

The *POT estimator for the expected shortfall S_q* is thus

$$\hat{S}_{q,u} = \frac{\hat{x}_q}{1 - \hat{\gamma}} + \frac{\hat{\beta} - \hat{\gamma}u}{1 - \hat{\gamma}},$$

where $\hat{x}_q$ is the POT quantile estimator.

17.4   Extreme Value Theory for Time Series

Let Z_t, $-\infty < t < \infty$, be a *strictly stationary time series*, as defined in Definition 10.6, that is the distribution of the data and its probability structure does not change over time. Each single observation Z_t has, among other things, the same distribution function F. To compare consider the i.i.d. random variables $X_1, X_2, \ldots$ with the same distribution F. Let $M_n = \max\{Z_1, \ldots, Z_n\}$, $M_n^x = \max\{X_1, \ldots, X_n\}$ be the maxima of n values from the time series respectively from n independent observations. A simple but basic relationship for the previous sections is (17.1), i.e.,

$$\mathrm{P}(M_n^x \le y) = \{\mathrm{P}(X_j \le y)\}^n = F^n(y),$$

where the independence of X_t is used. For dependent data this relationship does not hold and the distribution of the maximum M_n is not determined by F alone, but rather from the complete distribution of the time series. Luckily in many cases there is at least one comparable, approximate relationship:

$$\mathrm{P}(M_n \le y) \approx F^{n\delta}(y) \ge F^n(y) \quad \text{for large } n,$$

where $\delta \in [0, 1]$ is the so called extremal index. In order to find an exact definition, recall Theorem 17.2 for the independent case, whereby

$$n\overline{F}(u_n) \to \tau$$
$$\text{if and only if} \quad \mathrm{P}(M_n^x \le u_n) \to e^{-\tau}.$$

Definition 17.14 (Extremal Index)
$\delta \in [0, 1]$ *is called the* extremal index *of the time series* Z_j, $-\infty < j < \infty$, *when for certain* τ, u_n

$$n\overline{F}(u_n) \to \tau \quad and \quad \mathrm{P}(M_n \le u_n) \to e^{-\delta\tau}.$$

(If δ exists, then the value does not depend on the specific choice of τ, u_n).

From the definition the above claimed approximate relationship between the distribution of the maximum and the exceedance probability immediately follows:

$$\mathrm{P}(M_n \le u_n) \approx e^{-\delta\tau} \approx e^{-\delta n \overline{F}(u_n)} = (e^{-\overline{F}(u_n)})^{n\delta} \approx (1 - \overline{F}(u_n))^{n\delta} = F^{n\delta}(u_n),$$

when u_n is large and thus $\overline{F}(u_n) \approx 0$.

Pure white noise automatically has the extremal index $\delta = 1$, since Z_t here are independent. It is not obvious that all ARMA(p, q) processes (see Chapter 11) with normally distributed innovations also have an extremal index $\delta = 1$, its maxima thus behave like maxima from independent data. Intuitively this comes from, on the one hand, ARMA processes having an exponentially decreasing memory, i.e., the observations $Z_t, Z_{t+\tau}$ are for sufficiently large time periods τ practically independent, and, on the other hand, the probability of two extreme observations occurring within the same time interval, which is not too long, is small. These qualitative statements can be formulated as two precise criteria of time series that have an extremal index of 1, the exact formulation of which will not be given here.

For financial time series models the second condition is not fulfilled, because they contradict the presence of volatility clusters (see Chapter 12), i.e., the local frequency of extreme observations. The extremal index of an ARCH(1) process with parameters ω, α (see Definition 12.1) is, for example, always $\delta = \delta(\alpha) < 1$. It can be approximated for $\alpha = 0.5$, for example, $\delta \approx 0.835$.

Finally note that not every time series has an extremal index. A simple counter example is $Z_t = A \cdot X_t$ with i.i.d. random variables X_t, which are modelled by a random factor $A > 0$ that is independent of X_t. Since the factor A is contained in all observations, even in the most distant past, this time series has no decreasing memory. If the distribution of X_t has slowly decaying tails, i.e., they belong to the MDA of a Fréchet distribution, then it can be shown that Z_t can not have an extremal index.

The extreme theory for time series is still developing. The Fisher-Tippett theorem, however, exists as a central result in the following modified form:

Theorem 17.9
Let $\{Z_t\}$ be a strictly stationary time series with the distribution function F and an extremal index $\delta > 0$. Let $X_1, X_2, \ldots$ be i.i.d. with the same distribution function F. $M_n^x = max\{X_1, \ldots, X_n\}$. Let G_γ be a general extreme value distribution. We have

$$\mathrm{P}\left(\frac{M_n^x - d_n}{c_n} \leq x\right) \to G_\gamma(x)$$

if and only if $\quad \mathrm{P}\left(\frac{M_n - d_n}{c_n} \leq x\right) \to G_\gamma^\delta(x)$

for all x with $0 < G_\gamma(x) < 1$.

The maxima of the time series are standardized by the same series c_n, d_n and converge in distribution to the same type of asymptotic distribution as the maxima of the corresponding independent data, since G_γ^δ is itself a general extreme value distribution with the same form parameters as G_γ. For example, for $\gamma > 0$ it holds that

$$G_\gamma^\delta(x) = \exp\{-\delta(1 + \gamma x)^{-1/\gamma}\} = G_\gamma(\frac{x - \mu}{\sigma}), \ \ 1 + \gamma x > 0$$

with $\sigma = \delta^\gamma$ and $\mu = -(1 - \delta^\gamma)$, i.e., except for the location and scale parameters the distributions are identical.

Many of the techniques used in extreme value statistics, that were developed for independent data can be used on time series. To do this, however, one needs to have more data, because the effective size of the sample is only $n\delta$ instead of n. Besides that, additional problems appear: the POT method is perhaps in theory still applicable, but the excesses are no longer independent, especially when a financial time series with volatility clusters is considered. For this reason the parameters of the generalized Pareto distribution, with which the excess distribution is approximated, cannot be estimated by simply taking the maximum of the likelihood function of independent data. One way out of this is to either use special model assumptions, with which the likelihood function of the dependent excesses can be calculated, or by using a reduction technique, with which the data is made more "independent" at the cost of the sample size. One application, for example, replaces the cluster of neighboring excesses with a maximum value from the cluster, whereby the cluster size is so chosen that the sample size of the excesses is approximately reduced by the factor δ. Afterwards the POT estimators, which were developed for independent data, can be calculated from the reduced excesses.

Another problem is that the extremal index needs to be estimated in order to be able to use applications like the one just described. In the literature several estimation techniques are described. We will introduce only one here; one that can be described without a lot of technical preparation, the so called *Block method*. First the time series data $Z_1, \ldots, Z_n$ is divided into b blocks, each has a length l (size $n = bl$, b, l large). Let $M_l^{(k)}$ be the maximum of the observations in the k-th block:

$$M_l^{(k)} = \max(Z_{(k-1)l+1}, \ldots, Z_{kl}), \ \ k = 1, \ldots, b.$$

For a large threshold value u, let $N(u) = \#\{t \leq n; \ Z_t > u\}$ be the number of observations beyond the threshold and let $B(u) = \#\{k \leq b; \ M_l^{(k)} > u\}$ be the number of blocks with at least one observation beyond the threshold u. The estimator for the extremal index is then

$$\hat{\delta} = \frac{1}{l} \frac{\log\ (1 - \frac{B(u)}{b})}{\log\ (1 - \frac{N(u)}{n})}.$$

Heuristically this estimator can be derived from the following three observations:

(i) From the definition of the extremal index it follows that $P(M_n \leq u) \approx F^{\delta n}(u)$, when $n, u \to \infty$, so that $n\overline{F}(u) \to \tau$. Solving for δ it follows that

$$\delta \approx \frac{\log \ P(M_n \leq u)}{n \log \ F(u)}.$$

(ii) F can be estimated using the empirical distribution function $\hat{F}_n$, so that $F(u) = 1 - P(Z_t > u) \approx 1 - \frac{N(u)}{n}$.

(iii) With $n = bl$ it follows that

$$P(M_n \leq u) \ \approx \ \prod_{k=1}^{b} P(M_l^{(k)} \leq u) \approx \{P(M_l^{(1)} \leq u)\}^b$$

$$\approx \ \{\frac{1}{b} \sum_{k=1}^{b} \mathbf{1}(M_l^{(k)} \leq u)\}^b = (1 - \frac{B(u)}{b})^b.$$

By combining the three observations we have

$$\delta \approx \frac{b \ \log \ (1 - \frac{B(u)}{b})}{n \ \log \ (1 - \frac{N(u)}{n})} = \hat{\delta}.$$

17.5   Recommended Literature

Both of the basic theorems, Theorem 17.1 and Theorem 17.6, of this section go back to Fisher and Tippett (1928) respectively Pickands (1975). The essential notion of quantifying risk by coherent risk measures was introduced by Artzner et al. (1997).

A comprehensive summary of the modelling and statistical analysis of extreme results is given in the monograph from Embrechts et al. (1997). There one finds proofs as well as detailed mathematical and practical considerations of the content of this section and an extensive bibliography. Another actual and recommendable book on extreme value statistic is Reiss and Thomas (1997). A more in depth implementation of the method in the form of quantlets discussed in this last reference, which goes beyond the selection introduced in this section, can be found in Reiss and Thomas (2000).

A substantial problem that occurs when applying the methods of extreme value statistics such as the POT or the Hill estimators is the choice of the threshold value u or the corresponding number k of large order statistics. We have already mentioned how this choice can be made with the help of graphical representations. A more in depth discussion including the corresponding quantlet can be found in Reiss and Thomas (2000). Polzehl and Spokoiny (2003) and Grama and Spokoiny (2003) describe current procedures used for estimating the tail exponents, for which the choice of u respectively k, given the available data, can be adaptively and thus automatically chosen.

The methods described in this chapter give estimators for the Value-at-Risk as unconditional quantiles. Often one wishes to include financial data from the recent past when estimating risk, for example in a GARCH(1,1) model the last observation and the last volatility. In this case the Value-at-Risk is a conditional quantile given the available information. One possibility of using extreme value statistics in such cases is based on the assumptions of a specific stochastic volatility model which is parametric as in McNeil and Frey (2000) or nonparametric as in Chapter 13.

Given the assumptions of the model a conditional volatility σ_t is estimated given the past, which together with the data results in an estimator for the innovations Z_t. In calculating the conditional quantile it is not assumed that the Z_t are standard normally distributed, but instead the needed unconditional quantile of the innovations is estimated from the estimated innovations with, for example, the POT estimator. Alternatively one can estimate the conditional quantile also direct as nonparametric, in which the conditional distribution function is first estimated with a kernel estimator and then the inverse is taken. With moderately large quantiles, for example, with a 95% VaR, the method from Franke and Mwita (2003) gives good results, even for innovation distributions with heavy tails and infinite variance. For extreme quantiles such as the 99% VaR a semi-parametric method must be considered, as is the case with the POT method, in order to obtain useful results. Mwita (2003) estimates first a nonparametric, medium sized conditional quantile and modifies this estimator through the fitting of a Pareto distribution to the extreme excesses.

18 Neural Networks

A neural network is a non-linear system that converts a series of real input values $x_1, \ldots, x_p$ over several intermediary steps to one or more terminal variables $y_1, \ldots, y_q$. It represents a function $\nu : \mathbb{R}^p \to \mathbb{R}^q$:

$$(y_1, \ldots, y_q)^\top = \nu(x_1, \ldots, x_p),$$

that has a special form given by the network structure. This is graphically

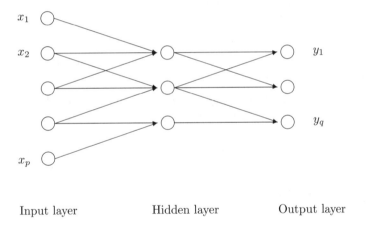

Input layer   Hidden layer   Output layer

Figure 18.1: Neural feed forward network with a hidden layer

displayed in Figure 18.1 in the form of a directed graph whose nodes are grouped in various levels. In the *input layer* each node represents an input variable; in the *output layer* each node represents an output variable. In between there are one or more *hidden layers*, whose nodes are neither sources nor layers of the graph. The network in Figure 18.1 contains only one hidden

layer. In additional it is a *feed forward network*, since it contains no edges
that begin in a node and end in the same node or in a different node from
the same or a previous layer.

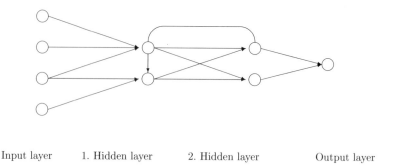

Input layer   1. Hidden layer   2. Hidden layer   Output layer

Figure 18.2: Neural feedback network with two hidden layers

Figure 18.2 displays a *feedback network*, in that there is feedback among the
nodes of the two hidden layers. In the following we will concentrate on the
feed forward network.

Neural network are used in financial statistics to represent functions, which,
for example, can represent the default probability of a credit, the forecast
of an exchange rate or the volatility of a stock. Here the emphasis is on
non-parametric applications, which in comparison to the local smoothing
function discussed in Chapter 13 require an advanced modelling and can
be quite involved to calculate. On the other hand it is still practical when
numerous variables need to be considered in forecasts or quantifying risk, i.e.,
when the dimension p of the function arguments is large.

Since neural networks are still relatively unknown tools in statistics, in the
first section we will give an elementary introduction in the structure of a neural network. It allows for the construction of complex functions using simple
elements. In the second section we describe the popular numerical application for fitting neural networks to the data, before we conclude with various
applications to financial problems and introduce the underlying assumptions.

18.1   From Perceptron to Non-linear Neuron

The perceptron is a simple mathematical model of how a nerve cell functions in receiving signals from sense cells and other nerve cells (the input variables) and from this sends a signal to the next nerve cell or remains inactive. In spite of all of the disadvantages the perceptron is very influential on the way of thinking with respect to neural networks, so that it is a good starting point for the discussion of components from which neural networks are constructed. The perceptron works in two steps:

– the input variables $x_1, \ldots, x_p$ are multiplied and added with *weights* $w_1, \ldots, w_p$,

– a *threshold operation* is applied to the result.

$x = (x_1, \ldots, x_p)^\top$, $w = (w_1, \ldots, w_p)^\top$ represent the input vector and weight vector respectively, and for a given b let $\psi(u) = \mathbf{1}(u > b)$ be the corresponding threshold function. The output variables $y = \psi(w^\top x)$ of the perceptron is 1 (the nerve cell „fires"), when the sum of the weighted input signales lies above the threshold and is 0 otherwise (the nerve cells remain inactive). The effect

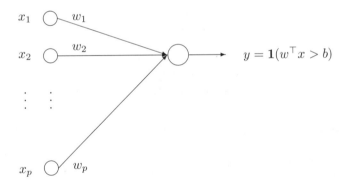

Figure 18.3: The perceptron

of the perceptron depends on the weights $w_1, \ldots, w_p$ and the threshold value b. An equivalent representation can be obtained by including the constant $x_0 \stackrel{\text{def}}{=} 1$ as an additional input variable, which has the weight $w_0 = -b$ and a threshold value of 0 is chosen since then

$$\mathbf{1}\left(\sum_{i=1}^{p} w_i x_i > b\right) = \mathbf{1}\left(\sum_{i=0}^{p} w_i x_i > 0\right).$$

This representation is often more comfortable since with the system parameters that can be freely chosen one does not have to differentiate between weights and threshold values.

A perceptron can be trained to solve classification problems of the following type: Given are objects which belong to one of two classes, C_0 or C_1. Decisions are made based on observations of the object $x_1, \ldots, x_p$, whether it belongs to C_0 or C_1.

The perceptron characterized by the weights $w_0, \ldots, w_p$ classifies an object as belonging to C_0 respectively C_1 when the output variable $y = y(x_1, \ldots, x_p)$ is 0 respectively 1. So that the classification problem "may be" solved, the weights $w_0, \ldots, w_p$ must be "learned". To do this there is a *training set*

$$(x^{(1)}, z^{(1)}), \ldots, (x^{(T)}, z^{(T)})$$

from T input vectors

$$x^{(t)} = (x_1^{(t)}, \ldots, x_p^{(t)})^\top$$

available whose correct classification

$$z^{(1)}, \ldots, z^{(T)} \in \{0, 1\}$$

is known. With the help from *learning rules* suitable weights $\hat{w}_0, \ldots, \hat{w}_p$ are determined from the training set.

In statistical terms the problem is to estimate the parameters of the perceptron from the data $(x^{(t)}, z^{(t)})$, $t = 1, \ldots, T$. A *learning rule* is an estimation method which produces estimates $\hat{w}_0, \ldots, \hat{w}_p$.

A learning rule is, for example, the Delta or *Widrow-Hoff learning rule*: The input vectors $x^{(t)}, t = 1, \ldots, T$, are used consecutively as input variables of the perceptron and the output variables $y^{(t)}$, $t = 1, \ldots, T$, are compared to the correct classification $z^{(t)}$, $t = 1, \ldots, T$. If in one step $y^{(t)} = z^{(t)}$, then the weights remain unchanged. If on the other hand $y^{(t)} \neq z^{(t)}$, then the weight vector $w = (w_0, \ldots, w_p)^\top$ is adjusted in the following manner:

$$w_{new} = w + \eta(z^{(t)} - y^{(t)}) x^{(t)}$$

η is a small relaxation factor which must eventually slowly approach zero in order to ensure convergence of the learning algorithm. The initial value of w

is arbitrarily given or randomly chosen, for example, uniformly distributed over $[0, 1]^{p+1}$.

The learning does not end when all of the input vectors are presented in the network, but rather after $x^{(T)}$ has been entered, $x^{(1)}$ is used again as the next input variable. The training set is tested multiple times until the network of all objects in the training set have been correctly identified or until a given quality criterion for measuring the error in classification is small.

The weights $w_0, \ldots, w_p$ can be identified up to a positive scale factor, i.e., for $\alpha > 0$, $\alpha\, w_0, \ldots, \alpha\, w_p$ lead to the same classification. By applying the learning rule, such as that of Widrow-Hoff, it can happen that $||w||$ continuously increases, which can lead to numerical problems. In order to prohibit this, one uses the so called *weight decay* technique, i.e., a modified learning rule in which $||w||$ remains stable.

Example 18.1 (Learning the OR-Function)
Let $p = 2$ and $x_1, x_2 \in \{0, 1\}$. The classifications that needs to be learned is the logical OR:

$$z = 1, \ \ if \ x_1 = 1 \ or \ x_2 = 1,$$
$$z = 0, \ \ if \ x_1 = 0 \ and \ \ x_2 = 0.$$

The following input vectors, including the first coordinate $x_0 = 1$

$$x^{(1)} = \begin{pmatrix} 1 \\ 1 \\ 0 \end{pmatrix}, \ x^{(2)} = \begin{pmatrix} 1 \\ 0 \\ 1 \end{pmatrix}, \ x^{(3)} = \begin{pmatrix} 1 \\ 1 \\ 1 \end{pmatrix}, \ x^{(4)} = \begin{pmatrix} 1 \\ 0 \\ 0 \end{pmatrix}$$

are used as the training set with the correct classification $z^{(1)} = z^{(2)} = z^{(3)} = 1$, $z^{(4)} = 0$. The perceptron with the weights w_0, w_1, w_2 classifies an object as 1 if and only if

$$w_0 x_0 + w_1 x_1 + w_2 x_2 > 0 \ ,$$

and as 0 otherwise. For the starting vector we use $w = (0, 0, 0)^\top$, and we set $\eta = 1$. The individual steps of the Widrow-Hoff learning take the following form:

1. *$w^{(1)}$ gives $y^{(1)} = 0 \neq z^{(1)}$. The weights are changed:*
   $w_{new} = (0, 0, 0)^\top + (1 - 0)(1, 1, 0)^\top = (1, 1, 0)^\top$

2. *$x^{(2)}$ is correctly classified with the weight vector.*

3. *$x^{(3)}$ is correctly classified with the weight vector.*

4. *For $x^{(4)}$ is $w^\top x^{(4)} = 1$, so that the weights are again changed:*
   $$w_{new} = (1,1,0)^\top + (0-1)(1,0,0)^\top = (0,1,0)^\top$$

5. *$x^{(1)}$ is now used as input and is correctly classified.*

6. *Since $w^\top x^{(2)} = 0$:*
   $$w_{new} = (0,1,0)^\top + (1-0)(1,0,1)^\top = (1,1,1)^\top$$

7. *Since $w^\top x^{(3)} = 3 > 0$, $x^{(3)}$ is correctly classified.*

8. *$x^{(4)}$ is incorrectly classified so that*
   $$w_{new} = (1,1,1)^\top + (0-1)(1,0,0)^\top = (0,1,1)^\top$$

Thus the procedure ends since the perceptron has correctly identified all the input vectors in the training set with these weights. The perceptron learned the OR function over the set $\{0,1\}^2$.

One distinguishes different types of learning for neural networks:

Supervised Learning: Compare the network outputs $y = y(x_1, \ldots, x_p)$ with the correct $z = z(x_1, \ldots, x_p)$. When $y \neq z$, the weights are changed according to the learning rule.

Reinforcement Learning: From every network output $y = y(x_1, \ldots, x_p)$ one discovers, whether it is „correct" or „incorrect" - in the latter case though one does not know the correct value. When y is „incorrect", the weights are changed according to the learning rule.

Unsupervised Learning: There is no feedback while learning. Similar to the cluster analysis random errors are filtered from the data with the help of redundant information.

For $y \in \{0,1\}$ supervised and reinforcement learning are the same. Included in this type is the Widrow-Hoff learning rule for the perceptron.

The perceptron can not learn all of the desired classifications. The classical counter example is the logical argument XOR = "exclusive or":

$$z = 1, \text{ if either } x_1 = 1 \text{ or } x_2 = 1,$$
$$z = 0, \text{ if } x_1 = x_2 = 0 \text{ or } \quad x_1 = x_2 = 1.$$

A perceptron with weights w_0, w_1, w_2 corresponds to a hyperplane $w_0 + w_1 x_1 + w_2 x_2 = 0$ in $\mathbb{R}^2$ space of the inputs $(x_1, x_2)^\top$, which separates the set using the perceptron of 0 classified objects from those classified as 1. It is not hard to see that no hyperplane exists for "exclusive or" where inputs should be classified as 1 $\binom{1}{0}, \binom{0}{1}$ can be separated from those to be classified as 0 $\binom{0}{0}, \binom{1}{1}$.

Definition 18.1 (linearly separable)
For $p \geq 1$ to subsets $\mathcal{X}_0, \mathcal{X}_1 \subseteq \mathbb{R}^p$ are called linearly separable *if $w \in \mathbb{R}^p$, $w_0 \in \mathbb{R}$ exists with*

$$w_0 + w^\top x > 0 \quad \text{for } x \in \mathcal{X}_1,$$
$$w_0 + w^\top x \leq 0 \quad \text{for } x \in \mathcal{X}_0.$$

The perceptron with p input variables $x_1, \ldots, x_p$ (with respect to the constant $x_0 \stackrel{\text{def}}{=} 1$) can exactly learn the classification that is consistent with the linearly separable sets of inputs.

If no perfect classification is possible through a perceptron, then one can at least try to find a "good" classification, that is, to determine the weights $w_0, \ldots, w_p$ so that a measurement for the amount of incorrectly identified classifications can be minimized. An example of such an application is given by the *least squares (LS) classification:*

Assuming that the training set $(x^{(1)}, z^{(1)}), \ldots, (x^{(T)}, z^{(T)})$ is given. Determine for some given weight w_0 the weights $w_1, \ldots, w_p$ so that

$$Q(w) = Q(w_1, \ldots, w_p) = \sum_{i=1}^{T} (z^{(i)} - y^{(i)})^2 = \min !$$
$$\text{with } y^{(i)} = \mathbf{1}(w_0 + w^\top x^{(i)} > 0), \ w = (w_1, \ldots, w_p)^\top$$

w_0 can be arbitrarily chosen since the weights $w_0, \ldots, w_p$ described above are only determined up to a scale factor. In the case of the perceptron, which takes on a binary classification, $Q(w)$ is simply the number of incorrectly defined classifications. The form mentioned above can also be directly applied to other problems. The attainable minimum of $Q(w)$ is exactly 0 (perfect classification of the training set) when both sets

$$\mathcal{X}_0^{(T)} = \{x^{(i)}, \ i \leq T; \ z^{(i)} = 0\}, \ \mathcal{X}_1^{(T)} = \{x^{(i)}, \ i \leq T; \ z^{(i)} = 1\}$$

are linearly separable.

The Widrow-Hoff learning rule solves the LS classification problem; there are, however, a series of other learning rules or estimation methods which can also solve the problem. The perceptron has proven to be too inflexible for many applications. Therefore, one considers general forms of *neurons* as components used to build a neuron network:

Error surface Q(w)   Error surface Q(w)

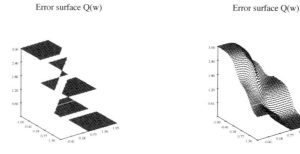

Figure 18.4: Error surface of $Q(w)$ given weight $w = (w_1, w_2)^\top$ with transform function: threshold function (left) and sigmoid function
(right)   **Q** SFEerrorsurf.xpl

Let $x = (x_1, \ldots, x_p)^\top$, $w = (w_1, \ldots, w_p)^\top$ be input and weight vectors respectively. For $\beta, \beta_0 \in \mathbb{R}$

$$\psi_\beta(t) = \frac{1}{1 + \exp(-\frac{t+\beta}{\beta_0})}$$

is the logistic function, which due to its form is often referred to as "the"
sigmoid function. One can also use other functions with sigmoid forms, for
example, the density function of a normal distribution. The output variable
of the neuron is $y = \psi_\beta(w^\top x)$.

For $\beta_0 \rightarrow 0+$ $\psi_\beta(t)$ approaches a threshold function:

$$\psi_\beta(t) \longrightarrow \mathbf{1}(t + \beta > 0) \qquad \text{for } \beta_0 \longrightarrow 0+ \ ,$$

so that the preceptron is a boundary of the neuron with a logistic activation function. An example of $Q(w)$ for neurons with threshold function and
sigmoid function as activation function is shown in Figure 18.4. The corresponding method is presented in Figure 18.5.

β_0 is often not explicitly chosen, since it can be integrated as a scale factor
in the other parameters $w_1, \ldots, w_p$, β of the neurons. If one also sets $w_0 = \beta$
and $x_0 \stackrel{\text{def}}{=} 1$,, then the output variables can also be written in the form:

$$y = \psi(w_0 + w^\top x) = \psi(\sum_{k=0}^{p} w_k x_k) \text{ with } \psi(t) = \frac{1}{1 + e^{-t}}.$$

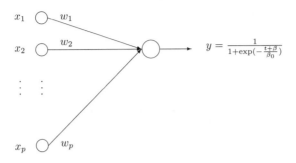

Figure 18.5: Neuron with a sigmoid transformation function

By combining multiple neurons with sigmoid or - in the limit case - threshold activation functions with a feed forward network one obtains a so called *multiple layer perceptron* (MLP) neural network. Figure 18.6 shows such a neural network with two input variables with respect to the constant $x_0 \overset{\text{def}}{=} 1$, two sigmoid neurons in the hidden layer that are connected by another sigmoid neuron to the output variables, where $\psi(t) = \{1 + e^{-t}\}^{-1}$ as above.

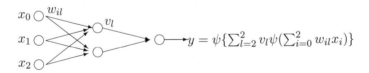

Figure 18.6: Multiple layer perceptron with a hidden layer

Neural networks can also be constructed with multiple hidden layers that give multiple output variables. The connections do not have to be complete, i.e., edges between the nodes of consecutive layers may be missing or equivalently several weights can be set to 0. Instead of the logical function or similar sigmoid functions threshold functions may also appear in some neurons. Another probability are the so called *radial basis functions* (RBF). To the former belongs the density of the standard normal distribution and similar symmetrical kernel functions. In this case one no longer speaks of a MLP, but of a RBF network.

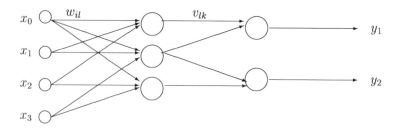

Figure 18.7: Multiple layer perceptron with two hidden layers

Figure 18.7 shows an incomplete neural network with two output variables. The weights $w_{13}, w_{22}, w_{31}, v_{12}$ and v_{31} are set to 0, and the corresponding edges are not displayed in the network graphs. The output variable y_1 is for example

$$y_1 = v_{11}\psi(w_{01} + w_{11}x_1 + w_{21}x_2) + v_{21}\psi(w_{02} + w_{12}x_1 + w_{32}x_3),$$

a linear combination of the results of the two upper neurons of the hidden layers.

Until now we have only discussed those cases that are most often handled in the literature, where a neuron has an effect on the linear combination of variables from the previous layer. Occasionally the case where the output of a neural of the form $\psi\left(\Pi_{i=1}^{p} w_i x_i\right)$ respectively $\psi\left(\max_{i=1,\dots,p} x_i\right)$ is considered.

Neural networks of MLP types can be used for classification problems as well as for regression and forecast problems. In order to find an adequate network for each problem, the weights have to be learned through a training set, i.e., the network parameters are estimated from the data. Since we are restricting ourselves to the case of supervised learning, this means that $(x^{(1)}, z^{(1)}), \dots, (x^{(T)}, z^{(T)})$ are given for the training set. The $x^{(i)} \in \mathbb{R}^p$ are input vectors, the $z^{(i)} \in \mathbb{R}^q$ are the corresponding desired output values from the network. The vectors $z^{(i)}$ are compared to the actual output vectors $y^{(i)} \in \mathbb{R}^q$ of the network. The weights are determined so that the deviations between $z^{(i)}$ and $y^{(i)}$ are small. An example of this is the *least squares (LS) application* already mentioned in the analysis of the perceptron:

Assuming that the training set $(x^{(1)}, z^{(1)}), \ldots, (x^{(T)}, z^{(T)})$ is given. The weights $w_{0l}, l = 1, \ldots, r$, $x_0 \overset{\text{def}}{=} 1$ are given, where r is the number of neurons in the first hidden layer. The weights of all the other edges in the network (between the input layer, the hidden layers and the output layer) are determined so that

$$\sum_{k=1}^{T} ||z^{(k)} - y^{(k)}||^2 = \min !$$

In the network given in Figure 18.7 the minimization is done with respect to the weights $w_{11}, w_{12}, w_{21}, w_{23}, w_{32}, w_{33}, v_{11}, v_{21}, v_{22}, v_{32}$. As for the perceptron the weights w_{01}, w_{02}, w_{03} can be set in order to avoid the arbitrage of scale factors.

Instead of the LS method also other loss functions can be minimized, for example, weighted quadratic distances or, above all in classification, the Kullback-Leibler distance:

$$\sum_{k=1}^{T} \sum_{i} \left\{ z_i^{(k)} \log \frac{z_i^{(k)}}{y_i^{(k)}} + (1 - z_i^{(k)}) \log \frac{1 - z_i^{(k)}}{1 - y_i^{k)}} \right\} = \min !$$

Since only the $y_i^{(k)}$ depend on the weights, it is equivalent to minimize the cross-entropie between z_i and y_i, which are both contained in $(0, 1)$:

$$-\sum_{k=1}^{T} \sum_{i} \left\{ z_i^{(k)} \log y_i^{(k)} + (1 - z_i^{(k)}) \log(1 - y_i^{(k)}) \right\} = \min !$$

18.2 Back Propagation

The most well known method with which the feed forward network learns its weights from the training set is the back propagation. The basic idea is non other than a numerical method to solve the (nonlinear) least squares problem that saves on memory on the cost though of eventually slower convergence and numerical instabilities.

To illustrate consider a neural network with an output variable y (i.e. $q = 1$) and a hidden layer with only one neuron:

$$y = \psi(w_0 + w^\top x).$$

ψ can be a logistic function, or some other transformation function. The training set is $(x^{(1)}, z^{(1)}), \ldots, (x^{(T)}, z^{(T)})$. The weight w_0 is held constant in order to avoid the arbitrary scale factor. The function to be minimized

$$Q(w) = \sum_{k=1}^{T}(z^{(k)} - y^{(k)})^2$$

is thus only dependent on the weights $w_1, \ldots, w_p$ of the input variables.

An elementary numerical method for minimizing Q is the *decreasing gradient method*. Given a weight $w(N)$ one calculates the next approximation by moving a small step in the direction of the steepest decline of Q:

$$w(N+1) = w(N) - \eta \operatorname{grad} Q(w(N)),$$
$$\operatorname{grad} Q(w) = -\sum_{k=1}^{T} 2(z^{(k)} - y^{(k)})\psi'(w^\top x^{(k)})x^{(k)}.$$

Error Surface: Learning weights

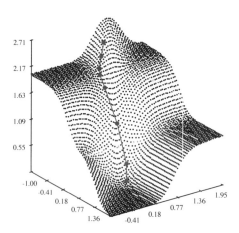

Figure 18.8: Gradients descent proceedings with goal vector $z = (0, 1, 0, 1)^\top$.

Q SFEdescgrad.xpl

To accelerate the convergence the small constant $\eta > 0$ can also converge to 0 during the iteration process. Figure 18.8 shows the path of optimizing $Q(w)$

evaluated in i-steps at $w_1, ..., w_i$, where each w is corrected according to the back propagation rule.

With the decreasing gradient method the quality of the weight $w(N)$, that is the actual network, is evaluated simultaneously using all the data in the training set. The network is applied to all $x^{(1)}, ..., x^{(T)}$, and only after this the weight vector is changed.

Back propagation is also a form of the decreasing gradient method with the difference that the network is repeatedly applied to the single $x^{(k)}$ and after every single step the weights are already changed in the direction of the steepest decline of the function $Q_k(w) = (z^{(k)} - y^{(k)})^2$:

$$
\begin{aligned}
w(N+1) &= w(N) - \eta \operatorname{grad} Q_k(w(N)) \ , \ k = 1, ..., T, \\
\operatorname{grad} Q_k(w) &= -2(z^{(k)} - y^{(k)})\psi'(w^\top x^{(k)})x^{(k)}.
\end{aligned}
$$

If in this process the training set has been gone through once, the iteration starts again from the beginning. T steps in the back propagation correspond then roughly to one step in the decreasing gradient method. Also by the back propagation algorithm it may be necessary to allow η to converge slowly to 0.

The Widrow-Hoff learning rule is in principle a back propagation algorithm. The threshold function $\psi(t) = \mathbf{1}(w_0 + t > 0)$ is non-differentiable, but after the presentation of $x^{(k)}$ the weights are changed in the direction of the steepest decline of $Q_k(w)$, i.e., in the direction of $x^{(k)}$ for $z^{(k)} = 1, y^{(k)} = 0$ and in the direction of $-x^{(k)}$ for $z^{(k)} = 0$, $y^{(k)} = 1$. By correct classifications the weights remain here unaltered.

Naturally one can apply every numerical algorithm that can calculate the minimum of a non-linear function $Q(w)$ to determine the weights of a neural network. By some applications, for example, the conjugate gradient method has proven to be the fastest and most reliable. All of these algorithms have the danger of landing in a local minimum of $Q(w)$. In the literature on neural networks it is occasionally claimed with the combination of training the networks such local minima do not occur. Based on experience of statistics with maximum-likelihood estimators of large dimensional parameters, this is to be expected since the training of neural networks for applications of regression analysis, for example, can be interpreted under the appropriate normality assumptions as the maximum-likelihood estimation technique.

18.3   Neural Networks in Non-parametric Regression Analysis

Neural networks of type MLP describe a mapping of the input variables $x \in \mathbb{R}^p$ onto the output variables $y \in \mathbb{R}^q$. We will restrict ourselves in this section to the case where the network has only one hidden layer and the output variable is univariate ($q = 1$). Then $y \in \mathbb{R}$ as a function of x has the form

$$y = v_0 + \sum_{h=1}^{H} v_h \psi \left(w_{0h} + \sum_{j=1}^{p} w_{jh} x_j \right) \stackrel{\text{def}}{=} \nu_H(x; \vartheta) \qquad (18.1)$$

where H is the number of neurons in the hidden layer and ψ is the given transformation function. The parameter vector

$$\vartheta = (w_{01}, \ldots, w_{p1}, w_{02}, \ldots, w_{pH}, v_0, \ldots, v_H)^\top \in \mathbb{R}^{(p+1)H+H+1}$$

contains all the weights of the network. This network with one hidden layer already has a universal approximation property: every measurable function $m : \mathbb{R}^p \to \mathbb{R}$ can be approximated as accurately as one wishes by the function $\nu_H(x, \vartheta)$ when ψ is a monotone increasing function with a bounded range. More precisely, the following result holds, Hornik, Stinchcombe and White (1989):

Theorem 18.1
Let $\psi : \mathbb{R} \to [0,1]$ be monotone increasing with $\lim_{u \to -\infty} \psi(u) = 0$, $\lim_{u \to \infty} \psi(u) = 1$, and let $J = \{\nu_H(x; \vartheta); H \geq 1, \vartheta \in \mathbb{R}^{(p+1)H+H+1}\}$ be the set which is mapped by a MLP function with a hidden layer from $\mathbb{R}^p$ to $\mathbb{R}$.

a) For every Borel measurable function $f : \mathbb{R}^p \to \mathbb{R}$ there exists a series $\nu_n \in J$, $n \geq 1$, with $\mu(x; |f(x) - \nu_n(x)| > \varepsilon) \longrightarrow 0$ for $n \to \infty$, $\varepsilon > 0$, where μ is an arbitrary probability measure of the Borel-σ-Algebra from $\mathbb{R}^p$.

b) For every increasing function $f : \mathbb{R}^p \to \mathbb{R}$ there exists a series $\nu_n \in J$, $n \geq 1$, with $\sup_{x \in C} |f(x) - \nu_n(x)| \longrightarrow 0$ for $n \to \infty$, where C is an arbitrary compact subset of $\mathbb{R}^p$.

The range of ψ can be set to any bounded interval, not only $[0,1]$, without changing the validity of the approximation properties.

The weight vector ϑ is not uniquely determined by the network function ν_H. If, for example, the transformation function is asymmetric around 0, i.e.,

$\psi(-u) = -\psi(u)$, then $\nu_H(x; \vartheta)$ does not change when
a) the neurons of the hidden layer are interchanged, which corresponds to a substitution of the coordinates of ϑ, or when
b) all input weights $w_{0h}, \ldots, w_{ph}$ and the output weight v_h of the neural are multiplied by -1.

In order to avoid this ambiguity we will restrict the parameter set to a fundamental set in the sense of Rüeger and Ossen (1997), which for every network function $\nu_H(x; \vartheta)$ contains exactly one corresponding parameter vector ϑ. In the case of asymmetric transformation functions we restrict ourselves, for example, to weight vectors with $v_1 \geq v_2 \geq \ldots \geq v_H \geq 0$. In order to simplify the following considerations we also assume that ϑ is contained in a sufficiently large compact subset $\Theta_H \subset \mathbb{R}^{(p+1)H+H+1}$ of a fundamental range.

Due to their universal approximation properties neural networks are a suitable tool in constructing non-parametric estimators for regression functions. For this we consider the following heteroscedastic regression model:

$$Z_t = f(X_t) + \varepsilon_t , \quad t = 1, \ldots, n,$$

where $X_1, \ldots, X_n$ are independent, identically distributed d-variate random variables with a density of $p(x), x \in \mathbb{R}^d$. The residuals $\varepsilon_1, \ldots, \varepsilon_n$ are independent, real valued random variables with

$$\mathsf{E}(\varepsilon_t | X_t = x) = 0, \quad \mathsf{E}(\varepsilon_t^2 | X_t = x) = s_\varepsilon^2(x) < \infty.$$

We assume that the conditional mean $f(x)$ and the conditional variance $s_\varepsilon^2(x)$ of Z_t are, given $X_t = x$, continuous functions bounded to $\mathbb{R}^d$. In order to estimate the regression function f, we fit a neural network with a hidden layer and a sufficiently large number, H, of neurons to the input variables $X_1, \ldots, X_n$ and the values $Z_1, \ldots, Z_n$, i.e., for given H we determine the non-linear least squares estimator $\hat{\vartheta}_n = \mathrm{argmin}_{\vartheta \in \Theta_n} D_n(\vartheta)$ with

$$\hat{D}_n(\vartheta) = \frac{1}{n} \sum_{t=1}^{n} \{Z_t - \nu_H(X_t; \vartheta)\}^2 .$$

Under appropriate conditions $\hat{\vartheta}_n$ converges in probability for $n \to \infty$ and a constant H to the parameter vector $\vartheta_0 \in \Theta_H$, which corresponds to the best approximation of $f(x)$ by a function of type $\nu_H(x; \vartheta), \vartheta \in \Theta_H$:

$$\vartheta_0 = \mathrm{argmin}_{\vartheta \in \Theta_H} D(\vartheta) \quad \text{with} \quad D(\vartheta) = \mathsf{E}\{f(X_t) - \nu_H(X_t; \vartheta)\}^2.$$

Under somewhat stronger assumptions the asymptotic normality of $\hat{\vartheta}_n$ and thus of the estimator $\hat{f}_H(x) = \nu_H(x; \hat{\vartheta}_n)$ also follows for the regression function $f(x)$.

The estimation error $\hat{\vartheta}_n - \vartheta_0$ can be divided into two asymptotically independent subcomponents: $\hat{\vartheta}_n - \vartheta_0 = (\hat{\vartheta}_n - \vartheta_n) + (\vartheta_n - \vartheta_0)$, where the value

$$\vartheta_n = \operatorname*{argmin}_{\vartheta \in \Theta_H} \frac{1}{n} \sum_{t=1}^{n} \{f(X_t) - \nu_H(X_t; \vartheta)\}^2$$

minimizes the sample version of $D(\vartheta)$, Franke and Neumann (2000):

Theorem 18.2
Let ψ be bounded and twice differentiable with a bounded derivative. Suppose that $D(\vartheta)$ has a unique global minimum ϑ_0 in the interior of Θ_H, and the Hesse matrix $\nabla^2 D(\vartheta_0)$ of D at ϑ_0 is positive definite. In addition to the above mentioned conditions for the regression model it holds that

$$\begin{aligned} 0 < \delta \leq s_\varepsilon^2(x) &\leq \Delta < \infty \quad \text{for all } x, \\ \mathsf{E}(|\varepsilon_t|^\gamma | X_t = x) &\leq C_\gamma < \infty \quad \text{for all } x, \gamma \geq 1 \end{aligned}$$

with suitable constants $\delta, \Delta, C_n, \gamma \geq 1$. Then it holds for $n \to \infty$:

$$\sqrt{n} \begin{pmatrix} \hat{\vartheta}_n - \vartheta_n \\ \vartheta_n - \vartheta_0 \end{pmatrix} \xrightarrow{\mathcal{L}} N\left(0, \begin{pmatrix} \Sigma_1 & 0 \\ 0 & \Sigma_2 \end{pmatrix}\right)$$

with covariance matrices

$$\begin{aligned} \Sigma_i &= \{\nabla^2 D(\vartheta_0)\}^{-1} B_i(\vartheta_0) \{\nabla^2 D(\vartheta_0)\}^{-1}, i = 1, 2, \\ B_1(\vartheta) &= 4 \int s_\varepsilon^2(x) \, \nabla\nu_H(x; \vartheta) \nabla\nu_H(x; \vartheta)^\top \, p(x) dx \\ B_2(\vartheta) &= 4 \int \{f(x) - \nu_H(x; \vartheta)\}^2 \nabla\nu_H(x; \vartheta) \nabla\nu_H(x; \vartheta)^\top p(x) dx \end{aligned}$$

where $\nabla\nu_H$ represents the gradient of the network function with respect to the parameter ϑ.

From the theorem it immediately follows that $\sqrt{n}(\hat{\vartheta}_n - \vartheta_0)$ is asymptotically $N(0, \Sigma_1 + \Sigma_2)$ distributed. Σ_1 here stands for the variability of the estimator $\hat{\vartheta}_n$ caused by the observational error ε_t. Σ_2 represents the proportion of asymptotic variability that is caused by the mis-specification of the regression function, i.e., from the fact that $f(x)$ is of the form $\nu_H(x; \vartheta)$ for a given H and no ϑ. In the case that it is correctly specified, where $f(x) = \nu_H(x; \vartheta_0)$, this covariance component disappears, since $B_2(\vartheta_0) = 0$ and $\Sigma_2 = 0$.

Σ_1, Σ_2 can be estimated as usual with the sample covariance matrices. In order to construct tests and confidence intervals for $f(x)$ a couple of alternatives to the asymptotic distribution are available: Bootstrap, or in the case of heteroscedasticity, the Wild Bootstrap method, Franke and Neumann (2000).

Theorem 18.2 is based on the theoretical value of the least squares estimator $\hat{\vartheta}_n$, which in practice must be numerically determined. Let $\tilde{\vartheta}_n$ be such a numerical approximation of $\hat{\vartheta}_n$. The quality of the resulting estimator $\tilde{\vartheta}_n$ can depend on the numerical method used. White (1989b) showed in particular that the back propagation algorithm leads under certain assumptions to an asymptotically inefficient estimator $\tilde{\vartheta}_n$, i.e., the asymptotic covariance matrix of $\sqrt{n}(\tilde{\vartheta}_n - \vartheta_0)$ is larger than that of $\sqrt{n}(\hat{\vartheta}_n - \vartheta_0)$ in the sense that the difference of the two matrices is positive definite. Nevertheless White also showed that by joining a single global minimization step, the estimator calculated from the back propagation can be modified so that for $n \to \infty$ it is as efficient as the theoretical least squares estimator $\hat{\vartheta}_n$.

Until now we have held the number of neurons H in the hidden layer of the network and thus the dimension of the parameter vector ϑ constant. The estimator based on the network, $\hat{f}_H(x) = \nu_H(x; \hat{\vartheta}_n)$ converges to $\nu_H(x; \vartheta_0)$, so that in general the bias $\mathsf{E}\{\hat{f}_H(x)\} - m(x)$ for $n \to \infty$ does not disappear, but rather converges to $\nu_H(x; \vartheta_0) - f(x)$. With standard arguments it directly follows from Theorem 18.2 that:

Corollary 18.1   *Under the assumptions from Theorem 18.2 it holds for $n \to \infty$ that*

$$\sqrt{n}\left\{\nu_H(x; \hat{\vartheta}_n) - \nu_H(x; \vartheta_0)\right\} \xrightarrow{\mathcal{L}} N(0, \sigma_\infty^2)$$

with $\sigma_\infty^2 = \nabla \nu_H(x; \vartheta_0)^\top (\Sigma_1 + \Sigma_2) \nabla \nu_H(x; \vartheta_0)$.

In order to obtain a consistent estimator for $f(x)$, the number of neurons H, which by the non-parametric estimator $\hat{f}_H(x)$ play the role of a smoothing parameter, must increase with n. Due to the universal approximation properties of the neural network $\nu_H(x; \vartheta_0)$ thus converges to $f(x)$, so that the bias disappears asymptotically. Since with an increasing H the dimension of the parameter vector ϑ increases, H should not approach ∞ too quickly, in order to ensure that the variance of $\hat{f}_H(x)$ continues to converge to 0. In choosing H in practice one uses a typical dilemma for non-parametric statistics, the bias variance dilemma: a small H results in a smooth estimation function $\hat{f}_H$ with smaller variance and larger bias, whereas a large H leads to a smaller bias but a larger variability of a then less smoothing estimator $\hat{f}_H$.

White (1990) showed in a corresponding framework that the regression estimator $\hat{f}_H(x)$ based on the neural network converges in probability to $f(x)$ and thus is consistent when $n \to \infty$, $H \to \infty$ at a slower rate.

From this it follows that neural networks with a free choice of H neurons in the hidden layer provides useful non-parametric function estimators in regression, and as we will discuss in the next section, in time series analysis. They have the advantage that the approximating function $\nu_H(x; \vartheta)$ of the form (18.1) is a combination of the neurons, which are composed of only a given non-linear transformation of an affine-linear combination of the variables $x = (x_1, \ldots, x_d)^\top$. This makes the numerical calculation of the least squares estimator for ϑ possible even when the dimension d of the input variables and the number H of neurons are large and thus the dimension $(d+1)H + H + 1$ of the parameter vector is very large. In contrast to the local smoothing technique introduced in Chapter 13, the neural networks can also be applied as estimators of functions in large dimensional spaces. One reason for this is the non-locality of the function estimator $\hat{f}_H(x)$. This estimator does not dependent only on the observations (X_t, Z_t) with a small norm $\|X_t - x\|$ and thus in practice it is not as strongly afflicted by the imprecation of dimensionality, i.e., even for large n there is a smaller local density of the observation X_t in large dimensional spaces.

Theoretically it is sufficient to consider neural networks of type MLP with one hidden layer. In practice, however, one can sometimes achieve a comparably good fit to the data with a relatively more parsimonious parameterization by creating multiple hidden layers. A network function with two hidden layers made up of H and G neurons respectively has, for example, the following form

$$\nu(x; \vartheta) = v_0 + \sum_{g=1}^{G} v_g \psi \left(w'_{0g} + \sum_{h=1}^{H} w'_{hg} \psi(w_{0h} + \sum_{j=1}^{d} w_{jh} \, x_j) \right),$$

where ϑ represents the vector of all the weights v_g, w'_{hg}, w_{jh}. Such a function with small H, G can produce a more parsimonious parameterized approximation of the regression function $f(x)$ than a network function with only one hidden layer made up of a large number of neurons. In a case study on the development of trading strategies for currency portfolios Franke and Klein (1999) discovered, that with two hidden layers a significantly better result can be achieved than with only one layer.

In addition the number of parameters to be estimated can be further reduced when several connections in the neural network are cut, i.e., when
the corresponding weights are set to zero from the very beginning. The large
flexibility that the neural network offers when approximating regression functions creates problems when creating the model, since one has to decide on
a network structure and thus ask:

1. How many hidden layers does the network have?

2. How many neurons does each hidden layer have?

3. Which nodes (inputs, hidden neurons, outputs) of the network should
   be connect, i.e., which weights should be set to zero from the very
   beginning?

Through this process one is looking for a network which makes it possible to
have a network function $\nu(x; \vartheta)$ that is parsimoniously parameterized and at
the same time for a suitable ϑ that is a sufficiently good approximation of
the regression function $f(x)$.

Similar to the classical linear regression analysis there are a comprehensive
number of instruments available for specifying a network structure consistent
with the data. For simplicity we will concentrate on the feed forward network
with only one hidden layer made up of H neurons.

a) *Repeated Significance Tests:* As with the stepwise construction of a linear
regression model we start with a simple network assuming that one additional neuron with the number H and v_H output weights has been added.
Whether in doing this the quality of the fit of the network has significantly
improved is determined by testing the hypothesis $H_0 : v_H = 0$ against the
alternative $H_1 : v_H \neq 0$. Since under H_0 the input weights $w_{0H}, ..., w_{pH}$ of
the neurons in question are not identifiable, i.e., they have no influence on
the value of the network function ν_H, this is no standard testing problem.
White (1989a), Teräsvirta, Lin and Granger (1993) have developed Lagrange
multiplier tests that are suitable for testing the significance of an additional
neuron. Going the other direction it is also possible to start with a complex
network with large H assumed neurons successively removing them until the
related test rejects the hypothesis $H_0 : v_H = 0$. To reduce the number of
parameters it makes sense to cut individual input connections, i.e., to set the
corresponding weight to zero. For the test of the hypothesis $H_0 : w_{jh} = 0$
against the alternative $H_1 : w_{jh} \neq 0$ classical Wald Tests can be applied due
to the asymptotical results such as 18.2 (see for example Anders (1997) for
applications in financial statistics).

b) *Cross Validation and Validation:* The resulting cross validation is usually eliminated due to the extreme amount of calculations to determine the order of the model, i.e., first of all the number H of neurons in the hidden layer. In order to calculate the leave-one-out estimator for the model parameters one must fit the neural network to the corresponding sample that has been reduced by one observation a total of n times, and this must be done for every network structure under consideration. A related and more known procedure from the application of neural networks in the regression and time series analysis is to take a portion of the data away from the sample in order to measure the quality of the model based on this so called validation set. In addition to the data (X_t, Z_t), $t = 1, \dots, n$, used to calculate the least squares estimator $\hat{\vartheta}_n$ a second independent subsample (X_t, Z_t), $t = n+1, \dots, n+M$, is available. By minimizing measurements of fit, such as,

$$V(H) = \frac{1}{M} \sum_{t=n+1}^{n+M} \left\{ Z_t - \nu_H(X_t; \hat{\vartheta}_n) \right\}^2$$

the order of the model H and the quality of the incomplete network structure can be determined, in which individual input weights have been set to zero.

c) *Network Information Criteria:* To compare the network structures some well known applications for determining order, such as the Akaike Information Criterion (AIC), can be used. The application from Murata, Yoskizawa and Amari (1994) called the *Network Information Criterion* (NIC) is specialized for the case of neural networks. Here it is implicitly assumed that the residuals ε_t are normally distributed with a common variance σ_ε^2.

18.4   Forecasts of Financial Time Series with Neural Networks

To forecast the future development of financial time series an autoregressive model is particularly suitable. The value of the time series at date $t + 1$ is a function of infinite many observations from the past in addition to an innovation independent of the past:

$$Z_{t+1} = f(Z_t, \dots, Z_{t-p+1}) + \varepsilon_{t+1}, \quad -\infty < t < \infty, \tag{18.2}$$

where ε_t, $-\infty < t < \infty$, is independently and identically distributed with $\mathsf{E}(\varepsilon_t) = 0$, $Var(\varepsilon_t) = \sigma_\varepsilon^2 < \infty$. The analogy of this formula for this nonlinear autoregressive model of order p (NLAR(p)) to the regression model considered in a previous section is obvious, where the p-variate random vector $(Z_t, \ldots, Z_{t-p+1})^\top$ takes the place of the d-variate independent variable X_t. The autoregression function $f : \mathbb{R}^p \to \mathbb{R}$ in this model immediately gives the best forecast for Z_{t+1} given the value of the time series up to date t:

$$\hat{Z}_{t+1|t}^0 = f(Z_t, \ldots, Z_{t-p+1}).$$

Since f is in general not known, it seems obvious in view of the last section to approximate the autoregression function with a neural network when observations of the times series $Z_1, \ldots, Z_{n+1}$ are available. For training the network, i.e., for estimating the network weights, the vector $(Z_t, \ldots, Z_{t-p+1})^\top$ is used as input values and as output values Z_{t+1} for $t = p, \ldots, n$, is used. We will restrict ourselves for simplicity to the MLP with one hidden layer. $\hat{\vartheta}_n$ again represents the least squares estimator for the weight vector:

$$\hat{\vartheta}_n = \operatorname*{argmin}_{\vartheta \in \Theta_H} \frac{1}{n-p+1} \sum_{t=p}^{n} \{Z_{t+1} - \nu_H(Z_t, \ldots, Z_{t-p+1}; \vartheta)\}^2$$

where ν_H is defined as in the previous section. We thus obtain a non-parametric forecast based on a neural network for Z_{t+1} :

$$\hat{Z}_{t+1|t} = \nu_H(Z_t, \ldots, Z_{t-p+1}; \hat{\vartheta}_n).$$

The result of this procedure is illustrated in Figure 18.9: it shows the forecasting of the exchange rate time series JPY/USD using neural networks considering 3 periods of time dependency.

The asymptotic normality of the parameters and of the function estimators and the consistency of $\nu_H(\cdot; \hat{\vartheta}_n)$ as an estimator of f for an increasing H remain robust even in the case where the stochastic process $\{Z_t, -\infty < t < \infty\}$ is α-mixing with exponentially decreasing mixing coefficients, White (1989b) and White (1990). Franke, Kreiss, Mammen and Neumann (2003) have formulated conditions for the case where $p = 1$ for the autoregression function f and for the distribution of the innovations ε_t, which guarantee for the NLAR(1) process the strongest β-mix properties with exponentially decreasing coefficients. Next to technical details it is essential that

$$\lim_{|x| \to \infty} |f(x)/x| < 1$$

is fulfilled, because it is sufficient for the innovation distribution that the density does not vanish anywhere. The last condition can be considerably weakened.

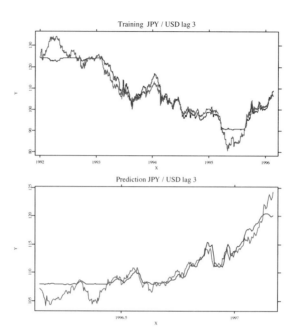

Figure 18.9: Approximation of exchange rate JPY/USD (red) through RBF
          neural network (blue): Training set(above) and forecasts(below)
          Q SFEnnjpyusd.xpl

The conditions on the autoregression function is comparatively weak and
obvious when one considers the stationarity conditions $|\alpha| < 1$ for linear
AR(1) processes $Z_{t+1} = \alpha Z_t + \varepsilon_{t+1}$, where $f(x) = \alpha x$. Accordingly also
for NLAR(p) process of large order ($p > 1$) it is sufficient to use weaker
conditions on f, which above all guarantees stationarity in order to make the
neural network a useful tool as a non-parametric estimator of f.

For the practical forecast one not only wants to use the last values in the
time series, but also economic data available at time t such as exchange
rates, index values, oil prices or the non-linear transformation of prices. To
do this the non-linear autoregressive process with exogenous components of
order p (NLARX(p)) process is suitable:

$$Z_{t+1} = f(Z_t, \ldots, Z_{t-p+1}, X_t) + \varepsilon_t, \quad -\infty < t < \infty, \qquad (18.3)$$

where the innovations ε_t, $-\infty < t < \infty$, are again independently and identically distributed with $\mathsf{E}(\varepsilon_t) = 0$, $Var(\varepsilon_t) = \sigma_\varepsilon^2 < \infty$, and X_t is the value of a d-variate stochastic process that contains all external information available at date t, which is used in the forecast.

The practical application of the forecast on financial time series with neural networks is illustrated with a pilot study that was done in cooperation with the Commerzbank AG, Franke (1999). The goal was to develop a trading strategy for a portfolio made up of 28 of the most important stocks from the Dutch CBS-Index. We will restrict ourselves here to the buy-and-hold strategy with a time horizon of a quarter of a year (60 trading days), i.e., the portfolio is created at the beginning of a quarter and then held for three months with no alterations. At the end of the three months the value of the portfolio should be as large as possible.

As a basis for the trading strategy a three month forecast of the stocks is used. S_t represents the price of one of the 28 stocks. To model the time series S_t we use a NLARX process of the form (18.3); the system function f is approximated with a network function $\nu_H(S_t, A_t, X_t; \vartheta)$. Here A_t is a vector made up of constant non-linear transformations of $S_t, ..., S_{t-p+1}$ that were taken from the technical market analysis, for example, a moving average, momentum or Bollinger-intervals, Müller and Nietzer (1993), Welcker (1994). The random vector X_t represents the chosen market data such as index prices, exchange rates, international interest rates, etc. As is expected with a forecast horizon of 60 units of time into the future, the actual forecasts of the stock prices in 60 days,

$$\hat{S}_{t+60|t} = \nu_H(S_t, A_t, X_t; \hat{\vartheta}_n),$$

is not very reliable. For making the decision whether a stock should be included in the portfolio or not, the general trend of the price developments are most important instead of the actual price of the stock at the end of the holding period. To realize this aspect in formulating the portfolio, it should be considered whether based on the network based forecast, $\hat{S}_{t+60|t}$, the price is expected to increase considerably (more than 5 %), decrease considerably (more than 5 %) or whether it is essentially expected to stay at the same level. The network based portfolio is composed of those stocks (with relative proportions that are taken from the stock's corresponding weight in the CBS Index) for which $(\hat{S}_{t+60|t} - S_t)/S_t > 0.05$. Here the *same* network function $\nu_H(S_t, A_t, X_t; \vartheta)$ is used for all 28 stocks taken into consideration whose price dependent arguments S_t actually take on the stock specific values.

In choosing a suitable network and in estimating the network weight vector ϑ the data from 1993 to 1995 is used. In choosing the network structure a statistical model selection technique and the experience of the experts was used. The resulting network is a multiple layered perceptron with one hidden layer made up of $H = 3$ neurons. The input vector (S_t, A_t, X_t) has the dimension 25, so that a parameter vector $\vartheta \in \mathbb{R}^{82}$ needed to be estimated.

To check the quality of the network based trading strategy, it is applied to the data from 1996. At the beginning of every quarter a portfolio made up of 28 stocks is created based on the network based forecast. At the end of the quarter the percentage increase in value is considered. As a comparison the increase in value of a portfolio replicating the CBS Index exactly is considered. Since in the years considered the market was of the most part in an increasing phase, it is known from experience that it is hard to beat an index. As Table 18.1 shows, the network portfolio achieved a higher percentage increase in value in every quarter than the index portfolio, that is in the quarters, such as the first and fourth, where the index has substantially increased, as well as in the quarters, such as the second, where the index has minimally decreased. Nevertheless the results need to be interpreted with a bit of caution. Even in the training phase (1993-1995) the CBS Index tended to increase, so that the network was able to specialize in a trend forecast in a generally increasing market. Presumably one would need to use a different network as a basis for the trading strategy, when the market fluctuates within a long-term lateral motion or when the index dramatically decreases.

	Quarterly returns			
	I.	II.	III.	IV.
Network portfolio	0.147	0.024	0.062	0.130
Index portfolio	0.109	-0.004	0.058	0.115

Table 18.1: Quarterly returns of a network portfolio and the index portfolio in 1996.

18.5   Quantifying Risk with Neural Networks

In the previous chapters the most popular measurements of risk, volatility and Value-at-Risk, have been introduced. Both are most often defined as conditional standard deviations or as conditional quantiles respectively, based on a given historical information set. As with other non-parametric methods the neural network can also be used to estimate these measurements of risk. The advantage of the neural network based volatility and VaR estimators lies in the fact that the information used for estimating the risk can be represented by a large dimensional data vector without hurting the practicality of the method. It is possible, for example, to estimate the conditional 5% quantile of the return process of a stock from the DAX given the individual returns of all of the DAX stocks and additional macroeconomic data such as interest rates, exchange rates, etc. In the following section we briefly outline the necessary procedure.

As in (13.1) we assume a model of the form

$$Z_{t+1} = f(Z_t, \ldots, Z_{t-p+1}, X_t) + s(Z_t, \ldots, Z_{t-p+1}, X_t)\,\xi_{t+1} \qquad (18.4)$$

to estimate the volatility, where ξ_t are independent, identically distributed random variables with $\mathsf{E}(\xi_t) = 0$, $\mathsf{E}(\xi_t^2) = 1$. $X_t \in \mathbb{R}^d$ represents as in the previous section the exogenous information available at date t which we will use in estimating the risk of the time series Z_t. The time series given by (18.4) is a non-linear AR(p) ARCH(p) process with exogenous components.

To simplify we use $Z_t(p) = (Z_t, \ldots, Z_{t-p+1})^\top \in \mathbb{R}^p$. Then it holds for $z \in \mathbb{R}^p$, $x \in \mathbb{R}^d$ that

$$
\begin{aligned}
\mathsf{E}[Z_{t+1}|Z_t(p) = z,\ X_t = x] &= f(z,x) \\
Var[Z_{t+1}|Z_t(p) = z, X_t = x] &= s^2(z,x) \\
&= \mathsf{E}[Z_{t+1}^2|Z_t(p) = z, X_t = x] - f^2(z,x).
\end{aligned}
$$

The conditional expectation function $f(z,x)$ is approximated as in the previous section by a neural network function $\nu_H(z,x;\vartheta)$ of the form (18.1). With the non-linear least squares estimator $\hat{\vartheta}_n$ we obtain for ϑ an estimator for f:

$$\hat{f}_H(z,x) = \nu_H(z,x;\hat{\vartheta}_n).$$

Analogously we could estimate the conditional mean

$$\mathsf{E}[Z_{t+1}^2|Z_t(p) = z,\ X_t = x] = g(z,x)$$

by approximating the function with a neural network with output function $\nu_G(z,x;\delta)$ and estimate its parameter δ with a least squares estimator $\hat{\delta}$ within a sufficiently large compact subset $\Delta_G \subset \mathbb{R}^{(p+d+1)G+G+1}$, such as Θ_H, chosen from a fundamental range:

$$\hat{\delta}_n = \underset{\delta \in \Delta_G}{\operatorname{argmin}} \frac{1}{n-p+1} \sum_{t=p}^{n} \left\{ Z_{t+1}^2 - \nu_G(Z_t(p), X_t; \delta) \right\}^2,$$

$$\hat{g}_G(z,x) = \nu_G(z,x;\hat{\delta}_n).$$

As an estimator for the conditional volatility we immediately obtain:

$$\hat{s}^2_{H,G}(z,x) = \hat{g}_G(z,x) - \hat{f}^2_H(z,x).$$

This estimator is in general guaranteed to be positive only for $G = H$. In order to avoid this restriction one can follow the procedure used by Fan and Yao (1998), who have studied a similar problem for the kernel estimator of the conditional variance in a heteroscedastic regression model. Using this application the residuals

$$\varepsilon_{t+1} = Z_{t+1} - f(Z_t(p), X_t) = s(Z_t(p), X_t)\,\xi_{t+1}$$

are approximated by the sample residuals

$$\hat{\varepsilon}_{t+1} = Z_{t+1} - \hat{f}_H(Z_t(p), X_t),\ t = p, \dots, n,$$

Since the ξ_{t+1} has mean 0 and variance 1,

$$\mathsf{E}[\varepsilon^2_{t+1}|Z_t(p) = z,\ X_t = x] = s^2(z,x).$$

We could approximate this function directly with a neural network with G neurons and the output function $\nu_G(z,x;\delta)$, whose parameter are estimated by

$$\hat{\delta}_n = \operatorname*{argmin}_{\delta \in \Delta_G} \frac{1}{n-p+1} \sum_{t=p}^{n} \left\{\hat{\varepsilon}^2_{t+1} - \nu_G(Z_t(p), X_t;\delta)\right\}^2.$$

The resulting estimators for the conditional volatility, which through the $\hat{\varepsilon}_t$ is also dependent on H, is then

$$\hat{s}_{H,G}(z,x) = \nu_G(z,x;\hat{\delta}_n).$$

Figure 18.10 shows the conditional volatilities estimated from the log returns of the exchange rate time series BP/USD together with some financial indicators using the procedure described above (3 periods are considered as time dependency and radial basis functions networks are used).

It is for arbitrary G, H automatically non-negative. Since the number of neurons essentially determines the smoothness of the network function, it can make sense when approximating f and s^2 to choose different networks with $H \neq G$ neurons when it is believed that the smoothness of both functions are quite different from each other.

When the distribution of the innovations ξ_t is additionally specified in the model (18.4), we immediately obtain together with the estimators of f and s^2 an estimator of the conditional Value-at-Risk. If the distribution of ξ_t

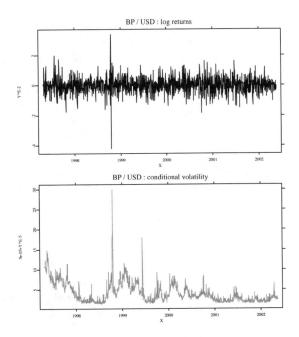

Figure 18.10: Log-returns of exchange rate BP/USD and the estimated conditional variances by RBF neutral network. ⊠ SFEnnarch.xpl

is, for example, N(0, 1), then the conditional distribution of Z_{t+1} given the information $Z_t(p)$ and X_t at date t is also a normal distribution with mean $f(Z_t(p), X_t)$ and variance $s^2(Z_t(p), X_t)$. If q_α° is the α quantile of the standard normal distribution, then the VaR process $\{Z_t\}$, i.e., the conditional α quantile of Z_{t+1} given $Z_t(p), X_t$ is:

$$VaR_{t+1} = f(Z_t(p), X_t) + s(Z_t(p), X_t)q_\alpha^\circ.$$

An estimator for this conditional Value-at-Risk based on a neural network can be obtained by replacing f and s with the appropriate estimator:

$$\widehat{VaR}_{t+1} = \hat{f}_H(Z_t(p), X_t) + \hat{s}_{H,G}^2(Z_t(p), X_t)q_\alpha^\circ. \tag{18.5}$$

In doing this we can replace the standard normal distribution with another distribution, for example, with a standardized t-distribution with mean 0 and variance 1. q_α° is then the corresponding α quantile of the innovation distribution, i.e., the distribution of ξ_t.

The estimator (18.5) for the Value-at-Risk assumes that Z_t is a non-linear ARX-ARCHX process of the form (18.4). Above all, however, it has the disadvantage of depending on the critical assumption of a specific distribution of ξ_t. Above all the above mentioned procedure, in assuming a stochastic volatility model from the standard normal distribution, has been recently criticized in financial statistics due to certain empirical findings. The thickness of the tails of a distribution of a financial time series appears at times to be so pronounced that in order to adequately model it even the distribution of the innovations must be assumed to be leptokurtic. Due to the simplicity of the representation a t-distribution with only a few degrees of freedom is often considered. In order to avoid the arbitrariness in the choice of the distribution of the innovations, it is possible to estimate the conditional quantile directly without relying on a model of the form (18.4). This application goes back to the regression quantile from Koenker and Bassett and has been applied by Abberger (1997) to time series in connection with kernel estimation. We assume that Z_t is a stationary time series. As in Chapter 17 P_{t+1} represents the forecast distribution, i.e., the conditional distribution of Z_{t+1} given $Z_t(p), X_t$. With F_{t+1} we depict the corresponding conditional distribution function

$$F_{t+1}(y|z,x) = \mathrm{P}(Z_{t+1} \leq y|Z_t(p) = z, X_t = x)$$

for $y \in \mathbb{R}$, $z \in \mathbb{R}^p, x \in \mathbb{R}^d$. $q_\alpha(z,x)$ is the conditional α quantile, i.e., the solution to the equation $F_{t+1}(q_\alpha(z,x)|z,x) = \alpha$. The conditional quantile function $q_\alpha(z,x)$ solves the minimization problem

$$\mathsf{E}\{\alpha(Z_{t+1} - q)^+ + (1 - \alpha)(Z_{t+1} - q)^-|Z_t(p) = z,\ X_t = x\} = \min_{q \in \mathbb{R}}! \quad (18.6)$$

where $y^+ = y - \mathbf{1}(y \geq 0)$ and $y^- = |y| \cdot \mathbf{1}(y \leq 0)$ represent the positive and negative parts of $y \in \mathbb{R}$. In order to estimate the quantile function directly with a neural network with H neurons, we approximate $q_\alpha(z,x)$ with a network function $\nu_H(z,x;\gamma)$ of the form (18.1), whose weight parameter γ lies in a fundamental range $\Gamma_H \subset \mathbb{R}^{(p+d+1)H+H+1}$. γ is estimated, however, not with the least squares method, but with the minimization of the corresponding sample values from (18.6):

$$\hat{\gamma}_n = \operatorname*{argmin}_{\gamma \in \Gamma_H} \frac{1}{n - p + 1} \sum_{t=p}^{n} \{\alpha[Z_{t+1} - \nu_H(Z_t(q), X_t)]^+$$

$$+(1 - \alpha)[Z_{t+1} - \nu_H(Z_t(q), X_t)]^-\}.$$

As an estimator for the quantile function we obtain

$$\hat{q}_{H\alpha}(z,x) = \nu_H(z,x;\hat{\gamma}_n)$$

and with this the estimator for the conditional Value-at-Risk given $Z_t, \ldots,$ Z_{t-p+1}, X_t

$$\widehat{VaR}_{t+1} = \hat{q}_{H\alpha}(Z_t, \ldots, Z_{t-p+1}, X_t).$$

White has shown that under suitable assumptions the function estimators $\hat{q}_{H\alpha}(z, x)$ converge in probability to $q(z, x)$ when the sample observations $n \to \infty$ and when at the same time the number of neurons $H \to \infty$ at a suitable rate.

18.6   Recommended Literature

One for mathematicians, statisticians and economists well accessible introduction to the area of the neural network is, e.g., Refenes (1995a). Haykin (1999) offers a comprehensive and effective overview about different forms and applications of neural network. Anders (1997) introduces neural networks from econometrical and statistical view and discusses applications from the finance mathematical areas such as option pricing and insolvency prediction. Ripley (1996) discusses in detail the application of neural network to classification problems and puts them in respect with the classical discriminant analysis. Numerous practical applications of neural network in the finance area are introduced in Rehkugler and Zimmermann (1994), Refenes (1995b), Bol and Vollmer (1996) and Franke (2000). The application described in the previous section, calculating the Value at Risk by adaptation of a non-linear ARCHX process based on DAX stocks is described in Franke and Diagne (2002).

19 Volatility Risk of Option Portfolios

In this chapter we analyze the principal factors in the dynamic structure of implied volatility *at the money* (ATM). The data used are daily *Volatility-DAX* (VDAX) values. By using principal component analysis we consider a method of modelling the risk of option portfolios on the basis of "Maximum Loss".

There is a close connection between the value of an option and the volatility process of the financial underlying. Assuming that the price process follows a geometric Brownian motion we have derived the Black-Scholes formula (BS) for pricing European options in Chapter 6. With this formula the option price is at a given time point a function of the volatility parameters when the following values are given: τ (time to maturity in years), K (strike price), r (risk free, long-run interest rate) and S (the spot price of the financial underlying).

Alternatively one can describe the observed market price of an option at a specific time point with the help of the BS formula using the so called "implied" volatility (see Chapter 6). In doing this one typically finds a U-shaped form for the resulting surface of the volatility over different times to maturity and strike prices. This phenomenon is also referred to as the "Volatility Smile". Figure 19.1 illustrates the typical form of a volatility surface using DAX options. Shown is the implied volatility as a function of the moneyness and the remaining time to maturity τ. Here the term *moneyness* $\frac{S}{K}$ refers to the ratio of the actual price S of the financial underlying and the strike price K of the respective option. It should be noted that options are only traded on the market on a discrete price basis and a discrete time to maturity. In determining the volatility surface, as in Chapter 13, a smoothing technique needs to be applied.

By observing the volatility surface over time, distinct changes in the location and structure become obvious. Identifying the temporal dynamics is of

Volatility Surface

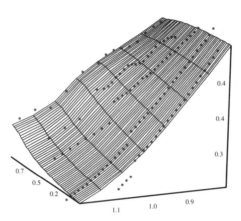

Figure 19.1: Implied volatility surface of the DAX option on July 18, 1998

Q SFEVolSurfPlot.xpl

central importance for a number of financially oriented applications. This is of particular importance for the risk management of option portfolios. To determine the volatility's dynamics, an application of principal component of analysis is quite suitable, see Skiadopoulos, Hodges and Clewlow (1998). The total temporal structure can be sufficiently represented by a small number of principal components so that the dimensions of the factor space for the purpose of risk analysis can be significantly reduced.

19.1   Description of the Data

DAX options belong to the most frequently traded derivatives of the German/Swiss derivative market "EUREX". On every trading day one can find a significant number of liquid time series with varying strike prices and maturities (K, τ) on the market, which in principle can be used to calculate implied volatilities. In view of the often limited data processing capacities, an updated calculation of numerous volatilities and partial derivatives of an extensive option portfolio is still not feasible. Even with the appropriate available information the isolated consideration of each implied volatility as a separate source of risk is problematic, since it results in an unstructured or "uneven" volatility surface. If one were to use generated volatilities in calibrating option prices, respectively risk models, this can lead to serious specification errors and significantly deteriorate the results of the corresponding trading and hedging strategies. As a result of principal component analysis a "smooth" volatility surface, in contrast to the one outlined above, can be generated with a manageable amount of information. This allows for a better calibration of the model and a more precise estimate of portfolio sensitivities.

For our study of the dynamics of implied volatility we use the volatility index (VDAX) made available by the German Stock Exchange (Deutsche Börse AG) respectively the closing prices of the corresponding VDAX subindices. These indices reflect the implied volatility of the DAX options "at the money" for times to maturity from one to 24 months. The corresponding values are determined by applying the Black-Scholes formula (6.23) using prices observed on the market:

$$C(S, \tau) = e^{(b-r)\tau} S \Phi(y + \sigma\sqrt{\tau}) - e^{-r\tau} K \Phi(y),$$

where Φ is the distribution function of the standard normal distribution and

$$y = \frac{\ln \frac{S}{K} + (b - \frac{1}{2}\sigma^2)\tau}{\sigma\sqrt{\tau}},$$

The only parameter from the BS formula that cannot be immediately observed on the market is the actual volatility σ of the price process. In principle the volatility of the process can be estimated from historical financial market data, see Section 6.3.4, however, it is commonly known that the assumption of the BS model, that the financial underlying has a geometric brownian motion, is in reality only approximately fulfilled. Alternatively the BS formula is also used in order to calculate the σ value as the implied volatility for a given market price of a specific option. This does not mean that the market participant should accept the assumption of the Black-Scholes method. On the contrary they use the BS formula as a convenient possibility to quote and price options with these parameters.

Given the observed implied volatilities from varying times to maturity τ at a specific time point and from a strike price K, the expectations of the market participants with respect to the future actual volatility of the underlying financial instrument can be estimated. In doing so one must remember that the implied volatility of the BS model does not directly apply to the actual variance of the price's process. Although the implied BS volatility reflects a market expectation, the theoretical relationship between it and the actual volatility can only be determined using specific assumptions, see Schönbucher (1998), Härdle and Hafner (2000).

Implied volatility for ATM-DAX options are calculated for various lengths of maturity by the German Stock Exchange AG. A detailed description of how the VDAX and its sub-indices are calculated can be found in Redelberger (1994). Since March 18, 1996 maturities of 1, 2, 3, 6, 9, 12, 18 and 24 months have been considered in the calculation. On this date the trading of so called "Long Term Options", i.e., trading of options with maturities of over 12 months, were added to the EUREX. Using closing prices the German Stock Exchange AG calculates for every trading day a total of eight VDAX sub-indices for the maturities mentioned above. These sub-indices reflect the volatility of the respective DAX option "at the money". The time to maturity structure for DAX options that are "at the money" can be determined for every trading day using the VDAX indices. Figure 19.2 illustrates a typical development of the structure, which shows strong changes in the positioning and form of the structure over time.

The analysis done here is not only restricted to specific maturities of liquid options, which are represented by the first four VDAX sub-indices. On the contrary, we include all eight sub-indices in the analysis for the following reasons:

First of all a brisk trade of even the "most distant" option contracts (i.e., the contracts with a remaining time of more than one year) take place on numerous trading days, so that excluding the pertaining sub-indices from the analysis would result in a loss of information. VDAX sub-indices for long maturities have been calculated by the German Stock Exchange since March 18, 1996. After the date of December 19, 1997 the quality of the data available to us declined considerably. In addition to the daily often unchanged prices, the entries corresponding to the removed sub-indices were usually missing. Given this we have restricted our analysis to the time period from March 18, 1996 to December 19, 1997.

Including relatively non-liquid DAX options with long maturities appears to make sense for another reason: For our analysis we require constant option maturities, since the daily shortening of the time to maturity can lead to enormous biases in the analysis results with data that has not been corrected. This especially holds for options with very short time to maturity. Thus we

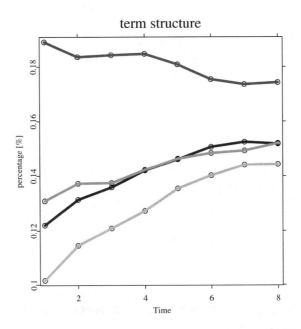

Figure 19.2: Time to maturity structure of implied DAX volatilities "at the money" 🔍 SFEVolaTermStructure.xpl

find it utterly necessary to use interpolated volatilities with corresponding constant time to maturities of the underlying option. Referring back to the calculation of the VDAX used by the German Stock Exchange AG we use the following linear interpolation:

For a fixed time to maturity of $\tau_1^* = 30, \tau_2^* = 60, \tau_3^* = 90, \tau_4^* = 180, \tau_5^* = 270, \tau_6^* = 360, \tau_7^* = 540, \tau_8^* = 720$ calendar days we calculate daily volatility indices $\hat{\sigma}_{I,t}(\tau_j^*), j = 1, ..., 8$, using the VDAX sub-indices with the next shorter respectively longer maturity $\hat{\sigma}_{I,t}(\tau_j^-)$ and $\hat{\sigma}_{I,t}(\tau_j^+)$ with

$$\hat{\sigma}_{I,t}(\tau_j^*) = \hat{\sigma}_{I,t}(\tau_j^-)\left[1 - \frac{\tau_j^* - \tau_j^-}{\tau_j^+ - \tau_j^-}\right] + \hat{\sigma}_{I,t}(\tau_j^+)\left[\frac{\tau_j^* - \tau_j^-}{\tau_j^+ - \tau_j^-}\right]. \quad (19.1)$$

This way, we obtain 8 volatility time series each with constant maturities. Every time series represents a weighted average of two consecutive VDAX

Sub 1	Sub 2	Sub 3	Sub 4	Sub 5	Sub 6	Sub 7	Sub 8
20.8	9.06	6.66	6.84	4.29	2.48	2.11	1.38
9.06	**9.86**	6.67	4.44	3.21	1.72	1.11	0.92
6.66	6.67	**6.43**	3.87	2.63	1.49	1.01	0.53
6.84	4.44	3.87	**4.23**	2.66	1.39	1.38	0.68
4.29	3.21	2.63	2.66	**2.62**	1.03	1.02	0.51
2.48	1.72	1.49	1.39	1.03	**2.19**	0.63	0.33
2.11	1.11	1.01	1.38	1.02	0.63	**1.76**	0.43
1.38	0.92	0.53	0.68	0.51	0.33	0.43	**1.52**

Table 19.1: Empirical covariance matrix $\hat{\Omega}$ of the first differences (all values have been multiplied by 10^5)   **Q** SFEVolaCov.xpl

sub-indices and is based on $n = 441$ daily observations of the implied DAX volatilities "at the money".

19.2   Principal Component Analysis of the VDAX's Dynamics

We will first check the data with the help of the "Augmented Dickey-Fuller" Tests (ADF-Test - see (10.46)) for stationarity. The null hypothesis of a unit root for the individual VDAX sub-indices $\hat{\sigma}_I(\tau_j^*)$ cannot be rejected at the 90% significance level. Obviously due to this result the first differences $x_{jt} = \Delta[\hat{\sigma}_{I,t}(\tau_j^*)] = \hat{\sigma}_{I,t+1}(\tau_j^*) - \hat{\sigma}_{I,t}(\tau_j^*), t = 1, ..., n - 1$, of the implied volatility indices will be used for further analysis. Additional ADF tests support the assumption of stationarity for the first differences.   **Q** SFEAdfKpss.xpl

Let $\bar{x}_j$ be the respective sample mean of the first differences x_{jt}. Table 19.1 contains the empirical covariance matrix $\hat{\Omega}$ used as an estimator for the 8×8 matrix Ω of the covariance $\mathrm{Cov}(x_{it}, x_{jt}), i, j = 1, ..., 8$. With help of the Jordan decomposition we obtain $\hat{\Omega} = \hat{\Gamma}\hat{\Lambda}\hat{\Gamma}^\top$. The diagonal matrix $\hat{\Lambda}$ contains the eigenvalues $\hat{\lambda}_k, k = 1, ..., 8$ of $\hat{\Omega}$, $\hat{\Gamma}$ are the eigenvectors. Time series of the principal components can be obtained with the help of $Y = X_C\hat{\Gamma}$, where X_C represents the 440×8 matrix of the centered first differences $x_{jt}^c = x_{jt} - \bar{x}_j, j = 1, ..., 8, t = 1, ..., 440,$. The 440×8 matrix $Y = (Y_1, ..., Y_8), Y_j = (y_{1j}, y_{2j}, ..., y_{440,j})^\top$ contains the principal components.

How accurately the first l principal components have already determined

Principal Component	Explaining proportion of variance	cumulative proportion
1	70.05	70.05
2	13.06	83.12
3	5.57	88.69
4	3.11	91.80
5	3.06	94.86
6	2.12	96.97
7	1.93	98.90
8	1.10	100.00

Table 19.2: Explained sample variance using principal components in percentage   **Q** SFEVolaPCA.xpl

the process of the centered first differences can be measured using the proportion of variance φ_l with respect to the total variance of the data. The proportion of explained variance corresponds to the relative proportion of the corresponding eigenvalue, i.e.,

$$\varphi_l = \frac{\sum_{k=1}^{l} \lambda_k}{\sum_{k=1}^{8} \lambda_k} = \frac{\sum_{k=1}^{l} \text{Var}(y_{tk})}{\sum_{k=1}^{8} \text{Var}(y_{tk})}, \tag{19.2}$$

where $\lambda_k, k = 1, ..., 8$ are the eigenvalues of the true covariance matrix Ω. An estimator for φ_l is

$$\hat{\varphi}_l = \frac{\sum_{k=1}^{l} \hat{\lambda}_k}{\sum_{k=1}^{8} \hat{\lambda}_k}.$$

In Table 19.2 the individual proportions of the variance $\hat{\lambda}_l / \sum_{k=1}^{8} \hat{\lambda}_k$ as well as the cumulative variance from the l decomposed proportions from the principal components, $\hat{\varphi}_l$, are displayed. It is obvious that the first principal component already describes 70% of the total variance of the underlying data. With the second principal component an additional 13% of the total variance within the observed time period can be explained. Together 83% of the variance of the analyzed first differences of our VDAX sub-indices can be explained with the help of the first and second principal components. Obviously the explaining power of the principal components significantly declines from the third principal component on.

By displaying the eigenvalues in a graph, a form with a strong curvature at the second principal component is shown. In accordance with the well

known "elbow" criterion, using the first two principal components with an
explanation power of over 80% of the total variance is considered to be sufficient in describing the data set. The remaining variance can be interpreted
for analytical purposes as the effect of an unsystematic error term. Figure
19.3 contains the factor loading of the first two principal components. Based
on the orthogonality of the components the loading factors can be estimated
using the least squares regression of the individual equations

$$x_{jt}^c = \sum_{l=1}^{2} b_{jl} y_{lt} + \varepsilon_t, \qquad (19.3)$$

Here ε_t is an independent error term.

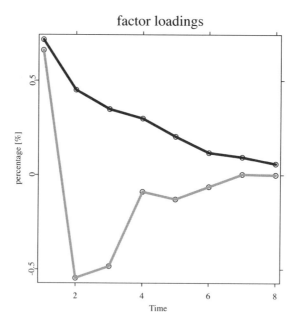

Figure 19.3: Factor loadings of the first and second principal components
Q SFEPCA.xpl

Based on the factor loadings it is clear that a shock to the first factor would
affect the implied volatility of all times to maturity considered in a similar
way, or would cause a non-parallel shift in the maturities' structure. A shock

Principal Components:	1	2	3	4	5	6	7	8
Weekly data 18.03.96-19.12.97	73.85	91.59	95.09	97.38	98.80	99.61	99.88	100
Daily data 18.03.96-19.12.97	70.05	83.12	88.69	91.80	94.86	96.97	98.90	100
Sub-period 1 18.03.96-05.02.97	83.36	91.84	94.65	96.39	97.76	98.78	99.52	100
Sub-period 2 05.02.97-19.12.97	68.22	82.21	87.99	91.35	94.64	96.93	98.86	100

Table 19.3: Explained portion of the variance (in percentage) in different sub-periods

to the second principal component, on the other hand, causes a tilt of the structure curve: while at short times to maturity it causes a positive change, the longer time to maturities are influenced negatively. The absolute size of the effect of a shock decreases in both factors with the time to maturity.

19.3   Stability Analysis of the VDAX's Dynamics

In order to sensibly apply the principal factors in measuring the risk of portfolios we have to study their stability over time. When the principal components and the factor loadings change significantly over time, a global analysis would not be suitable to illustrate the future variance of the implied volatility nor to judge the risks of the option portfolios with sufficient accuracy.

Our procedure considers two aspects: first whether the random portion in daily data is possibly significantly higher than in weekly data. A possible cause for this is the non-synchronous trading caused by a frequent realizations of the quotes in the liquid contracts with short time to maturity and sparsely available prices in the long running contracts. In order to distinguish the possible influences of this effect, we run our analysis analogously based on weekly data. By sufficient stability in the principal components the use of daily respectively weekly data should lead to similar results.

For the second aspect we divide our data into two non-overlapping periods of equal length. Each sub-period contains $m = 220$ daily observations of the process of the differences. We run for each sub-period a principal component analysis as described above and compare the respective size of the eigenvalues $\hat{\lambda}_k^i, k = 1, 2$, in both sub-periods $i = 1, 2$.

As already mentioned the effect of non-synchronous trading that appears in daily data can be eliminated by using weekly data. From Table 19.3 it emerges that the explanatory power of the first principal component is slightly higher in weekly data. This is not surprising given the expected size of the error terms proportion in daily data. Overall the explanatory proportions of the variance have similar values when using weekly data. This supports the stability of the analysis method used here w.r.t. the bias due to non-synchronous trading in daily data.

From Table 19.3 it emerges that the proportion of the variance explained by the first two principal components declines in the second sub-period. Based on this a stability test is necessary: A two sided confidence interval for the difference of the eigenvalues from both sub-periods is

$$\ln \hat{\lambda}_k^1 - 2q_\alpha \sqrt{\frac{2}{m-1}} \leq \ln \hat{\lambda}_k^2 \leq \ln \hat{\lambda}_k^1 + 2q_\alpha \sqrt{\frac{2}{m-1}}, \qquad (19.4)$$

where q_α represents the α quantile of a standard normal distribution, see Härdle and Simar (2003). From this it follows that

$$\mid \ln \hat{\lambda}_k^1 - \ln \hat{\lambda}_k^2 \mid \geq 2q_\alpha \sqrt{\frac{2}{m-1}} \qquad (19.5)$$

is a second test for $H_0 : \lambda_k^1 = \lambda_k^2$. Under the null hypothesis the respective eigenvalues are the same in both periods. The null hypothesis is rejected when the inequality is fulfilled for a corresponding critical value q. This would indicate an instability of the principal components over time.

Critical values for rejecting the null hypothesis are 0.313 (probability of error 10%), 0.373 (probability of error 5%) and 0.490 (probability of error 1%). The differences of the estimated eigenvalues are 0.667 and 1.183. Both differences are significantly larger than zero with an error probability of 1%. These results prove that the determining factors of the volatility dynamics changes over time. By the determination of the risk of option portfolios it therefore appears necessary to use an adaptive method of the principal components. Here the estimation is periodically done over a moving time window and the length of the time window is adaptively set, see Härdle, Spokoiny and Teyssiere (2000).

19.4   Measure of the Implied Volatility's Risk

The market value P_t of a portfolio consisting of w different options is dependent on changes of the risk free interest rate r_t, the prices S_t of the financial underlying, the time to maturity τ and the individual implied volatilities σ_I.

Changes in the portfolios value can be analytically approximated using the following Taylor approximation, where it is assumed that the options are all based on the same underlying.

$$
\Delta P_t = \sum_{u=1}^{w} \left\{ \frac{\partial V_{ut}}{\partial \sigma_I} \Delta \sigma_{I,t} + \frac{\partial V_{ut}}{\partial t} \Delta t + \frac{\partial V_{ut}}{\partial r} \Delta r_t \right.
$$
$$
\left. + \frac{\partial V_{ut}}{\partial S} \Delta S_t + \frac{1}{2} \frac{\partial^2 V_{ut}}{\partial S^2} (\Delta S_t)^2 \right\}
$$
$$
\Delta P_t = \sum_{u=1}^{w} \left\{ \frac{\partial V_{ut}}{\partial \sigma_I} \Delta \sigma_{I,t} + \Theta_u \Delta t + \rho_u \Delta r_t + \Delta_u \Delta S_t + \frac{1}{2} \Gamma_u (\Delta S_t)^2 \right\}
$$

Here V_{ut} describes the price of the u-th option with a time to maturity τ_u at date t, and $\Theta_u, \rho_u, \Delta_u, \Gamma_u$ are the characteristic values described in Section 6.3 of the u-th option. In practice option traders often insert "Vega" positions directly. In doing so they create portfolios whose profit and loss profile can be determined by the changes in the implied volatilities of the respective options, see Taleb (1997). Portfolios of this kind are called (Δ, Γ) and Θ neutral. The sensitivity of the option price under consideration to the changes in the volatilities is measured by the variable $\mathcal{V}$ ("Vega" - see (6.29)).

A well known strategy in utilizing the forecasted changes in the maturity structure of implied volatilities consists of buying and selling so called "Straddles" with varying maturities. A straddle is constructed by simultaneously buying ("Long Straddle") or selling ("Short Straddle") the same number of ATM Call and Put options with the same time to maturity. If a trader expects a relatively strong increase in the implied volatility in the short maturities and a relatively weaker increase in the longer maturities, then he will buy straddles with a short time to maturity and sell longer maturity straddles at a suitable ratio. The resulting option portfolio is (Δ, Γ) neutral and over a short time frame Θ neutral, i.e., it is insensitive with respect to losing value over time. The Taylor series given above can thus be reduced to:

$$
\Delta P_t \approx \sum_{u=1}^{w} \left\{ \frac{\partial V_{ut}}{\partial \sigma_I} \Delta \sigma_{I,t}^{(t)} \right\} \tag{19.6}
$$

The first differences of the implied volatilities can now be given as linear combinations of the principal components. By substituting the volatility indices $\sigma_{I,t}$, which are temporally next to the actual implied volatility $\hat{\sigma}_I(\tau_u^*)$, one obtains the following representation given (19.3):

$$
\Delta P_t \approx \sum_{u=1}^{w} \left\{ \frac{\partial V_{ut}}{\partial \sigma_I} \left(\sum_{l=1}^{2} b_{jl} y_{lt} \right) \right\} \tag{19.7}
$$

The number of principal components used in the previous expression can be reduced to the first two without any significant loss of information.

The following "Maximum Loss" (ML) concept describes the probability distribution of a short-term change in the portfolios value dependent on changes in the value of the underlying factors. The change in value of a (Δ, Γ) neutral option portfolio is substantially determined by the changes in the implied volatilities of the options contained in the portfolio. To determine the "Maximum Loss" it is necessary to have an adequate exact representation of the future distribution of the changes to the volatility of the options with varying time to maturity.

The "Maximum Loss" is defined as the largest possible loss of a portfolio that can occur over a specific factor space A_t and over a specific holding period τ. The factor space A_t is determined by a closed set with $P(A_t) = \alpha$. Here α is set to 99% or 99.9%. The ML definition resembles at first sight the "Value-at-Risk" Definition (see Chapter 15). There exists, however, an important difference between the two concepts: In calculating the "Value-at-Risk" the distribution of the returns of the given portfolio must be known, whereas the ML is defined directly over the factor space and thus has an additional degree of freedom, see Studer (1995).

In our analysis we have divided the maturity structure of the implied volatilities into two principal components, which explain a considerable portion of the variability of the structure curve. Thus the first two principal components represent the risk factors used in the ML model. The profit and loss profile of each portfolio held is determined by the corresponding changes in the risk factors using a suitable valuation model. In order to obtain this, a valuation of the underlying portfolios must theoretically occur for every point in the factor space. In the practical application the factor space is probed over a sufficiently small grid of discrete data points $y_1^z (z = 1, ..., N_1)$, during which the other risk factor is in each case held constant. Due to the orthogonality properties of the principal components, the profit and loss function $PL()$ is additive with $PL(y_1^{z_1}, y_2^{z_2}) = PL(y_1^{z_1}) + PL(y_2^{z_2})$.

Under the assumption of multivariate, normally distributed principal components confidence intervals can be constructed for the "Maximum Loss" over the total density

$$\varphi_2(y) = \frac{1}{(2\pi)\sqrt{\det \Lambda_2}} \exp(-\frac{1}{2} y^\top \Lambda_2^{-1} y), \qquad (19.8)$$

with $y = (y_1, y_2)^\top$. Here the matrix Λ_2 represents the 2×2 diagonal matrix of the eigenvalues λ_k, $k = 1,2$. The random variable $y^\top \Lambda_2^{-1} y = X_1^2 + X_2^2$ has a Chi-square distribution. The confidence interval for an existing portfolio is then $A_t = \{y; y^\top \Lambda_2^{-1} y \le c_\alpha\}$, c_α, where c_α is the α quantile of a random variable with a Chi-square distribution and 2 degrees of freedom.

19.5 Recommended Literature

The presentation of this chapter closely follows the work of Fengler, Härdle and Schmidt (2002). The principal components analysis is applied to the changes of implied volatilities for fixed ranges of days to maturity by Skiadopoulos et al. (1998) who find two principal components can already sufficiently explain the dynamics of smiles. The conditions to ensure the absence of arbitrage in the volatility models are derived by Schönbucher (1998). Furthermore, Härdle and Hafner (2000) show that the prices of out-of-the-money options strongly depend on volatility features such as asymmetry.

Härdle et al. (2000) develop an adaptive method of estimation which does not use any information about the time homogeneity of the observed process. It can be used to estimate the principal components. For the effect of the implied volatilities changes on the dynamic hedging of exotic and complex options we refer to Taleb (1997).

20 Nonparametric Estimators for the Probability of Default

The estimation of the probability of default based on information on the individual customer or the company is an important part of credit screening, i.e., judging the credit standing. It is essential for the establishment of a rating or for measuring credit risk to estimate the probability that a company will end in financial difficulties within a given period of, for example, one year. Also here nonparametric applications prove to be flexible tools in estimating the desired default probability without arbitrary assumptions. In this chapter we will give a brief overview of the various approaches for non- and semiparametric estimates of conditional probabilities.

20.1 Logistic Regression

In order to judge the credit standing of a customer a series of data are in general available. For a consumer credit there are, for example, in Müller (2000): *level of credit, age of the customer, duration of credit* as well as information on whether the customer is *unemployed* or not and whether there were problems in the past with *repaying a loan*. For the insolvency prognoses for a small company relevant information would be, for example, in Anders (1997): *age of the business, sales development* from the recent past, *educational degree of the entrepreneur, type of business* and the information on *liability*.

Some influential values are quantitative such as credit volume and sales development. Others are qualitative in nature and must be transformed into numbers for estimating the default probability. For dichotomic characteristics (unemployed, employed, limited liability, unlimited liability) indicator variables are set with values of 0 and 1. For characteristics with $d > 2$ possibilities and for categorical values $d - 1$ dummy variables are introduced, which also take on the value of 0 or 1. Coding the characteristics numerically the *type of business* and three clarifying variables *trade, processed business, other* are considered for which two Dummy variables, Z_1, Z_2, are used where $Z_1 = 1$ $(Z_2 = 1)$ if and only if the type of business is *trade (processed business)*. When $Z_1 = Z_2 = 0$, the firm considered belongs to one of the *other* types of business, for example, *services*. The case $Z_1 = Z_2 = 1$ can not occur.

If the values of the qualitative characteristics are hierarchically ordered, then it is possible to represent them with an integer valued random variable. The personal impression of the processor in the bank of the economic situation of a company: *very good, good, satisfactory, poor, very poor* can, for example, be transformed into a number of scale: *1, 2, 3, 4, 5*. Here one must be certain that every monotone transformation, i.e., where the order remains consistent, produces a different numerical code that can be used with the same justification. Instead of *1, 2, 3, 4, 5* one could also use *0, 1, 3, 6, 10* for instance. Using parametric applications such as the logistic regression one should specify the arbitrary setting of a numerical scale for the hierarchical characteristics. Through a monotone transformation of the scale better estimates can eventually be obtained for the default probabilities. Adequately flexible nonparametric and semi-parametric applications, in contrast, choose automatically a suitable scale.

In order to estimate the default probability of a credit, given the information available at the time the decision is made, we assume a random sample $(X_1, Y_1), \ldots, (X_n, Y_n)$ is independent, identically distributed. $X_j \in \mathbb{R}^d$ stands for the information available at the time the credit is issued to the j-th customer, where qualitative characteristics are already transformed into numerical values as described above. $Y_j \in \{0, 1\}$ is the indicator variable of the credit: it has a value of 0 when the loan can be paid back without any problems and 1 when the credit partially or completely defaulted. The default probability that is to be estimated is the conditional probability that $Y_j = 1$, given $X_j = x$:

$$\pi(x) = \mathrm{P}(Y_j = 1 | X_j = x), \ x \in \mathcal{X},$$

where $\mathcal{X} \subset \mathbb{R}^d$ represents the value space of X_j.

Since $\pi(x)$ only takes on the values between 0 and 1 given that it is a probability, linear regression models cannot be used for the function estimator. The class of generalized linear models (GLM) can, however, be used to estimate the probabilities. Here it is assumed that

$$\pi(x) = G(\beta_0 + \sum_{i=1}^{d} x_i \beta_i) = G(\beta_0 + \beta^\top x).$$

$G : \mathbb{R} \to [0, 1]$ is a known function that only takes on a value between 0 and 1, the real valued parameters $\beta_0, \ldots, \beta_d$ are unknown and need to be estimated. For the special case that G is chosen to be a logistic function ψ:

$$G(t) = \psi(t) = \frac{1}{1 + e^{-t}},$$

we obtain the model of the *logistic regression*: Given $X_1, \ldots, X_n$, the credit indicators $Y_1, \ldots, Y_n$ are independent Bernoulli random variables with parameters $\psi(\beta_0 + \beta^\top X_1), \ldots, \psi(\beta_0 + \beta^\top X_n)$. The conditional likelihood function is thus

$$L(\beta_0, \ldots, \beta_d) = \Pi_{j=1}^n [Y_j \psi(\beta_0 + \beta^\top X_j) + (1 - Y_j)\{1 - \psi(\beta_0 + \beta^\top X_j)\}].$$

Since Y_j only takes on a value between 0 and 1, the corresponding conditional log-likelihood function is

$$\log L(\beta_0, \ldots, \beta_d) = \sum_{j=1}^n [Y_j \log \psi(\beta_0 + \beta^\top X_j) + (1 - Y_j) \log\{1 - \psi(\beta_0 + \beta^\top X_j)\}].$$

Through maximizing L or $\log L$ one obtains the maximum likelihood estimator $\hat{\beta}_0, \ldots, \hat{\beta}_d$ of $\beta_0, \ldots, \beta_d$ and thus the maximum likelihood estimator for the default probability in the logistic regression model:

$$\hat{\pi}(x) = \psi(\hat{\beta}_0 + \hat{\beta}^\top x).$$

20.2 Semi-parametric Model for Credit Rating

The logistic regression model for the estimate of the conditional probability suffers under the same restrictions as the linear regression model when estimating the general functions. In order to avoid the dependence on the special parametric form of the model and to gain more flexibility in the function estimation it is suggested to estimate $\pi(x)$ nonparametrically, for example, with the LP-method given by (13.4) and (13.7). In doing this, however, it is not guaranteed that the function estimator will lie between 0 and 1. In order to enforce this possible, as was done in the previous section, we transform the value space of the estimated function to the interval [0,1] using a given function G:

$$\pi(x) = G(m(x))$$

where $m(x)$ is an arbitrary real valued function that can be estimated nonparametrically. For the estimate of the default probabilities the local smoothing methods are less suitable for two reasons. First of all x is often high dimensional in the application, for example, after adding the necessary dummy variables in the example considered by Müller and Rönz (2000) it has a dimension of 61, that even by larger local neighborhoods of x of the random sample, over which the estimation occurs, there are either too few observations or too large to produce a reliable estimate of $m(x)$. This problem can be solved by restricting ourselves to additive models

$$\pi(x) = G(\sum_{i=1}^{d} m_i(x_i)),$$

where $m_1(u), \ldots, m_d(u)$ are arbitrary functions of the one-dimensional variable u. It is however more critical that many of the coordinates of x take on a value of 0 or 1 in the credit rating, since they represent from the very beginning dichotomic characteristics or have been added as dummy variables for the unordered qualitative characteristics. Local smoothing functions would be suitable based on their underlying philosophy, but mainly for estimating functions with continuous arguments.

A combination of nonparametric and parametric applications offers the possibility to use the flexibility of the nonparametric method by credit rating, Müller and Rönz (2000). In doing so the influential variables are not combined in a random vector X_j, but are separated into two random vectors $X_j \in \mathbb{R}^p, Z_j \in \mathbb{R}^q$. The coordinates of Z_j represent several chosen exclusive quantitative characteristics and eventual hierarchical qualitative characteristics with sufficiently accurate subdivided value spaces. All remaining characteristics, especially the dichotomic and the dummy variables of unordered qualitative characteristics, are combined in X_j. In order to estimate the default probability we consider a generalized partial linear model (GPLM = generalized partial linear model) :

$$P(Y_j = 1|X_j = x, Z_j = z) = \pi(x, z) = G(\beta^\top x + m(z)).$$

G is again a known function with values between 0 and 1, for example, the logistic function ψ. $\beta_1, \ldots, \beta_p$ are unknown parameters, m is an arbitrary, unknown function that can contain an additive constant and thus can make an additional parameter β_0 superfluous. Müller (2000) has shown in an extensive case study that the additional flexibility from the nonparametric part $m(z)$ of the model results in a better estimate of the default probability than a pure parametric logistic regression.

There are various algorithms for estimating β and $m(z)$, for example the profile likelihood method from Severini and Wong (1992) and Severini and Staniswallis (1994) or the back-fitting method from Hastie and Tibshirani (1990). Essentially they use the fact that for the known function $m(z)$ of the parameter vector β can be estimated through maximization of the log-likelihood function analog to the logistic regression

$$\log L(\beta) = \sum_{j=1}^{n} [Y_j \log G(\beta^\top X_j + m(Z_j)) + (1 - Y_j) \log\{1 - G(\beta^\top X_j + m(Z_j))\}]$$

and for known β the function $m(z)$ can be estimated with local smoothing analog to the LP-Method (13.4), (13.7). Both of these optimization problems are combined in an iterative numerical algorithm.

Example 20.1

As an example we consider the rating of consumer credit already referred to above that Müller (2000) has done with a GPLM method. The data represent a part of the extensive random sample, which is described in detail by Fahrmeir and Tutz (1994). We use a total of $n = 564$ observations, in which 24.3 % of the cases have a problem with repaying the credit ($Y_j = 1$). From the 5 influential variables considered, two are dichotomic; they indicate whether the customer is unemployed or not (X_{j1}) and whether the customer had credit problems in the past or not (X_{j2}). The remaining three variables are quantitative: the duration of the credit (X_{j3} with values between 4 and 72 months), the level of the credit (between 338 and 15653 DM) and the age of the customer (between 19 and 75 years). We will take the logarithm of the last two variables and transform them linearly so that they take on a value in the interval $[0, 1]$. The data points, as can be seen in Figure 20.1, are dispersed comparatively homogenous over a part of the plane, which makes the local smoothing easier. These transformed variables are called Z_{j1} and Z_{j2}. We fit a GPLM

$$P(Y_j = 1 \mid X_{j1} = x_1, X_{j2} = x_2, X_{j3} = x_3, Z_{j1} = z_1, Z_{j2} = z_2)$$
$$= \psi\left(\sum_{k=1}^{3} \beta_k x_k + m(z_1, z_2)\right)$$

to the data and obtain the estimates (the corresponding standard deviation is given in parentheses)

$$\beta_1 = 0.965\,(0.249), \quad \beta_2 = 0.746\,(0.237), \quad \beta_3 = -0.0498\,(0.0115).$$

The probability of default on the credit increases when the customer is unemployed respectively when the customer had repayment problems in the past. It decreases with the duration of the credit. The dependence on the transformed

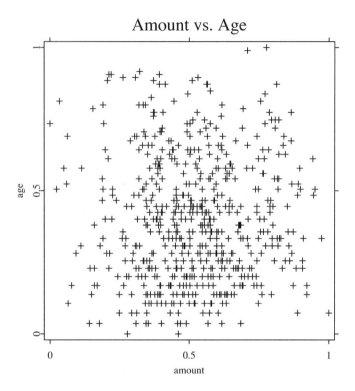

Figure 20.1: The scatter plot of the transferred variables: level of credit and age of the customers.   Q SFEgplm.xpl

credit levels and ages are nonparametrically estimated. From the Figure 20.2 it is obvious to see that the estimated function $\hat{m}(z_1, z_2)$ is clearly non-linear with a maximum by the average value of the credit level and age. The decrease in the probability of default by high levels of credit can be explained by the fact that the random sample contains only those credits that have actually been given and that the processor was essentially reluctant to give out large credits when the customer appeared to be unreliable. This effect, which is caused by the credit ratings from the past, occurs on a regular basis in credit rating. Even if a systematic, model based method was not used, that exclude the credit screening of extreme risks from the very beginning and thus these ratings no longer appear in the data. Thus it must be considered when *interpreting and applying a model.*

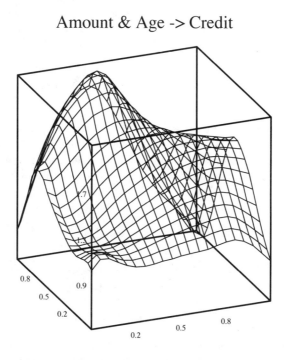

Amount & Age -> Credit

Figure 20.2: The estimated function with respect to level of credit and age of
the customers.   ▢ SFEgplm.xpl

20.3   Credit Ratings with Neural Networks

As with nonparametric fitting of financial time series models to the data, the
neural network also provides an alternative to local smoothing, as with LP
method, in estimating default probabilities. The logistic regression function
$\pi(x) = \psi(\beta_0 + \beta^\top x)$ is nothing more than a function defined by a neural
network with only one neuron in a hidden layer, when the logistic function ψ
is chosen as a transfer function. Through the combination of several neurons

in one or more hidden layers default probabilities can be estimated, as with the nonparametric regression analysis, with flexibility. In order to obtain estimates between 0 and 1, it is necessary to represent the function $\nu_H(x;\delta)$ given by (18.1), for example, with a function G over the interval $[0,1]$. We restrict ourselves to one hidden layer with H neurons and choose $G = \psi$, so that the default probability given by the neuron network has the form

$$\pi_H(x;\vartheta) = \psi(v_0 + \sum_{h=1}^{H} v_h\,\psi(w_{oh} + \sum_{j=1}^{d} w_{ih}x_i)),$$

where ϑ represents once again the parameter vector built from v_h and w_{ih}, $0 \leq i \leq d$, $0 \leq h \leq H$. To estimate the network weights from the data we will not use the least squares method, which makes sense for the regression model with normally distributed residuals, but instead we will maximize the log-likelihood function

$$\log L(\vartheta) = \sum_{j=1}^{n} [Y_j \log \pi_H(X_j;\vartheta) + (1 - Y_j)\log\{1 - \pi_H(X_j;\vartheta)\}]$$

following the procedure used in the logistic regression. By substituting in the estimator $\hat{\vartheta}_n$ we obtain an estimator for the default probability

$$\hat{\pi}(x) = \pi_H(x;\hat{\vartheta}_n).$$

In order to obtain an especially simple model with fewer parameters, Anders (1997) trivially modified the method for the insolvency prognoses for small and middle sized firms and assume a default probability of the form

$$\pi_H^l(x;\vartheta) = \psi(\beta^\top x + v_0 + \sum_{h=1}^{H} v_h\psi(w_{oh} + \sum_{i=1}^{d} w_{ih}x_i)),$$

which has obvious similarities to the general partial linear model, besides the fact that here a part of or all of the influential variables, i.e., the coordinates of x, can appear in linear as well as in nonparametric portions. The linear term $\beta^\top x$ can be interpreted as the value of an additional neuron whose transfer function is not the logistic function $\psi(t)$, but the identity $f(t) \overset{\text{def}}{=} t$. Estimating the network from the application of a model selection technique used to find the insolvency probability is surprisingly easy. It contains in addition to a linear term only one single neuron ($H = 1$). From the 6 input variables only 4 contribute to the linear part (Age of the business, sales development, indicator for limited liability, dummy variable for processed business), that means the other two coefficients β_i are 0, and only 3 (Dummy variables for processed business and for trade, indicator variable for educational degree of entrepreneur) contribute to the sigmoid part, that means the corresponding weights w_{i1} are 0. With this simple model using a validation data set, which is not used to estimate the parameters, a ratio of the correct identifications of 83.3 % was obtained for the insolvencies and of 63.3 % for the solvent firms.

A Technical Appendix

A.1 Integration Theory

Definition A.1
A decomposition $\mathcal{Z}$ of the interval $[a,b]$ is understood to be a set $\mathcal{Z} \stackrel{\text{def}}{=} \{t_0, t_1, \ldots, t_n\}$ of points t_j with $a = t_0 < t_1 < \ldots < t_n = b$. Through this the interval $[a,b]$ is decomposed into n sub-intervals $[t_k, t_{k+1}]$, where $k = 0, 1, 2, \ldots, n-1$. $|\mathcal{Z}| \stackrel{\text{def}}{=} \max_k(t_{k+1} - t_k)$, that is, the length of the largest resulting sub-interval and is referred to as the refinement *of the decomposition $\mathcal{Z}$.*

Definition A.2
For a function $w : [a,b] \longrightarrow \mathbb{R}$ and a decomposition $\mathcal{Z} \stackrel{\text{def}}{=} \{t_0, t_1, \ldots, t_n\}$ one defines the variation *of w with respect to $\mathcal{Z}$ as:*

$$V(\mathcal{Z}) \stackrel{\text{def}}{=} \sum_{k=0}^{n-1} |w(t_{k+1}) - w(t_k)|$$

$V \stackrel{\text{def}}{=} \sup_{\mathcal{Z}} V(\mathcal{Z})$ is called the total variation *of w on $[a,b]$. If $V < \infty$ holds, then w is of* finite variation *on $[a,b]$.*

Theorem A.1
For a function $w : [a,b] \longrightarrow \mathbb{R}$ it holds that:

1. *w is of finite variation when w is monotone,*

2. *w is of finite variation when w is Lipschitz continuous,*

3. *w is bounded when w is of finite variation.*

Moreover, sums, differences and products of functions of finite variation are themselves of finite variation.

Definition A.3
Given the functions $f, w : [a, b] \rightarrow \mathbb{R}$ and a decomposition $\mathcal{Z}$, choose for $k = 0, 1, \ldots, n - 1$ partitions $\tau_k \in [t_k, t_{k+1}]$ and form:

$$I(\mathcal{Z}, \boldsymbol{\tau}) \overset{\text{def}}{=} \sum_{k=0}^{n-1} f(\tau_k) \cdot \{w(t_{k+1}) - w(t_k)\}$$

If $I(\mathcal{Z}, \boldsymbol{\tau})$ converges for $|\mathcal{Z}| \rightarrow 0$ to a limiting value I, which does not depend on the chosen decomposition $\mathcal{Z}$ nor on the choice of the partitions τ_k, then I is called the **Riemann-Stieltjes integral** *of f. One writes:*

$$I = \int_a^b f(t) dw(t).$$

For $w(t) = t$ we get the **Riemann Integral** *as a special case of the Stieltjes Integrals.*

Theorem A.2 (Characteristics of the Riemann-Stieltjes Integral)

1. *If the corresponding integrals on the right hand side exist, then the linearity characteristics hold:*

$$\int_a^b (\alpha \cdot f + \beta \cdot g) \, dw = \alpha \int_a^b f \, dw + \beta \int_a^b g \, dw \quad (\alpha, \beta \in \mathbb{R})$$

$$\int_a^b f \, d(\alpha \cdot w + \beta \cdot v) = \alpha \int_a^b f \, dw + \beta \int_a^b f \, dv \quad (\alpha, \beta \in \mathbb{R})$$

2. *If the integral $\int_a^b f dw$ and the Integrals $\int_a^c f dw$ exist, then for $\int_c^b f dw$, $a < c < b$ it holds that:*

$$\int_a^b f dw = \int_a^c f dw + \int_c^b f dw$$

3. *If f is continuous on $[a, b]$ and w is of finite variation, then $\int_a^b f dw$ exists.*

4. *If f is continuous on $[a, b]$ and w is differentiable with a bounded derivative, then it holds that:*

$$\int_a^b f(t) dw(t) = \int_a^b f(t) \cdot w'(t) dt$$

5. Partial integration: *If $\int_a^b f dg$ or $\int_a^b g df$ exist, so does the other respective integral and it holds that:*

$$\int_a^b f dg + \int_a^b g df = f(b)g(b) - f(a)g(a)$$

6. *If w is continuous, it holds that $\int_a^b dw(t) = w(b) - w(a)$*

7. *If f is continuous on $[a, b]$ and w is step-wise constant with discontinuity points $\{c_k, k = 1, \ldots, m\}$, then:*

$$\int_a^b f dw = \sum_{k=1}^m f(c_k) \cdot \left\{ w(c_k^+) - w(c_k^-) \right\}$$

where c_k^+ (c_k^-) is the right (left) continuous limit and $w(c_k^+) - w(c_k^-)$ is the step height of w on $\{c_k\}$.

Theorem A.3 (Radon-Nikodym)
Let λ and μ be positive measures on $(\Omega, \mathcal{F})$ with

1. $0 < \mu(\Omega) < \infty$ *and* $0 < \lambda(\Omega) < \infty$

2. λ *is absolutely continuous with respect to μ, then from $\mu(A) = 0$ it follows that $\lambda(A) = 0$ for all $A \in \mathcal{F}$ (written: $\lambda \ll \mu$).*

When a non-negative $\mathcal{F}$-measurable function h exists on Ω, then it holds that:

$$\forall \mathcal{A} \in \mathcal{F} : \lambda(\mathcal{A}) = \int_A h \, d\mu.$$

In particular, for all measurable functions f it holds that:

$$\int f d\lambda = \int f \cdot h \, d\mu.$$

Remark A.1
One often uses the abbreviation $\lambda = h \cdot \mu$ in the Radon-Nikodym theorem and refers to h as the density of λ with respect to μ. Due to its construction h is also referred to as the Radon-Nikodym derivative. In this case one writes $h = \frac{d\lambda}{d\mu}$.

An important tool in stochastic analysis is the transformation of measure, which is illustrated in the following example.

Example A.1 *Let $Z_1, \ldots, Z_n$ be independent random variables with standard normal distributions on the measurable space $(\Omega, \mathcal{F}, P)$ and $\mu_1, \ldots, \mu_n \in \mathbb{R}$. Then by*

$$Q(d\omega) \stackrel{\text{def}}{=} \xi(\omega) \cdot P(d\omega) \quad with \quad \xi(\omega) \stackrel{\text{def}}{=} \exp\{\sum_{i=1}^{n} \mu_i Z_i(\omega) - \frac{1}{2}\mu_i^2\}$$

an equivalent probability measure Q for P is defined. For the distribution of the $Z_1, \ldots, Z_n$ under the new measure Q it holds that:

$$
\begin{aligned}
&Q(Z_1 \in dz_1, \ldots, Z_n \in dz_n) \\
=\ & \exp\{\sum_{i=1}^{n}(\mu_i z_i - \frac{1}{2}\mu_i^2)\} \cdot P(Z_1 \in dz_1, \ldots, Z_n \in dz_n) \\
=\ & \exp\{\sum_{i=1}^{n}(\mu_i z_i - \frac{1}{2}\mu_i^2)\} \cdot (2\pi)^{-\frac{n}{2}} \exp\{-\frac{1}{2}\sum_{i=1}^{n} z_i^2\} dz_1 \ldots dz_n \\
=\ & (2\pi)^{-\frac{n}{2}} \exp\{-\frac{1}{2}\sum_{i=1}^{n}(z_i - \mu_i)^2\} dz_1 \ldots dz_n,
\end{aligned}
$$

in other words $Z_1, \ldots, Z_n$ are, with respect to Q, independent and normally distributed with expectations $\mathsf{E}_Q(Z_i) = \mu_i$ and $\mathsf{E}_Q[(Z_i - \mu_i)^2] = 1$. Thus the random variables $\widetilde{Z}_i \stackrel{\text{def}}{=} Z_i - \mu_i$ are independent random variables with standard normal distributions on the measurable space $(\Omega, \mathcal{F}, Q)$.

Going from P to Q by multiplying by ξ changes the expectations of the normally distributed random variables, but the volatility structure remains notably unaffected.

The following Girsanov theorem generalizes this method for the continuous case, that is, it constructs for a given P-Brownian motion W_t an equivalent measure Q and an appropriately adjusted process W_t^*, so that it represents a Q-Brownian motion. In doing so the ("arbitrarily" given) expectation μ_i is replaced by an ("arbitrarily" given) drift, that is, a stochastic process X_t.

Theorem A.4 (Girsanov)
Let $(\Omega, \mathcal{F}, P)$ be a probability space, W_t a Brownian motion with respect to P, $\mathcal{F}_t$ a filtration in $\mathcal{F}$ and X_t an adapted stochastic process. Then

$$\xi_t \stackrel{\text{def}}{=} \exp(\int_0^t X_u dW_u - \frac{1}{2}\int_0^t X_u^2 du)$$

defines a martingal with respect to P and $\mathcal{F}_t$. The process W_t^* defined by

$$W_t^* \stackrel{\text{def}}{=} W_t - \int_0^t X_u du$$

is a Wiener process with respect to the filtration $\mathcal{F}_t$ and

$$Q \stackrel{\text{def}}{=} \xi_T \cdot P \qquad\qquad\qquad (A.1)$$

is a P equivalent probability measure Q.

The Girsanov theorem thus shows that for a P-Brownian motion W_t an equivalent probability measure Q can be found such that W_t, as a Q-Brownian motion at time t, contains the drift X_t. In doing so (A.1) means that:
$\int_\Omega \mathbf{1}(\omega \in A) dQ(\omega) = Q(A) \stackrel{\text{def}}{=} \int_\Omega \mathbf{1}(\omega \in A)\xi_T dP(\omega) = \mathsf{E}_P[\mathbf{1}(\omega \in A)\xi_T]$
for all $A \in \mathcal{F}$.

Remark A.2
With the relationships mentioned above ξ_t is by all means a martingale with respect to P and $\mathcal{F}_t$ when the so-called Novikov Condition

$$\mathsf{E}_P\left[\exp\left(\int_0^t X_u^2 du\right)\right] < \infty \quad \text{for all } t \in [0, T]$$

is met, that is, when X_t does not vary too much.

Another important tool used to derive the Black-Scholes formula by means of martingale theory is the martingale representation theory. It states that every Q-martingale under certain assumptions can be represented by a predetermined Q-martingale by means of a square-integrable process.

Theorem A.5 (Martingale Representation theorem)
Let M_t be a martingale with respect to the probability measure Q and the filtration $\mathcal{F}_t$, for which the volatility process σ_t of Q almost surely $\sigma_t \neq 0$ for all $t \in [0, T]$, where $\sigma_t^2 = \mathsf{E}_Q[M_t^2 | \mathcal{F}_t]$. If N_t is another martingale with respect to Q and $\mathcal{F}_t$, then there exists (uniquely defined) on $\mathcal{F}_t$ an adapted stochastic process H_t with $\int_0^T H_t^2 \sigma_t^2 dt < \infty$ with:

$$N_t = N_0 + \int_0^t H_s dM_s.$$

Example A.2 *It is easy to show that the standard Wiener process W_t with respect to the probability measure P is a martingale with respect to P and its corresponding filtration $\mathcal{F}_t$. If X_t is another martingale with respect to P and $\mathcal{F}_t$, then according to the previous theorem there exists a $\mathcal{F}_t$ adapted stochastic process H_t, so that*

$$X_t = X_0 + \int_0^t H_s dW_s.$$

Remark A.3
Writing the last expression in terms of derivatives:

$$dX_t = H_t dW_t.$$

The example shows once again that a martingale cannot possess a drift.

A.2 Portfolio Strategies

The portfolio of an investor at time t, i.e., the market value of the single equities (contracts) in his portfolio at time t, is dependent on the development of the price $\{\boldsymbol{S}_s; s < t\}$, $\boldsymbol{S}_s = (S_s^1, \ldots, S_s^d)^\top \in \mathbb{R}^d$ up to time t, that is, on the information that is available at that particular time point. Given this it is obvious that his strategy, i.e., the development of his portfolio's value over time, should also be modelled as a $\mathcal{F}_t$ adapted d-dimensional stochastic process ϕ_t. In doing so $\phi_t^i(\omega)$ represents how much is the security i in his portfolio at time t in state ω, where negative values indicate a short sell of the corresponding contract.

Definition A.4
Assume the following market model: $\mathcal{M} = (\Omega, \mathcal{F}, \mathrm{P}, \mathcal{F}_t, \boldsymbol{S}_t)$. *A d-dimensional stochastic process ϕ_t adapted on the filtration $\mathcal{F}_t$ is called a portfolio strategy. The stochastic process $V(\phi_t)$ with $V(\phi_t) \overset{\text{def}}{=} \sum_{i=1}^{d} \phi_t^i S_t^i$ is called the value of the strategy ϕ.*

Example A.3 *In the Black-Scholes model two financial instruments are traded on the market: a risky security S (stock) and a riskless security B (zero bond). As in Chapter 5, the stock price S_t is assumed to follow a geometric Brownian motion, so that the following stochastic differential equation is satisfied:*

$$dS_t = S_t(\mu dt + \sigma dW_t) \tag{A.2}$$

The price of the zero bond B_t satisfies the differential equation:

$$dB_t = r B_t dt$$

with a constant r. Without loss of generality it can be assumed that $B_0 = 1$, which leads to $B_t = \mathrm{e}^{rt}$.

The corresponding market model is thus $\mathcal{M}_{BS} = (\Omega, \mathcal{F}, \mathrm{P}, \mathcal{F}_t, \boldsymbol{S}_t)$, *where* $\boldsymbol{S}_t \overset{\text{def}}{=} (S_t, B_t)^\top \in \mathbb{R}^2$.

The two-dimensional stochastic process $\phi_t = (a_t, b_t)^\top$ now describes a portfolio strategy in which $a_t(\omega)$ gives the number of stocks and $b_t(\omega)$ gives the number of bonds in the portfolio at time t in state ω. The value of the portfolio at time t is then a random variable

$$V(\phi_t) = a_t S_t + b_t B_t.$$

A particularly important portfolio strategy is that once it is implemented it does not result in any cash flows over time, i.e., when the portfolio is re-balanced no payments are necessary. This means that eventual income (through selling securities, receiving dividends, etc.) is exactly offset by required payments (through buying additional securities, transaction costs, etc.) This is referred to as a self-financing strategy. One gets the impression that the change in value of the portfolio only occurs as the price of the participating securities changes.

Definition A.5
Let $\mathcal{M} = (\Omega, \mathcal{F}, \mathrm{P}, \mathcal{F}_t, \boldsymbol{S}_t)$ be a market model and ϕ a portfolio strategy with the value $V(\phi_t)$. Then ϕ is called

1. self-financing, *when $dV(\phi_t) = \sum_{i=1}^{d} \phi_t^i dS_t^i$ holds for P-almost sure,*

2. admissible, *when $V(\phi_t) \geq 0$ holds for P-almost sure.*

In the following the Black-Scholes model will be considered. The subsequent specification shows that arbitrage is not possible in such a market: There is no admissible self-financing strategy with a starting value of $V(\phi_0) = 0$, whose end value $V(\phi_T)$ is positive with a positive probability.

Lemma A.1
In the Black-Scholes model $\mathcal{M}_{BS} = (\Omega, \mathcal{F}, \mathrm{P}, \mathcal{F}_t, \boldsymbol{S}_t)$, $\boldsymbol{S}_t = (S_t, B_t)^\top$, the portfolio strategy $\phi_t = (a_t, b_t)^\top$ is exactly self-financing when the discounted process $\tilde{V}_t$ with $\tilde{V}_t = e^{-rt} V_t$ satisfies the stochastic differential equation

$$d\tilde{V}_t = a_t d\tilde{S}_t,$$

where $\tilde{S}_t = e^{-rt} S_t$ describes the discounted stock price.

The explicit specification of the corresponding strategy can be left out when it is clear from the context and V_t can be written as $V(a, b)_t$. With the help of the Girsanov theorem a P equivalent measure Q can be constructed, under which the process of the discounted stock prices is a martingale. Using (A.2) one obtains

$$d\tilde{S}_t = \tilde{S}_t\{(\mu - r)dt + \sigma dW_t\}. \tag{A.3}$$

By setting

$$X_t \stackrel{\text{def}}{=} -\frac{\mu - r}{\sigma}$$

the Novikov condition (see Remark A.2) is obviously fulfilled. Therefore, for Q with

$$
\begin{aligned}
\frac{dQ}{dP} = \xi_T &= \exp\left(\int_0^T X_u dW_u - \frac{1}{2}\int_0^T X_u^2 du\right) \\
&= \exp\left\{-\frac{\mu - r}{\sigma}W_T - \frac{1}{2}\left(\frac{\mu - r}{\sigma}\right)^2 T\right\}
\end{aligned}
$$

$W_t^* \stackrel{\text{def}}{=} W_t + \frac{\mu - r}{\sigma}t$ is a Q-Brownian Motion according to the Girsanov theorem. Because of (A.3) and using the definition of W_t^* it holds that

$$d\tilde{S}_t = \tilde{S}_t \sigma dW_t^*. \tag{A.4}$$

According to Itô's lemma this becomes

$$\tilde{S}_t = \tilde{S}_0 \exp\left(\int_0^t \sigma dW_u^* - \frac{1}{2}\int_0^t \sigma^2 du\right)$$

and solves the stochastic differential equation. Since σ is constant, for all t the Novikov condition holds

$$\mathsf{E}\left[\exp\left(\int_0^t \sigma^2 du\right)\right] < \infty.$$

According to Remark A.2

$$\exp\left(\int_0^t \sigma dW_u^* - \frac{1}{2}\int_0^t \sigma^2 du\right),$$

that is $\tilde{S}_t$, is also a Q-martingale.

Q represents with respect to $\tilde{S}_t$ a P equivalent martingale measure. It can be shown that given this form, it can be uniquely determined.

From the Definition of W_t^* and with the help of (A.2) one obtains

$$dS_t = S_t(rdt + \sigma dW_t^*),$$

i.e., under the measure Q the expected value of the risky securities is equivalent to the certain value of the riskless bonds. Because of this the martingale measure Q is also called the *risk neutral* probability measure and contrary to this P is called the *objective* or *physical* probability measure of the Black-Scholes markets.

As a result of the Q-martingale properties of $\widetilde{S}_t$, due to Lemma A.1, the discounted value of a self-financing strategy $\widetilde{V}_t$ is itself a local Q-martingale. Thus the value of every admissible self-financing strategy that is a non-negative local Q-martingale is a Q-super martingale. Consequently it holds that: If the starting value of an admissible self-financing strategy is equal to zero, then its value at all later time points t must also be equal to zero. Thus in using an admissible self-financing strategy, there is no riskless profit to be made: The Black-Scholes market is free of arbitrage.

The following theorem represents the most important tool used to value European options with the help of the Black-Scholes model. It secures the existence of an admissible self-financing strategy that duplicates the option, thus the value of which can be calculated using martingale theory.

Theorem A.6
Assume that the Black-Scholes model $\mathcal{M}_{BS}$ is given. The function X describes the value of an European option at the time to maturity T and is Q-integrable.

a) *Then an admissible self-financing strategy $(a_t, b_t)^\top$ exists, which duplicates X and whose value V_t for all t is given by*

$$V_t = \mathsf{E}_\mathsf{Q}[e^{-r(T-t)} X \mid \mathcal{F}_t]. \tag{A.5}$$

b) *If the value V_t in a) is dependent on t and S_t and is written as a function $V_t = F(t, S_t)$ with a smooth function F, then it holds for the corresponding strategy that*

$$a_t = \frac{\partial F(t, S_t)}{\partial S_t}.$$

Proof:

1. One defines V_t by (A.5), where the function is defined follows from the Q-integrability of X. Due to

$$\widetilde{V}_t = e^{-rt} V_t = \mathsf{E}_\mathsf{Q}[e^{-rT} X \mid \mathcal{F}_t]$$

one identifies $\widetilde{V}_t$ as Q-martingale. One should notice that $e^{-rT}X$, exactly like X, is only dependent on the state at date T and thus it can be classified as a random variable on $(\Omega, \mathcal{F}_t, Q)$.

$\mathcal{F}_t$ represents at the same time the natural filtration for the process W^*, which, as was seen above, is also a Q-martingale. Therefore, according to Theorem A.5 there exists using the martingale representation a process H_t adapted on $\mathcal{F}_t$ with $\int_0^T H_t^2 \sigma^2 dt < \infty$ Q-almost sure, so that for all t it holds that:

$$\widetilde{V}_t = \widetilde{V}_0 + \int_0^t H_s dW_s^* = V_0 + \int_0^t H_s dW_s^*.$$

Thus one sets:

$$a_t \stackrel{\text{def}}{=} \frac{H_t}{\sigma \cdot \widetilde{S}_t} \quad , \quad b_t \stackrel{\text{def}}{=} \widetilde{V}_t - a_t \widetilde{S}_t.$$

Then after a simple calculation it holds that:

$$a_t S_t + b_t B_t = V_t$$

and $(a_t, b_t)^\top$ is a X duplicating strategy. Furthermore, with (A.4) it holds for all t:

$$a_t d\widetilde{S}_t = a_t \widetilde{S}_t \sigma dW_t^* = H_t dW_t^* = d\widetilde{V}_t,$$

i.e., $(a_t, b_t)^\top$ is according to Lemma A.1 self-financing. Due to the non-negativity of X and the definition of V_t, $(a_t, b_t)^\top$ is also admissible.

2. For $V_t = F(t, S_t)$ it holds using Itô's lemma:

$$\begin{aligned}
d\widetilde{V}_t &= d\{e^{-rt}F(t, S_t)\} \\
&= \frac{\partial\{e^{-rt}F(t, S_t)\}}{\partial S_t} dS_t + A(t, S_t)dt \\
&= \frac{\partial F(t, S_t)}{\partial S_t} e^{-rt} S_t(rdt + \sigma dW_t^*) + A(t, S_t)dt \\
&= \frac{\partial F(t, S_t)}{\partial S_t} \widetilde{S}_t \sigma dW_t^* + \widetilde{A}(t, S_t)dt \\
&= \frac{\partial F(t, S_t)}{\partial S_t} d\widetilde{S}_t + \widetilde{A}(t, S_t)dt.
\end{aligned}$$

Since not only $\widetilde{V}_t$ but also $\widetilde{S}_t$ are Q-martingales, the drift term $\widetilde{A}(t, S_t)$ must disappear. According to part a) of the theorem the corresponding strategy is self-financing and thus using Lemma A.1 the claim follows.

□

Remark A.4 *With the relationships of the preceding theorems V_t is called the fair price for option X at date t, because at this price, according to the previous argumentations, there is no arbitrage possible for either the buyer or the seller of the option. Equation (A.5) is called the risk neutral valuation formula, since it gives the fair price of the option as the (conditional) expectation of the (discounted) option value at maturity with respect to the risk neutral measure of the Black-Scholes model.*

The result obtained from the last theorem was already formulated in Chapter 6 as equation (6.24).

Corollary A.1
The relationships of the preceding theorems hold. If the value X of the European option at date T is a function $X = f(S_T)$ dependent on the stock price S_T, then it holds that $V_t = F(t, S_t)$, where F for $x \in [0, \infty[$ and $t \in [0, T]$ is defined by:

$$F(t,x) = e^{-r(T-t)} \int_{-\infty}^{+\infty} f\left(xe^{(r-\frac{\sigma^2}{2})(T-t)+\sigma y\sqrt{T-t}}\right) \frac{e^{-\frac{y^2}{2}}}{\sqrt{2\pi}} dy \ . \qquad (A.6)$$

Proof:
With respect to Q, S_t contains the drift r and thus it holds that

$$S_t = S_0 \exp\{(r - \frac{\sigma^2}{2})t + \sigma W_t^*\}.$$

Thus S_T can be written in the following form:

$$S_T = S_t(S_T S_t^{-1}) = S_t \exp\{(r - \frac{\sigma^2}{2})(T - t) + \sigma(W_T^* - W_t^*)\}.$$

Since S_t is measurable with respect to $\mathcal{F}_t$ and $W_T^* - W_t^*$ is independent of $\mathcal{F}_t$, one obtains

$$\begin{aligned}
V_t &= \mathsf{E}_Q[e^{-r(T-t)} f(S_T) \mid \mathcal{F}_t] \\
&= \mathsf{E}_Q\left[e^{-r(T-t)} f(S_t e^{(r-\frac{\sigma^2}{2})(T-t)+\sigma(W_T^*-W_t^*)}) \mid \mathcal{F}_t\right] \\
&= \mathsf{E}_Q\left[e^{-r(T-t)} f(xe^{(r-\frac{\sigma^2}{2})(T-t)+\sigma(W_T^*-W_t^*)})\right]_{x=S_t}
\end{aligned}$$

From this it can be calculated that $V_t = F(t, S_t)$.   □

Example A.4 *Consider a European call $X = \max\{0, S_T - K\}$. Using (A.6) the value at date t is exactly the value given by the Black-Scholes formula in Chapter 6.*

$$C(t, S_t) \stackrel{\text{def}}{=} V_t = S_T \Phi(d_1) - K e^{-r(T-t)} \Phi(d_2)$$

with

$$d_1 \stackrel{\text{def}}{=} \frac{\ln(\frac{S_T}{K}) + (r + \frac{\sigma^2}{2})(T - t)}{\sigma\sqrt{T - t}}, \quad d_2 \stackrel{\text{def}}{=} \frac{\ln(\frac{S_T}{K}) + (r - \frac{\sigma^2}{2})(T - t)}{\sigma\sqrt{T - t}}.$$

Bibliography

Abberger, K. (1997). Quantile smoothing in financial time series, *Statistical Papers* **38**: 125–148.

Anders, U. (1997). *Statistische neuronale Netze*, Vahlen, München.

Ango Nze, P. (1992). Critères d'ergodicité de quelques modèles à représentation markovienne, *Technical Report 315, ser. 1*, C.R. Acad. Sci. Paris.

Artzner, P., Delbaen, F., Eber, F.-J. and Heath, D. (1997). Thinking coherently, *Risk Magazine* .

Baxter, M. and Rennie, A. (1996). *Financial calculus: An introduction to derivative pricing*, Cambridge University Press, Cambridge.

Black, F. (1976). Studies in stock price volatility changes, *Proceedings of the 1976 Meeting of the Business and Economic Statistics Section*, American Statistical Association, pp. 177–181.

Black, F. and Scholes, M. (1973). The pricing of options and corporate liabilities, *Journal of Political Economy* **81**: 637–654.

Bol, G., N. G. and Vollmer, K.-H. (1996). *Finanzmarktanalyse und -prognose mit innovativen quantitativen Verfahren*, Physica-Verlag, Heidelberg.

Bollerslev, T., Engle, R. and Wooldridge, J. (1988). A capital asset pricing model with time varying covariances, *Journal of Political Economy* **96**: 116–131.

Bollerslev, T. P. (1986). Generalized autoregressive conditional heteroscedasticity, *Journal of Econometrics* **31**: 307–327.

Bollerslev, T. P. (1990). Modelling the coherence in short-run nominal exchange rates: A multivariate generalized arch model, *Review of Economics and Statistics* **72**: 498–505.

Bollerslev, T. P. and Wooldridge, J. M. (1992). Quasi maximum likelihood estimation of dynamic models with time-varying covariances, *Econometric Reviews* **11**: 143–172.

Bossaerts, P. and Hillion, P. (1993). Test of a general equilibrium stock option pricing model, *Mathematical Finance* **3**: 311–347.

Box, G. E. P. and Jenkins, G. M. (1976). *Time Series Analysis: Forecasting and Control*, Holden-Day, San Francisco.

Briys, E., Bellalah, M., Mai, H. and de Varenne, F. (1998). *Options, futures and exotic derivatives*, John Wiley & Sons, Chichester.

Brockwell, P. and Davis, R. (1991). *Time Series: Theory and Methods*, Springer Verlag.

Campbell, J., Lo, A. and MacKinlay, A. (1997). *The Econometrics of Financial Markets*, Princeton University Press, Princeton, New Jersey.

Carroll, R. J., Härdle, W. and Mammen, E. (2002). Estimation in an additive model when the components are linked parametrically, *Econometric Theory* **18**: 886–912.

Chan, K. and Tong, H. (1985). On the use of deterministic Lyapunov functions for the ergodicity of stochastic difference equations, *Advanced Applied Probability* **17**: 666–678.

Chen, R. and Tsay, R. S. (1993a). Functional-coefficient autoregressive models, *Journal of the American Statistical Association* **88**: 298–308.

Chen, R. and Tsay, R. S. (1993b). Nonlinear additive ARX models, *Journal of the American Statistical Association* **88**: 955–967.

Cleveland, W. S. (1979). Robust locally weighted regression and smoothing scatterplots, *Journal of the American Statistical Association* **74**: 829–836.

Collomb, G. (1984). Propriétés de convergence presque complète du prédicteur à noyau, *Zeitschrift für Wahrscheinlichkeitstheorie und verwandte Gebiete* **66**: 441–460.

Comte, F. and Lieberman, O. (2003). Asymptotic theory for multivariate garch processes, *Journal of Multivariate Analysis* .

Copeland, T. and Weston, J. (1992). *Financial Theory and Corporate Policy*, Addison-Wesley.

Cox, J. C., Ingersoll, Jr., J. E. and Ross, S. A. (1985). A theory of the term structure of interest rates, *Econometrica* **53**: 385–407.

Cox, J. C. and Ross, S. A. (1976). The valuation of options for alternative stochastic processes, *Journal of Financial Economics* **3**: 145–166.

Cox, J., Ross, S. and Rubinstein, M. (1979). Option pricing: a simplified approach, *Journal of Financial Economics* **7**: 229–263.

Cox, J. and Rubinstein, M. (1985). *Options Markets*, Prentice-Hall, Englewood Cliffs.

Das, S. (1997). *Risk Management and Financial Derivatives*, McGraw-Hill, New York.

Davydov, Y. (1973). Mixing conditions for markov chains, *Theory of Probability and its Applications* **78**: 312–328.

Delbaen, F. and Schachermayer, W. (1994). A general version of the fundamental theorem of asset pricing, *Mathematische Annalen* **300**: 463–520.

Deutsch, H. and Eller, R. (1999). *Derivatives and Internal Models*, Macmillan Press.

Dewynne, J., Howison, S. and Wilmott, P. (1993). *Mathematical Models and Computation*, Oxford University Press.

Dickey, D. and Fuller, W. (1979). Distribution of the estimators for autoregressive time series with a unit root, *Journal of the American Statistical Association* **74**: 427–431.

Diebolt, J. and Guégan, D. (1990). Probabilistic properties of the general nonlinear autoregressive process of order one, *Technical Report 128*, Université de Paris VI, Paris.

Ding, Z., Granger, C. W. J. and Engle, R. F. (1993). A long memory property of stock market returns and a new model, *Journal of Empirical Finance* **1**: 83–106.

Doukhan, P. and Ghindès, M. (1980). Estimation dans le processus $x_{n+1} = f(x_n) + \varepsilon_{n+1}$, *C.R. Acad. Sci. Paris, Sér. A* **297**: 61–64.

Doukhan, P. and Ghindès, M. (1981). Processus autorégressifs non-linéaires, *C.R. Acad. Sci. Paris, Sér. A* **290**: 921–923.

Duan, J.-C. (1995). The GARCH option pricing model, *Mathematical Finance* **5**: 13–32.

Duan, J.-C. (1997). Augmented GARCH(p,q) process and its diffusion limit, *Journal of Econometrics* **79**: 97–127.

Duffie, D. (1996). *Dynamic asset pricing theory*, 2 edn, Princeton University Press, Princeton.

Embrechts, P., Klüppelberg, C. and Mikosch, T. (1997). *Modelling Extremal Events*, Springer Verlag, Berlin.

Embrechts, P., McNeil, A. and Straumann, D. (1999a). Correlation and dependence in risk management: Properties and pitfalls, *Preprint ETH Zürich* .

Embrechts, P., McNeil, A. and Straumann, D. (1999b). Correlation: Pitfalls and alternatives, *RISK* **May**: 69–71.

Engle, R. F. (1982). Autoregressive conditional heteroscedasticity with estimates of the variance of U.K. inflation, *Econometrica* **50**: 987–1008.

Engle, R. F. and Gonzalez-Rivera, G. (1991). Semiparametric ARCH models, *Journal of Business and Economic Statistics* **9**: 345–360.

Engle, R. F., Lilien, D. M. and Robins, R. P. (1987). Estimating time varying risk premia in the term structure: The ARCH-M model, *Econometrica* **55**: 391–407.

Engle, R. F. and Ng, V. K. (1993). Measuring and testing the impact of news on volatility, *Journal of Finance* **48**: 1749–1778.

Engle, R. and Kroner, F. (1995). Multivariate simultaneous generalized arch, *Econometric Theory* **11**: 122–150.

Fahrmeir, L. and Tutz, G. (1994). *Multivariate Statistical Modelling Based on Generalized Linear Models.*, Springer-Verlag, Heidelberg.

Fama, E. F. (1965). The behavior of stock market prices, *Journal of Business* **38**: 34–105.

Fan, J. and Gijbels, I. (1996). *Local polynomial modeling and its application – Theory and methodologies*, Chapman and Hall.

Fan, J. and Yao, Q. (1998). Efficient estimation of conditional variance functions in stochastic regression., *Biometrika* **85**: 645–660.

Fan, J. and Yao, Q. (2003). *Nonlinear Time Series: Nonparametric and Parametric Methods*, Springer Verlag, New York.

Fengler, M., Härdle, W. and Schmidt, P. (2002). An empirical analysis of the common factors governing implied volatility movements measured by the german vdax, *Financial Markets and Portfolio Management* **16**: 16–29.

Fisher, R. and Tippett, L. (1928). Limiting forms of the frequency distribution of the largest or smallest member of a sample, *Proc. Cambridge Philos. Soc.* **24**: 180–190.

Föllmer, H. and Schweizer, M. (1991). Hedging of contingent claims under incomplete information, *in* M.H.A.Davis and R.J.Elliot (eds), *Applied Stochastic Analysis*, Gordon and Breach, London, pp. 389–414.

Föllmer, H. and Sondermann, D. (1991). Hedging of non-redundant contingent claims, *in* W. Hildenbrand and A. Mas-Colell (eds), *Contributions to Mathematical Economics*, Amsterdam, North Holland, pp. 205–223.

Forsythe, R., Palfrey, T. and Plott, C. (1982). Asset valuation in an experimental market, *Econometrica* **50**: 537–567.

Franke, J. (1999). Nonlinear and nonparametric methods for analyzing financial time series, *in* P. Kall and H.-J. Luethi (eds), *Operation Research Proceedings 98*, Springer-Verlag, Heidelberg.

Franke, J. (2000). Portfolio management and market risk quantification using neural networks, *Statistics and Finance: An Interface*, London, Imperial College Press.

Franke, J. and Diagne, M. (2002). Estimating market risk with neural networks, *Technical report*, Department of Mathematics, University of Kaiserslautern.

Franke, J., Härdle, W. and Kreiss, J. (2003). Nonparametric estimation in a stochastic volatility model, *Recent advances and trends in Nonparametric Statistics* .

Franke, J., Härdle, W. and Stahl, G. (eds) (2000). *Measuring Risk in Complex Stochastic Systems*, Vol. 147 of *Lecture Notes in Statistics*, Springer Verlag, New York.

Franke, J. and Klein, M. (1999). Optimal portfolio management using neural networks - a case study, *Technical report*, Department of Mathematics, University of Kaiserslautern.

Franke, J., Kreiss, J. and Mammen, E. (2002). Bootstrap of kernel smoothing in nonlinear time series., *Bernoulli* **8(1)**: 1–37.

Franke, J., Kreiss, J., Mammen, E. and Neumann, M. (2003). Properties of the nonparametric autoregressive bootstrap, *Journal of Time Series Analysis* **23**: 555–585.

Franke, J. and Mwita, P. (2003). Nonparametric estimates for conditional quantiles of time series, *Technical report*, Department of Mathematics, University of Kaiserslautern.

Franke, J. and Neumann, M. (2000). Bootstrapping neural networks., *Neural Computation* **12**: 1929–1949.

Friedmann, R. (1992). Zur Güte von Einheitswurzeltests, *Technical report*, unveröffentlichtes Manuskript.

Glosten, L., Jagannathan, R. and Runkle, D. (1993). Relationship between the expected value and the volatility of the nominal excess return on stocks, *Journal of Finance* **48**: 1779–1801.

Gouriéroux, C. (1997). *ARCH Models and Financial Applications*, Springer Verlag.

Gouriéroux, C. and Jasiak, J. (2002). Nonlinear autocorrelograms: An application to inter-trade durations, *Journal of Time Series Analysis* **23**: 127–154.

Gouriéroux, C. and Monfort, A. (1992). Qualitative threshold ARCH models, *Journal of Econometrics* **52**: 159–199.

Gouriéroux, C. and Monfort, A. (1996). *Time Series Models*, Economica.

Gouriéroux, C., Monfort, A. and Trognon, A. (1984). Pseudo maximum likelihood methods: Theory, *Econometrica* **52**: 681–700.

Grama, I. and Spokoiny, V. (2003). Tail index estimation by local exponential modeling, *Technical report*, WIAS, Berlin.

Graumert, U. and Stahl, G. (2001). *Interne Modelle. Handwörterbuch des Bank- und Finanzwesens*, Schäffer-Poeschel Verlag, Stuttgart.

Gregory, A. (1989). A nonparametric test for autoregressive conditional heteroscedasticity: A markov chain approach, *Journal of Business and Economic Statistics* **7**: 107–115.

Hafner, C. (1998). Estimating high frequency foreign exchange rate volatility with nonparametric ARCH models, *Journal of Statistical Planning and Inference* **68**: 247–269.

Hafner, C. and Herwartz, H. (1998). Time-varying market price of risk in CAPM, approaches, empirical evidence and implications, *Finance* **19**: 93–112.

Hafner, C. and Herwartz, H. (2000). Testing linear autoregressive dynamics under heteroskedasticity, *Econometrics Journal* **3**: 177–197.

Hafner, C. and Herwatz, M. (2003). Analytical quasi maximum likelihood inference in bekk garch models, *Econometric Institute Report* **21**.

Hamilton, J. D. (1994). *Time Series Analysis*, Princeton Univ Press, Princeton, New Jersey.

Härdle, W. (1990). *Applied Nonparametric Regression*, Cambridge University Press, Cambridge.

Härdle, W. and Hafner, C. (2000). Discrete time option pricing with flexible volatility estimation, *Finance and Stochastics* **4**: 189–207.

Härdle, W., Lütkepohl, H. and Chen, R. (1997). Nonparametric time series analysis, *International Statistical Review* **12**: 153–172.

Härdle, W., Müller, M., Sperlich, S. and Werwatz, A. (2004). *Non- and Semiparametric Modelling*, MD*Tech, www.i-xplore.de.

Härdle, W. and Simar, L. (2003). *Applied Multivariate Statistical Analysis*, Springer Verlag, Heidelberg.

Härdle, W., Spokoiny, V. and Teyssiere, G. (2000). Adaptive estimation for a time inhomogeneous stochastic-volatility model, Discussion Paper, Sonderforschungsbereich 373, Humboldt University Berlin.

Härdle, W. and Tsybakov, A. (1997). Local polynomial estimation of the volatility function, *Journal of Econometrics* **81**: 223–242.

Härdle, W., Tsybakov, A. and Yang, L. (1996). Nonparametric vector autoregression, *Journal of Statistical Planning and Inference* **68**: 221–245.

Harrison, M. and Kreps, D. (1979). Martingales and arbitrage in multiperiod securities markets, *Journal of Economic Theory* **20**: 381–408.

Harrison, M. and Pliska, S. (1981). Martingales and stochastic integrals in the theory of continuous trading, *Stochastic Processes Applications* **11**: 215–260.

Hassler, U. (1994). Einheitswurzeltests – Ein "Uberblick, *Allgemeines Statistisches Archiv* **78**: 207–228.

Hastie, T. J. and Tibshirani, R. J. (1990). *Generalized Additive Models*, Vol. 43 of *Monographs on Statistics and Applied Probability*, Chapman and Hall, London.

Hastings, C. (1955). *Approximations for Digital Computers*, Princeton University Press, Princeton.

Haykin, S. (1999). *Neural networks: a comprehensive foundation*, Prentice-Hall.

He, C. and Teräsvirta, T. (1999). Properties of moments of a family of GARCH processes, *Journal of Econometrics* **92**: 173–192.

Heath, D., J. R. and Morton, A. (1992). Bond pricing and the term structure of interest rates: a new methodology for contingent claims valuation., *Econometrica* **60**: 77–105.

Hill, B. (1975). A simple general approach to inference about the tail of a distribution, *Annals of Statistics* **3**: 1163–1174.

Hornik, K., Stinchcombe, M. and White, H. (1989). Multilayer feedforward networks are universal approximators., *Neural Networks* **2**: 359–366.

Hull, J. C. (2000). *Options, Futures and other Derivatives*, Prentice Hall.

Hull, J. and White, A. (1987). The pricing of options on assets with stochastic volatilities, *Journal of Finance* **42**: 281–300.

Hull, J. and White, A. (1990). Pricing interest rate derivatives., *The Review of Financial Studies* **3**: 573–592.

Hutchinson, T. P. and Lai, C. (1990). Continuous bivariate distributions, emphasizing applications.

Ingersoll, Jr., J. E. (1987). *Theory of Financial Decision Making*, Rowman & Littlefield.

Jarchow, H.-J. and Rühmann, P. (1994). *Monetäre Außenwirtschaft I. Monetäre Außenwirtschaftstheorie*, Vandenhoeck & Ruprecht, Göttingen.

Jarrow, R. (1992). *Finance Theory*, 2 edn, Prentice-Hall, Englewood Cliffs, NJ.

Jaschke, S. and Küchler, U. (1999). Coherent risk measures, Discussion paper, No. 64, SFB 373, Humboldt-Universität zu Berlin.

Jeantheau, T. (1998). Strong consistency of estimators for multivariate arch models, *Econometric Theory* **14**: 70–86.

Jensen, B. and Nielsen, J. (1996). Pricing by no arbitrage, *in* D. Cox, D. Hinkley and O. Barndorff-Nielsen (eds), *Time series models in econometrics, finance and other fields*, Chapman and Hall, London.

Jorion, P. (2000). *Value at Risk: The New Benchmark for Managing Financial Risk*, McGraw-Hill, New York.

Karatzas, I. and Shreve, S. (1999). *Brownian motion and stochastic calculus*, Springer-Verlag, Heidelberg.

Katkovnik, V. (1979). Linear and nonlinear methods for nonparametric regression analysis (in Russian), *Avtomatika i Telemehanika* pp. 35–46.

Katkovnik, V. (1985). Nonparametric identification and data smoothing, Nauka.

Korn, R. (1999). *Optimal portfolios: stochastic models for optimal investment and risk management in continuous time*, World Scientific, Singapore.

Korn, R. and Korn, E. (1999). *Optionsbewertung und Portfolio-Optimierung*, Vieweg, Braunschweig.

Korn, R. and Korn, E. (2001). *Option pricing and portfolio optimization*, American Math. Soc., Providence.

Kreiss, J. P. (2000). Nonparametric estimation and bootstrap for financial time series, *in* W. Chan, W. Li and H. Tong (eds), *Statistics and Finance: An Interface*, Imperial College Press, London.

Krengel, U. (1995). *Grundkurs Stochastik*, Teubner, Stuttgart.

Krengel, U. (2000). *Einführung in die Wahrscheinlichkeitstheorie und Statistik*, Vieweg, Braunschweig.

Kwiatkowski, D., Phillips, P., Schmidt, P. and Shin, Y. (1992). Testing the null hypothesis of stationarity against the alternative of a unit root, *Journal of Econometrics* **54**: 159–178.

Leadbetter, M., Lindgren, G. and Rootzen, H. (1983). *Extremes and related properties of random sequences and processes*, Springer Series in Statistics, Springer-Verlag, New York - Heidelberg - Berlin.

Lee, S. and Hansen, B. (1994). Asymptotic theory for the GARCH(1,1) quasi-maximum likelihood estimator, *Econometric Theory* **10**: 29–52.

Lehrbass, F. (2000). A simple approach to country risk, *in* J. Franke, W. Härdle and G. Stahl (eds), *Measuring Risk in Complex Stochastic Systems*, Springer Verlag, pp. 33–65.

Leland, H. (1980). Who should buy portfolio insurance, *Journal of Finance* **35**: 581–594.

Lintner, J. (1965). Security prices, risk and maximal gains from diversification, *Journal of Finance* **20**: 587–615.

Liptser, R. and Shirjaev, A. (1980). A functional central limit theorem for martingales, *Theory of Probability and its Applications* **25**: 667–688.

Lubrano, M. (1998). Smooth transition GARCH models: A Bayesian perspective, *Technical report*, CORE, Louvain-la-Neuve.

Lumsdaine, R. (1996). Consistency and asymptotic normality of the quasi maximum likelihood estimator in IGARCH(1,1) and covariance stationary GARCH(1,1) models, *Econometrica* **64**: 575–596.

Maercker, G. (1997). *Statistical Inference in Conditional Heteroskedastic Autoregressive Models*, Shaker Verlag, Aachen.

Mandelbrot, B. (1963). The variation of certain speculative prices, *Journal of Business* **36**: 394–419.

McAllister, P. H. and Mingo, J. J. (1996). Bank capital requirements for securitzed loan portfolios, *Journal of Banking and Finance* **20**.

McKeague, I. and Zhang, M. (1994). Identification of nonlinear time series from first order cumulative characteristics, *Annals of Statistics* **22**: 495–514.

McNeil, A. and Frey, R. (2000). Estimation of tail-related risk measures for heteroscedastic financial time series: an extreme value approach, *Journal of Empirical Finance* **7**: 271–300.

Melino, A. and Turnbull, S. M. (1990). Pricing foreign currency options with stochastic volatility, *Journal of Econometrics* **45**: 239–265.

Merton, R. (1973). Theory of rational option pricing., *Bell Journal of Economics and Management Science* **4**: 141–183.

Mikosch, T. (1998). *Elementary stochastic calculus with finance in view*, World Scientific, Singapore.

Mills, T. (1993). *The cconometric modelling of financial time series*, Cambridge University Press, Cambridge.

Mokkadem, A. (1987). Sur un modèle autorégressif nonlinéaire. ergodicité et ergodicité géometrique, *Journal of Time Series Analysis* **8**: 195–204.

Mossin, J. (1966). Equilibrium in a capital asset market, *Econometrica* **34**: 768–783.

Müller, M. (2000). Generalized partial linear models, *in* W. Härdle, Z. Hlavka and S. Klinke (eds), *XploRe Application Guide*, Springer-Verlag, Heidelberg.

Müller, M. and Rönz, B. (2000). Credit scoring using semiparametric methods, *in* J. Franke, W. Härdle and G. Stahl (eds), *Measuring Risk in Complex Stochastic Systems*, Springer-Verlag, Heidelberg.

Müller, T. and Nietzer, H. (1993). *Das große Buch der technischen Indikatoren*, TM Börsenverlag.

Murata, N., Yoskizawa, S. and Amari, S. (1994). Network information criterion - determining the number of hidden units for an artificial neural network model., *IEEE Trans. Neural Networks* **5**: 865–872.

Mwita, P. (2003). *Semiparametric estimation of conditional quantiles for time series with applications in finance*, PhD thesis, University of Kaiserslautern.

Neftci, S. (1996). *An introduction to the mathematics of financial derivatives*, Academic Press, San Diego.

Nelsen, R. B. (1999). *An Introduction to Copulas*, Springer, New York.

Nelson, D. B. (1990a). Stationarity and persistence in the GARCH(1,1) model, *Econometric Theory* **6**: 318–334.

Nelson, D. B. (1990b). Arch models as diffusion approximations, *Journal of Econometrics* **45**: 7–38.

Nelson, D. B. (1991). Conditional heteroskedasticity in asset returns: A new approach, *Econometrica* **59**: 347–370.

Nummelin, E. and Tuominen, P. (1982). Geometric ergodicity of harris–recurrent markov chains with application to renewal theory, *Stoch. Proc. Appl.* **12**: 187–202.

Overbeck, L. (2000). Allocation of economic capital in loan portfolios, *in* J. Franke, W. Härdle and G. Stahl (eds), *Measuring Risk in Complex Stochastic Systems*, Springer Verlag, pp. 1–15.

Pickands, J. (1975). Statistical inference using extreme order statistics, *Ann Statist.* **3**: 119–131.

Pitman, J. (1997). *Probability*, Springer-Verlag, Heidelberg.

Polzehl, J. and Spokoiny, V. (2003). Local likelihood modeling by adaptive weights smoothing, *Technical report*, Department of Mathematics, University of Bremen.

Rabemananjara, R. and Zakoian, J. M. (1993). Threshold ARCH models and asymmetries in volatility, *Journal of Applied Econometrics* **8**: 31–49.

Rank, J. and Siegl, T. (2002). Applications of copulas for the calculation of value-at-risk, *in* W. Härdle, T. Kleinow and G. Stahl (eds), *Applied Quantitative Finance*, Springer Finance, Springer Verlag.

Redelberger, T. (1994). *Grundlagen und Konstruktion des VDAX-Volatilitätsindex der Deutsche Börse AG*, Deutsche Börse AG.

Refenes, A.-P. (1995a). *Neural networks for pattern recognition.*, Clarendon Press.

Refenes, A.-P. (1995b). *Neural networks in the capital market*, Wiley, New York.

Rehkugler, H. and Zimmermann, H. G. (1994). *Neuronale Netze in der Ökonomie*, Vahlen, München.

Reiss, R. and Thomas, M. (1997). *Statistical Analysis of Extreme Values*, Birkhäuser, Basel.

Reiss, R. and Thomas, M. (2000). Extreme value analysis, *XploRe Learning Guide*, Heidelberg, Springer, pp. 353–374.

Renault, E. and Touzi, N. (1996). Option hedging and implied volatilities in a stochastic volatility model, *Mathematical Finance* **6**: 277–302.

Ripley, B. (1996). *Pattern recognition and neural networks*, Cambridge University Press, Cambridge.

RiskMetrics (1996). Technical document, 4th edition.

Robinson, P. (1983). Non-parametric estimation for time series models, *Journal of Time Series Analysis* **4**: 185–208.

Robinson, P. (1984). Robust nonparametric autoregression, *in* J. Franke, W. Härdle and Martin (eds), *Robust and nonlinear time series analysis*, Springer-Verlag, Heidelberg.

Ross, S. (1994). *A first course in probability*, Macmillan, New York.

Rüeger, S. and Ossen, A. (1997). The metric structure of weightspace, *Technical report*, Technical University of Berlin.

Samaskij, A. (1984). *Theorie der Differenzenverfahren*, Akademische Verlagsgesellschaft Geest und Portig K.-G., Leipzig.

Schlittgen, R. and Streitberg, B. (1995). *Zeitreihenanalyse*, Oldenbourg.

Schönbucher, P. (1998). A market model for stochastic implied volatility, Discussion Paper, Department of Statistics, Bonn.

Severini, T. and Staniswallis, J. (1994). Quasi-likelihood estimation in semiparametric models, *Journal of the American Statistical Association* **89**: 501–511.

Severini, T. and Wong, W. (1992). Generalized profile likelihood and conditionally parametric models, *Annals of Statistics* **20**: 1768–1802.

Sharpe, W. F. (1964). Capital asset prices: A theory of market equilibrium under conditions of risk, *Journal of Finance* **19**: 425–442.

Shephard, N. (1996). Statistical aspects of ARCH and stochastic volatility models, *in* D. R. Cox, D. V. Hinkley and O. E. Barndorff-Nielsen (eds), *Time Series Models in econometrics, finance and other fields*, Chapman & Hall, London.

Skiadopoulos, G., Hodges, S. and Clewlow, L. (1998). The dynamics of implied volatility surfaces, Working Paper, Financial Options Research Centre, Warwick Business School University of Warwick, Coventry.

Sklar, A. (1959). Fonctions de répartition à n dimensions et leurs marges, **8**: 229–231.

Sklar, A. (1996). Random variables, distribution functions, and copulas – a personal look backward and forward, *in* L. Rüschendorf, B. Schweizer and M. Taylor (eds), *Random Variables, Distribution Functions, and Copulas – a Personal Look Backward and Forward*, Institute of Mathematical Statistics, Hayward, CA.

Stone, C. (1977). Consistent nonparametric regression, *aos* **5**: 595–645.

Studer, G. (1995). Value at risk and maximum loss optimization, Discussion Paper, ETHZ, RiskLab: Technical Report.

Taleb, N. (1997). *Dynamic Hedging: Managing Vanilla and Exotic Options*, John Wiley & Sons, New York.

Taleb, N. (2001). *Fooled by Randomness: The Hidden Role of Chance in the Markets and in Life*, TEXERE LLC, New York.

Taylor, S. J. (1986). *Modelling Financial Time Series*, Wiley, Chichester.

Teräsvirta, T. (1994). Specification, estimation, and evaluation of smooth transition autoregressive models, *Journal of the American Statistical Association* **89**: 208–218.

Teräsvirta, T., Lin, C.-F. and Granger, C. (1993). Power of the neural network linearity test., *Journal of Time Series analysis* **14**: 209–220.

Tong, H. (1983). *Threshold Models in Nonlinear Time Series Analysis*, Vol. 21 of *Lecture Notes in Statistics*, Springer Verlag, Heidelberg.

Tsybakov, A. (1986). Robust reconstruction of functions by the local-approximation method, *Problems of Information Transmission* **22**: 133–146.

Tweedie, R. L. (1975). Sufficient conditions for ergodicity and recurrence of markov chains on a general state space, *Stochastic Processes and their Applications* **3**: 385–403.

Vasicek, O. (1977). An equilibrium characterization of the term structure, *Journal of Financial Economics* **5**: 177–188.

Vieu, P. (1995). Order choice in nonlinear autoregressive models, Discussion Paper, Laboratoire de Statistique et Probabilités, Université Toulouse.

von Weizsäcker, H. and Winkler, G. (1990). *Stochastic integrals*, Vieweg, Braunschweig.

Wang, Y. (2002). Asymptotic nonequivalence of garch models and diffusions, *The Annals of Statistics* **30**: 754–783.

Weiss, A. A. (1986). Asymptotic theory for ARCH models: Estimation and testing, *Econometric Theory* **2**: 107–131.

Welcker, J. (1994). *Technische Aktienanalyse.*, Verlag Moderne Industrie, Zürich.

Welcker, J., Kloy, J. and Schindler, K. (1992). *Professionelles Optionsgeschäft*, Verlag Moderne Industrie, Zürich.

White, H. (1982). Maximum likelihood estimation of misspecified models, *Econometrica* **50**: 1–25.

White, H. (1989a). An additional hidden unit test for neglected nonlinearities in multilayer feedforward networks, *Proceedings of the International Joint Conference on Neural Networks, Zürich*, Washington DC.

White, H. (1989b). Some asymptotic results for learning in single hidden-layer feedforward network models, *Journal of the American Statistical Association* **84**: 1008–1013.

White, H. (1990). Connectionist nonparametric regression: multilayer feedforward networks can learn arbitrary mappings, *Neural Networks* **3**: 535–550.

Wiggins, J. (1987). Option values under stochastic volatility: Theory and empirical estimates, *Journal of Financial Economics* **19**: Journal of Financial Economics.

Williams, D. (1991). *Probability with martingales*, Cambridge University Press, Cambridge.

Wilmott, P., Howison, S. and Dewynne, J. (1995). *The mathematics of financial derivatives: a student introduction*, Cambridge University Press, Cambridge.

Yang, L., Härdle, W. and Nielsen, J. (1999). Nonparametric autoregression with multiplicative volatility and additive mean, *Journal of Time Series Analysis* **20**(5): 579–604.

Zakoian, J. (1994). Threshold heteroskedastic functions, *Journal of Economic Dynamics and Control* **18**: 931–955.

Zakoian, J. M. (1991). Threshold heteroskedastic models, *Technical report*, INSEE.

Index